GOING GLOBAL
WITH
EQUITIES

"Excellent, the best explanation and summary of the most important concept in fund management."

Mark Mobius
President, Templeton Emerging Markets Fund

"I was both impressed and entertained by *Going Global with Equities*. It is well-written, informative and interesting. It should prove useful as a source of basic facts and data and as an expression of a sensible and balanced professional investing philosophy."

James R. Vertin
President of the Research Foundation of the Institute of Chartered Financial Analysts (ICFA)

"Assembles valuable insight and information about global investing in a logical, readable way."

Keith P. Ambachtsheer
Principal, K.P.A. Advisory Services of Toronto

"The bible on global investing. A crystal-clear exposition of how to approach stocks and markets worldwide. Top marks."

Allen Keyte
Director, Centre for International Studies, London

"The world's mine oyster."

Pistol in *The Merry Wives of Windsor*,
by William Shakespeare

GOING GLOBAL
WITH
EQUITIES

Make investment gains
across frontiers

PAUL MELTON

FT
PITMAN
PUBLISHING

London · Hong Kong · Johannesburg · Melbourne
Singapore · Washington DC

PITMAN PUBLISHING
128 Long Acre, London WC2E 9AN
Tel: +44 (0)171 447 2000
Fax: +44 (0)171 240 5771

A Division of Pearson Professional Limited

First published in Great Britain 1996

© Pearson Professional Limited 1996

The right of Paul Melton to be identified as author of this work has been
asserted by him in accordance with the Copyright, Designs and Patents Act 1988.

ISBN 0 273 61973 X

British Library Cataloguing in Publication Data
A CIP catalogue record for this book can be obtained from the British Library.

1 3 5 7 9 10 8 6 4 2

Typeset by Pantek Arts, Maidstone, Kent
Printed and bound in Great Britain by Biddles Ltd,
Guildford and King's Lynn

*The Publishers' policy is to use paper manufactured
from sustainable forests.*

About the Author

Paul Melton writes *The Outside Analyst*, the only monthly newsletter that actually compares stocks globally. Since its inception in 1986, this wholly independent publication has earned a reputation for sound research. Mr Melton specializes in ferreting out the world's bargain equities, screening earnings estimates each month for more than 15,000 companies in over 40 countries. As the *International Herald Tribune* put it:

"*Mr Melton goes deep into the wilderness to find the best performance.*"

A popular speaker at investment seminars throughout the world, he has been quoted repeatedly in *Forbes, Portfolio International, Economia Internazionale, La Vie Française* and a host of other financial publications both in the US and Europe.

Mr Melton, a *cum laude* graduate of New York University's Washington Square College, has written and produced public affairs programs for CBS television, translated and directed plays, served as artistic director of one of Amsterdam's municipal theatres, created a Dutch television series on the 14th century, been senior portfolio manager of a British investment house and investment consultant to one of France's major insurance companies. He is a member of the International Society of Financial Analysts.

Acknowledgements

Working on this project, I often felt like a mouse hitching rides from elephants. I have been privileged to stand on the shoulders of giants, far too many to name, whom you will meet in the pages that follow. I have also benefitted from the generosity and advice of six colleagues who undertook the task of reading the whole manuscript. My sincere thanks to Keith Ambachtsheer, Gary Gastineau, Dean LeBaron, Mark Mobius, Bruno Solnik and James Vertin. I alone am of course responsible for any flaws that remain.

CONTENTS

allocation by market capitalization · Country allocation by gross
domestic product · Country allocation by equal weights · The role
of fuzzy logic

10 YOUR BENCHMARK 157

The suitability of common benchmarks
   Pension fund consultants
Constructing a global benchmark
   The equal global index
Benchmark worksheet
   In dollars · In Deutschmarks · In yen
Balancing risk and reward

11 ASSURING VARIETY 169

Developed markets
   Adjusting for country correlation: Global correlations · Diversifying
   within Europe · Forecasting correlations from the business cycle
Emerging markets
   Profiting from inefficiencies · Appropriate weighting · A role in
   reducing risk · Building a more stable portfolio

12 HANDLING CURRENCY RISK 184

In developed markets
In emerging markets

13 THE WORLD'S BEST BARGAINS 189

The bargain equities
   Expectations drive markets · The Institutional Brokers Estimate
   System · *The Outside Analyst* · The efficient market theory · The
   random walk approach · Market inefficiencies · How to find
   tomorrow's global winners· Technical and fundamental analysis ·
   Nonlinear models · Chaos theory · The theory of rational expectations ·
   Growth versus value · The danger in estimates · Detecting hidden worth ·
   Waltzing the wallflowers · Evaluating profitability · Comparing firms
   across borders
The bargain markets
   Adjusting for value: Bottom-up · Top-down · Combination methods
   Identifying the right countries: Rapid economic growth · Ratio of
   valuation to growth · Using GDP growth · Using aggregated earnings
   growth · Using estimate revisions · When to buy and sell · Pegging
   market cycles · Why price inefficiencies persist

PREFACE

"The important thing is not to stop questioning."
Albert Einstein (1879 – 1955)

Like any investment book, this is filled with half-truths. There is no other way of describing reality. No single formula applies to everyone, everything and everywhere ... no matter how clever we are.

Before the advent of modern portfolio theory, equity investors assembled holdings on a stock-by-stock basis, without regard to interaction. The importance of how securities movements differ, and the resulting benefits of diversification, were frequently ignored, as shown by this quote from Gerald M. Loeb, writing in the 1950s:

> Diversification is undesirable. One or two, or at most three or four, securities should be bought.

Since Harry Markowitz developed modern portfolio theory, however, stocks are no longer considered separate and distinct, but are judged in terms of their interaction with other stocks. And since William Sharpe subsequently formalized the relation between risk and return in his capital asset pricing model, stocks are evaluated on how their interaction affects these Siamese twins of investment. For their respective contributions to investment theory, Markowitz and Sharpe were each awarded the Nobel Prize.

Just as investment theory largely ignored the relation between risk and return until Sharpe, so physics largely ignored the relation between time and space until Einstein. The evolution of investment theory, in fact, much resembles how Newtonian physics evolved into quantum physics. Classical Newtonian physics saw the scientist as an observer detached from the physical world, carefully measuring its phenomena. Events were separate and distinct and could be precisely quantified. The universe was a sort of massive machine whose motions could be studied and known with certainty. This view changed as Einstein's relativity theory and Heisenberg's uncertainty principle became accepted.

Heisenberg's premise is this: Though physicists can measure a sub-atomic particle's position and its "momentum," defined as its mass times its velocity, they can never measure these two quantities with precision at the same time. The limitation has nothing to do with the imperfection of their measuring techniques. It is inherent in atomic reality. Light, for instance, cannot be observed directly without disturbing its behavior.

Modern portfolio theory, like modern physics, has discovered that awareness of interaction is essential to understanding physical reality.

In a further step, James Ware, whose article "Quantum Investing" sparked these introductory reflections, notes:

> Modern physicists are gradually coming to the same conclusion about physical reality that Eastern mystics have espoused for thousands of years – that is, that the ultimate reality of the physical world is not separate "balls" of matter colliding with one another, but rather interconnected, unseparated wholeness or "oneness."

1

WHY EQUITIES?

"It matters not whether a cat is black or white,
so long as it catches mice."
Deng Xiaoping, 1989

This book deals with shares, not with bonds, money-market funds, property or commodities. The reason? Over the long term, shares tend to give you a higher return and – believe it or not – a safer one.

The well-researched US market is a good guide to investment truisms, and a recent long-term study of that market by Jeremy J. Siegel, a finance professor at the University of Pennsylvania's Wharton School of Business Administration and academic director of the Securities Industry Institute, confirms the big edge that stocks have over bonds. In *Stocks for the Long Run* (Homewood, Illinois: Irwin, 1994), Siegel shows that, even though the stock market is more volatile than the bond market year by year, over every 30-year period since 1871 shares have done better than bonds.

This extrapolation from history is fundamentally flawed, says Nobel laureate Paul A. Samuelson, professor emeritus of economics at the Massachusetts Institute of Technology. Though US monthly performance records go back nearly 200 years, he finds that "too small a sample" to conclude that the healthy performance of stocks is a sure thing. "History," Keith Ambachtsheer recently wrote me, "is only one draw out of the great probability distribution in the sky."

Should we then ignore history? By no means. Though a compass seldom points true north, it remains a useful navigational tool. Similarly, though history provides no iron-clad guarantees, we can continue to be guided by it.

Adjusted for inflation, shares have never lost money over any period of 20 years or longer. By contrast, there have been several long stretches – most recently from 1961 to 1981 – when an investment in US Treasury bonds was a losing proposition.

Shares also have higher returns. Siegel writes: "Over the last century, accumulations in stocks have always outperformed other financial assets for the patient investor."

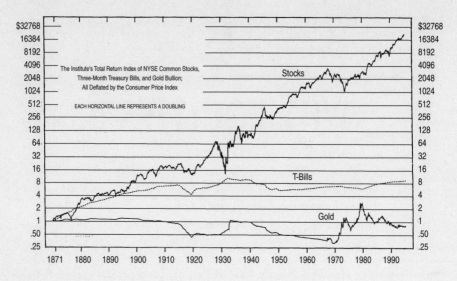

Fig 1.1 Stocks, Treasury Bills and Gold: Total returns after inflation, 1871–1995

An earlier historical analysis by Charles Ellis, described in his book *Institutional Investing,* led him to a similar conclusion: "A portfolio of conservative equities has been and is very likely to continue to be greatly superior to a bond portfolio on all counts."

The chart (see Figure 1.1) from the Institute for Econometric Research makes the point clear.

From 1871 through 1995, adding in dividends and ignoring taxes, US common stocks provided a spectacular 22,270 fold total return *after deducting losses of purchasing power due to inflation.* In other words, as the chart shows, $1 invested in a broadly-diversified portfolio of US stocks in 1871 grew in real value to $22,270. That's equal to a real compound return of 8.3 percent annually. In contrast, a dollar invested in three-month US Treasury bills grew only to $9.38, or a real compound return of 1.8 percent annually, while a one-dollar investment in gold fell in value to just 80 cents, adjusted for inflation and a modest 0.4 percent annual storage and insurance charge, over the 125-year span.

Most of the gain on bonds consists of interest, which as a rule is immediately taxable. Gains from stocks, on the other hand, come mostly from price appreciation, which isn't taxed until you sell – and in some jurisdictions, such as the Netherlands, not even then. Moreover, bonds often suffer the sort of price swings commonly associated with stocks. Bonds are also tricky to buy and sell. Unlike stocks, they have no central marketplace, so often in trading a bond you can't be sure you're getting a decent price. That's mainly a problem for individuals, though bond-fund managers can find it hard to get good prices too.

A solid profit frequently eludes bond investors, even if they guess right on interest rates. Many corporate and municipal bonds are callable much sooner than five years, so issuers can grab them back the minute it's to their advantage. Let's say you buy a long-maturity bond to lock in a super yield. As soon as interest rates start falling, and you think you've struck gold in your bond investment, the deal is cancelled and the postman brings your money back. As a bondholder, you have no more choice than a property owner whose building is condemned.

Buying bonds through a mutual fund is even more uninviting. For one thing, their costs badly erode returns. Municipal-bond funds levy average expense charges of 0.81 percent a year, according to Chicago-based fund researcher Morningstar Inc., while taxable-bond funds nail their shareholders for annual expense charges averaging 0.94 percent. These yearly fees are skimmed off bond-fund dividends – and loom large when most bonds are yielding less than 7 percent. Adding insult to injury, many bond funds also levy a commission when you buy or sell their shares.

Bond funds have a second drawback: you can't lock in a rate of return as you can with a single bond. Let's say you want to invest a sum for just five years. If you buy individual high-quality bonds that have good protection against calls and that mature in five years, you can be fairly certain how much money you will make. You know just how much interest you'll receive each year and you know just how much you'll get back when the bonds mature. Your only real doubt is what rate of return you'll get when reinvesting your interest payments. But stash that sum in a bond fund for the next five years, and everything is up for grabs. Bond funds – unlike individual bonds – generally don't mature. If you buy a medium-term bond fund, it remains a medium-term bond fund, year after year. The fund just keeps buying and selling medium-term securities. Result? You can't be sure how much income you'll get from the fund. And there is no guarantee, when the five years are up, that your shares will be worth what you paid for them. Bonds are a poor investment for long-term investors. Bond funds are even worse.

Peter Bernstein, who developed *The Journal of Portfolio Management* into a superb forum for exchanging ideas and experience among professional investors and academicians, says flatly that bonds generally have no legitimate place in a portfolio. In his article "How True are the Tried Principles?" in the March/April 1989 *Investment Management Review*, Bernstein compared the results of a portfolio consisting of 60 percent stocks, 40 percent bonds, and no cash with a portfolio consisting of 75 percent stocks, no bonds and 25 percent cash. "The results," he reported, "are clearly in favor of the bond-free portfolio, which provides higher returns with almost identical levels of risk. The bond-free portfolio outperforms the cash-free portfolio in 88 of the 138 quarters, or 64 percent of the time."

Common stocks indeed widely outperformed US Treasury bonds in the 68 years ending January 1, 1994, according to Ibbotson Associates of Chicago. US long-term government Treasury bonds had an average total return of 5.02 percent. During that same period, US inflation averaged 3.13 percent per annum. It doesn't take a rocket scientist to figure out that the inflation-adjusted return on those bonds was 1.89 percent. And that's before taxes on the 5.02 percent. Over the same period, the returns racked up on US equities trampled those meagre bond yields into the dust. Compounded annually over the 68 years, total return (income and growth) on the Standard & Poor's 500 averaged 10.33 percent, and on US small stocks 12.36 percent.

An investor who put $1 into US common stocks at the end of 1925 and reinvested the dividends would have seen that greenback grow to more than $800 by the end of 1993, despite some wide swings in the US stock market. Invested in small company stocks, the dollar would have become $2,757. That's a phenomenal long-term record for shares over a period that encompasses the Great Depression, wars, recessions and basic changes in the economy. In contrast, someone who put $1 into long-term Treasury bonds, steadily plowing coupon payments back into bonds of similar maturities, would only have squirreled away about $28 in the 68 years.

The same relationship also applies over somewhat shorter periods. Over any 10-year period, shares have outperformed bonds 82 percent of the time. Compound annual returns from US common stocks exceeded those from long-term Treasury bonds for the decades of the 1950s, 1960s, 1970s and 1980s.

Assuming dividends and capital gains were reinvested, an investment in the US stock market between 1966 and 1992 averaged a 4.2 percent annual return after inflation. A similar investment in long-term government paper yielded a mere 1.6 percent. Taking taxes into account makes the contrast even more striking. Siegel calculates that an investment in the stock market over the same period would have gained 1.8 percent annually, while an investment in bonds would have actually *lost* 1.7 percent each year.

Though bonds may be suitable for a portfolio with an investment horizon of less than five years, viewed long term, bonds are obviously legalized confiscation.

What about inflation-indexed bonds, you may ask? Britain has been selling indexed gilts since 1981. Australia, Canada, Sweden and New Zealand also issue index-linked debt, and the US announced in mid-1996 that it will shortly follow. Such bonds let a government initially finance its debt at lower interest rates. When an enconomy suffers a price surge, however, the government has to hike the coupon, enabling investors to pass their inflation loss on to the taxpayer.

But index-linked bonds are by no means risk-free. From 1985 through 1995, British investors in inflation-indexed bonds received an 8.8 percent annual return. Nice enough, but far short of the 15.1 percent yearly return from British stocks over the same period. More important (from the viewpoint of bond believers), over much of the 1980s the return on idexed gilts badly lagged that on conventional ones. In a period of low inflation, indexed bonds make little sense. People buy them nevertheless simply to avoid unpleasant surprises on the inflation front.

For the short term, a roughly 40 percent allocation to conventional bonds is generally deemed suitable. But investors who replace conventional bonds with those keeping pace with inflation can invest substantially more in stocks without taking on more risk. A mere 25 percent allocation to index-linked bonds will protect capital to the same extent. Oddly enough, therefore, Uncle Sam's recent embrace of inflation-indexed bonds is likely to mean a heavier long-term emphasis on equities. All to the good. A shift to equities should improve returns, especially for investors who diversify globally.

Even such debacles as the 1929 stock crash did not nullify the superiority of equities as long-term investments. True, a typical 1929 portfolio might have included Auburn, Cord, Missouri Pacific, Pierce -Arrow and Stutz, all of which went belly up. But that doesn't alter the basic picture. The Dow and reconstructed S&P averages from 1929 through 1942 take account of such firms at the closing price of the day after they declared bankruptcy. An investor who had the stomach to hold on to stocks through the 1929 crash would have ended up much better than someone who invested only in bonds. And on the long-term chart of stock-market values, at the beginning of this chapter (Figure 1.1), as you can see, the crash of 1987 is nothing but a blip – erased within two years. Moreover, the "normal" average annual gains from equities of 10 – 12 percent (ignoring inflation) can be improved by better-than-average share selection. As experience shows and this book demonstrates, prudent individuals can gain total equity returns of 15 – 18 percent over multi-year periods.

The superiority stocks have demonstrated over bonds for the long haul is by no means confined to the US. Over the past century, British equities have outperformed gilts by similar margins.

It can be argued, of course, that the reason American and British equities have outperformed bonds is simply that these two stock markets are odd. Odd because they have survived. The New York Stock Exchange began trading in 1792, when investors could buy shares in the financial markets of Britain, Holland, France, Germany and Austria.

But of these six markets, only those of the US and Britain have operated continuously since then. Moreover, of the 36 stock exchanges running at the beginning of the 20th century, more than half have undergone at least one major break in trading, through war or nationalization of large quoted companies. So anyone trying to evaluate the long-term reward from equities has little choice but to study the US and British markets. Their very survival, however, makes these markets unrepresentative.

This argument against the superiority of equities is advanced by Stephen Brown of New York University, and Stephen Ross and William Goetzmann, both of the Yale School of Management, in an article entitled "Survival" in the July 1995 issue of the *Journal of Finance*.

That panic button, however, is easily disconnected. Over the past 100 years, equity markets have had a roughly 50 percent survival rate. Let's assume that today's more stable capitalist systems provide a higher survival chance of, say, 80 percent over the next century. And assuming emerging markets have more risk of interruption, let's estimate their chances of long-term survival at 40 percent. Is this then a valid argument for buying bonds?

I think not. The following chapters in fact show you how to reduce both developed and emerging market risk to negligible proportions. So let's get back to comparing equities with bonds.

Investors needing income have generally looked to bonds to provide cash flow. But long-term bonds, unlike shares, offer no chance for growth – and little, if any, opportunity to improve performance. One 30-year government bond yielding 7 percent is much like another. You might enhance your total return on bond investments by successful market timing, but that is even trickier for bonds than for stocks. Granted, there are times to buy bonds: when their yields are historically high and interest rates are likely to tumble, pushing bond prices up. For 1982, the US long-term government Treasury bond had a total return of 40.36 percent; for 1985 30.87 percent; for 1986 24.53 percent; for 1989 18.11 percent; for 1991 19.30 percent; and for 1993 18.24 percent.

Nevertheless, for the long term, putting your retirement assets in bonds is buying fool's gold. To illustrate this, let's look at two investors, Squirrel Nutkin and Jiminy Cricket, each with a radically different approach to handling a nest egg of $500,000 at retirement.

Let's say both are in the 28 percent tax bracket – even though many governments are greedier – and seek net after-tax cash flow each year of about 5 percent of their portfolio's value to meet spending needs. We'll assume an inflation rate of 4 percent a year for the next 15 years. Naturally, both portfolios will fluctuate in value, but let's assume a steady annual rate of change for each.

Nutkin, figuring bonds will give him the income he needs, buys a mix of corporates with an average maturity of 15 years and a yield of 7 percent. After the first year, Nutkin indeed receives his $35,000 in dividends. He also incurs taxes of $9,800 on this ordinary income, leaving him with a net spendable income of $25,200 – roughly the 5 percent targeted. Though Nutkin's bonds are not called and continue paying the coupon over the entire 15 years, each year his fixed annual return of $25,000 in after-tax income shrinks by 4 percent in buying power. Nutkin is neither an interest-rate prophet nor a short-term trader, which is what one has to be to net more than the coupon rate on bond investments over the long term. So his portfolio provides no real growth from which to garner more income. Poor Nutkin soon has to cut back on his spending. After 15 years, his after-tax income has dwindled to a measly $13,661 in retirement-year dollars and his $500,000 portfolio, though nominally unchanged, has been nearly halved by inflation.

Jiminy Cricket, on the other hand, realizes that growth is essential to an enjoyable retirement and takes another path. He buys a solid equity growth fund that pays little or no income, but has a likely long-term growth rate of about 12 percent, only a bit above the US norm for total stock market return – income and growth – over the long haul. (UK shares averaged a 13.2 percent return from the end of World War II until 1994.) At the start of each year, after the first, Cricket takes enough money out of the fund to give him about $25,000 for living expenses after taxes (see Tables 1.1 and 1.2).

Cricket gets his cash flow from realized capital gains, not from ordinary income. Capital gains, in those countries where taxed, are adjusted for the cost basis before figuring the tax. So Cricket doesn't pay taxes on his first $26,000 withdrawal, but on that amount less the cost of the shares sold. The cost basis of the $26,000 sale in the first year is $23,214, so Cricket pays tax of only $780 on a capital gain of $2,786 ($26,000 minus $23,214).

Compare his tax burden with Nutkin's! As time goes by and the price of the fund rises, Cricket has to sell fewer shares to generate the same amount of cash, so his cost basis declines and his capital gains tax rises. Cricket's tax burden, however, remains much lighter than that on Nutkin's ordinary income. Even at the end of the 15th year, Cricket's effective tax rate is only 23 percent. Of course, each sale removes assets from the portfolio, unlike Nutkin's income check. But, as the rate of withdrawal is less than the rate of growth, Cricket's portfolio is still worth more after the first withdrawal – $534,000 – than Nutkin's stagnant $500,000. Adjusted for the first year's infla-

Table 1.1 Nutkin's $500,000 bond portfolio

	Year 2	Year 6	Year 11	Year 16
Portfolio value at beginning of year	$500,000	$500,000	$500,000	$500,000
Yield	35,000	35,000	35,000	35,000
Tax	9,800	9,800	9,800	9,800
Spendable cash flow	25,200	25,200	25,200	25,200
Adjusted for inflation	24,192	20,547	16,754	13,661
Remaining portfolio value	500,000	500,000	500,000	500,000
Adjusted for inflation	480,000	407,686	332,416	271,043

Table 1.2 Cricket's $500,000 growth fund portfolio with annual withdrawals

	Year 2	Year 6	Year 11	Year 16
Portfolio value at beginning of year	$560,000	$723,812	$987,890	$1,364,347
Withdrawal	26,000	36,000	48,500	61,000
Cost basis	23,214	20,427	15,616	11,144
Taxable gain	2,786	15,573	32,884	49,856
Tax	780	4,360	9,207	13,960
Spendable cash flow	25,220	31,640	39,293	47,040
Adjusted for inflation	24,211	25,798	26,123	25,500
Remaining portfolio value	534,000	687,812	939,390	1,303,347
Adjusted for inflation	512,640	560,823	624,537	706,526

tion, Cricket's portfolio is really worth only $512,640 in year-of-retirement dollars, but that's not bad considering the cash flow – and the fact that Nutkin's bonds, adjusted for inflation, have meanwhile eroded in buying power to $480,000.

Cricket also realizes that he needs to adjust his yearly fund redemptions to keep up with inflation and offset his increasingly heavier tax burden. So he adds another $2,500 each year to his annual redemption.

At the end of the 15th year of retirement, Jiminy Cricket is still whistling happily. His annual check is now for $61,000, which means he is netting $25,500 after tax in terms of the dollar's value in his year of retirement.

Thanks to the 12 percent growth rate, his portfolio, despite the yearly redemptions, passed the million-dollar mark in the 12th year and is now worth over $1.3 million. Though this is only $706,526 in real dollar terms, it represents a net yearly compound real return, after deductions for tax and inflation, of 2.34 percent. Cricket has successfully harnessed the powerful growth potential of equities.

The reason for the discrepancy in the two men's post-retirement fortunes is, of course, the lack of any real growth in Nutkin's fixed-income approach.

This is the basic argument for putting most of your investment funds into equities rather than into fixed-income securities or money-market funds.

But *which* equities?

The answer is simple. Whether you select equities for an institution, or just for your own portfolio, you naturally seek the highest return for the lowest level of risk. There's a proven way to make that job easier, gaining more chance of profit while gambling less. The key is simply investing *outside* your home market.

Going global tends to increase your profits and limit your risks. The aim of this book is to explain why – and to pull together all the information you need for a professional approach to trading equities worldwide. With it, you will be able to seize investment opportunities on a moment's notice – wherever they appear.

2

OUTSIDE INVESTMENT SNOWBALLS

*"Capital clearly has become global. Some $3 billion of
capital race around the world every day."*
Bill Clinton, 1993

No matter where you live, more of your country's currency is being invested *outside* its domestic markets than ever before. Buying shares across borders is of course not new. Europeans have been doing it for decades, most notably the British and, to a lesser extent, the Swiss. American Depositary Receipts (ADRs) – representing non-US shares – have been listed and traded in New York since the 1920s. What is new, however, is the *scale* of the global equities business.

MONEY HAS LOST ITS NATIONALITY

Today, there is a huge pool of hundreds of billions of dollars of global capital, from unit trusts and mutual funds, from pension plans, corporate investment accounts and private individuals. This pool of money flows from one continent to another, going where returns are highest and investors feel most safe. It has no national allegiance; for the smart money backs the best horse, regardless of where it was bred.

GLOBAL CAPITAL FLOWS

This global capital is snowballing rapidly, as shown in the following figures from the Bank for International Settlements. In 1970, US securities trades with foreigners – total purchases and sales of bonds and equities – were equal to 3 percent of the US gross national product. By 1990 this figure had soared to 93 percent. In West Germany it shot from 3 percent to 58 percent and in Japan from 2 percent (in 1975) to 119 percent. Thanks to the busy brokers in the City of London, Britain's cross-border securities trades scored even higher: no less than 368 percent of gross domestic product, even in 1985. Five years later this figure had nearly doubled, to 690 percent.

Between 1980 and 1990, the volume of worldwide cross-border transactions in equities alone grew at a compound rate of 28 percent a year, from $120 billion a year to $1.4 trillion. ("Trillion"is used throughout in the American sense of a million million – a one followed by 12 zeros – rather than the British, French and German meaning of a million million million – a one followed by 18 zeros.) Worldwide, says the US National Association of Securities Dealers, investing in foreign stocks is doubling every three years. It is projected to reach $5 trillion by the turn of the century, nearly the value of all goods and services produced in the US each year. A study by Michael J. Howell and Angela Cozzini of Baring Securities shows that the craving for foreign equities has grown so much that today one out of every four stock trades in the world involves either an overseas buyer or seller of a foreign stock. More shares are now dealt in Reuters, Akzo and L.M. Ericsson Telephone *outside* their home markets than in it. And foreign investors now own the majority of equity in Philips, Matsushita Electric and Sony Corporation – plus a big chunk of Dow Chemical and Elf Aquitaine.

This international flow of money includes small investors, who have been putting their nest eggs in ever more baskets, creating a boom for global mutual funds. Since 1989, stock assets overall have doubled, but assets of global stock funds have more than *tripled*, according to a 1993 report from the Investment Company Institute.

FOREIGN INVESTMENT BY PENSION FUNDS

A quiet revolution is also taking place in the way pension funds allocate their assets. In the mid-1980s, most pensioners were being paid from the profits of domestic investment in bonds and, to a limited extent, in equities. Today, pension funds throughout the world are increasingly looking abroad. The sums involved are huge. Global assets of pension funds are estimated at $7,053 billion, with $3,760 billion from the United States, $1,118 billion from Japan, $775 billion from the United Kingdom and $1,400 billion from other countries. This in 1994, according to a Connecticut investment consultancy, InterSec Research Corp., which predicts that, before the end of the century, the world's pension assets will total $11,236 billion. And these numbers do not include many countries which have a government pension system scheduled to be privatized.

Ever more of this capital too is being invested *outside* its domestic market. US pension assets have been flooding abroad at the rate of $50 billion a year. Since 1991, InterSec says, foreign securities held by tax-exempt US pension funds have more than doubled, from $125 billion to $300 billion – or 8.0 percent of total US pension assets. For Japan the figure is 7.6 percent, or $85 billion, for the United Kingdom 28.0 percent, or $217 billion, and for the world as a whole 11.2 percent, or $788 billion.

Hong Kong pension funds have a heady 56.8 percent of their assets in overseas equities and bonds – wholly comprehensible in the light of China's scheduled takeover of the colony in 1997.

By the end of 1999, InterSec projects that US pension assets invested abroad will rise to 12.2 percent of their total, for Japan to 14.4 percent and worldwide to 15.1 percent. By 1999, if we can believe InterSec, pension assets invested *outside* domestic markets will more than double, to over $1,702 billion, with non-domestic investment totalling $725 billion in the US, $313 billion in the U.K and $251 billion in Japan. Table 2.1 gives an overview.

Table 2.1 The world's pension funds (total pension fund assets in billions of dollars)

	Pension fund assets			Percentage invested abroad		
	1989	1994	1999 est.	1989	1994	1999 est.
United States	$2,425	$3,760	$5,936	3.7	8.0	12.2
Japan	513	1,118	1,750	8.4	7.6	14.4
Britain	453	775	116	22.7	28.0	28.0
Canada	181	238	381	6.4	17.0	19.0
Netherlands	202	264	361	11.5	18.7	22.8
Switzerland	133	191	343	4.3	12.3	15.3
Germany	84	124	177	4.5	3.6	5.3
Australia	42	82	166	17.5	16.1	20.9
Sweden	60	78	134	–	1.1	6.0
Denmark	33	53	96	–	7.7	11.4
France	19	57	61	2.0	6.0	8.0
Hong Kong	8	25	83	65.0	56.8	61.7
Ireland	9	20	24	25.0	37.5	37.5
Belgium	6	8	17	33.0	36.0	38.0
Norway	11	7	9	–	–	3.8
Rest of the World	159	253	581	2.8	8.7	12.2
Total	$4,338	$7,053	$11,236	7.0	11.2	15.1

Source: Intersec Research Corporation, 1995

THE GLOBAL SHIFT TO EQUITIES

Roger Smith, a partner at Greenwich Associates, another Connecticut-based investment consultancy, estimates that US pension plans could eventually end up with 70 percent of their assets in equities. Corporate pension funds in the US already have 57 percent of their assets in equities, up from 53 percent in 1994. The 1995 edition of the Greenwich annual survey of US corporate pension funds reveals that they intend to raise equity weighting to 60 percent by 1997. Interest in bonds has accordingly been reduced, with 1991's exposure of 27 percent likely to tail off to 22 percent by 1997.

Corporate funds represent only part of the $3,760 billion universe of US pension funds, and the rest – the public sector funds – are somewhat less aggressive. At present, they have an equity exposure of only 49 percent, but it too is on the rise.

These are dramatic and rapid changes. In the mid-1980s – a mere decade ago – most US pension funds had their assets split fairly equally between US bonds and equities. Now as much as $50 billion a year from US pension funds could flow abroad, mostly into foreign stocks, with the flight from domestic bonds most visible in the public sector.

The shift from bonds to equities is also evident in Europe. The change in attitude is most surprising in Germany, where antipathy towards equities dates back at least to the Wiemar Republic, which, unable to meet steep World War I reparation costs, saw the mark collapse and investors flee from securities of any kind. This distrust was exacerbated in the 1960s by the rise and fall of the late Bernie Cornfield's fund of funds, which older investors still recall with bitterness.

Germans remain skeptical about equity investments for another reason. Between 1987 and 1994, German bonds returned 5.6 percent, versus a total return of 4.5 percent for domestic equities. Naturally, the Bundesbank's seven years of high interest rates were a fleeting anomaly – and Germans who diversified globally had the likelihood of much higher returns. Nevertheless, German investors generally clung tenaciously to their beloved bonds.

The picture altered subtly at the end of 1991, when German insurance firms got permission to raise equity weightings from 20 percent to 30 percent of their assets. (Despite the greater leeway, most German insurers still hover around a 6 percent to 8 percent equity allocation.) In contrast, their French counterparts are allowed equity holdings of up to 65 percent of assets. Further, in late–1995 the French insurance industry created a Fr 14 billion ($2.53 billion) pension fund for its employees. The new fund is also permitted to invest almost two-thirds of its assets in shares.

Gradually, the elbowroom for equities recently granted to German insurers seems to be prodding other German companies awake. For years, German concerns have simply entered pension commitments as liabilities on the balance sheet, but now they have started to realize that this risks an eventual shortfall. To meet pension liabilities, German companies increasingly recognize the need for a so-called funded system where contributions go into a dedicated pool of assets, invested at least partially in equities.

In the summer of 1994, for instance, newly privatized national airline Deutsch Lufthansa announced it would provide a funded pension scheme for new employees.

The following year, German chemical giants Hoechst and Bayer each expanded the equity exposure of their pension funds. During 1995, Bayer cut back on domestic bonds so as to boost equity allocation from 16 percent to 20 percent of total assets. And Hoechst reduced its domestic bond weighting to raise its commitment to international equities from 20 percent to 25 percent of assets. Both firms increased their equity exposure through *Spezialfonds*, externally managed accounts that offer tax breaks to investors.

Consumer goods company Unilever, a Dutch–British hybrid, offers an even more striking example of this trend. Over the past decade, its pension funds in Belgium, Germany, the Netherlands, Sweden and Switzerland have nearly *doubled* their equity exposures, which now range from 26 percent for Unilever's German fund to 63 percent for its Swedish fund.

Public pension funds in Europe are going the same route. Traditionally, public funds have been vastly more conservative in investment approach than their corporate cousins. Not only do public pension funds tend to be more provincial and less exposed to new investment trends, but many are also forced to invest a minimum amount in government bonds.

Nevertheless, they too are slowly shedding old habits. Public funds in the Netherlands, which unlike Germany and France has had funded pension plans since the end of World War II, are leading the way. Until about 1980, Dutch public pension funds on average had less than 5 percent of their assets in equities. Now the urgent need for higher returns is driving many to a heavier equity weighting, and that snowball is gathering momentum.

The impact of the shift is most striking at the gigantic *f* 185-billion ($119 billion) Algemeen Burgerlijk Pensioenfonds, the Netherlands' public-employees fund. ABP – Europe's biggest pension fund – butted heads with the government for years for more freedom to invest as it saw fit – including higher legal limits on foreign and equity investing. In 1994, ABP – which was privatized at the beginning of 1996, freeing it from investment restrictions on governmental agencies – said it plans to triple equity allocation to 30 percent of assets by the end of the decade, approximately half invested outside the Netherlands.

Smaller public funds are following ABP's lead. In 1994, ABN AMRO bank did an asset-liability study for the *f* 6.3 billion Stichting Bedrijfspensioenfonds PTT Nederland, the postal and telecommunications workers' fund in Groningen. The result? PTT decided that to meet future pension liabilities, it had to shift from bonds and real estate into stocks. Accordingly, PTT is hiking its equity allocation from 36 percent of fund assets to 42 percent.

Dutch health and welfare pension fund PGGM plans to go even further, virtually doubling equity allocation to 50 percent to 60 percent of its f 50-billion ($32 billion) total investment portfolio.

Granted, British pension funds are heading the other way – but starting from a near-80 percent allocation to equities. Impelled by domestic inflation of over 25 percent, British pension funds began switching from domestic bonds into foreign shares in the 1960s.

The true revolution in Europe's buying of stocks, however, is reflected in the Continent's burgeoning mutual fund industry. Assets under management have zoomed in recent years, and in most countries equities are the main beneficiary.

In France, the banks, which dominate its mutual fund market, are witnessing a change in the public's attitude towards equities. But nowhere has the surge into equity mutual funds been more marked than in Italy, where domestic stock market limitations have virtually compelled investors to look elsewhere.

From German pension funds to French banks to Italian mutual funds, increased equity allocation is the order of the day. Though fixed-income diehards are still dragging their heels, especially in Germany, recent events have conspired to encourage the plunge into equities. Belief in the supposed safety of fixed-income instruments was badly shaken in 1995 by German interest-rate hikes that created huge losses in the world's bond markets. At the same time, thanks to performance benchmarks promulgated by Anglo-Saxon consultants, European pension funds finally began to twig that equities are unmistakably the best–performing long–term investment around.

Alas, traditional bookkeeping marks equities down at the lower of book or market value, thus rendering positive returns meaningless until the shares are sold. Perceiving that this distortion discourages equity investment, many European concerns have begun valuing equities at market value.

These factors, coupled with healthy cash flow and generally buoyant stock markets, have brought an impressive rise in the amount of equity held by European investors. The increase in equity weightings for pension and mutual funds in various European countries over the past few years is depicted in Figure 2.1.

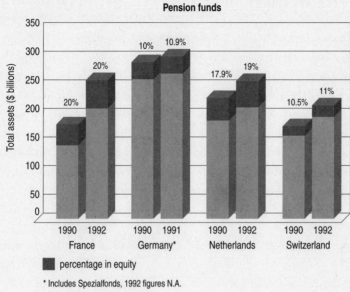

Pension funds

Total assets ($ billions)

	France		Germany*		Netherlands		Switzerland	
	1990	1992	1990	1991	1990	1992	1990	1992

percentage in equity

20% 20% 10% 10.9% 17.9% 19% 10.5% 11%

percentage in equity

* Includes Spezialfonds, 1992 figures N.A.

Source: UBS Asset Management

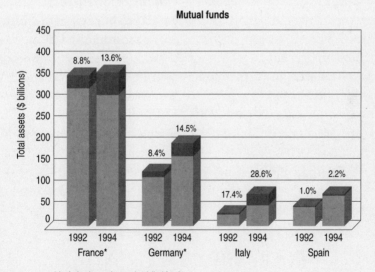

Mutual funds

Total assets ($ billions)

	France*		Germany*		Italy		Spain	
	1992	1994	1992	1994	1992	1994	1992	1994

8.8% 13.6% 8.4% 14.5% 17.4% 28.6% 1.0% 2.2%

* Includes Luxembourg-domiciled funds.

Source: Lipper Analytical European Fund Industry Data.

Fig 2.1 In some countries the shift is barely perceptible, but Europe's investors are slowly buying more equities

THE GLOBAL INVESTMENT PORTFOLIO

How big is the global pool of capital? Figures from US investment firm Brinson Partners show that global investment in real estate, cash, bonds and equities totalled no less than $28.5 trillion in early 1993. More than a third of this giant sum was in stocks, increasingly from outside the investor's domestic market, according to Salomon Brothers and Morgan Stanley. Indeed, in 1993 cross-border stock investment tripled on balance from the previous year, as investors purchased a record net $159.2 billion of stocks in other countries, well above the previous record of $100.6 billion, set in 1991.

WHERE THE MONEY CAME FROM

Purchases from the US led the pack. In fact, Americans, relative late-comers to international investing compared with the British, Dutch and Japanese, are gradually becoming a dominant force in global securities markets. According to London-based Baring Securities Ltd, of 1993's total $159.2 billion in net equity investment, US investors bought an estimated $66.4 billion, or 42 percent – with about half the purchases attributable to pension funds. Next in line were British investors, with $24.2 billion, followed by continental Europeans, with $21.0 billion, and the Japanese, with $15.3 billion.

The US Securities Industry Association – producing slightly different figures – says US investors purchased a net $67.8 billion in foreign equities, more than double the amount in 1992. That's a bigger total than the aggregate net acquisition of non-US stocks by Americans during the whole decade of the 1980s.

WHERE THE MONEY WENT

As for flows in the reverse direction, investors outside the US on balance bought $21.5 billion of US equities in 1993, after being net sellers in 1992. Of the net $159.2 billion that foreign investors poured into the world's equity markets in 1993, roughly 35 percent went to Europe (including Britain), 18 percent to the US and Canada and

13 percent to Japan. A whopping 33 percent flowed into the emerging stock markets of Asia, Latin America, Eastern Europe, the Middle East and Africa.

Of net foreign equity purchases of $67.8 billion by US investors, almost half were in Europe, with much of the rest split between Latin America ($12 billion) and Asia ($17 billion). Though Hong Kong ($6 billion) got much of the publicity, Mexico ($5 billion) got almost as much capital.

GLOBAL EQUITY ALLOCATION

How much of the global pool of capital is invested in shares – and how does it break down? Worldwide, says InterSec, in 1994 pension funds had $788 billion invested abroad, some 75 percent of it in equities. Another industry source, Technimetrics, estimates that European financial institutions managed over $204 billion in North American equities and over $369 billion in non-domestic European equities at end-1990, while Pacific Rim institutions managed over $122 billion in North American equities and almost $83 billion in European equities. At end-1990, US financial institutions managed an estimated $94 billion in international equities.

In early 1994, the world's equity markets totalled $10 trillion, broken down as shown in Figure 2.2.

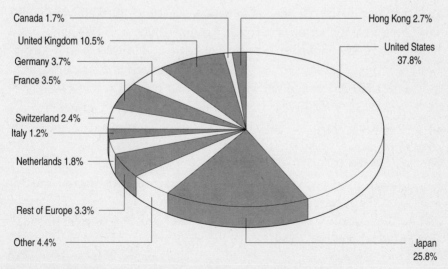

Canada 1.7%
United Kingdom 10.5%
Germany 3.7%
France 3.5%
Switzerland 2.4%
Italy 1.2%
Netherlands 1.8%
Rest of Europe 3.3%
Other 4.4%
Hong Kong 2.7%
United States 37.8%
Japan 25.8%

Fig 2.2 Distribution of world market capitalization, selected countries

Source: Lombard Odier & Cie

WHY BOURSES ARE BECOMING GLOBAL

Why is global investment now growing so rapidly? Why are foreign markets attracting so many institutional heavyweights?

Partly for the same reason Sir Edmund Hillary climbed Mount Everest. It was there. The microchip is here – and information technology is driving the globalization of equity markets. That should be no surprise. Throughout history, information technology has engendered financial developments.

In the 14th century, when travellers were the main conveyors of information, the Lombard banks created bills of exchange an itinerant monk could carry. A carrier pigeon is said to have made the Rothschilds rich in 1815 by bringing them a scoop on Wellington's victory over Napoleon.

Today, good-quality information on most markets is more readily available and ongoing improvement in communications is making it easier for bankers and securities firms to market shares to investors abroad. Moreover, few governments now impose exchange controls, which have restricted equity flows in the past. The scrapping of fixed commissions in the US two decades ago also helped by reducing dealing costs. Britain did the same in 1986 and other countries have followed suit.

In addition, national markets have been deregulated and opened to foreign investment, making share issues cheaper and more practicable for many companies. In 1990, the Securities and Exchange Commission reduced the paperwork needed to access US equity markets via depositary receipts, which trade as proxies for underlying non US shares. Such derivative products, lower transaction costs and advances in information technology have all encouraged investors to scour the globe.

But all these factors obviously do not add up to a full answer. They fail to explain why investors have taken so long to grasp outside opportunities. Foreign attractions haven't appeared magically overnight. No, the real question is why now, at the tail end of the 20th century, so many institutions are moving so much money so rapidly into foreign markets, with private investors riding their coat-tails or following their example.

The shift in emphasis seems to have two causes – one theoretical, one practical. Each has to do with *diversification*.

3

THE LOGIC OF DIVERSIFYING

"Tis the part of a wise man to keep himself today for tomorrow, and not venture all his eggs in one basket."
Miguel de Cervantes (1547–1616), *Don Quixote*

Imagine an island with only two businesses: one rents bikes and the other rents umbrellas. When the sun shines, the bike rentals boom and the umbrella rentals plummet. During rainy seasons, the bike man does poorly, while the umbrella lady enjoys high turnover and big profits. Table 3.1 shows some hypothetical earnings for the two ventures during the different seasons. Let's assume that all earnings are paid out as dividends, so these are also the returns paid out to investors.

Table 3.1 An example of diversification

	Umbrella Rental	Bike Rental
Rainy season	+50%	-25%
Sunny season	-25%	+50%

Suppose that, on average, half the seasons are sunny and half are rainy. In analyst-speak, the probability of a sunny or rainy season is one-half. If little Emily were to spend her dollar allowance to buy stock in the umbrella rental firm, she would earn a 50 percent return on the investment half of the time and a 25 percent loss the rest of the time. The average return would be 12.5 percent. This is what analysts call the expected return. Similarly, an investment in the bike rental firm would produce the same results. But investing in either one of these businesses would be fairly risky, because their results are quite erratic, and there could be several sunny or rainy seasons in a row.

Suppose, however, that instead of buying only one security, clever Emily waits a week until she has 2 dollars, and then diversifies, putting half her money in the business that rents umbrellas and half in the one that rents bikes. In sunny seasons, the 1-dollar investment in renting bikes would bring a 50-cent return, while the 1-dollar investment in renting umbrellas would lose 25 cents. Emily's total return would be 25 cents, or 12.5 percent of her total 1-dollar investment.

During rainy seasons, exactly the same thing happens – only the names are changed. Investment in umbrella rentals brings a solid 50 percent return, while the bike-rental investment loses 25 percent. Having diversified, however, Emily still makes a 12.5 percent return on her total investment. Whatever happens to the weather, and thus to the island economy, an investor who diversifies over both the firms is sure of making a 12.5 percent return each year.

The trick that makes the game work is that, while both firms are risky – i.e. returns are variable from year to year – each is affected differently by weather conditions. As long as firms react somewhat differently to an economy, diversification will always reduce risk. In the example above, where the firms' fortunes are negatively correlated (one always does well when the other does poorly), diversification can eliminate risk totally.

The rub is that the fortunes of most concerns move pretty much in tandem. When there is a recession and people are out of work, they may rent neither bikes nor umbrellas. So in practice you cannot expect the near total risk elimination just shown.

Nevertheless, since company fortunes do not always move wholly in tandem, investment in a diversified portfolio of stocks is likely to be far less risky than investment in one or two.

Just how many different stocks must you then buy to limit your investment risk?

A lot fewer than you may think. So-called naive diversification assumes that a portfolio made up of 200 different securities is ten times more diversified, and hence safer, than a portfolio of only 20 securities.

But it ain't necessarily so.

TWO KINDS OF RISK

Here's why: When you buy a stock you take on two kinds of risk: market and non-market.

Market risk

One reason it is hard to predict the future price of a share is our uncertainty about the future level of the overall market. This can be called the share's market risk, also known as systematic risk. Estimated at 25 – 50 percent of total risk, it stems from the tendency of stock prices in any one market to rise or fall in unison. The traditional notion of diversifying assets among many domestic firms is called the Noah's Ark technique: buy two of everything and wind up with a zoo. But no matter how many stocks you buy, the systematic risk within a single market stays roughly the same.

Specific risk

The second kind of risk is that unique to an individual firm or sector. A drop in earnings or earnings prospects, an accident or a scandal can put a dent in your stock's price. So even if you knew the future course of the market, some uncertainty would remain. This uncertainty can be called non-market risk. It is also known as specific or unsystematic risk.

Specific risk is notably high in the chemical sector. In late 1986, a fire at a Sandoz chemical plant in Switzerland released poisonous chemicals into the Rhine. Sandoz shares plummeted.

The year 1990 saw another textbook example of specific sector risk, when a number of airlines announced that they would wind up in the red, due mainly to higher fuel prices following Iraq's invasion of Kuwait. For the airlines, the price of fuel is an unsystematic risk.

Again, in the chemical sector, in early 1994 Dow Corning, Baxter International and Bristol–Myers Squibb were major signatories to the biggest product liability pact in the history of the US courts, a $4.75 billion settlement, for silicon breast implants that leaked.

Backed to the wall by the costs of that settlement, Dow Corning declared bankruptcy in May 1995.

Similarly, Dalkon shield liabilities are unique to A.H. Robins, while Johns Manville has a virtual monopoly on lawsuits for lung damage caused by asbestos insulation.

Abolishing specific risk

You can protect your investment portfolio against such risk. In fact – and this may surprise you – you get rid of specific risk almost entirely when you buy some fifteen diverse stocks in a single market.

That's because specific risks tend to cancel each other out. A few well-assorted stocks effectively reduce your specific risk to as good as zero: that is, your portfolio is then largely subject only to market risk.

That's logical. Specific, or unsystematic, risk is by definition unrelated to the market, so if you keep adding equities to your portfolio until it largely mirrors your domestic market, you obviously wipe out specific risk.

THEORETICAL BASIS

Trailblazer Benjamin Graham explained this encouraging fact in his definitive *Security Analysis* (New York, McGraw-Hill, 1934): "A group of, say, twenty or more common stocks will usually average out the individual favorable and unfavorable developments." Specific risk is thus virtually eliminated. This laid down the theoretical basis for delimiting diversification.

Evans and Archer

A key follow-up study appeared in the *Journal of Finance* in December 1968. Written by J.H. Evans and S.H. Archer, and entitled, if you'll forgive the mouthful, "Diversification and the Reduction of Dispersion: An Empirical Analysis," this study refines Graham's thesis. It shows that naive diversification will usually lower the unsystematic portion of total risk toward zero until you own about 15 different stocks. Adding more than this magical number of stocks to a one-market portfolio cannot be expected further to reduce its unsystematic risk.

Modigliani and Pogue

This argument was amplified by Franco Modigliani and Gerald Pogue, in a study on diversifying away risk, published in The *Financial Analyst's Handbook* (ed. Sumner Levine, Homewood, Illinois, Irwin, 1975). "All the risk in such a (well-diversified) portfolio," they wrote, "is a reflection of market risk. (There is a) ... rapid gain in diversification as the portfolio is expanded from one security to two securities and up to ten securities. Beyond ten securities the gains tend to be smaller."

J.C. Francis

The second edition of *Investments Analysis and Management* by Jack

Clark Francis (New York: McGraw-Hill, 1976) hammers the point home: "As the number of securities added to a naively diversified portfolio increases up to 10 or 15, the portfolio's risk will usually decrease toward the systematic level of risk in the market. After the portfolio's assets have been spread across more than 15 randomly selected securities, further decreases in risk usually cannot be attained by buying additional securities." This is shown in Table 3.2.

Table 3.2 Diversification and reduction of US specific risk*

Number of stocks in portfolio	Percentage of this risk eliminated
2	46%
4	72%
8	81%
16	93%
32	96%
64	98%
500	99%
All stocks in market	100%

*Individual stocks should be largely uncorrelated
Source: The Institute for Econometric Research

Domestic diversification

Granted, the risk of your equity portfolio lessens the more domestic issues you buy. But you quickly reach a practical limit in reducing risk this way. As you can see, a US investor holding 16 domestic stocks reduces the portfolio's specific risk only a mere 3 percent by adding another 16. Moreover, the total risk of any stock portfolio depends not only on the number of securities it holds, but also on the riskiness of each individual security and the degree to which these risks are independent of each other. A portfolio of ten electronics stocks is likely to benefit less from diversification than one made up of stocks selected from ten different industries.

The smaller or more uniform your home market, the less benefit you can generally derive from diversifying within it.

That's because you have fewer industries and a narrower range of stocks from which to choose. Conversely, domestic diversification in the United States provides more benefit than, for example, in Europe. The US market is so huge and varied that its non-diversifiable, or systematic, risk is a mere 27 percent.

Systematic risk in European countries looms much larger. In the United Kingdom, 35 percent of the typical risk of individual stocks cannot be diversified away. In Germany and Switzerland, the percentage of undiversifiable risk is even higher, at 44 percent. Most US firms publicly offer common stock, but a number of major European firms are still privately owned. With their domestic markets lacking the diversity of investment opportunities enjoyed by Americans, European investors naturally find the notion of investing abroad relatively more appealing.

Abating market risk

Though picking, say, 15 German stocks does tend to cancel out their individual risks, you're still highly vulnerable to the dangers of a single market. If it plummets, so will your portfolio. Happily, this problem too has an easy solution. Thanks to diversifying among those 15 well-assorted stocks, the only big risk remaining in your portfolio is that of the market itself. The next logical step is to whittle down that market risk as well. Fisher Black and Myron Scholes did demonstrate in "The Pricing of Options and Corporate Liabilities," published in 1973 in *The Journal of Political Economy*, that one can sharply reduce market risk by continuously hedging with options. But there is a simpler and cheaper long-term approach that achieves the same goal.

Several studies have shown stock price movements in different countries are virtually unrelated. These include H.G. Grubel, "Internationally Diversified Portfolios," in the December 1968 *American Economic Review*; H. Levy and M. Sarnat, "International Diversification of Investment Portfolios," in the same journal's September 1970 issue; and B.H. Solnik's work, *European Capital Markets*. (Rather than stud this book with footnotes, I have provided an extensive bibliography.)

Changes in price on the Paris Bourse seem independent of stock price fluctuations on the London exchange, and so on. When stocks in one country, say the United States, are doing worse than expected, another market is likely to be doing better, hence offsetting the losses. Therefore, just as you can virtually diversify away specific risk by holding various kinds of shares, so too you can substantially reduce market risk by holding investments in uncorrelated markets.

That means going global.

4

BEYOND BORDERS

"We are citizens of the world; and the tragedy of our times is that we do not know this."
Woodrow Wilson, 1917

There are two reasons to invest outside your home market. One is opportunity. The other is safety.

WHY FOREIGN STOCKS?

Although selecting, say, some 15 US stocks averages out their individual risks, it leaves you totally vulnerable to the risk of that single market. But diversifying into other markets tends to lower your market risk while increasing your chance of higher profits. What's more, foreign diversification cuts your currency exposure: a prime hazard today for any investor based in Eastern Europe or Latin America.

Marching to a different drum

Though the world economy is increasingly linked, world stock markets do not all move in tandem. Many foreign stock markets have their own unique quirks of behaviour. They react in ways quite different to your own, especially during economic recoveries, thus reducing the volatility of your portfolio. Your home market's ups and downs are generally offset by those in the foreign markets. That's why investing outside your home market can make your portfolio safer. Even when you invest in unlikely places.

Unseen dangers at home

Conversely, you substantially increase your investment risk by betting on any single country. Your home market is in fact riskier than it may seem. US stock returns over one-year periods since 1925 have zigzagged all over the map, from a 54 percent gain to a 43 percent loss. The added risk of a purely domestic portfolio is shown by a study, "International Equity Markets and the Investment Horizon." published by Israel Shaked in the Winter 1985 issue of the *Journal of Portfolio Management*. The study's conclusion? "There is substantial risk reduction available to those willing to diversify outside their own capital markets."

One reason why investing at home is riskier than you may think is that no market is immune to a shakeout. Ignoring the rest of the world means taking on unnecessary risk – risk that doesn't increase your chance of reward. So one compelling reason for going global is to increase safety by spreading risk. True, some investors use options to reduce the risk of a domestic portfolio. But such option hedging adds expense – and no profit opportunities.

More profit opportunities

The second pressing reason for going global is in fact to widen your chances of profit. Why bother? Why diversify outside your home market at all? Isn't there choice enough, especially in the United States, to make foreign investment wholly unnecessary?

To put it bluntly, no. Seven of the ten largest auto manufacturers, eight of the ten largest electronic companies, seven of the ten biggest chemical businesses and all ten of the biggest banks are headquartered outside the US.

Moreover, if your home market is a major one, such as the US, or for that matter the UK or Japan, it is not always the best place to invest. Especially these days. Figures from the International Finance Corporation show if you had put $1,000 in the average US stock in January 1985, ten years later at the beginning of 1995, it would have grown to only $3,818, as against $16,212 in Thailand, $23,209 in Mexico (despite 1994's steep peso devaluation), $48,023 in the Philippines, and no less than a whopping $64,707 in Chile.

That, however, is all water under the bridge. What matters is that you seize such opportunities today. If you're investing only at home, you're missing out on the rest of the world. But just as no market is immune to a shakeout, no single economy has a monopoly on dynamic growth. There is always a bull market somewhere. And if you widen your horizon, naturally you can find more bargains. So why limit your choice?

The second chapter posed the question of why just now, in the late 20th century, so many institutions are riding full tilt into foreign markets, with private investors in hot pursuit. The shift in portfolio emphasis, as I mentioned, seems to have two causes: one theoretical, one practical – each having to do with diversification. Here's the theory underlying that shift:

THE CONCEPT BEHIND GLOBAL INVESTING

The benefits of going global are set out by a prize-winning theory. Like all great ideas, it is simple. It also makes you an offer you'd be foolish to refuse: greater chance of profit with less risk. To reach this desirable goal, you combine assets whose price movements are highly unlike, yet all of which promise attractive rates of return. The idea, developed by Nobel Prize winner Dr Harry Markowitz, is called modern portfolio theory. An article by Markowitz, "Portfolio Selection," published in the *Journal of Finance* in March 1952, best spells it out.

Modern portfolio theory

The theory says you reduce risk by investing in asset classes that differ from each other – no matter what or where they are. A simplistic but graphic example is the behaviour of different groups of assets after the post-World War II oil-price shocks. Equities plunged, but anyone owning gold or oil assets did quite nicely.

Modern portfolio theory has been preaching the virtues of such diversification for over four decades. The ancient and modern attitudes to international investment can be summed up in the following paradox. Most investors who avoid foreign shares claim they're too risky and uncertain. Modern portfolio theory, on the other hand, says you should diversify your share portfolio globally precisely in order to *reduce* your risk.

You apply modern portfolio theory by going into other markets for a global mix of shares. In professional jargon, you seek a collection of attractive holdings whose covariance – how much their price movements tend to relate – is as small as possible. The guiding principle is not the item-by-item risk, but, rather, the *overall* level of risk in a portfolio.

This approach makes your portfolio more "efficient," improving the trade-off between lower risk and higher expected return. Global investing, in other words, tends to bring you higher returns for any given level of risk.

The prudent man rule

I am much indebted to Peter Bernstein for the following history.

Going global got its major boost in the United States, where modern portfolio theory led to a new interpretation of the prudent man rule: a legal test of how well a portfolio manager or other fiduciary has done his job. Since a landmark case in 1830 that involved Harvard University, the standard of investment selection by which fiduciaries are judged has come to be "how men of prudence, discretion and intelligence manage their own affairs."

Until modern portfolio theory came along, a fiduciary was on solid ground investing in IBM, even when it plunged 50 percent. After all, he'd done no worse than other members of his club: all presumed to be prudent. But with a 50 percent loss in South African gold or some obscure company like Philips, the money manager would find it tough to justify the investment decision to his trustees and the US legal system.

All this changed with the general acceptance of modern portfolio theory, which stated that the guiding principle for a fiduciary ought to be the *overall* level of risk in a portfolio.

Suddenly, an investment in a gold bar, a painting, a piece of real estate or a foreign stock was no longer inherently imprudent. What mattered was whether you invested 5 percent or 10 percent in a particular area – this being clearly prudent – or 50 percent, which could be deemed imprudent. Seemingly freed of the item-by-item standard of prudence, US money managers rode madly off in all directions to assemble non-US portfolios.

So much for theory.

Lessons from experience

Turning to the practical side, your home market isn't always going to be a winner.

In the crash during the last quarter of 1987, for instance, most major stock markets lost the gains they had racked up earlier in the year. Japan, however, ended 14.6 percent higher. Some minor markets, Korea and Finland, to name but two, finished the year even further ahead. Korea, for instance, was up over 80 percent.

Again, on the practical side, US investors once had seemingly convincing reasons not to venture abroad. In the post-war period, 1945–60, the US was enjoying a raging long-term bull market. But all good things must come to an end.

As the US market subsided and the grass in foreign fields began looking greener, President Kennedy brought in a hefty tax on foreign investment, called the interest-equalization tax. This penalty on foreign investment effectively fenced off the more attractive pastures abroad. Not until 1974, when the interest-equalization tax was finally lifted, did the US appetite for foreign stocks return. By a curious coincidence, this happened during the bear market of 1973–4, a mauling which taught US investors that, though their economy is many-sided, even *their* stock market is not diversified enough.

In October 1987, many yuppies discovered that too. Bear markets in other countries have taught local investors the same painful lesson: *truly broad diversification without foreign stocks is impossible.*

Meltdown Monday showed that in practice. A falling market is like a raid by the vice squad. When the paddy wagon pulls up, the good girls are carried off with the bad girls.

Likewise, when a market is on the skids, good and bad stocks take the fall together – and a portfolio that rises in value is almost impossible to find. The market largely determines what happens to individual securities and, even more, what happens to portfolios. That's our old friend, *covariance*.

Domestic stocks have strong *positive* covariance, which simply means they tend to move up or down together.

Investors have known this for centuries, but modern portfolio theory put it in a logical framework that offered more safety with no loss of profit. Investors – recently mauled by bear markets – found this an offer they couldn't refuse, leading to the awakened interest in modern portfolio theory. Negative covariance – the tendency for individual assets to dance to different rhythms and patterns – has now become the Holy Grail of professional investors. This has stimulated interest in fixed income securities and real estate at home, occasionally in gold, and especially in foreign securities of every sort. But the US, despite its contribution to the notion of going global, now lags when it comes to the practice. Granted, over the past 15 years or so, US purchases of foreign equities have grown at an impressive 22 percent annual compound rate, according to figures from the Securities Industry Association. Nevertheless, foreign stocks come to only 6 percent of the total equities held by US investors – this at a time when the capitalization of non-US equity markets has grown to well over 60 percent of total global market capitalization.

Investment isolationism

Brokers are partly to blame for US investment isolationism. A study of asset-allocation blends proposed by 13 major US brokerage-houses in periods ended June 30, 1995 is revealing. Despite the sound theory and proven benefits of diversifying abroad, the typical US broker virtually ignored foreign stocks in allocating assets. Only three of the 13 brokers surveyed by the *Wall Street Journal* (with help from Wilshire Associates in Santa Monica, California, and from Carpenter Analytical) even *mentioned* diversifying out of US stocks – and the highest non-US allocation was an embarrassingly lightweight 11 percent.

Instead, most of the brokerage houses sought another asset class solely in domestic bonds, even though shares in the long run clearly provide higher and safer returns than fixed-income instruments. The typical broker recommended that nearly 30 percent of an investment portfolio be allocated to such bonds (Table 4.1).

I mentioned earlier that more benefit is obtained from domestic diversification in the United States than in other countries. Doesn't that make going global less attractive for a US investor? Indeed, an argument often heard for such investment isolationism is that differences among national stock markets stem mostly from their disparate industry mixes. Thus, it is said, an index of Swiss firms will be weighted towards finance and an index of British firms towards utilities. This, the investment isolationists declare, is just industry diversification by another, and more expensive, means.

The basic question for a US-based investor is whether the diversification benefits of buying foreign securities outweigh the extra dealing costs involved. Perhaps an American could diversify simply by purchasing a varied collection of, say, Silicon Valley shares. Wouldn't the factors affecting each firm's performance largely balance out, thus eliminating specific risk? And if our American were to invest in US firms operating in disparate industries, wouldn't that reduce risk still further?

Table 4.1 Typical US asset allocations

Brokerage house	Performance			Recommended blend		
	Three months	One year	Five years	Stocks	Bonds	Cash
Goldman Sachs [a]	7.6%	20.3%	71.6%	60%	25%	10%
Dean Witter	8.2	19.5	63.5	60	35	5
Prudential	8.1	19.5	69.3	55	40	5
Merrill Lynch	7.6	18.8	69.0	55	35	10
Paine Webber	7.5	18.7	70.4	58	27	15
Kemper [b]	6.1	18.2	N.A.	60	20	20
Smith Barney	7.3	18.1	65.7	55	30	15
Edward D. Jones [c]	7.3	18.1	N.A.	65	25	10
A.G. Edwards	7.0	17.5	65.2	50	35	15
Salomon Brothers	6.6	16.6	N.A.	45	30	25
Lehman Brothers	6.7	17.1	64.6	55	30	15
CS First Boston	6.6	17.1	N.A.	60	35	5
Raymond James [d]	6.1	14.7	58.7	55	20	15
Average	7.1	18.0	66.4	56	29	13
Comparison yardsticks						
Fixed blend [e]	7.6	19.1	65.7	a Recommends 5% in commodities		
Stocks	9.5	26.1	76.7	b 45% U.S. stocks, 10% international		
Bonds	6.4	12.6	58.4	c 55% U.S. stocks, 10% international		
Cash	1.6	5.6	27.7	d 44% U.S. stocks, 10% international		
				e Constant mix of 55% stocks, 35% bonds, 10% cash		

N.A. = Not applicable (not in study for full period)
Sources: Company documents, Wilshire Associates, Carpenter Analytical
Performance of asset-allocation blends recommended by 13 brokerage houses in periods ended June 30 1995. Houses are ranked by 12-month performance. Also shown is the mix each house now recommends. Figures do not include transaction costs.

Yes. But the domestic portfolio would still underperform a global one. Going global has advantages because the returns on foreign stocks vary for reasons *beyond* their industries, such as government policies, demographics or weather. Later in this chapter I'll cite two studies which show that this is the case – and that diversifying abroad does indeed pay off. Therefore, investment advisers who tell you to diversify broadly within a single market – even one as varied as the US – do you a great disservice. They're ignoring not only a major source of risk, but also some of the world's fastest-growing economies and most attractive profit opportunities.

Causes of home bias

Like travel before the invention of the airplane, international investment diversification was once an expensive luxury for the privileged few. Today it is essential for any prudent investor. Despite these plain facts, many people still won't look beyond their domestic market. Preferring the devil they know to the devil they don't, they ignore the proven advantages of foreign diversification in making portfolio choices.

Globalization is still a relatively minor trend. Despite growing "outside" investment and the talk about globalization of capital markets, some 90 percent of the world's capital still stays at home. Mexico's economic crisis in December 1994, following peso devaluation, and the toppling shortly thereafter of Barings, Britain's oldest merchant bank, reinforced such home bias. Recent years have seen financial tourism by investors following one another to trendy foreign-investment hot spots such as Mexico. Then, when trouble strikes, the financial tourists pack their bags and head home. Investors simply do not have the commitment to foreign markets that they have to home markets.

Home bias by institutional investors may arise from the fact that the performance of fund managers is frequently assessed by referring to a local market index. This inevitably creates a strong incentive to own a good slice of the index's components.

Home bias by institutional investors is also often ascribed to government ceilings on the percentage of foreign assets that pension funds and insurance companies may hold. Apart from such institutional barriers, two other reasons commonly advanced for the widespread preference for home-country assets are discriminatory taxes and transaction costs and a desire to hedge against domestic inflation. But a study by Raman Uppal in the Autumn 1992 issue of the *Journal of International Financial Management and Accounting* finds all three of these reasons inadequate to explain the preference for domestic assets.

Still, the provincialism is understandable. People always tend to resist new ideas. Since ancient Egypt, it has been known that as a ship sails out of harbour, observers on shore first lose sight of the deck and then the sails and finally any pennant or flag flying from a high mast. In a flat world, a ship should appear to shrink progressively in observable size with no part vanishing before another. But most people preferred to ignore this fact and continued for centuries to believe that the world was flat. Similarly, most investors – even a few professionals – tend to go for what they know. That may be a dandy way to choose soap or toothpaste, but it can be deadly when applied to the serious business of protecting and increasing your net worth. Back in the 18th century, Antoine Lemierre put it neatly:

"It is a profound mistake to think the horizon the boundary of the world."

For a US investor, such myopia is especially dangerous, as it means ignoring far more of the world today than a quarter of a century ago. US stocks comprise a shrinking slice of the world's total equities. From 66 percent of the world total in 1970, they've dwindled to a mere 38 percent today, according to Lombard Odier & Cie. Figure 2.2 shows that investors who confine themselves to the US are turning their back on nearly two-thirds of the globe. (Obviously, non-US investors who stay at home are ignoring even more of the world.)

Inferior US returns

During World War II, the United States produced nearly two-thirds of the world's goods and services. That figure is now closer to a quarter. Moreover, the dollar, which may have been greatly respected by your grandfather back in 1913, will now buy less than 6 percent of the goods and services it did then. Should the old gent somehow return, in his eyes that greenback would now be worth less than six cents. In roughly eight decades, inflation has robbed the US dollar of more than 94 percent of its value. Silently and insidiously, inflation undermines investment returns. So let's look at *real* returns – deducting each year's nominal investment gains by the rate of inflation, reflected in the US consumer price index.

When it comes to investment, only real returns count. At first glance, on this score the US does not seem to have done badly. As noted in the first chapter, an investment in the US stock market between 1966 and 1992 averaged a 4.2 percent annual return after inflation, assuming reinvestment of dividends and capital gains. But – still assuming reinvestment – from 1984 through 1993, when US equities booked a real return averaging some 11 percent a year, French, Dutch and British equities posted annual real returns of better than 15 percent, according to a study by London brokers UBS. A $100 investment in French stocks in January 1984 would have risen to a princely $532 by December 1993, assuming dividend and growth reinvestment. In real dollar terms, deflating by the US consumer price index, French equities yielded an annual average return of 18.2 percent over the period, a whisker ahead of the roughly 17 percent average real dollar return on Dutch shares. The US real return pales in comparison.

Corrected for inflation, the Dow industrial average did not surpass its February 1966 high until January 1996. Underperformance by US shares may continue. The US, after all, has one of the world's most mature economies. Though studies in 1994 and 1995 by two Swiss think-tanks (the Geneva-based World Economic Forum and the Institute for Management and Development, or IMD, in Lausanne) dubbed the US world leader in economic competitiveness, the director of the studies warned that a third-world workforce of more than a billion people would soon threaten that position. At best, US growth will be steady and slow. So those who continue investing *exclusively* in US companies may see only modest returns. Returns even more modest when adjusted for inflation. Despite all this, the ratio of foreign investment by Americans is only half the world average. Most US investors are missing the boat.

The gains of going global

Obviously a US investor who selects 15 stocks from the hundreds listed on the New York and American stock exchanges is likely to be better diversified than one who selects only from among the 30 Dow Jones Industrials. Similarly, an internationally diversified portfolio is likely to carry much less risk than a typical domestic portfolio.

The gains from going global are substantial. Bruno Solnik was one of the first to publish on this subject in "Why Not Diversify Internationally Rather Than Domestically?" which appeared in the *Financial Analysts Journal* of July/August 1974. Using weekly price data for 1966 through 1971, Solnik assembled share portfolios of various sizes from the United States, the United Kingdom, France, the former West Germany, Italy, Belgium, the Netherlands and Switzerland. His conclusion? A well-diversified global equity portfolio is one-tenth as risky as a typical stock and half as risky as a well-diversified portfolio holding the same number of purely US stocks. Put another way, you get a higher return for the same level of risk. In a study in the March/April 1993 *Financial Analysts Journal*, "Lessons for International Asset Allocation," Solnik and Odier showed that from 1980 through 1990, a global equity portfolio bearing the same risk as a purely US portfolio achieved an annualized total return of more than 19 percent, versus 13.3 percent for the US portfolio. As noted earlier, the benefits of going global are even greater if you happen to live in Germany or Switzerland.

If you live in Germany, you may want to invest abroad to catch the upswing in Asian property or American technology. If you live in the

United States, you may want to invest in Europe to catch the cyclical upswing on the Continent. If you live in any major industrialized country, you may wish to enter other markets to catch the worldwide boom in telecommunications, infrastructure and the growing demand for global financial services, to say nothing of emerging markets that are reflecting the economic takeoff of Latin American and East Asia.

How widely should you diversify?

Expanding a global portfolio beyond 15 stocks brings far more risk reduction than going beyond 15 stocks in a domestic portfolio. Even a mutual fund with 50 different foreign stocks could benefit from additional holdings. But you certainly do not want to expand a portfolio beyond your capacity to track it. What rule of thumb should you use then to diversify your equity portfolio globally while still limiting the number of holdings?

A simple selection procedure would be to assure good geographical diversification by picking stocks across countries. The more conventional way is to select stocks across industries. Stocks from all countries can be classified by industry, so selection by industry automatically provides some international diversification. A third selection method combines the first two: choosing stocks across both countries and industries. Solnik's 1974 study tested all three approaches and found diversifying across countries generally brings you better investment results than diversifying across industries. That's because a stock's price movements correlate more with the market in which it is listed than with its industry. Swiss stock market trends, for instance, largely determine the price of Nestlé shares, even though more than 95 percent of Nestlé's cash flow is earned abroad.

Therefore, a portfolio diversified across countries is normally less risky than one (internationally) diversified across industries. And, as you might expect, combined industrial and geographic diversification gives slightly better investment results than pure country diversification alone.

More recently, Heston and Rouwenhorst reached similar conclusions, after examining monthly returns between 1978 and 1992 from the shares of over 800 companies, operating in seven different industry groups and 12 European countries. The differences in a country's industrial mix accounted for less than 1 percent of the variation in returns. In fact, of two portfolios with the same average return, diversifying across countries, but within a single industry, was less risky than diversifying across industries in a single country. This paper, "Does Industrial Structure Explain the Benefits of International Diversification?" appeared in the *Journal of Financial Economics* in August 1994.

Summary

Without foreign stocks, truly broad diversification is impossible. The well-diversified global investor experiences far less risk than the purely local investor. For optimal global equity diversification, it makes sense to select some 25 stocks, or their equivalents, from different countries and industries, placing more emphasis on country diversification than on industry diversification.

Before exploring the four paths to foreign investment, let's stop for a moment to consider risk and cost.

5

ESTIMATING RISK

"If only God would give me some clear sign. Like making a large deposit in my name at a Swiss bank."
Woody Allen, 1976

The patron saint of the Barcelona stock exchange is "Our Lady of Hope." Just as Odysseus sailed between Scylla and Charybdis, so investors have to navigate between fear and hope. We all hope for superior returns, yet fear loss of capital. We inhabit a world of uncertainty. The primary challenge for an investor is how to proceed in the face of this uncertainty. Long ago, natural scientists noticed the widespread presence of random variation in nature. This led to the development of laws of probability, which help predict outcomes. Though the toss of a coin is governed by chance, in a series of tosses perhaps we can have some idea of whether heads or tails is more likely. That brings me back to the subject of "risk," a term I've used repeatedly without fully defining it. The omission is intentional; for it is remarkably difficult to define that four-letter word in terms of investment. In fact, there is no general agreement on precisely what investment risk is or how best to measure it.

Nevertheless, within the framework of global investment this chapter tries to answer three questions:

- What is risk?
- Can you quantify it?
- If so, is that useful?

WHAT IS RISK?

Risk as an evolving idea

Risk is an idea. And ideas alter over the centuries. Sometimes an idea can change radically within the space of a decade. So too with the concept of risk, as Peter Bernstein spells out in "Risk as a History of Ideas." His intriguing thesis is as follows:

Perceptions of risk are the most telling symptoms of what a society is all about. Risk has always had two components: gut feeling and attempts at measurement. Sometimes one has predominated, sometimes the other. For most of human history, the future was a black hole. Risk was synonymous with blind chance. People, believing they had no control over the future, turned to oracles and priests to forecast it. But the random track records and murky techniques of these seers created little confidence in their predictions.

For centuries, the world lacked anything resembling the laws of probability as we know them today. Though evidence of gambling can be found from the earliest days of human history, systematic analysis of the likelihood of future events is less than 600 years old.

The Greeks, first civilization to be free of the intellectual strait-jackets imposed by secretive priesthoods, refused to accept the paradigms passed down by older societies. They insisted upon logical proofs.

But the Greeks too had their eyes shut to the laws of probability. They knew risk as a general idea, but did not try to quantify it because of their distinction between heaven and earth. The Greeks, superb astronomers, had discovered order, regularity and perfection in the skies. In contrast, they saw the earth as irregular and unpredictable. The notion of laws of probability for earthlings was thus a contraction in terms. There was no point in seeking order where no order could possibly exist. Chance still explained the entire outcome of taking risks.

That view vanished abruptly with the arrival of Christianity. Now random chance was out; God's will was in. "Thy will be done" became the basic rule of thumb for determining the future and explaining the past. Scientific research was crushed. In Alexandria in AD 380, the monks of St Cyril murdered Hypatia, a brilliant mathematician, by scraping her naked body with oyster shells.

The authority of religion crumbled in turn before the search for a better life on earth. The defining event was the Crusades and its attendant culture shock, particularly the numbering system the Arabs inherited from the Hindus nearly ten centuries earlier. It introduced the West, for instance, to the concept of zero, a notion of little use in daily life. No one goes out to buy zero fish. It also ushered Europe into the realm of negative numbers, which we as investors strive to avoid. Unlike the alphabetical numbering systems of the Hebrews, Greeks and Romans, Hindu numbers are *inputs* to calculations and are only incidentally used to record them. A whole new world of mathematics was opened, offering the abstract – not merely the tangible.

Using the new numbering system, Girolamo Cardano, a contemporary of Benvenuto Cellini and Copernicus, seems to have made the first effort to develop the principles of probability. In his treatise on gambling, *Liber de Ludo Aleae* – written in 1525, rewritten in 1565 and finally printed in Basle in 1663 – Cardano taught his readers, for one thing, that the probabilities on throws of two six-sided dice were to be based on 36 possibilities, not 12. He also uttered the theoretician's traditional lament:

> "These facts contribute a great deal to understanding but hardly anything to practical play."

Practical applications were not long in coming. At about the same time Cardano's book appeared, three Frenchmen set the stage for the work on probability theory that was to follow: a nobleman with an addiction to gambling, the Chevalier de Méré, and mathematicians Blaise Pascal and Pierre de Fermat. Then came the notion of normal distribution, published by Abraham de Moivre in 1733 and developed by Carl Gaus based on his own astronomical research from 1809 to 1816. Next were Galton's propositions of regression to the mean (i.e. things will return to "normal") and the coefficient of correlation, based on his studies of generations of sweetpeas in the 1880s. In this period, a Frenchman, Louis Bachelier, laid the mathematical foundations for analyzing stockmarket movements. He developed an equation based on Brownian motion for determining the value of a share option.

Without these pioneers, today's finance theorists would be lost – or at any rate, more so. A normal distribution, for one, is believed not only largely to predict noise in electromagnetic systems, the dynamics of star clustering and the evolution of ecological systems, but also next year's closing price for a stock-market index. We'll examine that last notion shortly.

Measurement was Galton's *idée fixe*, and one of his favourite expressions was "Wherever you can, count!" He noted down the size of heads, noses, arms, legs, heights and weights, as well as the colour of eyes, the sterility of heiresses and the number of fidgets made by people listening to lectures. He also classified the beauty of girls he passed on the street, pricking a hole in a left-pocket card when one was pretty and in a right-pocket card when she was plain. London girls scored highest; the girls of Aberdeen were at the bottom.

The big break in risk perceptions came when World War I blasted the smug wisdoms of the Victorian and Edwardian eras into smithereens. A world once deemed predictable and orderly was revealed to be unpredictable and disorderly in the extreme. It is no coincidence that John Maynard Keyne's *Treatise on Probability*, which appeared in 1921, is essentially an attack upon the notion that mathematics can define the future with any degree of certainty. Around then, G.K. Chesterson had reached a similar conclusion: "Life is not an illogicality; yet it is a trap for logicians. It looks just a little more mathematical and regular than it is." The pendulum had swung from measurement back towards gut feeling.

Risk perceptions shifted again after World War II, bringing us full circle: back, for one, to modern portfolio theory, summarized in the preceding chapter. This theory, you'll recall, demonstrates that risk is reduced by investing in asset classes that differ. The most rewarding way of applying the lesson is to assemble a global mix of equities, largely ignoring item-by-item risks in favour of the *overall* risk. The theory's philosophical roots stemmed from the optimism of the early postwar years – the 1950s and 1960s. Bernstein's article is studded with quotable gems, and his words neatly capture the flavor of this postwar environment:

> That was a time when people believed that men and women of good will could remake the awful world of the 1930s into a new world: well-behaved, functioning within clearly recognized standard deviations, and with generally accepted means to which matters would inexorably regress ... In such a world, financial markets are always orderly and risk is recognizable, measurable, manageable, and containable.

The drive to measure risk came even more to the fore after the oil shocks of the early 1970s. When the US stock market finally bottomed out in late 1974, prices had tumbled by 40 percent from their highs less than two years earlier. After adjustment for inflation, the entire bull move of the preceding 20 years had been obliterated. In the wake of such stunning losses of wealth, risk control became an explicit goal for the first time in many years – and the new theories of portfolio management and market behaviour seemed made to order. Investors had swung again from an intuitive approach to risk towards trying to measure it. Normal distribution, a popular technique, extrapolated future probabilities from past events. The following illustrations of normal distribution are drawn largely from Mark Kritzman's lucid essay "About Uncertainty."

Heads or tails is clearly governed by chance. So, too, is next year's closing price for the Standard & Poor's 500 – at least according to the laws of probability. To predict the S&P 500 return over the next 12 months, all you need do, the theory says, is count previous annual returns over a sample period. Table 5.1 shows the annual returns of the S&P 500 over the 40-year period from 1951 through 1990.

Table 5.1 Standard & Poor's 500 annual returns

1951	24.0%	1961	26.9%	1971	14.3%	1981	- 4.9%
1952	18.4%	1962	-8.7%	1972	19.0%	1982	21.4%
1953	- 1.0%	1963	22.8%	1973	- 14.7%	1983	22.5%
1954	52.6%	1964	16.5%	1974	-26.5%	1984	6.3%
1955	31.6%	1965	12.5%	1975	37.2%	1985	32.2%
1956	6.6%	1966	-10.1%	1976	23.8%	1986	18.8%
1957	-10.8%	1967	24.0%	1977	-7.2%	1987	5.3%
1958	43.4%	1968	11.1%	1978	6.6%	1988	16.6%
1959	12.0%	1969	-8.5%	1979	18.4%	1989	31.8%
1960	0.5%	1970	4.0%	1980	32.4%	1990	-3.1%

Source: Data through 1981 from Ibbotson and Sinquefield, Stocks, Bonds, Bills and Inflation: The Past and the Future (Charlottesville, VA: The Financial Analysts Research Foundation, 1982).

We can now simply count the number of returns between zero and 10 percent and the number of returns between 10 and 20 percent. Dividing each figure by 40 gives us the relative frequency of returns within each range. Six returns range from zero to 10 percent, while ten returns range from 10 to 20 percent. The relative frequency of these observations are 15 and 25 percent, respectively (Table 5.2).

Table 5.2 Distribution of S&P 500 annual returns

Range of Return			Frequency	Relative frequency
-30%	to	-20%	1	2.5%
-20%	to	-10%	3	7.5%
-10%	to	0%	6	15.0%
0%	to	10%	6	15.0%
10%	to	20%	10	25.0%
20%	to	30%	7	17.5%
30%	to	40%	5	12.5%
40%	to	50%	1	2.5%
50%	to	60%	1	2.5%

The relative frequency percentages are presented in Figure 5.1 in the form of a bar chart. The vertical axis shows the probability of a return within the ranges represented on the horizontal axis.

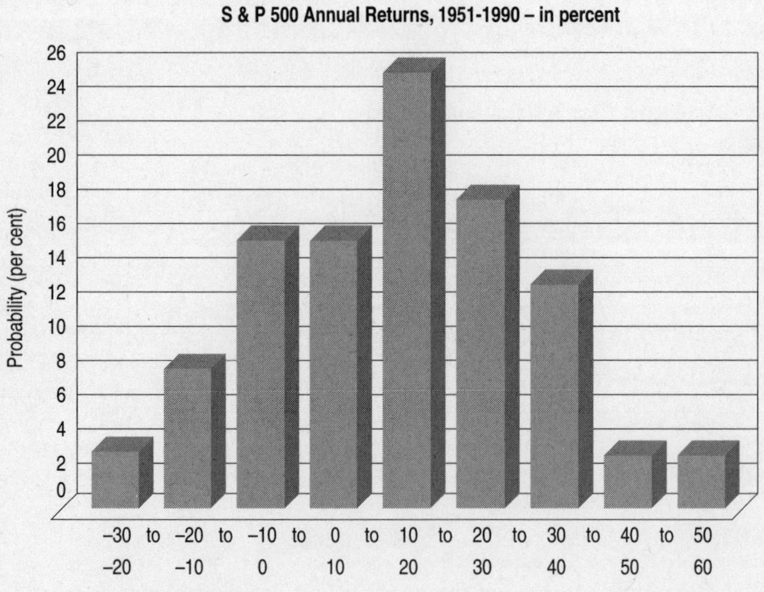

S & P 500 Annual Returns, 1951-1990 – in percent

Fig 5.1 Probability distribution, Standard & Poor's 500

This gives us only limited information. For one thing, the return ranges we've set are rather wide. For another, the sample captures only annual returns and covers just the past 40 years, thus excluding two world wars and the US depression.

Still, the sample seemingly tells us a number of things. As 25 is 66.7 percent more than 15, we're about two-thirds more likely to see a return between 10 to 20 percent than one from zero to 10 percent. Furthermore, adding up the relative frequencies for the three ranges below zero suggests there is a 25 percent chance the S&P 500 will post a loss for the year.

To make more precise deductions, we'd have to extend the measurement period or slice the data into narrower ranges. If we did so, the distribution of returns should in theory eventually come to resemble the familiar bell-shaped curve, or normal distribution (Figure 5.2). Beautiful, isn't it?

NORMAL DISTRIBUTION

The normal distribution is defined by two values: the *mean* of the observations and their variance. Frequency distributions can show you the general shape of a set of data, but some summary of averages or main tendency is also helpful in characterizing it.

MEAN RETURN

The most common average is the arithmetic mean, or simply the mean. To find the mean of any set of values, you just add them up,

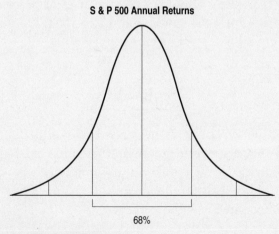

S & P 500 Annual Returns

68%

Fig 5.2 Normal probability distribution

then divide that sum by the number of values. Our 40 S&P 500 observations, for instance, add up to 518. Dividing 518 by 40 gives us the
mean return, which is 12.95 percent. The *mean return* of the S&P 500
will be its expected return (ignoring the effects of compounding).

Statisticians normally use the midpoint of each interval to represent
all the values that fall within it. The interval 10 percent to 20 percent
would be represented by 15 percent, 20 percent to 30 percent by
25 percent, and so on. To calculate the mean return for our S&P 500
sample using this shortcut, you can just multiply the midpoint of each
entry under the column "Range of Return" by its probability under
"Relative Frequency." Then you add up these values. Your worksheet
should look like Table 5.3.

Table 5.3 Distribution of S&P 500 annual returns

Midpoint of range		Relative Frequency		Total
−25%	x	2.5%	=	− 0.625%
−15%	x	7.5%	=	− 1.125%
−5%	x	15.0%	=	− 0.75%
5%	x	15.0%	=	0.75%
15%	x	25.0%	=	3.75%
25%	x	17.5%	=	4.375%
35%	x	12.5%	=	4.375%
45%	x	2.5%	=	1.125%
55%	x	2.5%	=	1.375%
				13.25%

This computation – the sum of observed returns times their probabilities of occurrence – also gives you the arithmetic mean. Adding up
the last column won't bring you out at *exactly* 12.95 percent – but at
13.25 percent you'll at least be close.

VARIANCE

To compute the *variance* of these returns, you deduct each annual
return from the mean return, square this value, add up the squared
values, then divide by the number of observations. This computation –
the average squared difference from the mean – gives the variance,
which in our example is 2.856 percent.

STANDARD DEVIATION

The square root of the variance, called the *standard deviation*, is commonly used as a measure of dispersion. The standard deviation of our example is 16.9 percent. (When checking these figures, remember that you're not dealing with whole numbers, but with *percentages*. We're not discussing the square root of 2.856, but that of 2.856 percent, or 0.02856.) Let's have a closer look at that beautiful bell-shaped curve (Figure 5.3).

CHARACTERISTICS

A normal distribution has several distinguishing features. First, it is *symmetric* around its mean, signifying that half the returns are below the mean return and half above it. Also, because of this symmetry, the *mode* of the sample – i.e. the most common observation – and the median – the middle value of the observations – are equal to each other and to the mean.

Moreover, as the illustration shows, the area enclosed within *one* standard deviation on either side of the mean covers 68 percent of the total area under the curve. The area within *two* standard deviations on either side of the mean encompasses 95 percent of the total area under

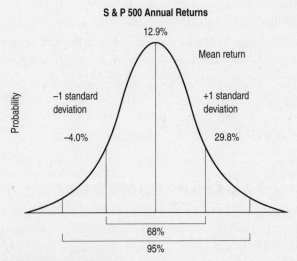

Fig 5.3 Normal probability distribution

the curve, and 99.7 percent of the area under the curve is within plus and minus *three* standard deviations of the mean.

CALCULATING PROBABILITIES

We can calculate several probabilities from this information. We "know," for instance, that 68 percent, 95 percent and 99.7 percent of returns, respectively, will fall within one, two and three standard deviations – plus and minus – of the mean return. Given these assumptions, it is reasonable to calculate the odds of returns one, two or three standard deviations away from the mean. There is roughly a 32 percent chance (100 percent minus 68 percent) of having returns more than one standard deviation above or below the mean return. That 32 percent chance is split equally between profit and loss, with a 16 percent chance of each. The *lowest* likely return within one standard deviation is -4.0 percent: the 12.9 percent mean minus one 16.9 percent standard deviation. The *highest* likely return within a single standard deviation is 29.8 percent: the 12.9 percent mean plus one 16.9 percent standard deviation. Accordingly, there is only a 16 percent theoretical chance that the S&P 500 will post an annual return lower than -4 percent or higher than 29.8 percent.

Such number games can be fascinating. But since the end of World War II, time has proven once more that things do not come in such tidy and familiar packages. In a world changing faster than any of us can grasp, risk seems less amenable to measurement than most investors had come to believe. Still, my attempt to define risk in today's terms will inevitably bring me back to that elegant bell-shaped curve, if merely to rebut its underlying theory. First, however, what are your *own* perceptions of risk? Perhaps you are a fund manager, who fears underperforming a benchmark. Or is your particular bugaboo that of having to subsist on dry crusts upon retirement?

RISK AS THE CHANCE OF LOSS

There are many concepts of risk. Like most people, I am still intuitively drawn to the definition of risk as the chance of *loss*. Yet the odds of losing money on an investment have not yet been calculated successfully.

As we have seen, risk is an elusive concept that is not handled easily with mathematical precision. Nevertheless, the *notion* of risk is central both to evaluating securities and to assembling a portfolio.

The major source of risk for an individual share is uncertainty about its future price. And the major source of risk for a portfolio is uncertainty about its future market value. Obviously, some shares are riskier than others and some portfolios riskier than others. It is also evident that the riskiness of a portfolio relates to the riskiness of the securities it holds. There is general agreement on these propositions, but not on how to quantify the uncertainties involved. The deficiency has become so pressing that in March 1995 the US Securities and Exchange Commission took the unprecedented step of asking individual investors how they would like to see risk defined. In a six-page questionnaire, the SEC asked investors what they think risk is and whether it is most easily understood in numbers, graphs or tables. At the end of June, having received a staggering 1,500 suggestions on defining risk, the SEC extended the comment period for another month. After collating the voluminous replies, the SEC hopes to recommend a standard, easy-to-read risk measure applicable to all investment funds – something which I, like many analysts, believe impossible.

RISK AS VOLATILITY

Nowadays, investment risk is equated wholly or partially with volatility: a measure of how widely the value of an investment fluctuates. Two similar funds or stocks might deliver identical returns over a given period, but one may have climbed steadily while the other repeatedly plunged and soared. Depending when investors pull out of the more volatile fund, they are likely to see bigger gains or losses than investors in the less volatile fund.

To complicate things further, there are *two* classical academic definitions of risk: absolute volatility (standard deviation) or relative volatility (beta). The first is the average percentage over time that a stock's value deviates from its mean, while beta estimates how much an individual holding exaggerates shifts in the value of a market index. More on these in a moment.

Equating volatility with risk embodies numerous absurdities. In the neat world of theoretics, a stock that rises 50 percent over a period in which the market advances 10 percent has a beta of 5.0 and is thus five times as "risky" as the market. I don't think so. The academic notion of volatility as risk might make slightly more sense if portfolio compositions remained more or less unchanged. After all, the composition of a market or its index is relatively static. But an astute global portfolio manager buys undervalued stocks that often fluctuate more than their home market. This means greater volatility than the home market, most often on the upside.

Here's the first place where reality shoves theory aside. When a stock becomes fully valued, an adroit manager sells it. The stock's volatile advance is terminated, so that it is no longer subject to the decline suffered sooner or later by its market. Naturally, a portfolio manager, no matter how adroit, will make mistakes and cannot always overcome market fluctuations. Studies such as Capaul, Rowley and Sharpe's "International Value and Growth Stock Returns" show, however, that undervalued shares tend to outperform their home markets.

Conclusion: *Over time, a consistently undervalued global equity portfolio will not only outperform a world stock-market index, but also tend to be less volatile than individual stockmarkets.*

Volatility as risk assuredly does not appeal to common sense, which, as noted, intuitively defines risk as the prospect of loss. As Norman Fosback points out in *Stock Market Logic*, it is not the *volatility* of the stock with wide price swings that makes it riskier – if, in fact, it is riskier – but rather that some of its swings may be on the downside, thus producing at least interim losses. Volatility itself is desirable in a rising market. Hence, it is loss, and not volatility, that is risk. Volatility is not the same as loss, because at least half of a stock's price swings are gains. Therefore, volatility is no rational measure of risk.

As a proxy for risk, volatility ascribes undesirable qualities to desirable results and favorable qualities to unfavorable results. A stock with only gains expected (no expected losses) would still be deemed risky if those gains varied widely, week to week or year to year. Conversely, a share which offers a single and certain loss would be called riskless.

Fosback poses this ironic question:

> If a highly volatile stock gained 50 percent one month, doubled the next, tripled the next, rose 50 percent the next – in short, racked up month after month of rising prices, never showing a loss – who in their right mind, based solely on that evidence, would call the stock risky?

Obviously, he replies, no one would ... in their right mind. Yet the academics do, because of the stock's exceptional volatility. Conversely, Fosback adds, they would declare a stock riskless if it fell in a smooth and continuous slide until worthless. And a portfolio wholly in cash, with its 0 percent rate of return, would be rated as providing a net "riskless" loss of 5 percent in an era of constant 5 percent inflation.

The Oxford dictionary calls *risk* "the chance of injury or loss." How then did the academics arrive at their definition of risk as volatility? Simple. Wanting to measure risk, they needed a quantitative surrogate. But the one they chose does not seem to measure the chance of injury or loss, either directly or indirectly.

BACK TO THE BELL-SHAPED CURVE

The quantitative-risk surrogate chosen focuses on rates of return. Investors cannot tell in advance what rate of return an investment will yield, but, as I've shown, they can formulate a probability distribution – that bell-shaped curve – of possible rates of return. The wider the bell, the more uncertainty, or risk. A probability distribution may be either subjective or objective. An objective probability distribution, like the previous S&P 500 example, is formed by measuring historical data. A subjective probability distribution is formed by simply writing down your hunches and assigning probabilities to them. As you saw, a *normal* probability distribution is symmetric, meaning the chance of, say, a 25 percent gain is equal to the chance of a 25 percent loss. It makes a beautiful bell, but no one would invest at those odds.

EMPIRICAL PROBABILITY DISTRIBUTION

An *empirical* distribution, on the other hand, is slightly skewed towards gains. Pick a price $10 higher and one $10 lower than today's quote on a stock, and the odds of reaching the higher price are somewhat greater than those of reaching the lower price. Nothing esoteric about this. It simply reflects the nature of stock price changes. Though it would be highly unusual for a stock selling today at $50 to soar by $60 in the next six months, a price change of that magnitude is possible. But it's impossible for the stock to plunge by $60 because its price cannot fall below zero. Allowing for this fact, over a period of six months the bell would look something like Figure 5.4.

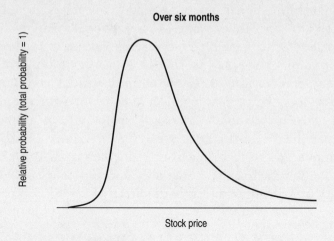

Fig 5.4 Empirical probability distribution

What is more, we know that over time equities in general tend to produce gains. In other words, probabilities shift more to the gain side of
the bell as time goes by. Gain and loss probabilities may be roughly symmetric for a holding a month after purchase, but the longer the holding
period, the more the symmetry of the bell decays. Five years later, the
probabilities are likely to be skewed even more sharply to the gain side.

We expect our *own* investment choices, moreover, to be skewed even
further towards gains. Call it hubris. But if we can indeed do no better
than blind chance, we'd be wiser to follow a passive index strategy – or
get out of the market altogether. (One theory maintains that security
prices are random, so the longer you hold an unchanged portfolio the
riskier it gets. More on this "random walk" idea later.)

Symmetric probability distributions clearly do not reflect the real
investment world. If risk is the chance of injury or loss, it seems more
logical to measure risk by the area in a probability distribution which
is *below* the expected return. This procedure is difficult, though, and
for a time academics seemed to prefer the easy way. Here, for instance,
is William Sharpe on standard distribution in the 1981 edition of his
book *Investments*:

> But why count happy surprises – those above the expected value – at all in
> a measure of risk? Why not just consider deviations below the expected
> return? Measures that do so have much to recommend them. But if a dis-
> tribution is symmetric, the results will be the same, since the left side is a

mirror image of the right! And in general, a list of portfolios ordered on the basis of "downside risk" will differ little if at all from one ordered on the basis of standard deviation.

LOGNORMAL DISTRIBUTION

Despite Sharpe's skepticism, statisticians still use so-called semistandard deviation or semivariance volatility measures in the hope of better reflecting the real world, where in the long run equities have more probability of gain than loss. Analysts therefore often try to approximate the stock price probability curve not by normal distribution, but by lognormal distribution. While normal distribution assumes a $60 price rise in a stock is just as likely as a $60 decline, lognormal distribution pegs the chances of a 100 percent price rise as equal to a 50 percent decline. Though lognormal distribution thus comes closer to matching the actual behavior of stock prices, it too fails to mesh neatly with the empirical data.

This was seen by Gary Gastineau and Albert Madansky in the early 1970s, while tinkering in Madansky's garage on developing an options analysis system. They were dissatisfied with the Black-Scholes options-pricing model, still used widely today, which largely assumes that the probability distribution of future stock prices is lognormal. As a result, the Black Scholes model tends to undervalue options. The model eventually developed by Mandansky, now a professor at the University of Chicago, and Gastineau, now a senior vice president of the American Stock Exchange, instead uses an empirical stock price distribution which fits short-term stock price data much better than the lognormal distribution does. It is indeed quite useful during the brief lifespan of options.

Global investors, however, need to focus on the longer term. Once we finally acknowledge that volatility is an imperfect definition of risk and start concentrating on the likely loss portion of the distribution, we might as well go the whole hog and acknowledge that it is the loss itself, and not the volatility of it, that counts as risk. Criticism of volatility as risk has been heard steadily for decades – and is growing. Despite my doubts, I do hope the Securities Exchange Commission eventually succeeds in redefining investment risk to reflect the real world.

Conclusion: *Volatility alone, no matter how measured, is a poor guide to risk.*

SIX COMMON NOTIONS OF RISK

Measuring the immeasurable

Which fund is most risky? The answer depends heavily on the "measure of risk" chosen. When it comes to funds, I'd say the biggest risk is a manager with a bad long-term record. But Morningstar prefers six other "measures" to rate the risks of US mutual funds. All, alas, ignore long-term performance.

Stock concentration

A fund invested in just a handful of stocks has climbed out on a limb. It may do much better than a broadly diversified fund but it may also do much worse.

Sector concentration

A fund concentrated on just one industry sector is also out on a limb. Even a sector that is deemed relatively safe can stumble badly, as utility investors learned to their sorrow in 1994.

Divergence of returns

As we've seen, standard deviation, beloved by academicians, gauges volatility, or how widely investment returns swing from one period to another. Standard deviation, which depicts the width of the number crunchers' pet bell-shaped curve, might show, for instance, how much a fund's monthly return can stray from its average return. Proponents of standard deviation maintain that a fund with volatile returns, even if it has usually posted gains, is more likely to show a big loss in a future period. That theoretical statement, however, has yet to be proven.

Beta

Beta, another measure of volatility, gauges market sensitivity: how much a fund exaggerates or buffers moves in its own stock market. A fund with a beta of 1.5 is a gunslinger's delight. It tends to rise 15 percent if the overall market is up 10 percent. But if the market falls

10 percent, that fund will probably fall 15 percent. A fund with a beta of 0.75 would be a conservative choice, normally moving only 75 percent as far as the overall market. Beta of course is meant to reflect the systematic risk discussed in Chapter 3.

Highest price/earnings ratio

Another way of assessing risk is to see which funds own the stocks with the highest price/earnings ratios – that is, stocks selling at the highest multiple of earnings per share. High P/E stocks are popular, typically those of successful, fast-growing companies. But any stumble can mean a deep and rapid plunge.

Largest monthly loss

A way of measuring risk familiar to commodities traders – and now gaining popularity in the stock market – is to tally the "maximum drawdown," the largest monthly or quarterly loss a fund has suffered. By those six yardsticks, at the end of June 1995 the riskiest funds among 1,800 diversified US stock funds monitored by Morningstar Inc are shown in Table 5.4.

Table 5.4 What's the riskiest fund of all?

MOST CONCENTRATED IN A FEW STOCKS [a]		LARGEST STANDARD DEVIATION	
Yorktown Classic Value	83%	Prudent Speculator	26
Sequoia	62	American Heritage	25
Steadman American Industry	61	Oberweis Emerging Growth	24
Progressive Value	55	Keystone Hartwell Emerging Growth	24
Steadman Investment	50	Bull & Bear Special Equities	24
MOST CONCENTRATED IN ONE SECTOR [b]		LARGEST BETA	
Copley Fund	86%	CGM Capital Development	1.6
Roberts Stephens Value + Growth	79	Met. Life State St. Res. Cap. Appr.	1.5
Keystone Hartwell Emerging Growth	76	State Street Research Capital	1.5
Eaton Vance Equity - Income	75	20th Century Giftrust Investors	1.5
20th Century Vista Investors	74	20th Century Vista Investors	1.5
HIGHEST AVERAGE P/E RATIO [c]		LARGEST MONTHLY LOSS	
Keystone Hartwell Emerging Growth	47	Prudent Speculator	-28%
USAA Aggressive Growth	36	Morgan Stanley Institut. Small Cap	-23
PBHG Emerging Growth	36	Bull & Bear Special Equities	-23
Smith Barney Special Equities	35	Security Ultra	-22
Govett Smaller Companies	35	Delaware Trend	-18

a. Percentage of fund's assets in top five holdings. b .Sector funds, which by definition invest in only one industry, are excluded.

c. Stock price, divided by past four quarters' per share earnings, averaged for all stocks in fund.

Source: Morningstar

Of the 30 places, it is notable that only four funds – Keystone, Bull &
Bear, 20th Century Vista and Edwin Bernstein's Prudent Speculator –
ranked among the five riskiest by more than a single "measure of risk."
Gertrude Stein's reaction to the California town of Oakland somehow
springs to mind: "When you get there, there isn't any there there." The
difficulty in quantifying risk is illustrated by the following example.

What is the risk of driving a car just slightly above the speed limit?
On a scale of ten, we might assign that risk the number two.

What is the risk then of running a red light? Common sense suggests that the second risk is much greater, so we might assign it the
number seven. Have we now measured risk?

No. We have *estimated* it. When we assign risk a number – *any*
number – it is wise to remember that we are engaged in this kind of
theoretical exercise.

The Hindu numbers we got from the Arabs do enable us to deal
with such abstractions as comparing one risk with another. But pinning arbitrary numbering systems to abstractions to aid comparison
by no means *measures* those abstractions.

*Conclusion: We cannot measure risk. We can only estimate it, and
there is no commonly accepted method of doing so. Different systems
of risk estimation will label different investments as "risky."*

Can you then quantify risk?

Yes. In a limited sense. Granted, an idea cannot be measured. Yet
risks can certainly be *compared*. Covering a war is clearly more risky
than sitting at home reading a book.

Though we cannot measure risk, we apparently can estimate it.

*Conclusion: Though we cannot measure risk, we can approximate (i.e.
quantify) it to make comparisons more discriminating.*

ARE RISK ESTIMATES USEFUL?

Sometimes the past is meaningful, sometimes not

Academics are fond of such yardsticks as Morningstar's because the
underlying data are easily quantifiable. But that doesn't automatically
make them useful. It simply raises the question of how much the past
has to do with the future.

US gross national product rose steadily from 1869 to 1900, with only 5 down years out of 31, so no wonder that a quant-oriented observer like Herbert Hoover – trained as an engineer – said before departing the presidency: "Prosperity is just around the corner." But it took a second world war to get the US back on its growth track. It also made little sense in 1995 to try predicting the future based on what German concerns were doing five years earlier, because – with the Berlin Wall demolished – things in Germany had changed.

Similarly, stock market trading records provide a rear view and ignore oncoming traffic. As the University of Chicago's Eugene Fama and Kenneth French have demonstrated, a fund's prior volatility says absolutely nothing about its future returns.

Standard deviation, in particular, says nothing about the risk that truly concerns investors: that of a one-time, substantial and sustained loss of capital, such as bond funds suffered in 1994. Just as a swimming pool's average depth is of little comfort to a man drowning at the deep end, a fund that usually varies by only 1 percent may, on occasion, zigzag wildly. Indeed, early in 1994, Morningstar assigned its highest, or safest, risk-return rating to the Piper Jaffray Institutional Government Income Portfolio. When the bond market crashed, the fund, stocked with high-octane derivatives, plummeted 25 percent.

Just before the crash, however, a Morningstar analyst had warned of the Piper Fund, "If interest rates move up again, this fund would be hurt far worse than its peers." The moral? Investors willing to face the hard slog of studying a fund's holdings can evaluate the fundamental risks of its actual assets. A numerical yardstick provides a quicker fix, but is sorely superficial. Beta is no substitute for brains.

Risk as volatility plus return

Despite its numerous shortcomings, risk as volatility does seem to have some limited predictive value. Volatility becomes a more useful predictive tool, however, when *performance* is included in the calculation. Fortunately, recent developments seem to trend in this direction.

The Sharpe ratio

The definition of risk most frequently used by professional investors is the ratio developed by Nobel Prize winner William Sharpe. The Sharpe ratio – my preferred method of sifting investment funds – measures an investment's return relative to its degree of risk. Essentially, you find the

Sharpe ratio by dividing the annualized rate of return over a fixed period, minus the risk-free rate, by the annualized standard deviation of returns. The risk-free interest rate, the one that could have been earned on a one-month interbank deposit, is the rate banks charge each other.

If you had a choice between two funds, one with a standard deviation of 5 percent and another with 10 percent, you'd probably choose the one with the lower figure. But when performance is added in, the picture can alter radically.

If the fund with a standard deviation of 10 percent is delivering an average return of 20 percent, while the fund with a 5 percent deviation delivers 5 percent, the more volatile fund is theoretically less risky.

The Sharpe ratio is often calculated over three years so as to take changing investment climates into account. To see how it works, let's turn this ratio loose on the 115 Dutch investment funds tracked by ABN AMRO bank. All meet these criteria:

- A minimum track record of three years
- Amsterdam-listed, Dutch-managed or Dutch-administered
- Registered with the central bank
- Assets no less than 15 million guilders ($1,000,000)
- Regular publication of share price
- Open to individual investors

From 1992 through 1994, the risk-free interest rate in the Netherlands averaged 7.7 percent. The return remaining after deducting that "riskless" 7.7 percent from a fund's average annual return over the three-year period may be either negative or positive. Either way, it is then divided by the risk incurred. That risk, under the Sharpe formula, equals standard deviation: how much a fund's price deviates from its average price. The wider the swings, the more your theoretical risk. In these calculations, funds with a high return can rank poorly if they carry substantial theoretical risk. In Table 5.5, according to the Sharpe ratio, are the current top ten among Holland's investment funds.

The Sharpe ratio, as I say, is useful for discriminating among funds. Managing *portfolio* risk, however, is chiefly a matter of diversification. In a global equity portfolio of 25 or more holdings, estimating the risk of individual stocks or funds is just not worth the trouble. It is far more important to assure that the portfolio reflect a wide range of countries and sectors. This simple method of risk reduction, unique to investing abroad, is spelled out in the chapters entitled "Allocating Assets" and "Assuring Variety."

Table 5.5 Scoreboard of Dutch investment funds per September 30, 1994

(Returns in guilders)	Last year	Place	Last 3 years	Place	Risk*	Place	Sharpe
ING Bank Dutch Fund	14.9%	10	17.8%	6	11.5	43	0.9
Asian Tigers Fund	25.8%	4	27.0%	4	24.4	87	0.8
Webefo	7.2%	22	12.5%	11	6.2	25	0.8
ABN AMRO Netherlands Fund	14.5%	11	18.7%	7	11.6	45	0.8
Asian Selection Fund	24.4%	6	28.8%	3	27.2	92	0.8
India Magnum Fund	52.2%	1	43.2%	1	49.2	99	0.7
Amsterdam EOE Index Fund	16.8%	9	15.9%	8	14.1	58	0.6
Indo Suez Himalayan Fund	38.9%	2	31.7%	2	47.7	98	0.5
ABN AMRO Obligatie Fonds	- 0.5%	59	9.5%	28	3.8	10	0.5
Obligatie Beleggingspool	- 0.7%	60	9.4%	29	3.7	7	0.5

*The risk proxy here is standard devaluation, measured over the last three years.
Source: The Outside Analyst

Conclusion: It is the risk of each market that concerns us – more than the risk of individual holdings.

Estimating aggregate market risks

One way to estimate your risk in a particular market is simply to average the volatility of your holdings in that market. Just as the beta of an individual stock or fund indicates how much it will exaggerate or dampen market swings, the beta of your holdings in a market lets you estimate how much that portfolio segment will rise or fall, given a specific swing in the underlying market. Several firms produce estimates of market sensitivity on a continuing basis. One readily accessible source is *Value Line*, covering some 5,000 US and Canadian firms. Merrill Lynch and a few other brokerage houses also rate the market risk of US stocks on a monthly basis. As for funds, the best known US rating service, Morningstar, as we've seen, uses six risk measurements, including beta. The two major UK fund rating services, Hardwick Stafford Wright (+ 44-1625-511311) and Micropal (+ 44-181-741-4100) calculate volatility figures as well. Micropal and HSW also produce figures combining risk rating with performance measurement for a risk-adjusted rate of return. UK fund managers can look up a local share's beta in the *London Business School Risk Measurement Service*, a quarterly for professionals. Using these figures, you can compute the beta of your own fund and than calculate whether you got a better return for the "risk" taken than you would have received by investing, for example, in an index fund.

If your portfolio holds approximately equal amounts in your home currency of a number of domestic stocks, figuring the portfolio's volatility is easy. You just average the beta ratings of all your holdings: that is, add up all the individual betas, then divide by the number of holdings. Your portfolio, however, is more likely to consist of unequal amounts of various holdings.

In this case, estimating portfolio volatility means a bit more work, but the technique is equally simple and straightforward. First, multiply the beta of each fund (or stock) by the *market value* of that holding. If your home currency is the guilder and you own 100 shares of Philips priced at *f* 60, its market value is *f* 6,000. Philips' beta, as reported in the local Dutch paper, is 1.56, so its guilder volatility is 1.56 times 6,000, or 9,360. Secondly, still assuming a single currency and a single market, add together all the numbers calculated in the first step. Thirdly, divide that sum by the total market value. The result is your volatility rating in that market. If your Dutch portfolio has a beta of 1.30, a 20 percent increase in Amsterdam's AEX index is likely to mean a 26 percent rise in the value of that portfolio (1.3 times 20). Conversely, the Dutch portfolio would probably reflect a 20 percent drop in the AEX by plunging 26 percent.

The three pillars of global investment

Things can get somewhat more complicated when you invest *outside* your domestic market. Now you have the opportunity to add value to your portfolio in three ways: *currency, market allocation and stock selection*. But this benefit is going to cost you time, effort – and especially thought. You no longer have the luxury of dealing purely with selecting attractive holdings. You're now also obliged to consider more than one currency – and the movements of more than one market. What we called guilder volatility for the Philips' holding would be sterling volatility for your holdings of, say, British Steel and Standard Chartered Bank – or dollar volatility if you happen to own Micron Technology. The volatility of your sterling and dollar portfolios can easily be calculated in the same way as the guilder-denominated portfolio. If the sterling portfolio has a beta of 1.10, it will tend to rise or fall 10 percent more than the FTSE index.

Now, however, we seem to have painted ourselves into a corner. Beta is highly sensitive to the market index selected. How then are we to deal with a global portfolio and its shifting mix of countries? You cannot just add up the volatilities for each currency and convert those sums to your home currency at the current exchange rate. That would be adding apples and pears. Beta compares a share's volatility with that of its home market. But what is the home market of a global portfolio? (A later chapter entitled "Your Benchmark" offers a pragmatic answer, useful in evaluating the performance of your global portfolio.) Here we have reached the practical limit in estimating risk. Some international managers, ignoring this fact, measure risk as the standard deviation of excess returns: how much a portfolio's gain deviates from its average value. As Fischer Black pointed out in "Global Portfolio Optimization," this is tantamount to having no benchmark, or defining the benchmark as a portfolio fully invested in the domestic short-term interest rate.

THE PRACTICAL LIMIT

Where estimating risk stops being useful

Quantifying risk is obviously useful in the context of a single market. It lets you compare your aggregate stock or fund holdings there with the movements of *that market* as a whole. But quantifying risk is of little use for a global equity portfolio. The rules covering a single market no longer apply.

Investing abroad is something like stepping off into space. The mother ship is your benchmark and earth is your home currency. Severed from the mother ship, the oxygen in your suit cannot last long. Calculating portfolio beta without a suitable global benchmark will fill your lungs no more than can the memory of a summer breeze. Likewise, calculating standard deviation without currency factors is as futile as trying to twirl a yo-yo in your weightless state. You can access the local currency return of a foreign stock market no more than you can survive on the planet Mars. You can receive the foreign return coupled with an exchange-rate return. Or you can get the foreign return hedged into your own currency. Those are the only options.

Country and currency factors

Over the long run, investment returns in your home market are largely determined by what stocks you pick. Short-term returns are of course another story. Now that you're investing globally, momentary swings in foreign markets and currencies can have a huge impact on your immediate performance. To keep things as simple as possible, let's assume that economic, inflation and interest-rate risks are all neatly reflected in stock market and currency movements.

You no longer have mainly one factor to consider, but rather three in each country: currency, market allocation and stock selection. The possible permutations of these three pillars of global investment are almost infinite. If you invest in just two foreign countries, the three factors determining your result in each of their markets will produce three times three, or nine possible permutations. This is commonly expressed as three to the second power, or three squared. If you double the number of foreign countries to four, the three determinant factors in each stock market will produce three times three times three times three, or 81 possible permutations, usually expressed as three to the fourth power.

If you widen your horizon to eight foreign countries, the number of permutations swiftly proliferates, becoming three to the eighth power, or 6,561. A global portfolio should certainly embrace no less than 15 foreign countries. The possible permutations of investing in 15 markets are mindboggling – over 14 million – even without the economic, inflation and interest-rate factors effectively excluded from this example.

Each country has its own peculiarities. One stock market's systematic risk is not automatically akin to that of another. Nor do the relative values of currencies long remain unchanged. Yet statisticians, ignoring the fundamental fallacy of applying the maths valid in a single market to that of multiple markets, often proceed to "measure" the risk adjusted return of a global portfolio without a suitable benchmark. The Sharpe ratio, which measures an investment's return relative to its degree of risk, is not applicable to a global portfolio because, as we've seen, that formula compares an investment's return relative to a riskless rate of return. But there is no global riskless rate. Ignoring this inconvenient fact, some statisticians simply use the US riskless rate, while others take a leap of faith: defining the risk-adjusted performance of a global portfolio as its mean return divided by its standard deviation. Moreover, lacking a global benchmark, beta, which estimates how much changes in a stock or fund price exaggerate shifts in the value of a market index, is not truly applicable to a global portfolio either. Nevertheless, investors sometimes compare a global portfolio's performance to that of their domestic index. This amounts to building sand castles. The key to estimating (and reducing) portfolio risk when investing globally lies elsewhere: in your country and currency decisions. Just as the specific (non-market) risks of individual stocks tend to nullify each other, so the economic and currency risks of different markets can be reasonably counterbalanced.

That has to do with how market movements correlate.

THE CAPITAL ASSET PRICING MODEL

Modern portfolio theory says that to the extent markets are efficient, high returns will carry high risk. Conversely, more risk generally means more likelihood of a big return. You get paid for taking on the extra risk.

A big advance in modern portfolio theory was seen in 1964, when William Sharpe published the Capital Asset Pricing Model, or CAPM, for which he subsequently won the Nobel Prize. The CAPM says the total risk of each individual security is irrelevant. Systematic (or market) risk, CAPM says, is the only one that matters, because, as Chapter 3 explained, stocks can be combined in portfolios to eliminate the other (specific) risk.

As we've also seen, systematic risk cannot wholly be diversified away. This, says the CAPM, is the only part of total risk you get paid for assuming. The CAPM declares, in other words, that returns for any stock will be related to beta, a proxy for systematic risk.

But beta is badly flawed. At the race track, long shots seem to go off at much lower odds than their probability of winning would suggest, while favorites go off at higher odds than jibe with their winning percentages. Similarly, low-risk stocks earn higher returns and high-risk stocks earn lower returns than beta theory predicts.

What is beta missing?

Plainly, *subjective input*. Beta is so severely objective that it totally ignores the key subjective component of share prices: the consensus of analyst earnings estimates. A recent study by Burton Malkiel, Professor of Economics at Princeton University, provides an attractive alternative to beta. He found that the dispersion of analysts' forecasts correlates best with expected returns and serves as a good proxy for a variety of systematic risks that beta sorely neglects. The following illustration is drawn from Malkiel's paper "Risk and Return: A New Look."

Suppose we have two companies: a steel firm that is highly sensitive to economic conditions and a pharmaceutical firm that isn't. Analysts may agree completely on how economic conditions affect the two concerns, yet differ greatly on their economic forecasts. If that should happen, earnings forecasts for the steel company might well diverge more than those for the pharmaceutical firm. Table 5.6 depicts this.

Table 5.6 How economic forecasts affect earnings forecasts

(Economic Forecast)	(Steel company forecast)	(Drug company forecast)
Analyst A: GDP: up sharply Inflation: down Interest rates: down	Sales up Raw material prices steady Borrowing costs down Strong earnings growth	Sales up whatever happens to GDP Uses few raw materials - no effect No borrowing - no effect Strong earnings growth
Analyst B: GDP: no growth Inflation: remains high Interest rates: remain high	Sales flat Raw material prices up Borrowing costs up Weak earnings growth	Sales up whatever happens to GDP Uses few raw materials - no effect No borrowing - no effect Strong earnings growth

Analyst A is optimistic about real growth and convinced that inflation and interest rates will fall.

Analyst B, on the other hand, predicts sluggish real growth but believes that inflation and interest rates will remain high.

Although the analysts agree on how economic conditions affect the two companies, their earnings forecasts differ because their economic forecasts differ and because the companies are not equally sensitive to these economic conditions. The steel firm is highly sensitive to GDP growth because it affects sales; to inflation because it affects raw material prices; and to interest rates because they affect borrowing costs. So Analyst A foresees strong earnings growth for the steel company, while Analyst B sees a very weak performance. As for the drug firm, assumed relatively immune to economic cycles, the analysts agree on their earnings forecasts despite differences in their economic forecasts.

The important point to note about this illustration is that the company for which the forecasts differed sharply was the one most sensitive to systematic risk factors, i.e. the company with the greatest sensitivity to economic conditions. Hence, differences in analysts' forecasts may be a most useful proxy for systematic risk in the broadest sense of the term. A firm for which earnings forecasts differ greatly is generally one highly sensitive to economic conditions, that is, to market risk. So the larger the dispersion of earnings forecasts (i.e. the wider the estimates are scattered) the larger your anticipated return ought to be.

Indeed, the dispersion of analysts' forecasts may be the best single approximation of systematic risk available. I'll explain how to use such forecasts in "The World's Best Bargains."

A global approach to risk

Strange as it may seem, in a global equity portfolio you are likely to achieve the highest return for any given level of risk by maximizing the risk of each individual market. As we have seen, market volatility does not equal risk. On the contrary, for the serious investor, volatility provides opportunity. Investment opportunity exists in the difference between reality and perception. High volatility widens that difference, increasing opportunity for the knowledgeable investor. Your aim in estimating the systematic risk of each market in which you invest is thus to assure that your stock selections within that market exaggerate its movements as much as possible.

You naturally want the largest likely portfolio rate of return for any given level of risk. Each part of the portfolio should therefore contribute as much as possible to the bottom line. This demands attention to the correlation among securities – how their rates of return interact. You seek stocks or funds whose rates of return are unrelated or – even better – move in opposition to each other. The final result will usually be to boost your portfolio return by letting you allocate a bigger slice to holdings with high expected returns. Inevitably, these will have higher systematic risk. More on this in "Allocating Assets."

Conclusion: For individual stocks, the dispersion of analyst earnings estimates seems to be the best proxy for market risk, and the wider such estimates are scattered the higher the return you can anticipate. In choosing individual holdings for a global portfolio, it is thus wiser to seek market risk than to avoid it.

Risk avoidance is already inherent in the overall composition of your portfolio. The standard deviation of a global portfolio will be much less than that of its typical holding. Though market risk cannot be eliminated, going global does reduce it sharply. This is in fact your most important technique for reducing risk.

Conclusion: Maximum risk reduction – reduction in the volatility of returns – is already inherent in the fact that you are investing worldwide.

The whole interminable discussion of how to define and "measure" risk may suggest medieval theologians debating how many angels can fit on the head of a pin. But as Malkiel notes in the study cited above:

> The quest for better risk measures is not simply an amusing exercise that accomplishes only the satisfaction of permitting academics to play with their computers. It has important implications for protecting investors.

Estimating risk is important so that you don't buy into more overall risk than you can stomach, then bail out when the going gets tough. Estimating risk also helps you measure your portfolio's performance against a benchmark.

Summary

There is no commonly accepted method of estimating risk. Different systems of risk estimation will judge different investments as "risky." Though you cannot measure risk, you can approximate (i.e. quantify) it so as to make comparisons more discriminating. Over time, a consistently undervalued global equity portfolio will not only outperform a world stock-market index, but also tend to be less volatile than individual stock markets. Volatility alone, however, is a poor guide to risk – no matter how it is measured. For individual stocks, the dispersion of analyst earnings estimates seems to be the best proxy for market risk, and the wider such estimates are scattered the higher the return you can anticipate. In choosing individual holdings for a global portfolio, it is thus wiser to seek market risk than to avoid it. The risk of each market should concern you more than the risk of individual shares. Quantifying risk is of little or no use for a global equity portfolio as a whole. The major factors in portfolio risk when investing globally are your country and currency choices. Just as the specific risks of individual stocks tend to nullify each other, so the economic and currency risks of different markets can be reasonably counterbalanced. Maximum risk reduction – if defined as reduction in the volatility of returns – is already inherent in the fact that you are investing worldwide. Once again, it is better to be approximately right than precisely wrong.

Though we cannot measure risk, we can measure *cost*. The next chapter reveals the hidden cost of investment fees.

6

MEASURING COST

"Beware of small expenses.
A little leak will sink a great ship."
Benjamin Franklin (1706–1790)

For every Deutschmark, franc or dollar skimmed from your investment capital today, you lose far more down the road. Those funds are gone forever. They can no longer help increase your assets. Money spent to pay commissions and expenses is money that fails to grow. The key to evaluating investment fees is to perceive that such expenses represent capital that would otherwise have been invested. The hidden cost of investment fees is their *future* cost: cumulative curtailment of your return.

Investing is a business. Business owners incur expenses to generate revenues. If they fail to keep track of those expenses, the business comes unraveled. Likewise, if you give all your attention in investing to the potential for big profits and fail to keep track of expenses, your portfolio will suffer.

INITIAL COSTS

Initial investment costs are frequently underestimated. Paying an 8.5 percent commission up front to invest in a fund, for instance, really means paying 9.3 percent, because that commission comes off the top. It reduces the size of your initial investment. If you invest $1,000 in a fund that charges 8.5 percent up front, your initial stake drops to $915. The $85 commission is 9.3 percent of $915. You have to earn 9.3 percent simply to have $1,000 again. Meanwhile, however, inflation has nibbled at the currency, so that $1,000 now buys at least two or three percent less than when you started.

RECURRING COSTS

Though investing regularly is a sound policy, doing so through a fund with an up-front commission charge can significantly undermine your total return. You're punished in the long run because you pay the commission repeatedly. Take a practical example from Britain: a seemingly modest 5 percent commission on a monthly contribution of £100. That's £5 a month, or £60 a year. Over 10 years, the face value of your commission costs for the privilege of investing amounts to £600.

But that calculation ignores the hidden cost. These fees are lost capital. Capital that would otherwise have been invested. Over the 10-year period, a regular monthly investment of £5 compounded at 10 percent would have grown to more than £1,024. If you could invest for 10 years at 10 percent without incurring commissions, a £100 monthly investment would grow to £20,484. The lost £1,024 has now reduced that sum to £19,460.

Commissions on funds or on share transactions are not the only recurring investment costs. Funds impose other recurring charges for various expenses, the steepest related to marketing. And some stock markets reflect prices set by buyers and sellers, while others create a spread between buying and selling prices. These spreads are profitable for the market-makers but mean you pay more each time you buy or sell.

Using a conservative 1 percent estimate for such recurring costs, the final value of your £100 monthly investment drops another £1,133 to £18,327. Over the ten years, total investment costs of £2,157 (£1,024 + £1,133) have sharply curtailed your return.

To make up that £2,157 difference, a fund with a 5 percent up-front charge and annual expenses of 1 percent would have to earn far more than 10 percent a year – nearly 11.75 percent, in fact, to approximate the "no-load" value. Although a fund may outperform others in some years by a 1.75 percent margin, that is a high hurdle over a 10-year investment horizon.

Because of the hidden cost of investment fees, from here on, where possible, I'll enumerate and compare such charges.

The next chapter describes the four paths you can take to global investment – and their various initial and recurring costs.

7

THE FOUR PATHS TO FOREIGN INVESTMENT

"When a road is once built, it is a strange thing how it collects traffic."

Robert Louis Stevenson, 1895

Global investing may sound a bit pretentious, but it is by no means only for an élite. You don't have to be wealthy or command huge corporate funds to invest outside your own home market. In managing your own portfolio, four paths can take you onto the global stage, each requiring only small sums. Two of these paths to foreign investment are direct and two are indirect. The direct way to diversify your portfolio internationally is to invest in foreign shares listed on your home market and on other exchanges. The indirect way is to invest through so-called depositary receipts – proxies for foreign shares – and through global, regional or country funds. Each of these four roads to foreign investment is collecting more and more traffic.

DIRECT INVESTMENT

Path one: Foreign shares listed on your home market

If you want to dip your toe in the global investment ocean, but aren't ready for the big plunge, one option is to become familiar with foreign stocks by buying some of those listed on your own home market. Trading foreign stocks on your home soil gives you the twin advantages of convenience and familiarity. Shares are quoted in your own currency, adjusted daily for fluctuations in exchange rates, and your broker can convert their dividends into the currency that suits you best.

On the other hand, there are drawbacks. The main one is the limited range of foreign stocks available at home. On your local stock market, the splendid array of world trade shrinks to a handful of corporate names.

Moreover, the foreign companies listed on your home exchange are among the best-known in their own countries. UK firm Reuters Holdings, for instance, is one of the most heavily traded stocks on the US Nasdaq Stock Market. But the prospects of finding bargains among such behemoths are small.

To find out whether you want to expand your efforts at global investing, the home-soil approach can nevertheless be useful as a first step in getting to know foreign companies. Investors in Switzerland, Hong Kong, Holland, Germany or Britain have the edge at home on their American counterparts. They can buy most foreign securities through neighborhood brokers. Dutch investors, for example, automatically compare US stocks with those in their home market. Not only that, they usually compare prices on all major world markets before deciding which stocks to buy or sell.

The path to foreign investment is rockier in the States.

In mid-1994, a mere 200 foreign stocks were listed directly on the New York Stock Exchange, 77 on the American Exchange and 323 on the Nasdaq. Price and availability of such stocks are no problem. Another 987 were traded over-the-counter, making it harder to get a fix on prices and trading volumes. Another 73 foreign stocks were available only to institutional buyers.

The major stock exchanges

If you live in the US or any other developed country, your domestic stock market is increasingly bringing foreign investment opportunities within easy reach.

The range of foreign securities available at home will continue to grow. The day of the global marketplace in which investors are able to trade securities electronically on just about any non-restricted exchange, is moving ever closer. Indeed, some firms in smaller countries now bypass their local markets to list shares directly in the markets of major countries. In December 1992, for instance, Brilliance China Automotive, a Chinese company, was listed on the New York Stock Exchange, bypassing a listing in Hong Kong or the possibility of listing "B" shares on the more volatile Shanghai or Shenzen exchanges. The issue was so well-received that the share price more than doubled, soaring from the $16 offer price to $33. This resounding success triggered a rush by mainland companies to list their firms on major exchanges outside their own Chinese markets. The world's major exchanges are of course the ones that transact the most business. They are shown in Figure 7.1 ranked by dollar volume of equity trading in 1994.

Today, in terms of total dollar volume of equity trading, the world's seven major markets are the United States, Britain, Japan, Germany, Switzerland, France and Canada. Sometimes they rise or fall together, but not always. If your home market is one of the major ones, you'll find that roughly 100 to 500 foreign equities are already listed there.

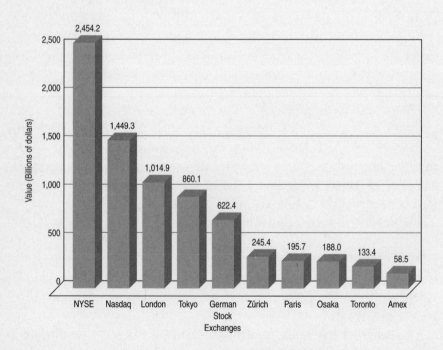

Fig 7.1 1994 Dollar volume of equity trading in major world markets

But the fact that an exchange has high turnover does not automatically mean that it can deal efficiently with your foreign share transactions.

Path two: Foreign shares listed on other exchanges

Sometimes an exchange with relatively modest turnover can be more tuned in to global diversification. Paris, for instance, lists more foreign equities directly than Switzerland, Germany, Nasdaq or the New York Stock Exchange. And Amsterdam, despite its relatively low turnover, lists just as many foreign equities as the New York Stock Exchange (NYSE). Table 7.1 displays the number of foreign equities listed on several major exchanges with their 1994 foreign equity turnover in sterling.

Table 7.1 Foreign equities listed directly on major exchanges

Total number of foreign companies listed at end- 1994		Value of 1994 foreign-equity turnover (£m)
Amsterdam	217	125*
Brussels	141	2,441
Germany (Federation of Exchanges)	227	11,760*
Nasdaq (includes 104 ADRs)	325	50,006
New York (includes 152 ADRs)	217	158,768
Amex (includes 8 ADRs)	74	3,966
Paris	338	2,532
Switzerland (Association of Exchanges)	242	10,210
Tokyo	93	481
London	464	359,333*
Vienna	46	391

* Turnover has been halved for comparison purposes
Sources: London Stock Exchange, Nasdaq

Many so-called London trades are done by British brokers on the Dutch and German exchanges. To avoid double counting and provide a better basis of comparison, turnover has been halved for these three markets. London, as you can see, has a greater value of foreign equity transactions than the NYSE and Nasdaq – though if you add in domestic equities, each of the latter has higher total turnover. (The stock exchanges of Athens, Helsinki, Korea, Lisbon, Mexico and Taiwan list no foreign shares at all.)

Let's look at some of the major markets more closely:

The New York Stock Exchange

In dollar volume, more than half of all US stock market business is transacted on the New York Stock Exchange. Known as the Big Board, it lists more than 3,000 stocks, all of which must meet stringent requirements. Though the NYSE handles the largest dollar volume, it is not necessarily the best place for trading. In recent years, the NYSE has lost ground, moving from an 85 percent share of the total market in 1960 to its current 55 percent.

The American Stock Exchange

The American Stock Exchange (Amex) is also located in New York. Many blue-chip companies, including General Motors and Standard Oil, were first listed on the Amex before moving to the Big Board. All major US brokerage houses have seats on the Amex, as well as on the NYSE. But the Amex is shrinking. During 1995, it lost 28 companies to competing exchanges and delisted another 38 itself. After adding 52 new listed companies, the most since 1991, the Amex had a net decline of 14 companies. By comparison, the NYSE added a net 105 companies. The declining trend at the Amex has been visible for sometime. In 1970, it listed 1,222 companies, just short of the Big Board's 1,311 at the time. Since then, the NYSE list has grown past 3,000 while the Amex list has dwindled to less than 900.

Regional exchanges

There are numerous other US regional exchanges. These include the Pacific Stock Exchange, the Philadelphia Stock Exchange and the Midwest Stock Exchange in Chicago. All regional exchanges specialize in the growth companies in their own regions.

   The regional exchanges do not meet the NYSE's size and volume requirements, but they are more likely to have new issues, small growth companies, local utilities and other stocks with greater growth potential. Many local exchanges carry the Big Board stocks as well.

Nasdaq

In 1971, Washington-based Nasdaq became the world's first electronic stock market. Unlike the NYSE, Amex and regional exchanges, with auction floors where brokers buy and sell face-to-face, Nasdaq – owned by the National Association of Securities Dealers – is an association of some 500 market-maker firms linked by phone and computer. In January 1993, for the first time, more shares were traded via Nasdaq's electronic quotations systems than via the order-pads and computers of the NYSE's specialist floor-traders. Despite NYSE claims of the superiority of its auction-specialist-based market over Nasdaq's quote screens, many Wall Street brokers say Nasdaq's lower costs and faster execution have made it the preferred market. Partly for this reason, the Nasdaq Stock Market is the fastest-growing equity market in the United States. More foreign-based firms now trade there than on all other US stock markets combined.

In 1992, Nasdaq overtook the Tokyo Exchange as the world's second largest equity market in dollar terms, also leaving London's International Stock Exchange far behind. In 1994, the dollar value of trading in Nasdaq-listed foreign securities and American Depositary Receipts totalled more than $80.8 billion. At the end of the year, Nasdaq had 221 foreign firms listed (135 in Canada), versus 66 for the Amex and 65 for the NYSE. Nasdaq also had 104 issuers of American Depositary Receipts, as against 152 for the NYSE and 8 for the Amex.

There are significant disadvantages to trading through Nasdaq, some related to the absence of market-making specialists to provide liquidity when order imbalances threaten to halt trading. A couple of Nasdaq's drawbacks – volatility and riskiness – are simply those of trading in any small stock at a time of heavy demand, particularly from very large buyers.

Nasdaq's main disadvantage is that commissions and spreads between bid and offer price can vary too widely. For illiquid stocks, the cost between buying and selling may reach 10 percent or more, meaning the shares must rise by at least that much for you to break even, let alone make a profit.

There are also recent allegations of collusion by Nasdaq market-makers in quoting prices. Nasdaq is a "quote-driven" market in which market-makers display buy-and-sell prices, while the NYSE and Amex are "order-driven," with the bid-offer spread calculated from the trades that have been done. In an order-driven market like the NYSE, dealers rely mainly on commissions for their profits. In a quote-driven one like Nasdaq, dealers make their profits from spreads between the bid and ask price – and a 1994 study by economists William Christie and Paul Schultz in the *Journal of Finance* concluded that Nasdaq dealers had been conniving to keep spreads on stocks artificially wide.

It based this conclusion on a look at dealers' quotes for 100 of Nasdaq's most heavily traded stocks in 1991.

Share prices in the US and Canada are not yet quoted under the decimal system, but in eighths. The study – "Why do Nasdaq market-makers avoid odd-eighth quotes?" – found that for many stocks the dealers, surprisingly, almost never made quotes ending in odd-eighth amounts: i.e. one-eighth, three-eighths, etc. In fact, for more than half of the stocks, including such heavyweights as Apple Computer and Lotus Development, odd-eighth quotes appeared less than 2 percent of the time.

Christie and Schultz suggested that this reflected an implicit agreement among Nasdaq market-makers. By rounding all price quotes to the nearest quarter-dollar, they could guarantee themselves a minimum spread between buying and selling of 25 cents. Spreads of one-eighth and three-eighths, the study found, are common on the NYSE and Amex, occurring more than 20 percent of the time, but they are rare on Nasdaq. Applying that 20 percent guideline to Nasdaq, the alleged overcharges mount up. An extra eighth of a point may not sound like much, but on a 1,000-share transaction it comes to $125. In the eleven years from 1983 through 1993, the average number of shares traded on Nasdaq per year was 33.9 billion. If Nasdaq dealers indeed conspired to fix prices on some 20 percent of these transactions, or 6.8 billion shares, the overcharges were – hold on to your hat – about $847 million per year.

In the summer of 1994, following a report of the study in the *Los Angeles Times*, over 20 lawsuits were filed accusing dealers who make markets on Nasdaq of price-fixing. The lawsuits alleged that market-makers enforce price-fixing by steering business away from any dealer who steps out of line. They also contended that such arrangements are common knowledge among Nasdaq insiders, and that traders are taught them as part of their training.

One piece of damning evidence was the behaviour of Nasdaq prices in the wake of the study. After it came out, odd-eighth quotes suddenly became more common and many published spreads narrowed. In early May, Apple Computer's spread was 25 cents 70 percent of the time and otherwise 50 cents. By the end of May, the respective figures were $12\frac{1}{2}$ cents and 25 cents.

In the summer of 1995, the *Los Angeles Times* reported that the Securities & Exchange Commission will file civil charges against the National Organization of Securities Dealers for failing to halt these illegal practices and others that increase small investors' costs. Nasdaq will have to end such violations, perhaps by introducing order-matching and the decimal system.

The moral? Whether you invest at home or globally, vigilance is the watchword. Even the best markets are prone to abuses. Nasdaq nevertheless remains the prototype of the future global marketplace, where investors will be able to trade securities located anywhere on the planet. Nasdaq is being emulated not only in the stock markets of London, Paris, Frankfurt, Sydney and Toronto, but also in those of Argentina, Korea and Taiwan.

In addition to Nasdaq's 216,056 terminals in the United States, another 29,942 can be viewed in 52 countries around the world. The number of Nasdaq terminals ranges from 10,412 in Canada and 6,340 in Switzerland to 3 in New Zealand and 1 in Jordan.

For a list of terminal locations in your own country and more information on trading foreign equities, you can write Nasdaq at 1735 K Street N.W., Washington, DC 20006-1500, USA, or phone them on + 1 202-728-8000. Three of their booklets are especially informative: *Nasdaq Fact Book & Company Directory, The ADR Handbook* and *The Investor Glossary.*

Easdaq

The year 1996 saw a European version of Nasdaq: the European Association of Securities Dealers Automated Quotation System, or Easdaq. Trading is quote-driven, with European and US market makers displaying competing prices, and the system focuses on smaller growth companies. For information, you can write Easdaq at 7 Limeharbour, Docklands, London E14 9NQ, or phone + 44-171-515-3095.

Direct US listings of foreign shares

Non-US firms that meet the strict accounting and disclosure rules of the US Securities & Exchange Commission, plus NYSE, Amex or Nasdaq standards, may have their shares listed just like those of any qualifying US firm. So-called "New York" shares of other foreign firms, denominated in dollars, also trade directly in the US, mostly over-the-counter, with some quoted on Nasdaq. Reports and dividends on "New York" shares can be a problem.

The London Stock Exchange

Operating in the European time zone, London is the natural apex of the global financial triangle, situated in a key position between New York and Tokyo. It speaks the only language that dealers in both those cities more or less understand. By European standards, telecommunications are cheap. More international telephone calls originate in London than anywhere else on earth. It has two of the five largest international airports and is being cabled with optical fibre faster than any other major city.

Elimination of foreign exchange controls in 1979 paved the way for UK institutions to invest in foreign securities. For the first time, members of the exchange faced competition from overseas brokers. But the London firms were relatively small. Some lacked capital to trade in volume and so were unable to compete successfully. Under government pressure, major trading changes – the Big Bang – were implemented in October 1986. Outside corporations could now own member firms, which thus enjoyed a larger capital base. Many London brokerages were snapped up by UK and overseas banks or major overseas securities firms. Today, the London Stock Exchange permits trading in securities listed on any bourse it recognizes. London's importance to global investing is reflected in the fact that 464 foreign firms have elected to be listed there, more than on any other stock exchange.

The London Stock Exchange, like Nasdaq, is an OTC market. It posts market-makers' prices and reports trades, but does not execute them. Also like Nasdaq, the London Stock Exchange lacks a facility for order-matching, in which buyers and sellers of shares indicate the price at which they are ready to deal.

The London Stock Exchange claims to handle around 60 percent of all share trading outside domestic markets. Within Europe, the Exchange says, that figure rises to over 90 percent. But London's share of the European market has been dwindling, due to its lack of order-matching, more readily available on the continent.

Moreover, the assertion that some 60 percent of business consists of foreign shares doesn't really hold water. Members of the London Stock Exchange have to count *all* European trades, even though some are done in local markets. The exaggerated claims, however, do not nullify London's value to you as an investor. The concentration in London of major fund managers, global banks and securities houses means its exchange will continue to be the leading marketplace for trading foreign equities.

Today, the London exchange is underpinned by two electronic price quotation systems: Stock Exchange Automated Quotations (SEAQ) for the UK equity market and SEAQ International for most foreign equities. These systems are used by competing market-makers to supply

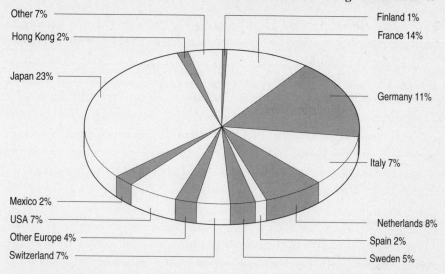

Other 7%

Hong Kong 2%

Japan 23%

Mexico 2%

USA 7%

Other Europe 4%

Switzerland 7%

Finland 1%

France 14%

Germany 11%

Italy 7%

Netherlands 8%

Spain 2%

Sweden 5%

Fig 7.2 Turnover in foreign equities transacted on the London Stock Exchange by country sector

quotes to member firms, who, following Nasdaq's example, now deal from screens in their own offices instead of face-to-face on the market floor. In 1994, the average transaction size on SEAQ International was almost £240,000 (£207,000 in 1993), reflecting the dominance of institutional business. The companies quoted on SEAQ International benefit from exposure to an international market, while investors gain a visible and regulated trading facility. The system is divided into 18 developed countries plus a developing markets division.

London's 52 market-makers represent major international securities houses and quote continuous firm or indicative two-way prices. Share prices are usually quoted in the home currency of each major country, with transactions completed through the local market.

The developing markets division covers companies based in Latin America and Asia as well as newly privatized companies from Eastern Europe. Bearing a health warning about the unsuitability of these stocks for private investors, it is supported by 18 market-makers, who in early 1995 were quoting 48 emerging market securities.

London's growth in international equity trading has been truly mindboggling, with the value of turnover growing six-fold from 1987 through 1993. In 1994, London's busiest year ever for trading non-UK equities, the exchange averaged 11,986 such transactions per day. Foreign equity turnover in 1994 was £719 billion, up 24 percent on 1993's record £579 billion. European equities, at £429 billion, accounted for nearly 60 percent of the trades, including £103 billion in French equities and £81 billion in German equities. Japan was largest in the single country category, with £165 billion (Figure 7.2).

In 1994, the London exchange also posted record share turnover in several emerging markets: Argentina £2.7 billion, Brazil £1.8 billion, India £3.7 billion, South Korea £2.6 billion, Taiwan £1.2 billion and Thailand £2.3 billion.

By the summer of 1997, SEAQ will operate side-by-side with a more up-to-date system called SEQUENCE. The new system will provide the long-needed capacity for order-matching, giving you sharper prices on trades in foreign equities. Commissions, however, are another story.

Commission comparisons

The Big Bang of 1986 abolished minimums. But the London Exchange was embarrassed six years later, when a survey it had commissioned revealed that small investors in Britain got the worst deal in Europe when they sold shares worth up to 1,000 European Currency Units ($1,150).

Publication of the survey was "postponed," then squelched. The statistics showed that in 1992, British brokers charged an average 2.4 percent commission on a 1,000 ecu transaction, much steeper than 0.74 percent in Milan, 0.80 percent in Luxembourg and 0.98 percent in Madrid. Costs of dealing in other markets were also cheaper.

But charges were sometimes confusing. German brokers, for instance, had a commission rate of only 1 percent, but there was an extra charge of around 0.6 percent from the Kursmakler (market intermediary).

Total charges in Amsterdam and Paris worked out to 1.75 percent and 1.29 percent respectively.

The picture with slightly larger transactions was similar. Up to 10,000 ecu ($11,500), Madrid was the cheapest, with a price war driving the rate down towards the prescribed minimum of 0.25 percent. Milan was the second cheapest, charging 0.75 percent.

London was again relatively expensive, with a commission rate of 1.82 percent – even though some 43 percent of all British share deals take place at between 1,400 ecu ($1,620) and 7,000 ecu ($8,100).

The Dublin market was the dearest, with charges of 2.2 percent.

Prices fell dramatically for larger value transactions, with Madrid again the cheapest exchange in Europe for trades in shares of up to 100,000 ecu ($115,000). There, costs per trade dropped to just 0.27 percent.

Much to the relief of British statisticians, here London came in second, with costs of 0.59 percent. A 1995 study by Birinyi and Associates, a Connecticut Consulting firm, showed dealing spreads on the London Stock Exchange still among the widest in the world: The median spread for the most-liquid shares was 1.44 percent of the purchase price in London, compared with 0.32 percent on the New York Stock Exchange and 0.30 percent on the Paris Bourse.

Regulations imposed by the European Union should level commissions on buying and selling equities throughout the continent from 1996 on.

You can obtain information on buying and selling foreign equities through the London Stock Exchange by writing to them at Old Broad Street, London EC2N 1HP, or telephoning + 44–171–797–3628.

Two of their booklets are particularly useful: *How to Buy and Sell Shares* and *Introduction to the London Stock Exchange.*

You may also wish to request a guideline to current commission rates, not only in London, but on one or more of these other European exchanges as well:

European stock exchanges

Austria
Vienna Stock Exchange
Wipplingerstrasse 34, A–1011 Vienna
  Contact: Ulrich Kamp
  Phone: (+ 43–1) 534–990   Fax: (+ 43–1) 535–6857

Belgium
Brussels Stock Exchange
Palais de la Bourse, B–1000 Bruxelles,
  Contact: Michel Touzeau
  Phone: (+ 32–2) 509–1211   Fax: (+ 32–2) 509–1212

Denmark
Copenhagen Stock Exchange
Nikolaj Plads 6, DK–1007 Copenhagen K
  Contact: Hans Henrik Munch-Jensen
  Phone: (+ 45–33) 93–3366   Fax: (+ 45–33) 12–8613

Finland
Helsinki Stock Exchange
PO Box 361, 00131 Helsinki
  Contact: Maija Särömaa
  Phone: (+ 358–017) 33–01   Fax: (+ 358–017) 33–0399

France
Sócíété des Bourses Françaises
39/41, rue Cambon, F–75001 Paris
  Contact: Catherine Goffin
  Phone: (+ 33–1) 4927–1043   Fax: (+ 33–1) 4927–1604

Germany
Deutsche Börse AG
Börsenplatz 4, D–60313 Frankfurt am Main
  Contact: Werner G. Seifert
  Phone: (+ 49–69) 299 77 219   Fax: (+ 49–69) 299 77 579

Greece
Athens Stock Exchange
10, Sofokleous Street, Athens 10559
  Contact: Alexandra Psyrri
  Phone: (+ 30–1) 321–0424   Fax: (+ 30–1) 321–3938

Ireland
The Irish Stock Exchange
28, Anglesea Street, Dublin 2
  Contact: Tom Healy
  Phone: (+ 353–1) 677–8808   Fax: (+ 353–1) 671–9029

Luxembourg
Bourse de Luxembourg
11, avenue de la Porte–Neuve, L–2227 Luxembourg
  Contact: Michel Maquil
  Phone: (+ 352) 4779–36 272   Fax: (+ 352) 4779–36 205

The Netherlands
Amsterdam Stock Exchange
Beursplein 5, NL–1012 JW Amsterdam
  Contact: Shirley van der Linden
  Phone: (+ 31–20) 523–4054   Fax: (+ 31–20) 624–8062

Norway
Oslo Stock Exchange
Postboks 460 – Sentrum, 0105 Oslo 1
  Contact: Roy Halvorsen
  Phone: (+ 47–22) 34–1700   Fax: (+ 47–22) 41–6590

Portugal
Bolsa de Valores de Lisboa
Rua dos Fanqueiros 10, 1100 Lisboa
   Contact: Rui Alberto Saraiva Ambrosio Tribolet
   Phone: (+ 351–1) 888–2738   Fax: (+ 351–1) 886–4231

Spain
The Madrid Stock Exchange
Plaza de la Lealtad 1, E–28014 Madrid
   Contact: Ramon Adarraga
   Phone: (+ 34–1) 589–1362   Fax: (+ 34–1) 581–2290

Sweden
Stockholm Stock Exchange
P.O. Box 1256, SE 111 82 Stockholm
   Contact: Leif A. Vindevag
   Phone: (+ 46–8) 613–8880   Fax: (+ 46–8) 24–6861

Switzerland
Swiss Stock Exchange
Selnaustrasse, 32, CH–8021 Zürich
   Contact: Dieter Sigrist
   Phone: (+ 41–1) 229–2828   Fax: (+ 41–1) 229–2833

Geneva Stock Exchange
15, rue de la Cité, CH–1204 Genève
   Phone: (+ 41–22) 310–0684   Fax: (+ 41–22) 311–2576

Basel Stock Exchange
   Phone: (+ 41–61) 272–0555   Fax: (+ 41–61) 272–0626

Foreign shares listed on local exchanges

Lower costs and better liquidity have long been the rationale for buying any foreign stock on its home exchange. Direct dialling makes it almost as easy to telephone a foreign broker as one in your own country, preferably one who speaks the same language and is accustomed to dealing with foreign clients.

Instead of dealing directly with a foreign bank or broker, you can also use an institution in your home market as go-between. That organization can then set up your trading arrangement with one or more foreign investment firms. Either route leads to a much wider universe of foreign investment opportunities.

The Appendix lists emerging market stock exchanges and discusses various ways you can trade directly in foreign-listed shares. Jon Golding of London-based Sterling Westminster Group (+ 44–171–581–3551) can track such direct foreign stock market investments in one unified report, denominated in the currency of your choice.

INDIRECT INVESTMENT

Indirect investment, in its various forms, ushers you into the global investment arena primarily via your home market.

Path three: Depositary receipts

A depositary receipt is a negotiable certificate representing ownership of ordinary shares of a company outside your home market. The shares are deposited with a custodian in their own market and the depository bank issues you a sort of claim check, called a "depositary receipt."

The prime advantage of such depositary receipts is that they let investors in America and Europe buy foreign shares without leaving their home market.

Depositary receipts are also sometimes cheaper to buy than the underlying shares themselves. For example, transaction costs to buy an Australian stock directly in Sydney are at times steeper than those to buy a depositary receipt on that stock in New York.

Not entering a foreign market directly also avoids substantial administrative complications.

Dividend collection and distribution is more efficient, with the sponsoring bank collecting all dividends and distributing them to the depositary receipt holders after conversion into US dollars or the holder's own currency. The Appendix shows a present count of some 1,800 depositary receipts from 64 countries.

There are three kinds of depositary receipts: American, International and Global.

American Depositary Receipts

American Depositary Receipts (ADRs) provide a way to invest worldwide via Wall Street. Most ADRs are shares of non-US corporations packaged into negotiable receipts by major banks. When you take this route to buy stock in a non-US company, a broker purchases the shares on that company's home stock market, then deposits the shares in the foreign office of a US bank or one of its correspondent banks abroad. The US bank issues you a receipt confirming ownership. This receipt can represent single or multiple shares, or fractions of shares. To sell the shares, you can either sell the receipt on a US stock exchange or return it to the depository for cash, in which case the foreign shares are put up for sale on their home exchange. American Depositary Receipts are by no means only for Americans. Regardless of where you live, you can buy and sell these receipts through any US broker just like US stocks. The trades clear within five market days in the US and as an ADR-holder you are entitled to all the advantages and rights of shareholders in the company's home country.

ADRs have been around since 1927, when J.P. Morgan set up a depository for shares of Selfridge's, a popular British department store. Because the concept was developed in Europe, most ADRs – like most European stocks – are issued in bearer form. The person holding the ADR is presumed to be the owner. The receipt was created chiefly to eliminate the long and cumbersome practice of shipping stock certificates by steamer back and forth across the Atlantic, in an era when the actual paper often had to be submitted to receive a dividend payment. Though that purpose is *passé*, the basic structure of the ADR hasn't changed much since.

An ADR can be "sponsored," created by a single depository bank, or "unsponsored," created by several. Depository banks create unsponsored ADRs when they think there is market demand, or when requested to do so by a foreign issuer – or, more typically, a broker. "There is increased retail interest in international investing, and there are thousands of retail brokers trying to find the next thing to sell to their client base," says Bill Treut, who heads ADR sales for Latin America at Citibank. Citibank, along with Bank of New York and J.P. Morgan, dominates the depositary business.

ADR trading costs

With this trio of New York commercial banks dominating the ADR market, you could easily be gouged on price. Under an anti-trust waiver, banks are allowed to set uniform fees for an unsponsored ADR. The fees are uniform because unsponsored ADRs have to be interchangeable. But the fees set are often uniformly excessive.

Brokers pay fees to the depository banks for the creation of ADRs, adding to the cost of their purchase, or for their destruction, adding to the cost of their sale. On unsponsored ADRs, the depository banks charge fees for foreign exchange and transaction costs on distributing dividends. Banks can also make money at the expense of the ADR's owner on non-cash distributions, such as rights, which are prohibited by the SEC, and so cannot be distributed to US shareholders.

There is considerable anecdotal evidence of massive fees being charged by banks when one ADR company is taken over by another. There are also stories of banks using currency exchange rates that never appeared in the market on the date the dividend was paid, charging for the exchange at rates unfair to the shareholder or paying dividends with a huge time lag, meanwhile profiting from the float. Banks also charge for distributing proxies or providing information about stockholder meetings, rights or other non-cash benefits to shareholders. Banks will also bill shareholders on a per share basis for issuing cash in lieu of rights. This can mount up in the case of low-priced shares, such as those in Mexico, where investors often own thousands of shares in a single company.

As examples of recent fee excesses, in 1993 Citibank kept 18.5 percent of a dividend payment from an Australian company, Ashton Mining, and, on another dividend distribution, Bank of New York charged 10 percent to convert Thai baht to dollars.

The cartel's days of high fees and poor service, however, seem numbered. Under US law, a depository can be either a commercial or an investment bank. The trio has been joined by Morgan Stanley, a brokerage house, which in mid-1993 filed requests to offer ADRs for three European stocks. Chase Manhattan and German banking giant Deutsche Bank are also setting up as depository banks. These moves have already prompted New York banks to improve the way they treat ADR owners. For the first time, one bank is actually helping ADR owners recover foreign taxes withheld.

The Security Exchange Commission's Rule 144A
This fast lane to placing depositary receipts in the United States is only of interest there to "qualified institutional investors," who since 1990 have been permitted by SEC Rule 144A to trade privately placed securities without the two-year waiting period formerly required.

The big drawback to 144A placements is that they narrow the investor base, totally excluding individuals and smaller institutions. Moreover, in the US such private placements trade on the Portal secondary markets system, where liquidity is often inadequate. For this reason, even qualified institutional investors feel more comfortable buying public stock offerings. So despite the speed of the 144A process, there is currently a clear trend away from such issues towards full registration with the SEC. For many countries, SEC filings are no longer seen as a barrier. In fact, a number of companies that originally came to the market via 144A are now upgrading to public ADRs.

ADR trading volume
Today, ADRs are the fastest-growing class of securities traded in the United States. Just one single ADR, that of Teléfonos de Mexico, now averages a higher volume of daily transactions than General Motors. Some ADRs are listed on the New York Stock Exchange, Amex or quoted on Nasdaq. Total ADR trading volume on these three bourses soared from less than $50 billion in 1988 to some $278 billion in 1995.

Unlisted ADRs
Any brokerage firm can enter a trading order for any listed stock on the NYSE, Amex or Nasdaq. Other ADRs are unlisted, trading either on the over-the-counter (OTC) market or on the private markets. More than 80 percent of foreign-stock ADRs are traded OTC or via the National Daily Quotation Service, known as the "pink sheets," a system that works by telephone rather than via a computer screen, like Nasdaq – or on a trading floor, like the NYSE or Amex. Trading a stock listed in the "pink sheets" entails a call to a designated market maker, so many brokers either refuse to offer this service or charge extra for it. Trades of OTC stocks not in the pink sheets are more problematic and often are handled only by specialized brokers.

The three ADR levels
The US Securities & Exchange Commission recognizes three levels of ADRs. Level One trades over-the-counter, through the OTC Bulletin Board or the "pink sheets." The issuing company has to file a registration statement with the SEC but can get an exemption from filing annual reports.

Companies issuing Level Two ADRs, which can trade on Nasdaq, the Amex or the NYSE, must file an annual report on Form 20-F – comparable to a US company's 10-K – and partially reconcile their financial statements to US accounting principles.

Levels One and Two ADRs are for shares that already exist in a non-US market.

Level Three ADRs are for new shares sold by non-US companies seeking to raise additional capital. These offerings may be publicly traded equity or private Rule 144A placements with institutional investors.

Additional public ADRs can be created simply by going into the company's home-country market and buying shares, then exchanging them for depositary receipts. Likewise, if excessive numbers of ADRs are for sale, the underlying shares in the home country will probably be sold and the ADRs cancelled.

Beyond these basic features, each company's ADR can differ slightly. It is up to the issuing company, for instance, to determine how many of its ordinary, or common, shares are represented by each ADR.

ADR attractions

Foreign companies establish ADRs primarily for two reasons: to broaden their shareholder base to US investors and to raise fresh capital in quantities unavailable at home. US investors buy ADRs to diversify their equity portfolios internationally without having to face the traditional problems associated with direct foreign investment.

One such problem confronts mutual funds, pension funds and other institutions whose charters restrict or prohibit them from investing directly in non-US securities. Such an institution, however, can often buy ADRs and benefit from an internationally diversified portfolio while still adhering to its charter.

US residents, and, increasingly, non-US residents as well, invest in foreign shares through ADRs to avoid the following problems, real or imagined: undependable settlements, costly currency conversions, unreliable custody service, poor information flow, unfamiliar market practices and confusing tax conventions. Moreover, by using ADRs, global custodian safekeeping charges are eliminated.

ADRs are quoted in dollars and also pay dividends or interest in dollars. In addition, some ADRs are quoted in US dollars on non-US markets during the hours when US markets are closed. Dollar pricing doesn't mean of course that ADRs are immune to currency fluctuations. The ADR price will swing as the value of the yen, franc or other currency changes against the dollar. ADRs are popular with US investors because they trade and settle just like US securities. In contrast, US investors holding foreign shares directly are subject to settlement conventions governing the home market which differ from US practices.

ADR drawbacks

Outside the US, you can choose from tens of thousands of equities, including the small and obscure. The biggest drawback of ADRs, apart from the heavy bank fees, is that they narrow this choice to a few hundred of the largest non-US stocks. About 80 percent of ADR stocks come from just 10 countries. And mineral or oil exploration stocks make up much of the total.

What's more, ADRs focus mainly on superstars: the largest, most popular and widely researched foreign equities, which are less likely to provide positive earnings surprises than the tiny wallflowers. Over a number of years, using the criteria enumerated in Chapter 13, I've observed that relatively few bargain equities are found among the ranks of ADRs.

The ease of trading ADRs and their blue-chip character sometimes makes them more volatile and dangerous than smaller, locally listed firms. ADRs are the main vehicle for tourists: the more fickle investors who have no long-term commitment to a region. When a market is popular and foreign demand for shares heats up, ADRs can trade above the value of the local stocks they represent. Conversely, when a market cools, ADRs can plunge to a discount. This happened when Mexico devalued its peso in December 1994. Roughly half the country's shares were held at the time by foreigners and these were first to be sold off, causing ADR prices to collapse ahead of shares traded locally. A recent study by the Boeing pension fund showed that ADRs also have a high correlation with the S&P 500, and so as a group are not significantly different from investing in the US market.

Another disadvantage of investing abroad via ADRs, at least those traded via the over-the-counter "pink sheets," is the difficulty of getting accurate quotes in US dollars. Many are not quoted as ADRs, but only as foreign shares on overseas exchanges. So first you have to obtain and peruse the appropriate foreign financial papers. To convert a foreign stock quote into a US dollar price for your ADR, you then need two more bits of data: the exchange rate between the foreign currency and the dollar, and the conversion ratio, how many foreign shares per ADR. The issuing bank can tell you both.

With unsponsored ADRs and "New York" shares (actual foreign stocks that trade in the US without the intermediate step of ADRs), you may have trouble in getting dividends and regular reports. Therefore, it's a good idea to write the foreign firm's investor relations officer directly to ask to be put on their mailing list. The depository usually won't bother.

Finally, most ADRs are so illiquid, especially the 80 percent trading over-the-counter, that there are only a few market makers. Often just one. That tends to make bid-offer spreads excessive, so your broker should price the foreign shares in their home market as well as the ADR in the US, especially on a "pink sheet" transaction. Most major broker-age houses can get quotes of foreign shares priced in dollars, frequently a cheaper and easier way to buy non-US shares than the ADR detour.

Trading symbols

To recapitulate, foreign equities in the US trade largely in three forms: regular listed shares, ADRs and New York shares. Foreign stocks listed on the NYSE or Amex have trading symbols like those of any other stock. On Nasdaq and OTC, though, most follow a convention setting them apart from US stocks. A five-letter symbol ending in Y (****Y) denotes an ADR. One ending in F (****F) generally denotes a New York share.

ADR coverage

Good coverage of the still relatively tiny ADR universe is offered by Vivian Lewis in *Global Investor* (tel: + 1–800–950–1577; $99 a year) and by David G. Muller, Jr. in his more modestly titled *Foreign Markets Advisory* (tel: + 1–703–425–5961; $225 a year). For $89, Lewis will send you her *Global Investing Comprehensive Guide to American Depositary Receipts*, while Muller's subscribers get a free annual *Directory of Foreign Stocks Traded in the US*. Both newsletters also cover regional and country closed-end funds readily available to the US investor.

Morningstar Inc., a Chicago research firm best known for its in-depth coverage of mutual funds, publishes another newsletter, *Morningstar ADRs* (tel: + 1-312-696–6000; $195 a year). Each biweekly issue features profiles of 70 ADR stocks. In all, 700 stocks representing more than 30 countries are covered and updated over a 20-week period.

International Depositary Receipts

International Depositary Receipts (IDRs) are similar to ADRs, but designed for non-US investors who wish to hold US shares. A company wishing to raise equity both in the United States and in Europe can utilize a two-tier structure: an ADR for the US and an IDR for Europe.

IDR drawbacks

The basic weakness of this two-pronged approach is that the ADR is issued, traded and settled only in the US and the IDR is issued, traded and settled only in the European markets. The two individual securities operate under two settlement conventions and have no direct links with each other. The ADR/IDR structure breaks the share offering into two distinct parts in two separate markets. The ADR and the IDR are not interchangeable.

Global Depositary Receipts

In contrast, Global Depositary Receipts (GDRs) enable firms to tap international capital markets by *simultaneously* issuing a *single security* in multiple markets – public or private, US or non-US.

GDRs can be, and are, registered, issued and traded in the US public markets and listed on major US and non-US exchanges, especially London and Luxembourg. When 144A placements are done as a GDR, private investors outside the US can generally trade them freely.

The first Global Depositary Receipt was developed by Citibank for Samsung Co. Ltd., a Korean trading company, in December of 1990. Samsung wanted to raise equity capital in the US, but also had a strong European investor base it wished to include in the offering. To solve this problem, Citibank came up with the GDR.

Teléfonica de Argentina is one of several firms that switched from an IDR to a GDR. In March 1994, the company had an exchange offer for its Rule 144A ADRs, which had originally sold in a global offering. At that time, the two-tier structure had to be put in place in order to separate the IDRs trading on London's SEAQ system and the Rule 144A ADRs trading on Portal.

Since the exchange offer, Teléfonica de Argentina now has only one class of Global Depositary Receipts – each representing one share – listed on both the New York Stock Exchange and SEAQ. The Teléfonica exchange offering has introduced the company to the vast US retail market.

A GDR drawback

Cumbersome settlement procedures, notably in India, can make GDRs an attractive way for international players to invest. On the other hand, a GDR, like an ADR, can trade at a premium or discount to the underlying share. Such premiums or discounts sometimes fluctuate widely. In the first quarter of 1996, the average Indian GDR traded at a 20 percent premium to the underlying market.

Path four: Global, regional and country funds

Why funds are popular

One reason funds are popular is simply lack of money. A preceding chapter showed why it makes sense to select some 25 stocks, or their equivalents, from different countries and industries, placing more emphasis on country diversification than on industry diversification. However, minimum dealing costs and higher commission rates for smaller transactions make modest investments disproportionately expensive. For that reason, a minimum investment of $3,000 to $5,000 in each company's shares should be the aim. That suggests you need at least $75,000 to $125,000 to invest in shares for a good global spread of risk. If your assets don't yet run to this, a portfolio of global, regional or country funds may be the better option.

Moreover, some countries are less internationally minded than others. The paucity of foreign shares directly available to US buyers, for instance, coupled with unfamiliarity in researching and monitoring them, partially explains why global, regional and country funds are more popular with US investors than foreign shares themselves. But, as Bailey and Lim recently pointed out in The *Journal of Portfolio Management,* although country funds offer some diversification bene-fits, they are usually poor proxies for country indexes or direct holdings of foreign equities – especially in the Pacific Rim. This is probably because country funds as a rule do not invest in the broad market, but in the equity of larger companies.

Fund advantages

"Union gives strength," wrote Aesop in *The Bundle of Sticks.* The fable, published about 600 BC, contrasts the weakness of one stick with the strength of several tied together. Substituting "stocks" for "sticks" gives a parable of the advantages offered by a fund.

Diversification

Your stake is pooled with thousands of others, enabling a fund to assemble a portfolio of at least 50 to 100 stocks: a selection more than broad enough to protect you from the specific risk of any catastrophe affecting a single company.

Cost savings

Funds also buy and sell stocks in large blocks, so they often command lower brokerage commissions than a smaller investor. Funds, in other words, generally pay a lower percentage of the total value of a trans-action. (But, as the next chapter will show, not always.)

Low initial investment

Most funds will let you open an account for the equivalent of $1,000 or less. Some impose no minimum at all. And many funds let you build your stake in increments of $100 or less.

Professional management

Though I'm listing this as a plus, a strong case can be made for considering it a minus. True, a handful of fund managers have managed to outperform the market averages over many years. But most funds are lucky to keep up with the market. That's because they *are* the market. Institutions such as mutual funds, pension funds and insurance companies now account for the bulk of trading volume on the major stock exchanges. No wonder, then, that the typical fund is hard put to beat "the market" after you deduct its advisory fees and administrative expenses.

Therefore, it is wise to keep a weather eye on commissions and other costs here as well. These are listed at the beginning of every prospectus. To help you make astute choices among the various kinds of funds, the following discussion enumerates their costs – and how high they can go.

The two basic fund structures are closed-end and open-end.

Open-end funds

Open-end funds – known in the US as mutual funds and as unit trusts in the UK – issue new shares as needed, buying and selling them at net asset value, with a profitable spread for the fund managers between bid and offer price. The proceeds from the sale of shares are then used to buy additional securities for the fund's investment portfolio. Shares in an open-end fund are generally bought or sold via an agent on behalf of the firm that runs it. There is no secondary market. Many open-end funds have stiff initial sales charges and even redemption fees. The buzz word for such charges is the "load."

The front-end charge, traditionally levied by fund managers around the world, goes solely to promotion and to reward the agent. Fund sales can easily constitute one-fourth of a broker's income. In addition, an open-end fund may charge an advisory – or management – fee, usually ranging from a half to three-quarters of 1 percent.

In the US, you may also be saddled with a so-called 12b-1 fee, named after the SEC rule permitting it, which can oblige shareholders to subsidize costs of "distribution." This is really another sales charge, which can reach 2 percent, though most funds charge less than a half percent. Like the advisory fee, this is paid yearly to the fund's management out of the fund assets. Funds with 12b-1 fees are sometimes touted as no-loads, so here again it pays to read the fine print.

To confuse things further, some funds have inactive 12b-1 plans. The dormant cookie monster is there in case they want to impose a 12b-1 fee in future, but it doesn't cost you anything at the moment. Again, a careful reading of the prospectus will help.

Some open-end funds also have diverse redemption or contingent deferred sales charges. Redemption fees, intended to deter active trading, are generally 1 to 2 percent. Contingent deferred sales charges – which larger brokerage houses often impose on their so-called "no-load" funds – can be especially costly. Some funds sponsored by major brokerage houses mug you for as much as 5 or 6 percent of the value of your investment if you redeem your shares in the first year. In most cases, thankfully, these charges come down annually, eventually vanishing after the fifth or sixth year. These so-called no-loads are really "low-loads," because they slap you with the back-end fee if you quit the ship earlier than they'd like.

Managers running back-loaded funds cover the commission cost themselves. That cost is finally recouped from you via the back-load when the fund is cashed in. The broker still receives an up-front commission payment, but nothing is deducted from the amount you invest. On the other hand, funds claiming to be no-load which pay the broker a commission of, say 4 percent, out of a high recurring 12b-1 fee are conning you. They assert, truthfully enough, that your full equity is invested from day one, but somehow fail to mention their plan to nibble away at that equity each year. You can easily pigeonhole open–end funds despite their bewildering range of fees. Imagine the mutual–fund universe divided, like Gaul, into three parts: load funds, no–load funds and rolling–load funds. Members of the rapidly growing rolling–load group do not have front–end or back–end charges. Instead, you pay annual sales fees – often 1 percent to 1.5 percent of assets – that roll along year after year: precisely the kind of recurring charge I warned you about in the previous chapter. You're most likely to encounter the rolling load if you buy a fund through a financial adviser who charges an annual fee rather than collecting an initial commission.

Rolling–load funds include all those in the popular Charles Schwab Institutional Funds network, Fidelity Institutional Funds Network and similar broker programs. Boston–based Putman Investments also recently jumped on this bandwagon, making its funds available to advisors through the Fidelity program. That kind of announcement can elicit wild cheers from investors who believe that a bunch of load funds have suddenly become load–free, or load–waived. The broker may even claim you're being offered a net asset deal. No way. The load has simply been carved up into several annual charges. Rolling–load funds, for instance, prohibit advisers from cutting their fees below a minimum, typically 0.75 percent. You're being offered a load fund in disguise. The various charges can really add up. Take a front–load example. You've paid, say, an initial 5 percent, plus, each year, three-quarters of one percent advisory fee, plus a 12b-1 fee of, let's say, a half percent. But there's more. The fund itself has naturally incurred expenses for administration, bookkeeping, rent, salaries and so forth. As a rule, these expense charges vary from a half to a full percent of net assets. During the first year, ignoring any possible redemption charges, before you know it you've paid some 6.75 percent over net asset value for the privilege of investing in an open-end mutual fund or unit trust.

To put that in perspective, if your fund shows a 7.5 percent increase for the year (from the factual base of 93.25 percent of your initial stake), nominally you'll just about break even.

The load means that despite a seemingly decent return, you won't have managed even to keep pace with inflation.

Increasing competition for business and a growing realization that investors are being turned off by high fees is at last bringing value-for-money to fund management.

The main target for change is the front-end load.

Since the mid-1970s, when front-end charges in the US reached a peak of 8.5 percent of the amount invested, direct marketing has become increasingly popular. This broader distribution is boosting competition and giving investors a wider choice.

An indirect result is that the front-end loads still levied tend to be much lower. In Britain, where front-end loads are still common, the average charge is now about 5 percent.

According to Erick Kanter, vice president of the Investment Company Institute, a New York-based trade group, in the US and Canada, only around half of all new fund investment is still front-loaded.

But other markets are proving tougher to crack.

In Europe, this is mostly due to the long-standing tradition of commissioned agents. Though US discount broker Charles Schwab & Co. has introduced no-load funds in Europe through its London office, the firm admits price competition is evolving slower in Europe than it has in the United States.

In Southeast Asia, where the picture is more complicated, three factors impede a wider sale of funds. First, only a few regions of Asia have recently become affluent enough to consider anything other than deposit accounts as a means of saving.

Second, Asian culture tends to regard stock investment, like horse-racing, as an amusing distraction.

The insult that finally slams the door is the widespread prevalence of front-end loads. Asian investors are reluctant to sacrifice up to 5 percent of their hard-won savings by moving into front-loaded funds, no matter how large the prospect of gains.

Investment International magazine, at 91 Charterhouse Street, London EC1M 6HR, lists non-US open-end funds around the globe together with their terms and track records, as does *The International*, Greystoke Place, Fetter Lane, London EC4A 1ND. Each is sent only to non-US addresses.

No-loads and low-loads

No-load funds carry no sales charges and sell at net asset value. That's possible because they don't employ agents or salespeople. You can only buy shares directly from the fund.

Moreover, as you don't have to fill out the revealing forms required by brokerage firms, no-loads give you more privacy.

The first no-loads were started by investment firms in the 1920s as a receptacle for small, nuisance accounts. A wealthy client would send his cook to the firm with a note requesting that her savings be placed in growth equities rather than an interest-bearing account. Her assets were too meagre to be invested on their own, so the firm maintained a fund into which it dumped all such accounts, investing them collectively. No-load funds have come a long way from those early days, when they were largely scorned by the industry.

As you might surmise, your broker is unlikely to recommend no-load funds or funds that charge only a modest front-end fee, because they usually don't pay a commission.

Do higher fees mean better performance?

Brokers sometimes claim a higher-commission fund is worth the extra money, because its better performance makes up for the higher load in time. That's baloney, no matter how you slice it. The sales charge goes to the broker, who has nothing to do with how the fund performs.

The higher-commission funds offered by major stockbrokers are in fact lousy investments. Four of the five top Wall Street firms had fund performance results ranging from slightly above average to terrible, according to a ten-year study by Boston-based fund-research firm Kanon Bloch Carre & Co. Only Merrill Lynch made it into the top-ten fund families.

One reason for this poor performance is the heavy front-end fee most big brokers slap on. You begin automatically with a 5–8 percent handicap.

Forbes magazine, which ranks mutual funds in a special issue every September, has found no difference in performance between load and no-load funds. Its honour roll includes both. (*Forbes'* performance figures reflect the impact of annual fund expenses, but not loads or sales charges.) Subscription address: PO Box 10048, Des Moines, IA 50340-0048, USA.

Expense ratios

Funds that charge sales loads justify their added fees by claiming that the use of a sales force cuts marketing and advertising expenses, thus reducing overall fund costs. Therefore, they maintain, front-loads are cheaper than no-loads or low-loads.

How true is that? Morningstar compared the expense ratios of more than 2,000 load funds, pure no-loads and no-loads that deduct an annual 12b-1 charge from net asset value to cover marketing costs. The conclusion? Pure no-loads are cheapest. Second come the load funds, with an annual expense ratio of 1.32 percent of assets, while the so-called "no-loads" with 12b-1 fees have a slightly higher expense ratio of 1.48 percent. Morningstar's study reveals that funds with any type of redemption or contingent deferred sales charge have the industry's highest expense ratios. Pure no-loads, with annual average annual expenses of 0.97 percent, are the best deal going: cheaper to buy and cheaper to hold.

Conclusion: No one knows which open-end funds will produce the best gains in the future, so unless you have some compelling reason to do otherwise, it's best to choose pure no-load funds.

Among several newsletters that compare the performance data on such funds are *NoLoad Fund*X* (tel: + 1–415–986–7979; $119 a year) and *The No-Load Fund Investor* (tel: + 1–914–693–7420; $125 a year).

Extra fees

Concealment of charges is a dangerous precedent – no matter how small initially. As an Arab proverb says: Do not let the camel get his nose in your tent. Open–end funds in the US have recently taken a page from banks and begun levying all sorts of separate charges for services that used to be free. Fund companies argue that if each investor pays for services used, expenses stay low for others. But it can be tricky to figure out the impact of a fund's extra charges on a portfolio – or even what those charges are. In fact, when funds charge on an item-by-item basis, it becomes nearly impossible to figure out how expensive or cheap the fund really is.

Unlike sales loads and expense ratios, fees for shareholder services are not published in newspapers' performance tables or quarterly rankings. Such fees are often not even found in a fund's prospectus. But they are pervasive. Only three of 61 fund groups surveyed recently by Boston consulting firm Dalbar Inc. offered all their services at no extra cost: G.T. Global Group, GE Funds and the Mariner Group.

Closed-end funds

Closed-end funds sell a limited number of shares and invest the proceeds in securities. Unlike open-end funds, closed-ends generally do not buy their shares back from investors who wish to cash in their holdings. Instead, fund shares trade on an exchange, like any other stock. This means you can buy them through a discount broker for very little commission, often below 1 percent, depending on how many shares you want.

In contrast, when you buy an open-end with an up-front load, you have no choice. You always pay the net asset price plus, say, 5–8 percent. For this reason alone, a closed-end fund can save you a lot of money. What is more, the structure of closed-end funds means they cannot hit you with extra fees. Obviously, you want to look at factors other than fees in choosing funds. And funds with low annual expenses may still be bargains, even with fees, compared with high-expense funds that impose few or no extra fees.

As closed-end funds, unlike open-ends, do not have to keep cash to meet redemptions, they tend to be more fully invested. Closed-ends are able to take positions in risky, smaller markets that are less liquid. A closed-end fund is therefore likely to hold more risky investments than an open-end fund invested in the same region. But thanks to that extra risk, closed-end funds also tend to outperform their open-end counterparts.

Premiums and discounts

The closed-end route to global investment also has a third compelling attraction. In contrast to the open-end funds, which are sold by legions of energetic and persuasive salespeople, closed-end funds have no one especially interested in distributing them. It is no wonder then that while most open-end funds are sold at a premium above net worth (mostly to cover the seller's commission), the majority of closed-end shares have been consistently available at *less* than their asset value. Unlike open-end funds, whose shares are bought and sold by the fund companies themselves, the price of closed-end funds is set by supply and demand. A closed-end fund cannot redeem shares or issue new ones, so when demand is higher or lower than supply, the price gets uncoupled from the asset value.

When demand for a closed-end fund is weak, its price falls, no matter what the fund is intrinsically worth. This can create rewarding loopholes for the canny investor. Conversely, when a closed-end fund is popular, investors bid its price up to a premium over net asset value, creating traps for the unwary. In Europe a few years ago, the future seemed so rosy that speculators bid up the price of European funds to two or three times net asset value. In 1989, the price of shares in the NYSE-traded Spain Fund doubled to a premium of nearly 200 percent in a few short weeks, simply because buyers outnumbered sellers. That price, like others, dived soon after and has not since come close to reaching previous heights.

Conclusion: High premiums mark the end of periods of good performance, not the beginning.

Closed-end funds listed outside the United States tend to be more attractively priced than the US-listed funds. In the US, closed-ends average only an 8 percent discount, but in Britain the average closed-end fund – known as an investment trust – traded recently at 14 percent below net asset value, according to the British Association of Investment Trust Companies. Bigger disparities can often be found in similar pairs of funds. On 31 July 1994, for instance, US-listed Indonesia Fund sold at a 35 percent premium, while the London-listed Indonesian Equity Fund was selling at a 21 percent discount. Prices tend to be lower in London because some fund buyers are institutions that tend to be more aware of alternative investments elsewhere. If Templeton's Emerging Markets Investment Trust were to become too expensive, investors might buy the open-end Templeton fund based in Luxembourg. Alas, US investors in many of the country funds do not have as many alternatives among domestic open-end funds. For such a US investor, Luxembourg open ends and UK investment trusts can be attractive alternatives. London-based Warburg Securities publishes a regular list pinpointing the largest discrepancies between US and UK closed-end funds with similar investment policies. But US investors thinking of buying UK investment trusts need to consider a number of factors. Currency risk, for one: UK funds are of course denominated in sterling. Another factor is the wide variety of tax implications. The Association of Unit Trusts and Investment Funds, a UK fund industry

association, says taxation is extremely complicated and can be puni-
tive. Moreover, even though a US fund may seem more expensive than
a UK equivalent, that appearance may be deceptive. So if you choose a
UK closed end over a US equivalent, or switch out of a US fund to one
in the UK, it is advisable to make sure there is a discrepancy of at least
10 percent in favour of the UK fund. You need that edge to cover the
additional costs and risks.

Conclusion: *If you can, buy your closed-end funds in London.*

Closed-ends versus open-ends

As Benjamin Graham pointed out in *The Intelligent Investor*, you can
often get more for your money from closed-end shares. If you buy a
fund at, say, a 10 percent discount, you will pay only £9 for each £10
worth of stock. On the other hand, if you pay 10 percent more than
net asset value, that same £10 worth of underlying stock will cost you
£11. So in electing to build a global equity portfolio by putting money
in investment funds, it is wiser to buy a group of closed-end shares at
discounts of 15 to 20 percent from asset value, rather than paying premiums of some 5 to 8 percent above asset value for shares in open-end
funds. If future dividends and changes in asset values continue to be
about the same for the two groups, you will get nearly 25 percent
more for your money from the closed-end shares.

The mutual fund salesman, Graham predicts, will be quick to
counter: "How do you know what price you will get when you sell the
closed-end shares? Their discount may widen. But we guarantee you can
always redeem your open-end shares at 100 percent of asset value."

The following variant on the old master's elegant refutation of this
sales argument calls, like the original, for a little arithmetic. Assume that
Jack buys some open-end funds at 107 percent of asset value, while Jill
purchases closed-end funds at 85 percent of asset value, plus 1.5 percent
commission. Both sets of shares earn and pay 30 percent of this asset
value in, say, four years and end up with the same value as at the beginning. Jack turns in his shares at 100 percent of value, losing the
7 percent he paid. His overall return for the period is 30 percent less
7 percent, or 23 percent on asset value. This, in turn, is 21.5 percent on
his investment. How much does Jill have to realize on her closed-end
shares to obtain the same return on her investment as Jack?

Jill's overall return was 30 percent less 1.5 percent, or 28.5 percent
on asset value. To realize 21.5 percent on her investment, as Jack did
on his, Jill need only to sell her shares at 75 percent of asset value, or a

discount of 25 percent. In other words, the market discount on Jill's portfolio of closed-end funds could widen an unlikely 10 percentage points before her return would be as poor as Jack's. If Jack were to substitute a portfolio of pure no-load funds, Jill's advantage would of course diminish, but she would still have the edge.

Conclusion: *Other things being equal, closed-end funds trading at a discount are more attractive than open-end funds.*

Should you only buy closed-ends at a discount?

The fact that some closed-end funds sell at premiums greater than the true 7 percent charge on most mutual funds introduces a separate question. Should you follow the advice of those who warn you never to buy a closed-end fund at a premium but only at a discount, selling if the fund goes to a premium? I consider that advice wrongheaded – or at least simplistic. True, as we've seen, investing in deeply discounted closed-end funds does tend to help you outperform most open-end funds and market averages. But you need to know more than the discount or premium to judge whether a closed-end fund is a bargain. It is certainly not prudent to grab a glamorous fund at a premium price. Nor should you be seduced by a big discount, if that is the fund's only selling point. There can be good reasons to pay a modest premium on a closed-end fund. And there can be good reasons to shun a fund selling at a discount. To identify these reasons, let's see why premiums and discounts arise in the first place.

Why the closed-end discounts?

Why are many closed-end country and regional funds often available at discount prices? What makes them go unwanted? One answer is that brokers don't particularly want to sell them. Many brokers have come to think it beneath them to bother with retail clients, preferring to trade for institutions or underwrite offerings. Your broker's lack of enthusiasm for closed-end funds may also be related to their fee structure. When closed-end funds are first issued to the public, brokers hawk them feverishly because the fees they get then are up to eight times more than their normal commission for selling the same number of shares. But once a fund starts trading, many brokers lose interest. It is hard for them to interest institutional investors in closed-end funds. Big investors pick stocks for a living, after all, and don't especially relish paying management fees to someone who does it for them. The exodus of institutions from investment trusts largely explains the huge discounts in Britain. When the megabuck men move out of funds, others have to move in. The problem is there aren't enough other investors to take up the slack. The big discounts in London also reflect a ban on country-fund advertising. Moreover, London punters are more confident than most about investing in Asian markets without the costly intermediation of country funds. And investors overall are turned off by high expense ratios, the prime curse of small funds – often those that invest in regions or single countries. The discounts in part reflect that too. Then there are taxes. Some closed-end funds are pregnant with unrealized capital gains from positions held for many years. When those gains are taken, the funds' asset values stay the same – though they now have cash instead of stock – but the gains may be taxable to shareholders, especially in the United States, where treatment of capital gains is particularly unkind. Closed-end fund discounts reflect this too.

Another element in such discounts is liquidity. Stocks in a closed-end portfolio have a market value based on their latest closing prices, but if the manager were to dump them into a thinly traded market, those prices would then plummet, dragging down the fund's net asset value and eventually its price. And if the fund itself is also thinly traded, a large sale of its shares would clobber their price at once. Finally, the conventional wisdom about closed-ends is based mostly on experience with funds that invest in US equities. Because you can easily invest in the same shares on your own, there is indeed little reason to pay a premium for such a fund. For this reason, closed-ends that invest in US equities traditionally trade at substantial discounts, reflecting lack of interest by investors.

Why the closed-end premiums?

Premium and discount levels reflect investor sentiment about a region. Closed-ends that invest in non-US stock markets, especially those not readily accessible to US investors, often trade at a premium because their growth potential far exceeds that of the mature United States. The more promising a foreign market, the higher a closed-end premium tends to be. Closed-end funds that reflect the vibrant Asia-Pacific economies have routinely been valued higher than those that mirror geriatric Europe. Valuation of Latin American funds has shuttled between high and low as the area's economic prospects have altered. Moreover, funds are the only way to invest in some promising countries

– at least for the time being. The premium on such closed ends, as John Templeton suggested in 1988, may well be "a bonus for ability to invest in blocked country markets." South Korea, which caps foreign invest-ment, and India, with problems in settling trades, are prime examples. It is hardly surprising that a closed-end fund letting you leap such barri-cades carries a high premium, especially if it's the only game in town. The premium stayed relatively high even after two other Korea funds were launched. For a long period, India Growth, also NYSE-listed, was the only way to invest in India, but reflecting the lack of interest in the country it bore no high premium. When attention suddenly focused on India in 1993, the premium shot up to more than 25 percent, hovering there for long periods. But India rapidly lowered its investment barriers, and three more India funds came to market in early 1994. The premium immediately evaporated.

Conclusion: A country fund selling at a premium may be the only way to enter an emerging market priced at a low multiple of earnings.

A new market indicator

Market sentiment seems to play a major role in closed-end discounts. Sector discounts among closed-end funds are widest at market bot-toms. The discounts get squeezed as a market rises, and are narrowest at market tops. Just before the October 1987 crash, according to a 1992 study by London stockbroker Smith New Court, discounts on UK investment trusts were narrower than ever. They were wide in the middle and end of 1988, just prior to strong market advances. Autumn of 1989 saw the next historically wide discounts, again pre-dating a market rise, and end-1989 saw narrow discounts, in front of a poor year for equities. Once more, at end-1990, narrow discounts coincided with a market top, while in spring 1992 wide discounts again preceded the next rally. Much of the price variation of closed ends is thus apparently due to psychology, rather than to other factors – such as taxation, expenses or liquidity – that could warrant a big discount.

Conclusion: As premiums and discounts on closed-end funds are largely attributable to market sentiment, narrow discounts often denote market tops and wide discounts market bottoms.

Fears and fads

Similarly, equities, as measured by price/earnings ratios, are relatively expensive at market tops and cheap at market bottoms. A price/earnings (P/E) ratio compares a firm's share price with its earnings per share, showing how many years the company would need, at current earning power, to cover its share price. If the P/E ratio is above average, investors expect profits to rise. The higher the P/E, the greater their confidence in the firm. Because P/E ratios reflect demand, market tops are marked by high P/E ratios and market bottoms by low P/E ratios.

Just as a P/E ratio reflects market demand for a stock, a premium or discount obviously reflects market demand for a closed-end fund. If the premium is above average, investors expect that fund to rise. The higher the premium, the greater their confidence in the fund. The market anticipates a higher return from a fund with a premium and a lower return from one with a discount. Long term, the market is generally right. But sometimes, gripped by fears or fads, the market is dead wrong. Excessive optimism inflates both earnings multiples on stocks and premiums on closed-end funds. That is a time to tread carefully. Conversely, excessive pessimism deflates P/E ratios on stocks and hammers down premiums on closed-end funds. At that point, it is often wiser to be bold.

The fact that a closed-end fund sells at a modest premium by no means rules it out as a bargain. For virtually the entire period from January 1991 through mid-July 1994, Templeton Emerging Markets Fund traded at a premium – often considerable. The premium swung widely, averaging 17 percent. Worldwide Value Fund, on the other hand, traded consistently at a discount, averaging 14 percent. But if you had refused to buy Templeton until it went to a discount, you could never have got into the fund after the first few months. And if you had snapped up Worldwide Value purely because of the discount, you were in for a big disappointment. Over the three-and-a-half-year period, counting cash distributions, Worldwide had a 24.5 percent total return, while Templeton racked up 271 percent. Several times during that period, you could have bought Templeton at a premium of about 10 percent, well below its average.

Purchases at such points are obviously going to give you a better return than those made when premiums spike up to 30 percent or more. The secret is not to buy only at a discount, but when a promising fund sells at a higher discount or lower premium than its average. Indeed, with fear and hope largely determining discounts, the best bet might be a closed-end country fund undervalued for political reasons.

In retrospect, the best moment to have bought Hong Kong shares was in June 1989, just after Tiananmen Square.

Conclusion: A promising closed-end fund selling at a higher discount or lower premium than its average can be a bargain.

Initial public offerings

A word of caution. Though it may be acceptable to pay a modest premium for a promising closed-end fund, that applies only to the premium set by the market. Another kind of premium is set by fund underwriters and brokerages: the fee on an initial public offering. As Mark Skousen makes clear in his useful and amusing *Scrooge Investing*, the fee structure starts you off on the wrong foot.

A typical closed-end country fund is issued at a share price of $15. Yet the net asset value, before the portfolio manager is able to buy a single share, is about $14, putting the fund at a premium of some 7 percent on its first day of trading. The missing dollar, give or take some change, has been pocketed by the firms who brought the fund to market. Due to the nature of closed-ends, those firms are not going to make any money placing new shares, so they need to make their money up front. Fine. They've supplied a service and have a right to get paid. But who says you have to be the one to pay them?

Besides, as Mark notes, a newly issued country fund usually tumbles at least a point or two from its offering price in its first three months. A study on closed-end funds by John W. Peavy III, published in the *Financial Analysts Journal,* concluded, "Shares of newly issued closed-end equity funds perform poorly relative to the overall stock market and to seasoned funds already trading." A 1989 study of the performance of the initial public offerings of closed-end funds, conducted by the Securities & Exchange Commission, showed that after 24 weeks, US closed-end equity funds had an average discount of 10 percent. Non-US closed ends had an average discount of 11.4 percent.

The lesson is clear: it pays to wait.

Conclusion: Never buy a closed-end fund at its initial public offering.

Barron's, a weekly publication you can buy at many newsstands, lists closed-end funds traded on the world's stock exchanges and notes their premium or discount to net asset value. Subscription address: PO Box 2845, 6401 DH Heerlen, The Netherlands. Premiums and discounts on closed-end funds also appear in the Monday editions of the *International Herald Tribune* and the *New York Times*. The *Financial Times* carries similar data daily on British closed-ends under the heading "Investment Trusts."

Information on closed-end funds listed outside the United States can be obtained from four sources. One is British broker Olliff & Partners Plc, 10 Eastcheap, London EC3M 1AJ; telephone: + 44–171–374–0191. Second is The Association of Investment Trust Companies, Durrant House, 8-13 Chiswell Street, London EC1Y 4YY. The third is my own newsletter, *The Outside Analyst*, which also covers US funds. Fourth and most extensive is *Lipper International Closed-End Funds Service*, which carries detailed information on both US and non-US funds and is priced at some $4,000 per year. Their address is 74 Trinity Place, New York NY 10006; telephone: + 1–212–393–1300. Lipper has been tracking premiums and discounts on the world's closed-end funds since 1990.

For US data only, you may wish to check out *The Investor's Guide to Closed-end Funds*, published by Thomas Herzfeld. Each monthly issue covers some 40 closed-ends, including four years of performance data and the range of premium or discount. A yearly subscription is $325, including a free copy of *Herzfeld's Guide to Closed-end Funds* (McGraw-Hill, 1993). PO Box 161465, Miami, FL 33116; telephone: + 1–305–271–1900.

Global funds

Global funds know no geographic bounds. They invest anywhere they can find a bargain – including the United States. Naturally, the more scope you give a fund's portfolio manager, the wider the return variation you can expect. The global funds really give a manager his head, and that's evident in their widely mixed results. In the five years to 1 June 1995, data from Hardwick Stafford Wright showed Duncan Lawrie International down 23.3 percent in US dollar terms, while GAM Global scored a gain of 70.9 percent, a yearly compound average just short of 11.5 percent. What's more, global fund portfolios are spread very widely. Sometimes too widely. They can include a whole basket of markets, some of which are booming, while others are not. So despite GAM Global's admirable result, the average global fund is unlikely to produce superior returns. On the contrary, the average global equity fund is likely to underperform a world stock-market index. In the five years to 1 June 1995, for example, Morgan Stanley's

MSCI World Index was up 44.1 percent in dollar terms, while the 88 global equity funds tracked by Hardwick Stafford Wright rose an average of only 33.7 percent.

Conclusion: Choosing a global fund as proxy for a worldwide fund portfolio surrenders global asset allocation to a manager who is likely to lag the averages. Even worse, if a global fund posts a loss without other holdings to offset it, your entire portfolio winds up in the red.

Regional funds

A fund which invests anywhere but the United States is commonly called an "international" rather than a "global" fund. International funds are aimed at US investors seeking global diversification. Regional funds – those encompassing several countries – are superficially more attractive than those covering only one. After all, the reasoning goes, why stake your money on a single country when there are plenty of broad-based area funds more stable and offering similar returns?

On the other hand, a regional fund implies more risk than a broader, more diversified portfolio. With regional funds, you're less protected against potential bad choices. If a regional fund's markets do poorly, its price may lag the averages – or even drop. All the same, regional funds give you a better chance than global ones of outperforming the averages. Moreover, there is less risk in a group of regional funds than in buying individual stocks, because most regional funds give you a wide range of stocks in each country they cover.

That regional funds can be both more rewarding and more mercurial than the global funds was driven home in 1991 by Micropal, which reported that for the year to 1 September, the average US dollar return on the 189 international equity funds it tracked was only 3.9 percent, despite a top return of 155.7 percent for the crapshooter's Genesis Chile Fund. During the same period, Micropal also computed the average return on 128 European Equity funds at 40.0 percent. Yet, showing the greater risk inherent in area funds, the 22 Australian funds Micropal tracked showed an average 1.4 percent loss. In general, you would have been wiser during 1991 to invest in a European rather than an Australian fund. But not just any old fund. The CEF German Warrant Fund, though European, would have given you a 34.7 percent loss, but First Australia Prime more than a 21 percent gain, despite its location down under.

The lesson – that regional funds can be both more rewarding and more mercurial than the broader international funds – was repeated in

1993. Micropal tracking showed the average US dollar return on 196 international equity funds was only 15.7 percent, while the average return on the 136 North American equity funds it follows was more than double that, at 34.9 percent. But again demonstrating the greater risk of regional funds, the 119 European funds tracked by Micropal in 1993 showed only an average 1.5 percent gain. Careful fund selection, you can see, is vital.

Country funds

When investing globally, the countries you choose can be more crucial than the stocks you actually buy. A country's economic and political climate can have such a strong impact on stock market performance that individual shares are swept along, whatever their merits. Morgan Stanley says that over time, some 75 percent of its profits from international investing have come from getting the country choice right.

By emphasizing the country choice in investing abroad, you also cut down on portfolio turnover. The factors making a country a good or bad place to invest generally do not change all that rapidly or often. An attractive alternative to buying individual stocks or funds that seem too broadly based is a country fund – with its assets invested in just one country or a small group of related countries. This way of investing abroad entails fewer headaches than nearly any other, and lets you enter markets normally more difficult to access.

But you have to be even more finicky in choosing such a country fund than in picking a stock. That's because you'll probably want to allocate more of your portfolio to a basket of stocks balanced to reflect the local market than to shares in any single firm. This automatically raises your commitment and risk.

Country funds are by no means equal, and performance by funds investing in the same country can vary widely. In the twelve months that ended 1 July 1995, one Japanese open-end warrant fund, Gartmore Japan Warrant, was down 80.2 percent, while another, GT Japan Warrant, rose 101.5 percent.

Even more striking, among open-end funds investing in the US, Kestrel US Dollar Shares managed to fall by nearly 40 percent in the three years ending 1 July 1994, while in the same period TSB Offshore Investment Pan American soared over 238 percent.

Such country funds have become the fastest-growing vehicle for international investment, and the trend is likely to snowball in coming years. The reason is simple. It can be extremely difficult, costly and time-consuming to put together a portfolio of foreign stocks. Many can only be bought on foreign exchanges, after converting currency and forking out commissions – sometimes double commissions: one to your local bank or broker and one to the foreign broker. It may also take time to acquire the stocks and there can be annoying delays in selling them. Above all, you have to know which stocks to buy. Most of these problems are solved by a country fund, which can be purchased and sold in short order. The fund's manager picks the stocks and shapes the portfolio. I tend to prefer country funds over regional funds: a rifle rather than a buckshot approach.

There's another sound reason to emphasize country funds. To earn decent returns, you have to take risks. That means buying more aggressive funds – and closed-end country funds are among the most aggressive. The trick is not to overdo it. You can make owning these riskier funds less unnerving by holding them as part of a diversified fund portfolio that reflects a variety of regions and sectors. In this way, following the tenets of modern portfolio theory, you reduce your *overall* risk.

Summary

Paris lists more foreign equities directly than Switzerland, Germany, Nasdaq or the New York Stock Exchange. Amsterdam, despite its relatively low turnover, lists just as many foreign equities as the New York Stock Exchange. However the concentration in London of major fund managers, global banks and securities houses means its stock exchange will continue to be a leading marketplace for foreign equities. Regardless of where you live, you can buy and sell American or Global Depositary Receipts as proxies for foreign shares. Such receipts entitle you to all the rights of shareholders in a firm's home country. Investing in foreign shares via depositary receipts avoids such problems as slow settlements, costly currency conversions, unreliable custody service, poor information flow, unfamiliar market practices and confusing tax conventions. However, ADRs as a group tend to reflect the movements of the US market and most are highly illiquid.

Minimum dealing costs and higher commission rates for smaller deals make modest investments disproportionately expensive, so a minimum investment of $3,000 to $5,000 in each firm's shares should be the aim. That suggests you need at least $75,000 to $125,000 to invest in shares for a good global spread of risk. If your assets don't yet run to this, a portfolio of global, regional or country funds may be *the better option. Among open-end funds, it is best to choose pure no-loads, unless you have some compelling reason to do otherwise.*

Among closed-ends, high premiums mark the end of periods of good performance, not the beginning. Closed-end funds are generally cheaper in London than in New York. Never buy a closed-end fund at its initial public offering. Other things being equal, closed-ends trading at a discount are more attractive than open-ends. As premiums and discounts on closed-end funds are largely attributable to market sentiment, narrow discounts often denote market tops and wide discounts market bottoms. A promising closed-end fund selling at a higher discount or lower premium than its average can be a bargain.

The average global equity fund is likely to lag a world stock-market index. A portfolio of country funds is usually only slightly riskier than one of regional funds, but can focus on the most promising markets. Country funds should be held as part of a diversified portfolio reflecting a variety of regions and sectors.

All well and good. But how do you go about picking the funds in which to invest? The next chapter will answer this question.

8

PICKING FUNDS

"Examine the contents, not the bottle."
The Talmud

If your global portfolio is to consist wholly of equities rather than one or more fund equivalents, you can readily skip to the next chapter, which deals with allocating assets.

You may, on the other hand, wish to pick a single fund as the most practical means to enter a certain market. Alternatively you may wish to pick several so as to create a well-diversified global fund portfolio. Either way, you now face the same problem: how to choose astutely.

To help you in this effort, the previous chapter spelled out the differing costs of various types of funds – e.g., open-end versus closed-end, load versus no-load. Two questions remain unanswered:

- Is there any way you can assure yourself of better than average results by choosing the right funds?
- If not, how can you avoid choosing funds that will give you poorer than average results?

Before trying to answer these questions, let's review the performance of the fund industry as a whole. Has it done a good job for its shareholders? How have fund owners generally fared as against those who invested directly?

The simplest queries are often the hardest to answer. Here is a case in point:

ARE FUNDS A GOOD INVESTMENT?

Investment funds in the aggregate, as Benjamin Graham observed in
The Intelligent Investor, serve three useful purposes:

- They encourage good habits of savings and investment.
- They protect countless individuals against costly mistakes in the
  stock market.
- They bring their shareholders income and profits equal to the overall returns from common stocks.

In all fairness, the fund industry cannot be criticized for doing no better
than the market as a whole. Funds account for so big a slice of all listed
stocks that what happens to the market as a whole must inevitably
happen to the sum of their assets. The combined decisions of professional
investors largely determine the movements of the stock averages, and the
movements of the averages largely determine the aggregate results of
investment funds. As I said earlier, most funds fail to beat the market
because they are the market. What is more, as I'll demonstrate, the cost of
investing in funds seems to exceed that of buying stocks directly.

Nevertheless, over the past decade the average fund participant has
probably done better than the average direct buyer of stocks. Graham
made a similar observation nearly a quarter of a century ago. Now, as
then, the real choice for the average person is probably not between
assembling a well-balanced stock portfolio or doing the same thing, at
greater expense, by buying funds. More likely, the choice is between
swallowing a fund salesman's pitch or that of the more dangerous ped-
dlers of second- and third-rate new issues.

Moreover, the average individual who opens a brokerage account
with the notion of building a conservative portfolio of shares is often
nudged willy-nilly toward speculation and speculative losses. Such
temptations loom less large for the fund buyer.

THE ROLE OF REDEMPTIONS

Whether a fund is a good investment inevitably depends on the skills
of the manager in deciding when and where to invest. Right?

Not necessarily. Sometimes the tail wags the dog. The flight of capital from Latin American (and Far Eastern) markets in the wake of

Mexico's 1994 peso devaluation suggests that fund managers, far from being masters of the financial universe, are in fact servants of those whose money they manage.

Many open-end fund managers were forced to retreat from emerging markets because investors were screaming for their money. Instead of buying on weakness and selling into strength – the classic recipe for success – these managers were forced to liquidate assets into a market where they really wanted to buy. That did not apply to the managers of closed-end funds, whose investment policies are less affected by redemptions.

HOW FUNDS FARE AGAINST THE MARKET

Over the period 1986 through 1995, according to Micropal, a mere 7 of the 277 UK(open-end) unit trusts in the equity growth category managed to beat the All-Share index. Figures for UK investment trusts, pension funds and life funds tell a similar story.

As for the US, two well-known studies in the 1960s by Sharpe and Jensen showed that mutual (open-end) funds underperformed common market indexes. But in 1989, Richard Ippolito published an article in the *Quarterly Journal of Economics*, estimating minimum and maximum total yearly expenses incurred by mutual funds over four periods covering the years 1971 through 1984. The study was cited, though not updated beyond 1984, in another Ippolito article in the *Financial Analysts Journal* of January/February 1993. The expenses, shown in Table 8.1, include investment fees, expense charges and trading costs, but exclude load charges.

Table 8.1 Annual expenses of mutual funds

Period	Percentage of assets	
	Minimum	Maximum
1971 – 1974	1.50	2.06
1975 – 1977	1.56	2.06
1978 – 1981	1.69	2.36
1982 – 1984	1.87	2.77

Source: "On Studies of Mutual Fund Performance," Financial Analysts Journal

With expenses ranging from 1.5 percent to more than 2.75 percent a year, the mutual funds should have badly lagged the market average.

But over these years in fact, they didn't. Mind you, Ippolito was not talking about *beating* the market – just about keeping up with it. "These results," he reported, "suggest that mutual funds, on average, are sufficiently successful in their trades to offset their expenses." In other words, the risk-adjusted performance of open-end funds, net of expenses, was shown to resemble that of index funds. Fund expenses of course are largely research. These findings do not imply that all funds are always clever in buying research, nor do they mean that funds as a whole spend money wisely in every period. But the study did suggest that a sizable number of funds are successful enough so that industry experience matches the returns from index funds – after subtracting expenses and adjusting for risk. If true, this would make indexing a less efficient way of imitating a market than investing in a diversified basket of funds. But *is* it true?

Not always. From 1984 through 1994, in contrast to the two previous decades, mutual funds did badly lag the market. Few investors need to be reminded that 1994 was a poor year for funds. The average US open-end (mutual) fund lost 3.6 percent, while the S&P 500 index gained 1.3 percent. Eight out of ten of the well-paid experts who manage funds for the big investment houses failed to beat the market. During the decade, such dismal performance was par for the course. According to the Vanguard group, from 1984 through 1994, US stock funds posted an annual return 15 percent below the return of the S&P index. The conclusion of the 1960s studies – mutual funds underperform common market indexes – was seemingly reconfirmed.

Did something change in the investment environment during the late 1980s and early 1990s that might explain this recent poor performance by mutual funds? I believe it did. This may surprise you, but these days chances are that an individual incurs a lower brokerage commission on a typical $100,000 trade than does a $1 billion mutual fund. A recent study of fund commission costs by finance professors Miles Livingston and Edward O'Neal shows that US mutual funds pay an average 6.2 cents a share in brokerage commissions. That's hardly dirt-cheap, the study notes, because a deep-discount broker would handle a $100,000 trade on a $45 stock for half that amount – less than three cents a share.

How is that possible? Don't mutual funds have a lot more clout to negotiate low commission rates than most of us?

Sure. But size isn't the whole story, according to the study, which argues that a big reason funds pay so much for their trades is the arcane Wall Street practice known as "soft-dollar payments." In practice, a mutual fund trading through a brokerage firm doesn't pay commissions merely for getting its trades done. It also pays for stock-picking research and other services. The extra payment above the bare-bones cost of trading a stock is called the "soft-dollar" payment.

And who foots the bill? You do.

You thought you already were being charged for research in the annual management fee?

True. You're paying for it twice.

The study also raises an intriguing question: Why do funds with the highest operating expenses tend to pay the highest brokerage commissions? This surprising pattern holds true, the study found, even after screening out funds that might be expected to pay higher commissions, such as foreign-equity funds.

Perhaps this is the answer: Another common practice in the fund industry is to use soft-dollar commissions to pay for computers, office furniture and subscriptions to publications. At many mutual fund groups it is also an accepted practice to direct trading to brokerage firms that sell the group's funds. The practice is legal, as long as it is disclosed to investors and as long as the brokers can provide "best execution" of the trade. That means the broker is supposed to buy the stock as cheaply as competitors and charge low commissions.

Disclosure of the brokerage commissions paid by funds is currently quite limited. But since November 1995, each prospectus has to reflect mutual fund expenses such as printing and custodial costs picked up by third parties: that is, costs paid by brokers as part of soft-dollar arrangements. Fund companies are now required to track the average commission they pay per share. But don't hold your breath. US mutual funds won't be required to report this figure to investors until early 1997.

Confronted with the recent miserable performance, and doubting that open-end funds truly perform like index funds, an investor has three courses of action:

- Buy an index fund whose portfolio is *structured* to mirror an appropriate index. The next chapter expands on the merits and shortcomings of indexing.
- Somehow find funds that consistently beat the averages. This chapter maps the steps in that search.

- Forget funds – wholly or partly – and build your own stock portfolio: a process traced in "Allocating Assets," "Your Benchmark," "Assuring Variety," "The World's Best Bargains" and "Producing Steady Profits."

WHICH FUNDS?

Anyone betting at the track has two decisions to make. The first is to work out which is the best horse. The second is to discover whether the jockey is good enough. Similar logic applies to choosing the right funds. First you have to pick the right regions. Then you have to ensure that you don't trash that careful research by choosing the financial equivalent of a bad jockey: a bad fund manager. To draw a winning fund, you need to pick both the right region and the right manager.

THE RIGHT REGIONS

Basically, medium to long term, share prices reflect earnings growth. In turn, corporate earnings tend to rise most when general economic growth is strong. So your first step is to find those countries with the most vigorous economic growth. This often includes countries about to pull out of recession and those freeing their economies from state control. More on freedom's vital economic role when we discuss top–down investing in Chapter 13.

Your second standard for country choice is value. How expensive are stocks in the light of the growth anticipated? As with individual company stocks, markets trading at a low average price/earnings ratio frequently offer superior returns. And among low P/E markets, those with the highest growth rates generally perform best.

Your third yardstick is country risk. How shaky is the government? Are its economic policies given to rapid shifts? Is the country running a huge deficit? Is a coup, revolution or invasion brewing?

Let's examine these three criteria of growth, value and country risk.

Country risk

In Chapter 1, we estimated chances of survival over the next 100 years for the average developed market at 80 percent, and at 40 percent for the average emerging market. The following discussion, particularly the chapter on allocating assets, will show you how to reduce such country risks to negligible proportions.

Nascent markets in Eastern Europe, Middle East and Africa have the potential to deliver solid returns for the next decade, but may also give you a petrifying rollercoaster ride. The myriad challenges investors face in these regions include a lack of liquidity, unstable currencies, political conflicts and wars. How can you assess such risks? The Economist Intelligence Unit, or EIU, a branch of the London-based Economist group, stands ready with an answer: its country-risk service. For a hefty £10,000 a year (about $15,000), this service rates some 180 countries on political, economic and investment prospects, providing quarterly reviews, a telephone inquiry contact and an annual seminar. The reports are also available online, on CD-ROM and in microform.*

Alas, estimating risk on a country-by-country basis will not help you find promising regions or show you where to expect the highest investment return. Indeed, estimating individual country risk is actually of little value to a global equity portfolio. A first step that makes far more sense is simply to decide which regions you find most attractive in terms of potential return.

Relative value

In surveying major markets, it is often useful to see how historical prices relate to current prices. Based on average earnings per share, a market's average share price can be expressed as a multiple of earnings. This price/earnings ratio, or P/E, is a useful way of flagging promising markets. You simply look for a P/E ratio that is cheap relative to similar markets and to its own historical norms.

As I write this, most major stock markets are trading above their average price-earnings ratio during the 15-year period from March 1973 to March 1988. The first column in Table 8.2 gives you the 15-year average P/E, the second the bear market P/E in 1974, the third the bear market P/E in 1981 and the last the rounded-off P/E on consensus estimates of 1996 earnings, as published by the Institutional Brokers Estimate System on 17 August 1995.

---

* For more information, you can write to the EIU at P.O. Box 200, Harold Hill, Romford RM3 8UX; Tel: + 44–171–830–1007; Fax: + 44–171–830–1023.

Table 8.2 P/E Market Comparisons

Country	Average P/E	1974 P/E	1981 P/E	1996 P/E (est.)
Canada	13.7	6.8	7.6	10.9
France	19.2	5.6	4.2	12.9
Germany	11.6	9.0	7.2	16.8
Hong Kong	14.6	6.4	11.7	9.5
Japan	24.4	12.3	15.9	44.5
Switzerland	11.4	5.9	10.1	13.3
United Kingdom	9.4	3.1	6.1	12.4
USA (S&P 500)	11.0	7.2	7.4	13.2

These relative price/earnings ratios seem to say that at present, among major markets, Japan, the United States and Germany are historically overpriced, while Canada, France and Hong Kong are relatively cheap. But that doesn't automatically mean the latter three countries are bargains. What is cheap is not always a bargain. In fact, appraising a market by its *relative* value begs the question of what that market is actually worth.

Intrinsic value

If markets in general are priced too steeply, the cheapest may also be expensive. It is thus wiser to appraise a market by *intrinsic* rather than relative value. Intrinsic value is present where stocks sell at a low multiple of expected earnings. Even more intrinsic value can be found where corporate profits are expanding and where analysts keep raising earnings estimates.

Economic growth

Some investors simply assume that countries with the strongest economic growth will provide the strongest stock market performance and delimit themselves largely to those markets. Other investors favour countries that combine relatively strong economic growth with a strong currency. More sophisticated investors also take note of such factors as prospective recovery from recession, as set out later in the discussion of market cycles. Earnings estimates, when aggregated, are also a useful indicator of future economic growth. The chapter entitled "The World's Best Bargains" evaluates these various approaches to finding the most promising regions.

Okay. Let's say you have now found what you consider to be the "right" regions. Should you invest only in these countries? Not unless you're absolutely sure of your choices. And also quite certain that over the next 12 months no other stock markets will produce better returns. But that kind of certainty is largely reserved to soothsayers and lunatics. If, like most of us, you can peer but dimly into the future, you are wiser to hedge your bets.

And why not? You have set out, after all, to construct a global portfolio, not a regional one. So by all means emphasize the markets that seem most attractive. Just don't ignore the others. A simple rule of thumb in building a long-term global fund portfolio is to place a third of your equity investments in each of three areas: your home country, developed international markets and emerging markets. The next chapter goes into such asset allocation considerations.

No fund is a global portfolio

A word of warning before we move on to evaluating managers. As the preceding chapter pointed out, it is most unwise to choose any one fund as a proxy for your "global fund portfolio" because you then delegate asset allocation to a fund manager who is likely to lag a world stock-market index. What is more, if a global fund posts a loss without other holdings to offset it, your whole portfolio winds up in the red. Pinning all your hopes on a single global fund is thus a foolish gamble. No one fund will always be tilted towards the fastest-growing markets – another prime reason you need more than a single fund. You can't know for certain which portfolio manager will be best able to take advantage of each new turn of the global markets.

Conclusion: *Finding and monitoring a global fund that consistently outperforms a world stock-market index is more difficult and less prudent than assembling a global portfolio of funds.*

THE RIGHT MANAGERS

Once you've found the most promising regions, you can then think about selecting an appropriate fund to reflect each market. With more than 22,000 funds available internationally, you're certainly spoilt for choice. The US alone has some 7,400 mutual funds, roughly three times the number of stocks on the New York Stock Exchange. This embarrassment of riches makes picking the funds to invest in an increasingly daunting task. Even beginning to narrow down the field poses a number of fundamental concerns. How relevant are past returns? Does the manager truly matter? How important is the fund family? These are among the questions answered in this chapter.

So just how are you to choose a fund? Though there is no magic formula, you can take a structured approach. Moreover, being a global investor gives you a tremendous advantage in threading the labyrinth of choice. You'll generally be looking for a fund that covers a specific region. This at once narrows the field sharply, often to a mere handful of funds.

On the other hand, certain factors make selection of a regional or country fund difficult, such as the currency in which it is denominated. It is obviously impossible to make a fair comparison between a fund denominated in, say, US dollars and another in Japanese yen. So, the first step in trying to choose between funds is to use a common currency. Here I use US dollars throughout. That makes comparison easy, but has a weakness. Favorable exchange-rate fluctuations can mask poor performance by a fund manager. And unfavorable moves in exchange rates may conceal good investment management.

There are three main things to decide about a fund. First, will it score good results? Second, how much will you have to pay to get that performance? And third, how wild a ride can you expect from gyrations in its price? The last two questions are relatively easy to answer. The subject of performance, on the other hand, can be as difficult as you choose to make it. In Ernest Hemingway's *For Whom the Bell Tolls*, set in the Spanish Civil War, the American Robert Jordan says to Pilar: "You are a very hard woman."

"No," she replies. "But so simple I am very complicated." You can choose to follow so-called "expert" advice complicated enough to make your head spin. Or you can select country or regional funds using a deceptively simple system, outlined later in this chapter.

Performance criteria

As you've seen, performance by funds investing in the same country can vary widely. Conventional wisdom says a fund's performance has a lot to do with who is running it. If that's true, selecting a specific country fund should involve examining track records and what strategies the various portfolio managers follow. Many investors start therefore by poring over performance tables published by such fund-trackers as Hardwick Stafford Wright (HSW) (+ 44–1625–511311), Lipper Analytical (+ 1–908–273–2772), Micropal (+ 44–181–741–4100) and Morningstar (+ 1–312–696–6000).

Perils of picking winning funds

This apparently logical approach is sown with booby traps. A fund that has shown terrific returns over a recent period may seem an irresistibly warm place to hatch your nest egg. But past performance, as they say, is no reliable guide to future returns. A fund may look good over one, three and five years, despite doing badly over four of those years, just because it had one sensational year. And a fund may have done well over the past three or five years only because its investment style has been in vogue – and is on the verge of going out of favor. The latter point is crucial and I'll return to it shortly.

One kind of past performance *is* a good guide to the future: Bad performance tends to continue. Yet even bad funds sometimes rank as number one performers. According to Lipper Analytical, Nautilus Fund was the top US mutual fund in 1980, Lexington Strategic Investments claimed that honour in 1979, 44 Wall Street Fund in 1975 and Sherman Dean Fund in 1974. All four funds were among the nation's worst performers over the decade ended in 1993. Long-term losers are often number one performers over short time periods. By choosing the proper category and the proper time period, virtually any fund in existence can claim to be "number one."

Pursuing consistency

According to the experts, therefore, looking at two arbitrary points in time says nothing. They say you also need to examine the *consistency* of returns. Following this well-meant advice, many investors launch a search for the Holy Grail: the fund that steadily performs well in its market without ever hitting the top of the charts. If a fund's performance has been in the upper quartile in its region for, say, three consecutive six-month periods, it is said to have demonstrated consistency. And if a fund has scored consistent returns in the past, many investors believe the odds are it will be consistent in the future.

Fine. Let's assume, for the moment, that it makes sense to pursue the will-o'-the-wisp of consistency. Say you've dug through reams of historical data and have found a few country funds with a consistent track record of high returns relative to the market in which they were achieved. As of 31 August 1995, Gartmore American Emerging, for instance, was ranked by HSW among the top ten gainers among UK unit trusts over one, three, five and ten years. Is the search now over?

Not by a long shot, say the fund experts, who urge you to pose the following questions as well: How were those consistently high returns attained? Was it luck or judgment that produced the good performance? Was the strategy high-risk or low-risk? What are the charges? Is the investment process repeatable? Does the whole team understand its investment strategy? Would new money adversely affect performance? Have managers invested their own money? How much does the team depend on one person's talents?

Who is now in charge?

At a bare minimum, the experts say, before reaching for your checkbook you should ring up the company to learn the details of its fee structure and precisely who is currently running the fund. There is a surprisingly high turnover of managers, so the one who racked up the impressive gains may have been poached by a rival firm.

Keeping track of who is managing each fund recently became somewhat easier in the United States. In July 1994, the Securities and Exchange Commission made it mandatory for funds managed by one person to disclose that person's name in their annual prospectus. Of course if a manager leaves a month after the prospectus has been sent out, you may not hear about it for another eleven months.

The Securities and Exchange Commission, by the way, has a public reference branch in Washington, DC, which will verify by telephone whether a fund is registered. The background information that the SEC will provide includes a fund's initial registration statement, prospectus and annual reports. These documents can yield information both on the fund manager and on the kind of investments the fund says it intends to make. Fund experts note that the same general approach applies to any global locale. If you're interested in a Channel Islands fund, for instance, you can contact the offshore domicile's Financial Services Department, a regulatory agency, to find out if the fund is properly registered, whether there have been any complaints about it and who the manager is.

The you name it, we sell it, fund

Even more obvious advice from the experts is to make sure that the fund you have in mind really does what it says it does. Advisers warn you not simply to accept a general description of a fund's investment approach, such as "European Small Companies," "Indian Communications" or "China Opportunities." Instead, they say, request a detailed outline of the portfolio, because it can yield valuable additional information. Of the huge array of funds investing in China, the spread of performance to March 1994 was enormous, with the best up 62 percent and the worst down 6 percent. The reason for the diversity in results? Many of the funds also invested in Hong Kong and Taiwan. Others were venture capital funds. Examination of the portfolios would have revealed that.

"Mutual Fund Styles," a recent study by Stephen Brown, an economist at New York University, and William Goetzmann, an economist at Yale University, suggests that some funds in fact deliberately mislead their clients about the strategy they pursue. A fund can choose the benchmark that shows it in the best light simply by switching categories at the end of the year. The two economists studied the performance of 48 US mutual funds that altered their stated investment style. In each case, they compared a fund's performance in the year preceding the switch with the average return in its old category and the average return in its new one. Surprise! On average, the switch in styles improved the benchmark-adjusted return by nearly 1 percent.

Conclusion: *The name of a fund does not always reflect its investment style.*

Evaluating the managers

Fund experts also have a number of tips on finding the right managers, ranging from good common sense to the absurd. The theatre of the ridiculous includes those who tell you to read the annual report to see if the fund's manager writes decent prose, on the assumption that someone who can write clearly is likely to have a carefully planned strategy.

Finding pertinent background information on a specific manager, whether in New York, Guernsey or Hong Kong, can require persistence. Fund groups sometimes try to obscure who the manager actually is, fearing those managers who become known as successful will leave, taking customers with them. Assuming you've been able to pry loose a name, the experts suggest you find out how long the manager has been with the fund and then check to make sure it is the same type of fund as those on which that person's overall track record is based.

Make sure, they add, that a manager's style matches your investment objective. Clues to the thinking of fund managers can be found in shareholder letters written by the managers themselves, as opposed to public-relations people. Such letters generally offer a fairly candid view of what has gone right with the fund and what has not. Other useful background information on managers can often be obtained directly from the company. If you request copies or reprints of manager interviews that have been conducted by financial publications, fund companies as a rule are happy to send them to you. But background information on a portfolio manager can become obsolete if the manager changes investment style. It doesn't happen often, but, say the experts, it's worth asking if the manager's investment style has changed while running the fund.

To determine how a manager performs in a bear market, another question experts often suggest you ask is, "What is the most money I could have lost in this fund if I had bought and sold it at the worst time?" Another favourite question is to what extent a manager's performance has been buoyed or hurt by general market conditions. A manager whose country fund rises 10 percent in a period when that particular market gains 20 percent may not be the genius you're looking for.

People who select fund managers on a full-time basis agree that it is not easy. They also generally agree that on-site interviews with fund management groups are indispensable. Talking regularly with managers and monitoring subsequent performance in the light of their words can make you effective in what at bottom are subjective assessments. But there are no guarantees. Picking funds involves probabilities, not certainties. The various questions posed by the fund pickers are intended to differentiate between luck and skill – the key to evaluating a fund manager. The aim is to discover which part of a fund's returns are due to markets, which part to investment style and which part to stock-picking. Obviously the process can be laborious: mostly a matter of putting in hours. But there are easier ways to choose a manager.

Finding a local hero

A simpler and more pragmatic approach to discovering the right manager for a country fund is to go with a local hero. A recent study by

London-based Micropal for the *Wall Street Journal* indicates that the best returns among funds covering a single country will generally be scored by local managers. The study showed that while foreign funds investing in German equities only rose an average 8.8 percent over the three years ended February 1995, home-grown equity funds were up 15.5 percent over the same period. A comparison of foreign and domestic-registered funds investing in UK, French and Swiss equity markets led to the same conclusion (Table 8.3).

Table 8.3 Local managers do better

	One year		Three years	
French equity funds				
Domestic	-21.29%	(111)	+9.86%	(83)
Foreign	-23.54%	(32)	+0.92%	(28)
German equity funds				
Domestic	-7.21%	(68)	+15.48%	(56)
Foreign	-9.79%	(48)	+8.84%	(37)
Swiss equity funds				
Domestic	-15.74%	(19)	+40.39%	(15)
Foreign	-18.48%	(16)	+28.95%	(11)
UK equity funds				
Domestic	-12.88%	(427)	+39.00%	(399)
Foreign	-13.35%	(104)	+27.28%	(86)

Source: Micropal Ltd.
Average performance of foreign-registered equity funds compared with funds registered in their home markets. Performance is measured to 1 February 1995. (Figures in parentheses show the number of funds included in survey.)

Conclusion: *You're likely to do best by picking a local team, if available, to manage a country fund.*

Does the manager really matter?

The only known study to analyze performance as a function of change in portfolio management, carried out by US fund data group CDA/Wiesenberger, surveyed 40 diverse equity funds. It showed that top performers fell to 10 percent below the norm in the five-year period after their managers had left.

Conversely, the study showed that returns from poor performers soared from 69 percent below the norm to 27 percent above average in the five years after a new manager was hired.

That improvement seems logical. If a fund company is sufficiently motivated to change managers, chances are it will go out and find a good one. Take the $137 million American Heritage Fund, for instance. After losing more than 42 percent from February 1986 to February 1990, it decided to switch managers. From 1 February 1990, when Heiko Thieme took over, to 31 March 1994, American Heritage rose more than 92 percent, or an annualized return of 16.4 percent.

Conclusion: *Poor fund performers that do not change managers tend to stay poor performers.*

The impact of group style

If a fund has scored consistent returns in the past, do the odds favour good returns in the future, as we assumed earlier? Sometimes. A change in manager may not matter if a fund group has a consistent approach to investing, so another tip from the experts is to check if the group has posted solid performance in its other funds. Individual funds can have a great run for a while because they're invested in a particular country that is currently top of the pops. But for the long haul, common wisdom has it, your best chance of achieving decent returns is to invest in several country or regional funds run by one, two or three fund management groups with the best all-round performance. (There is the added advantage of reduced costs should you decide to switch funds within a group.)

In this case, common wisdom is right. There can be wide differences in how much latitude an individual manager is permitted by the company he works for. Some companies give their managers free rein to pursue investment opportunities as they see fit, while others demand stricter adherence to a "house" approach.

It doesn't much matter who is cooking at McDonald's. The product is rigidly defined by portion and menu control, with recipes followed to the letter. At De Trechter in Amsterdam, on the other hand, Jan de Wit creates dishes according to the season and his own fancy and still turns out great food night after night. The loss of the chef would obviously have a much greater impact on the second restaurant than the first. Fund companies have just as much disparity between styles, so the fund family's overall style can be of paramount importance in judging a manager's effect on performance, especially if you're taking the regional route. In that case you're best off seeking steady returns in a group with solid performance in a number of funds.

Conclusion: When investing in regional funds, it is wise to choose those run by fund management groups with a consistent approach and the best all-round performance.

A detour around high loads

Here's another useful tip from Mark Skousen's enjoyable *Scrooge Investing*. Fund families that normally impose fat 5 to 9 percent loads have recently begun offering closed-end funds listed on stock exchanges. Mark, a celebrated tightwad, suggests buying such funds through a discount broker for a rock-bottom commission, often less than 1 percent. You can also place a limited buy order below the current asking price, which might get you a better deal on the fund.

Some high-load fund families that offer closed-end funds:

- Foreign & Colonial Emerging Middle East Fund (NYSE: EME): Foreign & Colonial, the oldest fund group in the UK, charges front-end loads up to 5 percent and back-end fees of up to 1 percent. But you can get their expertise at a cut-rate price on the New York Stock Exchange.
- GT Greater Europe Fund (NYSE: GTF): London's GT group specializes in foreign equities. You can buy the GT Europe Fund and pay a 4.75 percent load, or get virtually the same thing, without a load, through the GT Greater Europe Fund on the New York Stock Exchange.
- Templeton Global Income Fund (NYSE: GIM), Templeton Global Government Fund (NYSE: TGG) and Templeton Emerging Market Fund (NYSE: EMF): A thousand dollars placed in 1954 in Sir John Templeton's Templeton Growth Fund would have grown to $218,000 by the end of 1993. But why pay a 8.5 percent load for the Templeton name when you can join the same fund family for a modest brokerage fee?
- A number of London-listed closed-end country funds are also run by well-known management groups, including Foreign & Colonial, GT, Old Mutual International, Perpetual and Templeton. You can find them in the *Financial Times* under investment trusts. The Association of Investment Trust Companies, which represents over 90 percent of investment trusts, can tell you about them and their performance. Write to The Private Investor Helpdesk, AITC, Durrant House, 8 – 13 Chiswell Street, London EC1Y 4YY.

Conclusion: You can sometimes join a high-load fund family at a discount through a closed-end regional fund.

The past as prologue

The fact that you cannot predict future performance does not mean you should wholly ignore past performance. There is some relationship between a fund's past and future performance. Roger Ibbotson, president of Ibbotson Associates, a Chicago investment-consulting firm, looked at US stock-fund performance for the period 1976-1987. He found that funds that ranked in the top 25 percent of their category during the past three years had a better than 60 percent chance of being in their category's top half during the next three years.

London-based Fund Research, which analyzes UK unit trusts for professional financial advisers, has found that one in five of the funds in the top quarter of a league table are likely to remain in the top quarter over the next five years. In an attempt to find the funds which do consistently well, Fund Research breaks the five-year period down into five separate one-year periods. Then, in harmony with the Ibbotson study, the selection process weights each fund's performance heavily towards the last three years.

Alas, the fact that a fund has done moderately well for three years, or even for five, does not mean it will excel as time goes by. Quite the contrary – especially if your own performance standards are more demanding. In 1990, Burt Berry of DAL Investment Co., which publishes *No-Load Fund*X*, tracked the records of the best-performing US funds for 17 five-year periods, starting with 1971. Of the top 25 funds in each of the five-year periods, an average of only two or three were in the top 25 in the following year or in the following five years. "Worse," Berry adds, "many of the top 25 ended up near the bottom of the heap in the following year as well as in the following five years."

Conclusion: A fund that has done well for three years or five will not necessarily excel as time goes by. The performance of most funds decays over time – regresses to the mean – and a prudent investor takes account of this fact.

AVOIDING THE WRONG FUNDS

In fund investment, as I mentioned, your biggest risk is a manager with a bad long-term record. But fund returns swing so widely that it takes quite a while before you can be really sure that a fund manager is incompetent. In this environment, it is easy to see how a market in "lemons" can arise. But there is an easy way to avoid the non-performers, particularly among no-load funds.

The polar bear strategy

When an ice floe has melted substantially, the polar bear springs to another. Similarly, if a fund's relative performance has dwindled badly over a year or so, you simply step to a leader. Within a single sector, be it a country or a region, you just stay with the winning funds until they are no longer winners, then move on to the new leaders. A study by Harvard professors Hendricks, Patel and Zeckhauser, done for the US National Bureau of Economic Research over a 17-year period, tested the results of buying the top five performing open-end funds each year, holding them for one year then switching to the new top five. Called "Hot Hands in Mutual Funds: The Persistence of Performance," it concluded that this technique outperformed the market by 5 to 10 percent a year. This approach seems to work in strong and weak environments – or at least it has for the past 19 years. Though you do not know for sure which portfolio manager will profit most from each new turn of the global markets, betting on those doing well at the moment helps you to be right most of the time.

A recent study by the *Wall Street Journal* confirms that one year is more predictive of fund performance than five years. This makes sense, because though market conditions change, a fund manager's approach usually does not. Most fund managers have a certain philosophy of how to invest. Some like large capitalization stocks and some small. Some accentuate blue chips while others avoid them. So-called "value" managers look for stocks priced relatively low in terms of a firm's assets or its eventual ability to make money, while a "growth" fund manager typically prefers glitter to diamonds in the rough. Growth managers are willing to pay premium prices for the shares of companies with earnings in a strong uptrend. These personal styles generally do not vary, but markets do. Managers in tune with the market shine brightly as it rewards their particular style. Their stars dim as another market sector comes to the fore. In 1991, Donald Yacktman won the Morningstar Mutual Funds Manager of the Year award. During the 1980s and earlier 1990s, Mr Yacktman distinguished himself as a leading portfolio manager, guiding the Selected American Shares fund to a 16.6 percent annual gain over nine years, versus 14.7 percent for the S&P 500. In March 1992, he left Selected American to start his own fund, called the Yacktman fund, which was launched four months later. In the year ended 31 December 1993, with dividends reinvested, the S&P 500 had gained 10.0 percent but the Yacktman fund had lost 6.6 percent. Nothing had happened to Mr Yacktman. The market had simply rotated, and his style didn't fit any more. (He subsequently narrowed the gap somewhat, scoring 24.1 percent in the year ended September 30, 1995 as against 29.3 percent for the S&P 500.)

The polar bear strategy puts you into a top-performing country or regional equity fund in each sector, automatically weeding out the laggards. The bottom line is all that counts. Once you abandon the search for long-term consistency, you no longer need to differentiate between luck and skill. You no longer care which part of returns are due to markets, which to investment style and which to stock-picking. In fact, with inept managers weeded out, it doesn't much matter who runs a fund.

Conclusion: One year is more predictive of fund performance than five years. Stay with the winners in each country or regional sector by upgrading your open-end funds at least annually.

As a rule, this technique works nicely for no-load funds, but not as well for closed-ends. If you were regularly to replace each closed-end country fund that gets bumped from the lead in its sector, commissions and taxes would eat you alive. So if the market in question remains attractive, switch out of a closed-end country fund only if it badly lags its stock-market index. Most markets you choose *will* remain attractive, because the factors making a country a good place to invest do not alter all that rapidly or often. A list of attractive stock markets and suitable closed-end country funds appears each month in my newsletter *The Outside Analyst*.

Conclusion: Replace a closed-end fund that gets bumped from the lead in an attractive country sector only if the fund also badly lags its stock-market index.

Where to find data on funds

If you have a closed-end fund in mind, find out how its present price compares with the average premium or discount over the last year or so. The lower its relative premium or the higher its relative discount, the better off you are. Historical data on closed-end premiums and discounts can be found in *Morningstar Closed-End Funds* and *Foreign Markets Advisory*, both cited in the preceding chapter. Morningstar, by the way, offers a monthly computer diskette, "OnFloppy," with data on over 500 US closed-end funds (tel: + 1–312–696–6000; $185 a year). Other relevant publications cited in the preceding chapter include *Barron's*, the *International Herald Tribune*, the *New York Times*, the *Financial Times, Investor's Guide to Closed-end Funds* and *Lipper International Closed-End Funds Service*.

The performance of US mutual (open-end) funds is regularly reported by major financial publications, including *Business Week, Forbes, Money* and *The Wall Street Journal*. Here are some other sources of this information:

- *Morningstar Mutual Funds* (tel: + 1–800–876–5005; $375 a year). Reviews more than 1,500 funds biweekly.
- *Value Line Mutual Fund Survey* (tel: + 1–800–284–7607; $295 a year). Similar in type and scope to the data provided by Morningstar.
- *Mutual Fund Profiles* (tel: + 1–800–221–5277; $152 a year), published quarterly by Standard & Poor's, with Lipper Analytical. Covers 750 fund families.
- *CDA/Wiesenberger Mutual Funds Update* (tel: + 1–800–232–2285; $295 a year). Covers over 5,400 funds and is updated monthly.

Pinchpenny vs. Prodigal

Given equal risk-adjusted performance, a fund with a low expense ratio stacks the odds in your favor. Over 10 years, an annual difference of even 1 percent has a measurable impact on your wallet. Suppose two fund managers rack up a compound return before expenses of 10 percent annually for 10 years. Pinchpenny has an expense ratio of 1 percent. Prodigal, on the other hand, runs through 2 percent each year for overhead. After 10 years, $10,000 invested with Pinchpenny will grow to $23,674. The same sum placed with Prodigal will rise to only $21,589. By choosing Prodigal, you've tossed away $2,085 – a year's worth of heat and electricity at my house, or two day's rent on a three-bedroom flat in the Peak district of Hong Kong.

The cookie monster

Recurring annual expenses can have a severe impact on fund performance, especially that of open ends. Steadman American Industry Fund,
worst-performing US stock fund for the five years ended December
1993, managed to lose 25 percent of shareholders' money while Standard & Poor's 500-stock index soared 97.1 percent. Stock-picking was
only partly responsible for the rotten results. According to Morningstar,
this open-end fund actually gained 45.1 percent if you ignore yearly
costs. But its annual expenses were outrageous, gobbling up more than
12 percent of the assets each year from 1990 through 1993. Investors
are often only dimly aware of this cookie monster's impact on returns.
For many open-ends, annual expenses made the difference between
beating and lagging the market in the five years from end-1988 through
1993. Before expenses, these funds soared an average 108.1 percent in
that period, versus 97.1 percent for the S&P 500. But after expenses,
they returned a market-lagging 95.3 percent. Yearly expenses can bite
painfully into short-term performance as well. Morningstar figures that
the average diversified US stock fund returned 12.6 percent in 1993, as
against 10.1 percent for the S&P 500 index. But cut out yearly expenses
and fund returns jump to almost 14 percent.

Charges can vary widely from fund to fund. Charges are often not
highlighted in sales brochures or in annual reports, the only figure
clearly visible being the management fee – normally from 0.5 percent to
1 percent. A low management fee can thus easily mislead you into thinking you are buying a low-cost fund. But other costs include the
commission the fund pays brokers to buy stock, plus the cost of custody
to keep the stock, audit fees and directors' fees. After these charges are
tacked on to the management fee, you may be startled to see the cookie
monster has nibbled several percentage points off your reported return.

Offshore fund charges

When it comes to fees, the real chamber of horrors is found in offshore funds, those domiciled in a country known for minimal
regulation and low taxes. Offshore funds are often domiciled in such
places as Bermuda, Cayman, the Channel Islands and Malta. Seeking
to stimulate investment, some non-island locations, including Dublin
and Luxembourg, have reduced regulation so that they are also considered offshore. Offshore rules on fee disclosure are thus somewhat
more lax than in the UK or the US.

According to the report "Offshore Fund Expenses," aimed at financial advisers and fund managers, total annual costs of an offshore fund can be about six times the quoted annual charge. Worst offenders are funds such as Citiportfolios Emerging Asian Markets, which quotes a yearly management fee of 1.5 percent, but in 1993 had total charges of 9.78 percent. Other firms whose funds generally rank badly for their extra charges include Templeton, and Von Ernst, a German company whose funds were previously branded Hill Samuel. A consumer version of the report costs £124 and can be obtained from Fitzrovia (tel: + 44–171–370–0084).

Conclusion: Other things being equal, funds with low expense ratios are preferable.

A hidden flaw in performance reports

Most open-end fund performance tables are highly misleading. Investment results are usually described as "performance" or "total return" – a combination of dividends paid to shareholders, plus realized profits to be paid as capital gain distributions, plus or minus unrealized capital gains or losses resulting from market action. If a fund pays a 5 percent dividend over any period of time but loses 5 percent in market value over the same period, the total return for that period would be zero. But if you've paid 6 percent commission to buy the fund (or unit trust), your experience and the fund's experience would differ vastly, since you got only $94 worth of shares for the $100 you laid out. You'd be down 6 percent for the year.

Most fund performance statistics are reported as fund experience, including widely quoted HSW, Lipper and Morningstar. In other words, most reported performance results treat all funds as no-load.

Conclusion: If you're considering buying a load fund of any kind – full-load, low-load or back-end load – study investor experience rather than fund experience in your selections.

Ultimately, all you can do to avoid high fund fees is to be vigilant:

- Check out the costs. These are disclosed within the first few pages of a fund's prospectus, the official sales document sent to prospective investors.
- Find out how much commission you are paying the broker or financial intermediary.

- Ask to see "load-adjusted" performance figures from the fund-rating agencies.
- Finally, read annual reports carefully to search for hidden costs.

Conclusion: *If a fund company's charges are significantly out of line with most others, don't even consider it.*

If you want to concentrate on true no-load funds, you can get a list of all those in the US by writing to:

No-Load Mutual Funds Membership List, Investment Company Institute, 1600 M Street NW, Suite 600, Washington, DC 20036
Tel: + 1–202–293–7700

The Individual Investor's Guide to Low-Load Mutual Funds, at $24.95, covers 800 no-load and low-load funds. It is published annually by the American Association of Individual Investors, a non-profit organization that provides members with a monthly journal, real-time price quotes on mutual funds and several free books. Dues are $49 per year. You can reach AAII at:

625 North Michigan Avenue, Chicago, IL 60611
Tel: + 1–312–280– 0170.

Sheldon Jacobs' annual *Handbook for No-Load Fund Investors*, at $45, is the most comprehensive source of information on no-load funds, covering 1,304 no-load and low-load funds. To order: call or write to:

The No-Load Fund Investor,
PO Box 283, Hastings-on-Hudson, NY 10706
Tel: + 1–914–693–7420.

The best research to implement the polar bear strategy outlined here for no-load funds is available from the newsletter *No-Load Fund*X* ($119 a year), published by DAL Investment Co.

235 Montgomery St, San Francisco CA 94104–2994
Tel: + 1–415–986–1595.

Editor Burt Berry ranks more than 700 no-loads by risk and return over the past 1-, 3-, 6- and 12-month periods, with the funds rising and falling in ratings like football teams from season to season.

MAKING FUND RISK IRRELEVANT

A fund's historical price gyrations can give you a good fix on how muc.. the price will bounce around in future. But just as estimating country risk is of little value to a global equity portfolio, estimating the risk of any single fund in a global portfolio is also largely a waste of time.

With funds, it's the basket you want to watch, not the eggs. The risk of each individual fund is far less important than the riskiness of your entire portfolio. Indeed, funds that on their own are deemed highly risky – and might be labelled as such under any rule the SEC may devise – can actually seem fairly tame when hitched with others to a fund portfolio. That's because funds don't all move in lockstep. Some will stumble, but others may take up the slack. So a well-diversified fund portfolio generally does fairly well, both in return and in smoothing out price gyrations of its various holdings.

For proof, consider this investment mix: 45 percent in US large-company stocks, 20 percent in smaller-company shares, 15 percent in European stocks, 15 percent in the Pacific Rim and 5 percent in emerging markets. That's spicy enough for many investors. Yet over the 10 years ended in December 1994, this hypothetical portfolio would have given its owner a remarkably smooth ride. The portfolio's performance was tracked by using five stock-market indexes – the blue-chip S&P 500, the Wilshire 4500 index of smaller-company stocks, Morgan Stanley's averages for European and Pacific shares and the International Finance Corp.'s emerging-markets index. The data were provided by Ibbotson Associates and Vanguard Group.

During the ten calendar years, there were some hairy moments for each of the five indexes and the markets they represent. US large-company stocks posted one calendar-year loss, and smaller companies had three down years. Meanwhile, Pacific, European and emerging-market shares all had a pair of losing years. But amidst all the hurly burly, the portfolio barely twitched. US securities took a beating in both 1987 and 1994, but foreign stocks – especially Japanese – saved the day. The tables were turned in 1992, when foreign shares were ambushed and the US cavalry thundered to the rescue. In fact, during the decade, the portfolio had just one losing year, an 11.3 percent drop in 1990, when all five indexes were hammered, with losses ranging from 3.1 percent to 34.4 percent.

You can't win them all.

Despite the drubbing in 1990, the portfolio racked up an impressive gain of 344 percent over the ten-year stretch, well ahead of the 281.7 percent earned by those who stuck only with the blue gyps in the S&P 500. The moral? Don't get hung up on the riskiness of any one fund. As we've discussed, your aim is to assemble a spectrum of funds that comply with modern portfolio theory by reflecting disparate regions and sectors, thus reducing your overall risk.

Conclusion: *To assure the necessary range of regions and sectors, no single holding should comprise more than roughly 7 percent of a global fund portfolio.*

Summary

Finding and monitoring a global fund that consistently outperforms a world stock-market index is more difficult and less prudent than assembling a global portfolio of funds. The name of a fund does not always reflect its investment style. You're likely to do best by picking a local team, if available, to manage a country fund.

When investing in regional funds, it is wise to choose those run by fund management groups with a consistent approach and the best all-round performance. You can sometimes join a high-load fund family at a discount through a closed-end regional fund. If you're considering buying a load fund of any kind – full-load, low-load or back-end load – study investor experience rather than fund experience in making your selections. Other things being equal, funds with low expense ratios are preferable. If a fund company's charges are significantly out of line with most others, don't even consider it.

Poor fund performers that do not change managers tend to stay poor performers. A fund that has done well for three years or five will not necessarily excel as time goes by. The performance of most funds decays over time – regresses to the mean – and a prudent investor takes account of this fact. One year is more predictive of fund performance than five years. Stay with the winners in each sector, by upgrading your open-end funds at least annually. Replace a closed-end fund that gets bumped from the lead in an attractive country sector only if the fund also badly lags its stock-market index.

To assure the needed diversification, a global portfolio should cover at least 15 regions and sectors.

Again all well and good. But how do you go about weighting the countries and shares, or equivalents, in which you invest? How can you determine the best *allocation of assets* for your global equity portfolio? The next chapter answers this question.

9

ALLOCATING ASSETS

"And before him shall be gathered all nations: and he shall separate them one from another, as a shepherd divideth his sheep from the goats."
Matthew, XXV, v. 32

Bonds, stocks and cash are the chocolate, vanilla and strawberry of traditional asset allocation. This chapter is plain vanilla: how to divide a global equity portfolio among countries. All countries experience bull and bear markets, but often at different times. Diversifying across borders therefore gives you a better chance of avoiding the shrinkage in market value periodically suffered by investors in a single country. It helps you follow John Templeton's sage advice: "Be sure not to have all your eggs in the wrong basket at the wrong time."

TECHNIQUES OF ASSET ALLOCATION

Institutions and individuals have similar concerns

Institutional and individual asset allocation have the same goal. Pension funds and charitable foundations normally judge asset mix strategies according to how likely such strategies are to meet future financial commitments for the least amount of ongoing funding. This trade-off between future benefits and present costs applies to individual investors as well. As an individual, you try to accumulate enough capital to support yourself in retirement, but at the least possible sacrifice of current consumption. In other words, both institutions and individuals seek to fund a future liability at the lowest current cost.

Giraffes and gerbils

When it comes to asset allocation, however, several practical distinctions are visible between institutions and individuals. Just as nations can be divided into sheep and goats, investors can be divided into giraffes and gerbils.

The giraffes – institutions – own nearly 75 percent of the total market value of stocks listed on the New York Exchange. On an average day, they also account for 80–90 percent of total trading dollar volume. Like giraffes, institutional investors browse upon tall and familiar trees. But individual investors, like gerbils, can scurry around below: an area where small investors have the edge.

While the giraffes browse upon, say, Philip Morris, gerbils can often find better nourishment in the underbrush. Here many a choice morsel is ignored by the herd. Morgan Stanley put it this way in a 1986 report quoted by Strebel and Carvell's *In the Shadows of Wall Street*:

> The performance of institutionally overowned stocks relative to institutionally underowned issues is embarrassing. You would make money if you simply bought every stock the learned institutions sold.

Not that the giraffes are stupid. They just have their own logic and priorities. Institutions, mutual funds, banks and money managers concentrate on the taller trees in the investment forest both as a matter of preference and for sound structural reasons.

The megabuck mandate

The giraffes cannot invest easily in firms or stock markets with small capitalizations. Here's why: First, an institution usually has more money to invest than an individual. Heavy investment in a security with low capitalization, which is thinly traded, can affect not only its price but also its liquidity. It is easier to find a buyer for a thousand shares at $50 than for a hundred thousand. Second, investment in a low-cap stock can often result in more than 5 percent ownership, which in several countries requires an insider's report to comply with security regulations. Third, such an institutional holding can easily loom large enough to require a voice in the company's affairs, which may fall outside an institution's interest and expertise.

Apart from these three structural reasons, there is also the matter of preferences. Institutional fund managers sometimes wish to avoid the greater risk they think associated with small firms and small markets. The megabuck men are expected to follow a prudent investment policy, which, alas, often translates into doing just what everybody else does. What's more, many institutions demand that investments yield dividend income, which shares of small firms rarely do.

As Avner Arbel noted in "Giraffes, Institutions and Neglected Firms," these diverse constraints on the investment choices of financial institutions cause them to neglect certain securities and certain countries. The chapter entitled "The World's Best Bargains" shows how you can benefit from this neglect.

Conclusion: Shares and countries ignored by institutions can provide individual investors with superior returns.

Two practical differences

In asset allocation, there are two other key differences between institutions and individuals. Individuals pay taxes and so invest in tax-favored assets, such as the personal equity plans now encouraged by countries including the US, the UK, the Netherlands, France and Belgium. Therefore, in contrast to institutions, individuals see some of their investments compound at a pre-tax rate of return and others at an after-tax rate of return.

Individuals also have more clustered and less predictable cash flows than institutions. Pension funds have relatively smooth cash flows because actuarial and accounting procedures are designed precisely to that end. In contrast, individuals face a wide variety of less foreseeable cash flows, due to such financial jolts as tuition payments, major purchases and medical emergencies. Though these distinctions are important, they do not alter the prime significance of asset allocation – either for gerbils or giraffes.

Conclusion: Whether you're investing for an institution or for yourself, asset allocation is the key to managing your portfolio. It is especially crucial when investing globally.

Country selection

Logically, the first step in global equity investment is to make up your mind how much money to invest in which countries. This vital decision will shape most of the performance and risk of your global equity portfolio. A recent study found that an average of roughly 90 percent of the monthly variation of returns on a large sample of US mutual funds is explained by asset allocation, and only 10 percent by security selection.

It should be no surprise then that country selection turns out to be the dominant factor in global equity returns. Though industry and fundamental factors are important, most of the time the choice of country matters most. Country selection, however, is complicated by lack of comparability. Each country has its own accounting quirks. The term "generally accepted accounting standards" is an oxymoron. Further, you naturally need some valid and reliable standard against which to compare the performance of your global portfolio. Picking or constructing a benchmark is thus essential.

The stock market – any stock market – is a moving target. At a given moment, some markets seem to be priced at approximately twice what they should be and others at about half. Markets constantly swing from periods of being overvalued to periods of being undervalued. Such discrepancies – or "inefficiencies" – are transitory. Illustrating this, Table 9.1 shows the range of returns within the Morgan Stanley Capital International Europe, Australia and Far East (EAFE) Index basket from 1980 through 1994.

Table 9.1 Range of market returns: EAFE countries (1980–1994)

	Best	*EAFE Index*	*Worst*
1980	80%	23%	−19%
1981	38	− 2	−29
1982	24	− 2	−44
1983	81	24	−7
1984	46	7	−36
1985	176	56	−23
1986	121	69	− 2
1987	56	25	−24
1988	57	28	−13
1989	104	11	− 9
1990	10	−23	−37
1991	50	13	−17
1992	32	−12	−28
1993	117	33	22
1994	52	8	−29

Source: The Outside Analyst

In 1980, most volatile of the first five years, the EAFE Index was up 23 percent, while the best market posted an 80 percent gain and the worst market a 19 percent loss. In the second half of the eighties, the gaps between the leading and lagging markets were even wider. In 1985, with the EAFE Index up 56 percent, the best market soared 176 percent and the worst dropped 23 percent. In 1993, no EAFE market posted a loss. The best rose 117 percent and the worst "only" 22 percent. In 1994, with the EAFE up 8 percent, the best market jumped by 52 percent and the worst plunged 29 percent.

Great opportunity obviously exists here for investors who are good at identifying the right countries: a subject treated shortly.

Imitating an index

Doubting their ability to recognize the right countries (or to control trading costs), some pension fund managers assemble an international portfolio in a way about as simple as it gets. They buy all the shares of a particular index and weight the fund so that it effectively becomes a mini-version of the index itself. In theory, this means the fund should never do worse than its benchmark index. In practice, however, managers do allow for a small percentage of tracking error, both upside and down. Index-tracking is mostly in vogue with highly conservative institutions and pension funds aiming at steady long-term growth. You know you won't do much worse than the index. Alas, you won't do better, either.

A more serious disadvantage of index-tracking is that not all indexes are easily replicated. Certain shares are restricted to local investors or simply not available in the quantities needed. To get round this, some index trackers only partially mimic their benchmark index. That's not only more complicated, but can lead to a higher tracking error.

Benefits from tracking error

Not that a tracking error is always something to avoid. Pure indexers try to maintain perfect index-like portfolio compositions and consider minimizing trading costs a secondary matter. Rex Sinquefield's article "Are Small-Stock Returns Achievable?" reports that among indexers these portfolios have the lowest returns. At the other extreme, some indexers stress minimal trading costs at the expense of perfect portfolio composition. They permit higher tracking error. Among indexed portfolios, Sinquefield found that these have the highest returns.

Take the Vanguard Index Trust-500 Portfolio, for instance, oldest and biggest of the Standard & Poor's 500 index funds. This Vanguard fund, based in Valley Forge, Pennsylvania, climbed 287 percent during the decade ended April 30, 1995, slightly lagging the 297 percent gain for the S&P 500 stock index. Lest you think this Vanguard fund merely guarantees mediocrity, actively managed US stock funds returned an average of just 239 percent, far worse than either the Vanguard fund or the S&P 500. In fact, over the ten-year stretch, Vanguard's S&P 500 fund beat 77 percent of US stock funds. Bearing out Sinquefield's study, a lot of the excess return comes down to costs. The Vanguard fund charges just 0.19 percent in annual expenses and spends precious little on trading, because it rarely buys and sells stocks. The same pattern is found in Standard & Poor's Depositary Receipts, so-called "spiders" that imitate the performance of the S&P 500 index. In contrast, the typical US stock-fund manager trades up a storm, levying 1.35 percent in annual expenses. These hefty expenses have proven a millstone for most actively managed stock funds.

The Russell Rampage and S&P Stampede

Indexing, however, can also force you to trade heavily, with attendant costs. Take the Russell Rampage, for instance: the annual reconstitution of the Russell 2000 Index of small stocks. This phenomenon is making the small-stock arena increasingly tricky for investors. Some $13.9 billion is run by US fund managers who merely try to match the Russell 2000 – and who thus have no choice but to jump in or out of stocks being added or delisted. And other fund managers, aiming to beat this Russell benchmark, base many of their decisions on what is in the index. The result? Small stocks, which can be swayed by just a few investors, are bouncing up and down ever more widely for no fundamental reason. The swings are due to buying and selling by herds of giraffes. Companies dropped from the index tend to fall, while ones joining it tend to rally.

A few years ago, Standard & Poor's took steps to ease the so-called S&P Stampede that used to accompany changes in its index. Moreover, S&P makes these changes throughout the year, thus softening their impact. But the Russell 2000, with four times as many stocks, is revamped in one fell swoop each year. In 1995, a hefty 25 percent of its members were shown the door. For index-linked small-stock funds, this is a procedural nightmare.

Why indexing is on the march

The passive approach of indexing has grown steadily more popular in recent years for two structural reasons. Some investors, believing stock markets are efficient in pricing assets, conclude that it is virtually impossible to achieve consistently superior returns. Others believe – rightly – that orthodox, active money managers generally underperform the market due to high transaction costs. If you contemplate imitating an index, be sure to know why; for these two reasons carry highly different implications. If you believe a market return is the best you can hope for, your best approach to asset allocation is indeed a passive investment program replicating the market.

When passive is active

That rules out a number of indexes, including the S&P 500 – not only a poor proxy for the US market but in fact actively managed as well. In the past decade, Standard & Poor's has made several hundred additions and deletions to its portfolio, creating transaction costs for holders of S&P index funds. Nor have those changes been consistent or predictable. Rather, they represent individual judgments of the S&P staff, based on a combination of research and intuition: precisely the approach used by old-fashioned, active portfolio managers. Nevertheless, indexing – in the US at least – has become synonymous with buying an S&P fund. According to data from fund researchers Lipper Analytical Services, S&P funds have garnered roughly 70 percent of US investment in stock-index funds. Yet the companies making up the S&P 500 account for only 70 percent of the US stock market and US shares less than 40 percent of the global stock market.

The coffee can portfolio

If, on the other hand, you have concluded that transaction costs are the main deterrent to superior investment returns, you might briefly consider what Robert Kirby calls the "Coffee Can" portfolio. This concept harkens back to America's Old West, when people put their valuable possessions in a coffee can and kept it under the mattress. The coffee can involved no transaction costs – or, for that matter, any costs at all. Its eventual return depended wholly on the wisdom and foresight used to select the objects placed in the coffee can to begin with. Similarly, argues Kirby in the Fall 1984 issue of *The Journal of Portfolio Management*, why not have your passive portfolio represent the best possible selection, rather than a changing list of stocks selected by Standard & Poor's?

> "I suggest," he writes, "that you find the best investment research organization you can and ask them to select a diversified portfolio of stocks with the knowledge that the portfolio will not be re-evaluated or re-examined for a period of at least 10 years."

Tongue in cheek? Sure. As Kirby himself admits, the notion of a coffee can portfolio has two fatal flaws. First, who's willing to buy something that takes ten years to evaluate? Second, who will pay the huge up-front fee necessary to support the kind of top-notch research organization that can select a superior 10-year portfolio? Nevertheless, the idea has a certain attraction, if only because it sharpens your awareness of transaction costs.

Conclusion: To curb transaction costs, the wise investor abstains from frequent rebalancing of an equity portfolio.

Using funds to index globally

For most global investors, especially individuals, the index imitation approach is hampered by the fact that no investment fund yet truly mirrors a major global index. But if, despite its pitfalls, you are determined to take the index imitation route to global investing, there are several ways you can surmount this. For one thing, the Charles Schwab discount brokerage has set up its own index of the world's 350 largest firms – and a fund that tracks it. This is in fact about the only way an individual investor with limited assets can imitate a global index.

That's just as well, because individual investors who imitate an index are surrendering their edge over the institutions. The very notion of index imitation arises from the various constraints faced by institutional investors, for whom this part of the chapter is meant. If you're more gerbil than giraffe, you may wish to skip to the next section, headed "Three basic approaches."

But, if you insist on indexing, Table 9.2 shows some suitable no-load funds that mirror a US market index.

Table 9.2 No - load US Index Funds

Index fund	Duplicates composition	Annual fee %
Benham Gold Equities (+ 1 – 415 –965 –427)	30 leading North American gold equities	0.75
Dreyfus Small Cap – Growth (+ 1 – 718 –895 – 1206)	Wilshire 5000 "growth" stocks	0.30
Dreyfus Small Cap – Value (+ 1 – 718 –895 – 1206)	Wilshire 5000 "value" stocks	0.30
Dreyfus Mid-Cap – Value (+ 1 – 718 –895 – 1206)	S&P 400 Mid-Cap Index	0.30
Federated Mid-Cap (+ 1 – 412 – 288 – 1900)	S&P 400 Mid-Cap Index	n.a.
Federated S&P 500 (+ 1 – 412 – 288 – 1900)	S&P 500 Index	n.a.
Fidelity Spartan Market (+ 1 – 617 – 523 – 1919)	S&P 500 Index; can use options and futures	0.45
Gateway Index Plus (+ 1 – 513 – 248 – 2700)	S&P 100 Index; sells call options on S&P 100	1.15
United Services All-American (+ 1 – 512 – 523 – 2453)	S&P 500 Index	1.00
Vanguard Index Trust 500 (+ 1 – 215 – 648 – 6000)	S&P 500 Index; uses options	0.22
Vanguard Quantitative Index (+ 1 – 215 – 648 – 6000)	S&P 500 Index; uses computer models	0.48
Vanguard Index Trust Extended (+ 1 – 215 – 648 – 6000)	Wilshire 5000 Index minus 500 stocks in S&P 500	0.23
Vanguard Index Trust Total (+ 1 – 215 – 648 – 6000)	Wilshire 5000 Index	0.23
Vanguard Index Trust Growth (+ 1 – 215 – 648 – 6000)	"Growth" stocks from S&P 500; uses options	0.35
Vanguard Index Trust Value (+ 1 – 215 – 648 – 6000)	"Value" stocks from S&P 500; uses options	0.35
Vanguard Small Cap (+ 1 – 215 – 648 – 6000)	Russell 2000 Index (smallest companies)	0.31

There are only a handful of no-load funds that mirror a regional or emerging markets index. These are shown in Table 9.3.

Table 9.3 No - load Emerging Market Index Funds

Index Fund	Duplicates composition	Annual fee %
Schwab International Equity Index	Largest 350 non-US. companies	0.40
United Services European Equity	Selected stocks in MSCI International Index	1.00
Vanguard International Equity Index – Emerging Markets	MSCI Select Emerging Markets Free Index	0.40
Vanguard International Equity Index – Europe	MSCI Index – Europe	0.40
Vanguard International Equity Index – Pacific	MSCI Index – Pacific	0.35

For an institutional investor, it is certainly feasible to construct a global index portfolio by cobbling together funds that track various regional indexes. There are myriad funds tracking almost any index of the US market you care to name. The US market as a whole is best represented by the Wilshire 5000 Stock Index, though it is impractical to use the entire Wilshire 5000, even if you rank as an heavyweight giraffe. The last 1,000, or so, stocks in that index barely qualify as publicly owned and are roughly as marketable as three-day old bread. On the other hand, a tailor-made "Wilshire 1000" should represent 87 percent of the Wilshire 5000 and be a reasonable proxy for "everything out there," nicely mirroring US market results. To continue on this course, obviously you also have to index non–US issues in both major and minor markets. There are also many funds that track a single–country index, enabling investors to place high–risk bets on individual markets. Two such instruments were set up in 1996: World Equity Benchmark Shares, or WEBS, developed by Morgan Stanley, and CountryBaskets, developed by Germany's Deutsche Bank. Each is a listed security based on an ordinary mutual fund owning equities in a particular country. They are a relatively low–cost way to invest in equities mirroring a country index.

Normal mutual funds are priced once a day, but WEBS and Country-Baskets, like closed–end country funds, are repriced continuously over the course of a day. Unlike closed ends, however, these new tools generally trade at prices close to the net asset value of their underlying equities. They do so because each product has a mechanism enabling institutional investors to swap the new securities easily for a fat basket of the equivalent underlying equities – or vice versa. The two products, whose various country offerings have annual expenses of between 0.8 percent and 1 percent of assets, are cheaper than closed–end country funds, whose annual expenses average 1.8 percent. They also offer better diversification benefits than closed–end country funds. Initially, CountryBaskets covered nine countries, with performance designed to track the Financial Times/Standard & Poor's Actuaries World Indices. WEBS covered 17 countries, with performance designed to mimic the relevant Morgan Stanley indexes. (The WEBS designation is an allusion to the American Stock Exchange "spiders," or Standard & Poor's Depositary Receipts, that mimic the performance of the S&P 500 index, including dividends.) To invest $1,000 or $100,000 in a CountryBasket or WEBS single-country index fund, you simply call your broker. WEBS, listed on the ASE, were initially priced at between $10 and $20, while CountryBaskets, trading on the NYSE, were initially priced at between $30 and $50.

Other index derivatives

The high cost of researching specific firms worldwide has led many global portfolio managers to focus on broad asset allocation strategies, relying on the paramount importance of country selection. This has made the low–cost strategy of indexation more popular. In addition to savings on analysis on research, an index portfolio generally has lower turnover, and thus lower execution and settlement costs.

Even more appealing, exchange–traded futures and options contracts, as well as swaps, are now available on major equity indexes. If you run an institutional portfolio, these derivatives enable you to invest globally in equities without costly changes to your organization. Equity derivatives also enable you to take a position in a foreign stock market without the custody costs and withholding taxes normally associated with direct investment in shares or in ADRs. Transaction costs are lower too, particularly for rebalancing. Though a typical stock index futures position has to be rolled over four times a year to maintain an equity position with futures, it is far easier to execute a large trade in many futures markets than in the market for the underlying shares. Institutions, you may gather, are increasingly using such instruments to implement a global equity investment program.

Summary
Shares and countries ignored by institutions can provide individual investors with superior returns. Whether you're investing for an institution or for yourself, asset allocation is the key to managing your portfolio, especially when investing globally. To curb transaction

costs, the wise investor abstains from frequent rebalancing of an equity portfolio. Exchange–traded futures and options contracts, as well as swaps, now enable institutions to implement a low–cost global equity investment program made up of country indexes.

Three basic approaches

Apart from imitating an index, there are three ways investors normally determine country allocation. One method weights countries to reflect the size (i.e. capitalization) of their equity markets. A second approach allocates assets to reflect each country's contribution to the world's total gross national product. The third approach simply weights major markets equally. Let's examine the attractions and drawbacks of these three allocation techniques. Most striking initially is that over the long run they differ very little in risk and return. David Umstead's article "The Portfolio Management Process," reports that their risk and return profiles were virtually identical from 1970 through 1989. More about that fateful year 1989 in a moment, though.

Allocation by market capitalization

Earlier, I noted that investors who confine themselves to the US renounce nearly two-thirds of the global equity market – and that non-US investors who stay at home are spurning even more of the world. As that is part of my argument for going global, you might well expect me to favor weighting countries to reflect the size of their stock markets. But allocation in ratio to the size of stock markets has a number of severe drawbacks. For one thing, it hands you a rubber yardstick, because the size of each country's capitalization relative to the whole expands or shrinks as that particular market rises or falls.

You can see that reflected clearly in a capitalization-weighted index. Japan's weight within the EAFE capitalization-weighted index was less than 15 percent on December 31, 1969, when EAFE was created. It swelled to almost 70 percent by 1989 – and is now just over 40 percent. The big jump in Japan's weighting in the EAFE Index came at the expense of virtually all other EAFE stock markets. Such instability in country allocations is an inevitable and unwelcome byproduct of splitting your assets among countries based purely on the size of their stock market. It also makes you scramble to stay in one place, busily rebalancing your portfolio every few months as capitalization ratios shift. That's both impractical and expensive.

Besides instability, capitalization-weighted asset allocation creates severe distortion. Some countries have thinner public stock markets than one might expect from the size of their economy. Germany has a big economy and equity market, but, with most equities privately held, its various exchanges add up to a relatively tiny public stock market. So allocating assets by stock market size inevitably underweights Germany in a global equity portfolio.

Conversely, most Japanese companies are publicly listed and trade at much steeper earnings multiples than the rest of the world. Japan's relative stock market capitalization thus looms far larger than its relative economic production.

This distortion is compounded by cross-holdings of Japanese company shares. By "cross-holding" I mean the ownership by one listed company of shares in another listed company. Sony, for example, owns large blocks of stock in Matsushita, so allocation of investment funds in proportion to the value of Sony and Matsushita stock outstanding involves counting some of the Matsushita shares twice. This so-called *mochiai* effect thus artificially inflates reported market capitalization.

Cross-holdings (and the resultant double counting) do also exist in other markets, but nowhere near their extent in Japan. During the 1980s, according to a study by Oyvind Bohren and Dag Michalsen, cross holdings on the Oslo Stock Exchange averaged 16 percent of the market's total size, but were dwarfed by Japan's 47 percent. In other words, Japan's market capitalization was 47 percent higher than its underlying economic value.

The *mochiai* effect exacerbates the underlying distortion created by Japan's inflated earnings multiples. Allocating assets by stock market capitalization thus tilts a global equity portfolio far too heavily towards Japan.

This can lead to crazy imbalances. It did so in 1989, when firm followers of the capitalization-weighted approach had allocated no less than a mind-boggling 70 percent of their assets to Japan. These supposedly prudent institutional investors were just in time to participate almost fully in that market's giddy rollercoaster ride over the next three years: a 36 percent plunge in 1990, followed by a 9 percent rise in 1991 and a subsequent drop of 21 percent in 1992. On average, even ignoring rebalancing and associated expenses, those three years wiped out more than 45 percent of the heavy asset allocation to Japan. By allocating assets to mirror the size of stock markets, these unreflecting organizations had put nearly all their eggs in the wrong basket at the wrong time – precisely the blunder asset allocation is meant to avoid.

Investors clutch at the notion of a capitalization-weighted index only when global diversification comes up. No sensible investor holds domestic equities in proportion to capitalization weights. Why then impose such ratios on foreign equities?

Conclusion: Splitting assets among countries based on the size of stock markets creates distortion and instability in country allocations.

Allocation by gross domestic product

Then how about allocating assets to reflect each country's contribution to the world's total gross national product? Such benchmarks are easy to construct and readily available. Morgan Stanley, for instance, has a GDP-weighted EAFE Index alongside its capitalization-weighted index. Table 9.4 shows the EAFE Index allocations, weighted by GDP and by market capitalization.

Table 9.4 Morgan Stanley international EAFE index

GDP	Weight as a percentage of	Capitalization
1.43	Austria	0.38
1.96	Belgium	1.15
1.21	Denmark	0.82
1.05	Finland	0.62
12.02	France	6.25
16.00	Germany	6.72
0.46	Ireland	0.28
7.92	Italy	2.20
3.13	Netherlands	3.89
0.99	Norway	0.42
3.81	Spain	1.69
1.84	Sweden	1.74
2.42	Switzerland	5.32
9.05	United Kingdom	16.48
2.47	Australia	2.56
0.89	Hong Kong	3.17
31.70	Japan	42.21
0.60	Malaysia	2.44
0.48	New Zealand	0.42
0.57	Singapore	1.24
100%		100%

Source: The Outside Analyst - 1995

GDP weights are appealing not as a theoretically perfect solution, but because they eliminate the distortions caused by shifts in market values and produce a far more stable and uniform distribution of capital around the world. Although such GDP weights better reflect the underlying economic relationships of major markets, this approach too has severe drawbacks.

For one thing, some governments own a huge chunk of an industry. Banks and utilities are part of French GDP, but until recently you couldn't buy shares in French banks and utilities because they were government owned. And big slices of Argentina's largest privatizations are still in government hands.

Conclusion: Asset allocation reflecting GDP weights is subject to distortion by government-owned firms whose shares are not traded on any stock exchange.

The common flaw of market-size and GDP weightings

Where does a 400-pound gorilla sit? Anywhere it likes. Likewise, a huge multinational also can sit where it likes. But how does that affect the GDP of, say, Hong Kong or Singapore? Many of their firms operate globally, with little or no relation to where corporate headquarters is located. As I mentioned, Nestlé earns more than 95 percent of its cash flow outside Switzerland. Should companies that just happen to be based in a particular country but do most of their business elsewhere properly be counted in GDP? Weighting by GDP obviously tilts a portfolio towards markets dominated by multinationals or national firms.

On this score, weighting to reflect market size is no better; for it automatically emphasizes big companies as well. The ten largest quoted firms make up over half of total stock market capitalization in Switzerland, Holland, Singapore, Sweden, Italy and Spain. Switzerland's top ten account for a hefty 68 percent of the total, slightly more than Holland's 67 percent. No single firm accounts for a bigger slice of its national stock market than Royal Dutch Petroleum: a whopping 25 percent. Its $67,894 million capitalization (June 1, 1995) exceeds that of several European countries: Austria, Denmark, Finland, Luxembourg and Norway.

So whether you weight by GDP or by capitalization, the result will be a portfolio badly tilted by uninvited 400-pound gorillas.

What's wrong with big-company bias?

Two things. First, in the aggregate, assuming equal risk, shares in big concerns tend to produce smaller returns than shares in small concerns. This was first demonstrated in 1981 by Rolf Banz in "The Relationship Between Return and Market Values of Common Stock." Two years later, in a study entitled "Transaction Costs and the Small Firm Effect," Paul Schultz showed that, even allowing for trading costs, the superiority of small firms held. Tilting your portfolio toward countries dominated by huge multinationals thus can lower your likely gains, if by default you buy the big and well-known concerns. The second (and more basic) disadvantage is that your country allocation can become lopsided, even if you substitute, say, smaller Swiss companies for Nestlé and Roche or smaller Italian companies for Assicurazioni Generali. Despite such tinkering, your global portfolio will still be badly tilted towards Switzerland or Italy at the expense of more promising markets.

Conclusion: Both GDP weightings and weightings by market size are biased towards markets dominated by big multinationals.

Allocation by equal weights

Weightings by GDP or market size, despite their veneer of rationality, are clearly unstable and quite arbitrary. As with Japan, these two approaches can be dangerous as well. As a portfolio manager, whether institutional or private, you're unlikely to be able to forecast returns in large markets any better than returns in small markets. It makes no sense, therefore, to let yourself be forced to bet more heavily on a market simply because it is large.

What's needed is a safe method of asset allocation, easily applied in the marketplace as a long-term, low-cost, passive strategy. By this yardstick, equal allocation is the ultimate in diversification. This seemingly haphazard (and also arbitrary) approach emphasizes no country at the expense of others. Any weighting other than equal weights requires a forecast. One way to grasp this is to ask yourself the following question: What would you do if a trusted advisor were to offer you a choice of 22 stocks with a guarantee that, in the aggregate, they would perform extremely well?

Barring any further information, it would obviously seem wise to buy an equally weighted portfolio. Any other set of weights would make sense only if you had additional information about the expected returns or covariances of the 22 stocks. Neither allocation by market size nor by GDP embodies a particularly good forecast of these elements.

The role of fuzzy logic

Back in 1890, William James said, "The art of being wise is the art of knowing what to overlook." By common agreement, the human race has chopped the globe into 24 time zones, creating a magical stripe across the Pacific Ocean that separates one day from the next. The date border was intentionally placed at sea, but who knows how accurately? Maybe there's an ill-favoured island somewhere on which you can stand with one leg in Monday and the other in Tuesday. In what date are you living then?

The classic logic of Aristotle is based on two foundations. The first is the law of contradiction: if statement "A" is true, then its opposite (not "A" or "-A") cannot be true at the same moment. The other law is that of the excluded third or *tertium non datur*: one of the two possibilities "A" or "-A" must always be true, so no third possibility can exist between them. The two laws are often valid. The statement: "Sixteen is a quadrate" is true, while its opposite "Sixteen is not a quadrate" is false. There is no middle ground. Aristotelian logic was later expanded by an Englishman, George Boole, into a usable system enabling one to test the truth of all kinds of compound statements. Our digital computer is wholly based on Boolean logic. That's no surprise, because the machine's physical foundations dovetail nicely with the theory: a true statement is represented by a small amount of electricity (a logical 1) and a false statement by nothing (a 0). A switch can be either on or off, and according to the law of the excluded third there is no middle ground.

But the world consists of more than numbers and switches. People, for instance, are masters of foggy definitions and vague descriptions. That's why on that hypothetical island straddling the date border it can be Monday and Tuesday at the same time, and a philosopher from another island – Crete – can maintain that he always lies.

His statement embodies a paradox that baffles the rigid laws of Aristotle. If the Cretan philosopher is speaking the truth, then, according to his own statement, he is lying. On the other hand, if he is lying, then the statement "I always lie" is untrue, and he is speaking the truth.

There is no way out of this dilemma – unless you assume that the statement is half true and half false.

That is precisely what Lotfi A. Zadeh of the University of Berkeley proposed 30 years ago: let's not cling to the notion that something is always either true or false.

Classic logic is "crisp" and permits no nuance. But people don't generally view the world in such black and white terms. Therefore, crisp logic is a clumsy tool when you want a computer program to react to human input. So Zadeh proposed using another sort of logic, one that leaves room for half truths. He called it "fuzzy" logic.

Let's face it: an element of guesswork is present in all investing, however sophisticated. As the Roman poet Horatio observed:

To know all things is not permitted.

Your aim is to assemble a global portfolio offering the most possibility of profit with the least threat of loss. To this end, remember that you are selecting countries to be *combined*. Careful construction of your total portfolio is thus far more important than the accuracy of individual country choices and weightings.

Conclusion: Fuzzy logic is useful in asset allocation.

In "Risk, Market Sensitivity, and Diversification," William Sharpe makes a similar point about individual securities:

> A number of rather inaccurate estimates for securities may combine to form an exceptionally accurate estimate for a portfolio, thanks to the law of large numbers. The estimate for one security may be too high, and another too low, with the result that the average is "just right."

The more equal your company weightings, the less impact any one security has on the whole. Similarly, the more equal your country weightings, the less impact any single country is likely to have on your global portfolio's overall performance. Equal weighting of countries produces a global equity allocation that is widely diversified and stable over time. Though not an all-purpose elixir, it is clearly your most practical point of departure for global asset allocation. It offers you the best protection against the unknown – and avoids big-firm bias.

Summary

Country weightings largely determine the performance of a global equity portfolio. Splitting assets among countries based on the size of their stock markets causes both distortion and instability. Asset alloca-tion reflecting GDP weights is subject to distortion by government-owned firms whose shares are not traded on any stock exchange. Both GDP weightings and weightings by market size are biased towards markets dominated by big multinationals. For most investors, there-fore, the most practical point of departure for global asset allocation is to use fuzzy logic, assigning the major markets equal weights. It is better to be approximately right than precisely wrong.

10

YOUR BENCHMARK

"Take thine own measure."
George Herbert, 1633

For a valid and reliable standard against which to compare the performance of your global portfolio, you need a benchmark. A benchmark will provide valuable information on the sources of your return and risk. Morgan Stanley Capital International, based in Geneva, creates and maintains 3,500 different international-market indexes that are the standard for the industry. Should you pick such a benchmark – or construct one? Because foreign markets differ so widely, the choice of a global benchmark has many of the characteristics of an asset allocation decision. It is commonly believed that a mega-portfolio restricts the asset allocation decision – and thus the choice of a benchmark. The larger your portfolio, the argument goes, the less you can invest in smaller markets, because of liquidity constraints. Yet an index equally weighted in 22 developed countries has an allocation of just over 4.5 percent in each. How many developed markets are so illiquid they cannot absorb 4.5 percent of a portfolio? Equal asset allocation is thus clearly feasible even if you're an institutional heavyweight. You just need a suitable benchmark.

WHICH INDEX?

The suitability of common benchmarks

Let's examine the suitability of common benchmarks for practical portfolio management. Alas, allocating assets in the same ratio as an existing benchmark will almost inevitably paint you into a corner. As a rule, index weights are very unevenly distributed, badly hampering the split of assets among countries.

For example, 15 of the 20 countries in the capitalization-weighted EAFE benchmark represent only 23 percent of the index. (You can check this by turning back to page 151.) If you were to use this index as the point of departure to assemble a global equity portfolio according to your own lights, you would have trouble in underweighting Austria, because it is already only an infinitesimal 0.38 percent of the index. You'd have no way of allocating assets so as to reflect bearishness on Austria.

The same applies to Ireland, Norway and New Zealand, each representing less than a half of 1 percent of the index. What's the use of including a market like Ireland, capitalization-weighted at 0.28 percent, if it cannot support a modest overweighting from time to time? Surely Ireland cannot make much difference if its weight can never go above 0.28 percent.

If you believe that either the Japanese equity market or the yen are overvalued, a benchmark based on market size confronts you with a similar dilemma. Japan's weighting in an index based on market capitalization is determined by the average share price times the total number of listed shares times the yen's exchange rate. An overvaluation of either market prices or the yen's exchange rate against your own currency thus means overweighting Japan just when you would prefer to underweight it.

Global investors deal with this dilemma in a number of ways. The majority continue using a capitalization-weighted benchmark, while trying to underweight Japan. But this puts them in a tricky position. The more aggressive global investors become, the more their portfolio performance is dominated by the decision on Japan. A simple example, similar to one used by David Umstead in "Selecting a Benchmark for International Investments," will demonstrate this.

Table 10.1 reflects Morgan Stanley's capitalization-weighted World Index, which adds Canada and the United States to the 20 EAFE countries. I've ranked these 22 countries in order of attractiveness, based largely on which markets are most undervalued at this moment in terms of expected earnings growth.

Though Japan – with the Nikkei index well below its peak – is still no bargain, it is not as overvalued as in the recent past.

Table 10.1 Capitalization weights versus equal weights

Attractiveness rank	Market	Capitalization weight	Equal weight
1	Finland	0.36%	4.55%
2	Norway	0.24%	4.55%
3	Malaysia	1.43%	4.55%
4	Ireland	0.16%	4.55%
5	Sweden	1.02%	4.55%
6	Austria	0.23%	4.55%
7	Denmark	0.48%	4.55%
Total attractive:		3.92%	31.85%
8	Australia	1.50%	4.55%
9	Hong Kong	1.87%	4.55%
10	Netherlands	2.29%	4.55%
11	Canada	2.27%	4.55%
12	United States	38.85%	4.55%
13	United Kingdom	9.70%	4.55%
14	Japan	24.85%	4.55%
15	New Zealand	0.25%	4.55%
Total average:		81.58%	36.40%
16	France	3.68%	4.55%
17	Spain	1.00%	4.55%
18	Switzerland	3.15%	4.55%
19	Singapore	0.73%	4.55%
20	Germany	3.96%	4.55%
21	Belgium	0.68%	4.55%
22	Italy	1.30%	4.45%
Total unattractive:		14.50%	31.75%

Obviously, neither you nor I can perfectly predict relative performance. Let's suppose, though, that you believe that you can at least identify three groups within the 22 countries: seven likely to outperform, eight likely to provide average returns and seven likely to underperform. Even if you're right, you'll have considerable difficulty in exploiting this information.

The capitalization weights given in Table 10.1 highlight Japan's dominance. Of the 22 markets, 16 have capitalization weights of less than 2.5 percent. For practical purposes, only five non-US countries matter – and four of them (France, Germany, Switzerland and the UK) add up to less than 85 percent of the size of the fifth (Japan). The heavy tilt in these capitalization weights severely hampers your ability to benefit from the accuracy of your forecasts. The six most attractive countries add up to only 3.92 percent, and you will find it extremely difficult to get them up to even 20 percent of the total portfolio. Here's why.

Your success as a global portfolio manager will be measured by how much you outperform your benchmark. The benchmark on the preceding page has six countries likely to underperform, but the aggregate weight of these six countries is only 14.50 percent. Even if your forecasts are on the nose, your ability to benefit from them is limited because only 14.50 percent of your portfolio can be reallocated to exploit your brilliant insights. The only way you can be more aggressive is to move further up the list, liquidating positions in markets which you are far less certain are overvalued. Adding a seventh country to the sell list in this example accomplishes little: New Zealand adds only 0.25 percent to the amount sold.

Adding an eighth country, however, changes things considerably. Now, all of a sudden, an additional 24.85 percent of the portfolio is available for reallocation. Until this point, your biggest sell decision has been a reallocation of 3.96 percent out of Germany. Does it make sense to allocate much more out of a country which you believe, at best, only slightly overvalued?

This example makes it clear that the diversification derived from spreading country-allocation decisions across 22 markets is severely hampered by a capitalization-weighted benchmark. And, as we've seen, country allocation is not much improved by shifting to a GDP-weighted benchmark. Such limitations stem purely from the composition of the index.

The limitations disappear if the benchmark is altered to an equally weighted mix of the 22 countries. You are then able to exploit any special knowledge of promising or unpromising markets uniformly across all countries. In an equally weighted index, the bottom seven countries represent a third of the portfolio and you are always able to act decisively on your forecasts.

If, despite the proven drawbacks, you elect to allocate by GDP or market size, benchmark selection becomes relatively simple. You merely choose an appropriate market-capitalization or GDP index. US-based investors often choose two indexes, one for the US, such as the Wilshire 5000, and one *outside* it, such as the EAFE Index of Morgan Stanley. As we've seen, that firm also has a World Index weighted by GDP or market size. You can phone Morgan Stanley in London on + 44–171 –513–8000 and in New York on + 1–212–703–4000.

On the other hand, you can vastly improve your balance of risk and return by refusing to be a prisoner of any such aggregate index. Countries need to be looked at individually, if you are not to wind up with a benchmark that is less than optimal for your own investment parameters.

As I mentioned, existing non-US indexes such as the EAFE do not adequately reflect global equity markets. The markets outside the US are quite dissimilar, so why lump them into a single non-US index? The differences between various foreign markets are in fact just as great as their differences with the US. Australia is just as different from Austria as it is from the US. It is thus naive to speak of a US stock market and an international market that includes every other country. Not only does this approach ignore reality, it also undermines portfolio performance. The same can be said of aggregate "world" indexes – even those promulgated by Morgan Stanley.

An alternative, proposed by Gary Brinson in "Setting the Global Asset Allocation Mix," is investing in *separate* indexes of US, Japanese, German, British and Canadian stocks that have their own risks, correlations and returns. For any level of risk, this approach produces a higher return, and for any level of return, a lower level of risk. The notion of utilizing separate indexes for each country clearly warrants further development.

Such multiple benchmarks do already exist, the best and most readily available being the FT/S&P Actuaries World Indices. Published daily in the *Financial Times*, these 26 country indexes (which include Mexico, South Africa and Thailand) are denominated in dollars, sterling, marks and yen.

Alas, the global benchmark derived from these indexes is not equally weighted. To fill this gap, I have constructed a global index which combines the notion of separate country indexes with the pragmatic approach of weighting major markets equally. More on that in a moment.

Pension fund consultants

Here are four well-qualified consultants that can help select an appropriate benchmark for a pension fund: InterSec Research Corp., Brinson Partners, Frank Russell Associates and Boston International Advisors.

InterSec favors the Morgan Stanley benchmarks and is skeptical about specific-country allocation, which it views largely as a means of increasing consultants' fees. InterSec has branches or associates in Australia, Canada, Japan, Switzerland and the United Kingdom. Its president is Christopher A. Nowakowski and the US headquarters are located at:

6 Gatehouse Road, Stamford, CT 06902.
Telephone: + 1–203–348–7101; Fax: + 1–203–348–1906.

Brinson Partners runs a low-risk global balanced portfolio that has outperformed the S&P 500 since its inception in 1981. President Gary Brinson, a Chartered Financial Analyst (CFA), favors a unique non-aggregate benchmark for each client. The firm is located in the US at:

209 South LaSalle Street, Chicago, IL 60604–1295.
Telephone: + 1–312–220–7100; Fax: + 1–312–220–7199.

Boston International Advisors encourages equal country allocations. David Umstead, also a CFA , is managing director. Their office is at:

75 State Street, Boston MA 02109–1807.
Telephone: + 1–617–345–9550.

Frank Russell Co., which advises more than 200 major pension funds and gives emerging markets suitable attention, is located in the US at:

909 South "A" Street, Tacoma, WA 98401–1616.
Director of consulting is Michael J. Philips.
Telephone: + 1–206–591–3500; Fax: + 1–206–596–3282.

A smaller but highly competent consultant for setting a global benchmark is Martingale Asset Management, at:

222 Berkeley Street, Boston MA 02116.
One of the principals is Arnold Wood, past president of the International Society of Financial Analysts.
Telephone: + 1–617–424–4700; Fax: + 1–617–424–4747.

Nelson's *Guide to Pension Fund Consultants* ($335) can also be useful here. Updated annually, it gives you an in-depth look at over 300 pension/endowment consulting firms, identifying their services, philosophy, background and qualifications, as well as any affiliation with banks or brokerage houses. You can write to Nelson Publications at:

PO Box 591, Port Chester, NY 10573,
or fax them on + 1–914–937–8709.

Constructing a global benchmark

One common method of constructing a global benchmark is to apportion a third of assets to each of the US, Europe and the Far East.

One variant cuts Japan's weighting proportionately, spread reduction equally among the other countries. Another approach weight countries equally, lowering weights for countries where li ity is deemed a problem.

The Equal Global Index

As equal weighting of the major equity markets is the most practical launching pad for global asset allocation, I've set up a multi-currency global index based on separate indexes for each country. The Melton Equal Global Index, or MEG Benchmark, assigns North America, Europe and the Far East roughly equal weights of, respectively, 23.7 percent, 23.8 percent and 22.5 percent. The widely diversified US gets 20 percent of portfolio assets and Canada 3.7 percent. Fourteen European markets each get 1.70 percent, while Australia, Hong Kong, Japan, Malaysia, New Zealand and Singapore get 3.75 percent apiece (see Table 10.2).

Table 10.2 Melton's equal global index (MEG)

Country	Weight as percentage
Canada	3.70%
United States	20.00%
Austria	1.70%
Belgium	1.70%
Denmark	1.70%
Finland	1.70%
France	1.70%
Germany	1.70%
Ireland	1.70%
Italy	1.70%
Netherlands	1.70%
Norway	1.70%
Spain	1.70%
Sweden	1.70%
Switzerland	1.70%
United Kingdom	1.70%
Australia	3.75%
Hong Kong	3.75%
Japan	3.75%
Malaysia	3.75%
New Zealand	3.75%
Singapore	3.75%
Emerging Markets	30.00%
	100%

Source: The Outside Analyst

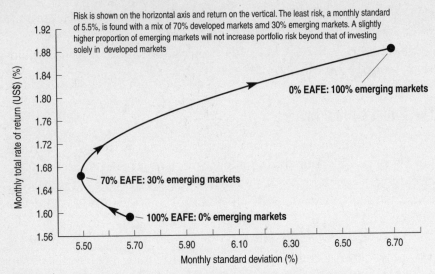

Fig 10.1 The optimal portfolio mix of developed and emerging markets
Source: Morgan Stanley Research

You'll note that the allocations to developed markets add up to only 70 percent. The other 30 percent is allocated to emerging countries.

"Whoa!" you may think, "isn't that a big slice of assets to entrust to such volatile stock markets?"

Granted, this allocation is significantly higher than the average emerging markets weighting in a typical institutional portfolio. But numerous studies show that adding emerging markets to a balanced, developed markets portfolio not only cuts risk but also boosts return.

At the vanguard of this thinking is Morgan Stanley. Their work shows that optimum investment performance at lowest risk – the so-called "efficient frontier" – is achieved with an EAFE weighting of 70 percent and an IFC Emerging Markets Composite weighting of 30 percent. Figure 10.1 demonstrates this clearly.

So though 30 percent may seem like a heavy allocation to emerging markets, trust me. I'll come back to this point in the next chapter.

MEG BENCHMARK WORKSHEET IN US DOLLARS

Suitable both for institutions and individuals, the MEG Index is both a global benchmark and a point of departure for adjusting weights for value and for correlations between markets. In the MEG Benchmark, the 1st of January 1995 equals 100. On that inception date, the various country indexes comprising the MEG Index stood as shown in Table 10.3 in US dollar terms:

Table 10.3 Melton's equal global index (MEG) – US$ (worksheet)

Weight	Country	Index 1 Jan 1995	Index Today	MEG Benchmark
3.70%	Canada	129.39		
20.00%	United States	187.76		
1.70%	Austria	182.74		
1.70%	Belgium	168.43		
1.70%	Denmark	251.81		
1.70%	Finland	185.96		
1.70%	France	163.55		
1.70%	Germany	143.31		
1.70%	Ireland	206.23		
1.70%	Italy	75.29		
1.70%	Netherlands	216.88		
1.70%	Norway	213.17		
1.70%	Spain	131.96		
1.70%	Sweden	231.11		
1.70%	Switzerland	165.19		
1.70%	United Kingdom	194.83		
3.75%	Australia	171.64		
3.75%	Hong Kong	326.14		
3.75%	Japan	156.94		
3.75%	Malaysia	479.37		
3.75%	New Zealand	70.45		
3.75%	Singapore	373.04		
30.00%	Emerging Markets	307.40		
100%		100		

Source: The Outside Analyst   1 January 1995 = 100

The proxy for emerging markets is the IFCI (Investable) Price Index, published by the International Finanace Corporation. The country indexes are the FT/S&P Actuaries World Indices that appear regularly in the *Financial Times*. I have intentionally left the two right columns blank, so that you can photocopy this table to use as a worksheet. You simply fill in the appropriate indexes on a monthly or quarterly basis to determine the rise or fall in the MEG Benchmark in dollar terms.

In Table 10.4, for instance, I have filled in the various indexes as of June 30, 1995:

Table 10.4 Melton's equal global index (MEG) – US$

Weight	Country	Index 1 Jan 1995	Index 30 Jun 1995	MEG Benchmark
3.70%	Canada	129.39	143.07	110.57
20.00%	United States	187.76	222.54	118.52
1.70%	Austria	182.74	197.48	108.07
1.70%	Belgium	168.43	194.40	115.42
1.70%	Denmark	251.81	276.53	109.82
1.70%	Finland	185.96	236.22	127.03
1.70%	France	163.55	181.35	110.88
1.70%	Germany	143.31	157.49	109.89
1.70%	Ireland	206.23	236.59	114.72
1.70%	Italy	75.29	73.33	97.40
1.70%	Netherlands	216.88	249.89	115.22
1.70%	Norway	213.17	233.14	109.37
1.70%	Spain	131.96	147.24	111.58
1.70%	Sweden	231.11	269.58	116.56
1.70%	Switzerland	165.19	201.52	121.99
1.70%	United Kingdom	194.83	213.27	109.46
3.75%	Australia	171.64	163.98	95.59
3.75%	Hong Kong	326.14	359.51	110.23
3.75%	Japan	156.94	142.49	90.79
3.75%	Malaysia	479.37	530.02	110.57
3.75%	New Zealand	70.45	78.86	111.94
3.75%	Singapore	373.04	383.37	102.77
30.00%	Emerging Markets	307.40	281.84	99.97
100%		100		107.92

Source: The Outside Analyst   1 January 1995 = 100

The percentage of growth or decline in each index is added or deducted to the base of 100 in ratio to that country's weighting. If a European market, for instance, were to rise 10 percent, you would add 0.17 percent (1.7 percent x 10) to the MEG Benchmark, raising it to 100.17. Conversely, if the US index were to decline 3 percent, you would deduct 0.6 percent (20 percent x 3) from this equal global index, thus lowering it to 99.4.

Between January 1, 1995 and June 30, 1995, as you can see, the MEG Benchmark rose 7.92 percent in dollar terms.

Worksheets for the MEG Index denominated in sterling, marks and yen appear in Tables 10.5 and 10.6. The two right columns have again been left blank, so that you can fill in the appropriate index monthly or quarterly to see the rise or fall in the MEG Benchmark in the currency of your choice.

Table 10.5 MEG benchmark worksheets in sterling and in yen

Melton's equal global index (MEG) – £ Sterling

Weight	Country	Index 1 Jan 1995	Index Today	MEG Benchmark
3.70%	Canada	122.62		
20.00%	United States	177.93		
1.70%	Austria	173.18		
1.70%	Belgium	159.62		
1.70%	Denmark	238.63		
1.70%	Finland	176.23		
1.70%	France	154.99		
1.70%	Germany	135.81		
1.70%	Ireland	195.44		
1.70%	Italy	71.35		
1.70%	Netherlands	205.53		
1.70%	Norway	202.01		
1.70%	Spain	125.05		
1.70%	Sweden	219.02		
1.70%	Switzerland	156.54		
1.70%	United Kingdom	184.63		
3.75%	Australia	162.66		
3.75%	Hong Kong	309.07		
3.75%	Japan	148.73		
3.75%	Malaysia	454.29		
3.75%	New Zealand	66.77		
3.75%	Singapore	353.52		
30.00%	Emerging Markets	291.31		
100%		100		

Source: The Outside Analyst   1 January 1995 = 100

Meltons' equal global index (MEG) – ¥ Yen

Weight	Country	Index 1 Jan 1995	Index Today	MEG Benchmark
3.70%	Canada	81.60		
20.00%	United States	118.41		
1.70%	Austria	115.25		
1.70%	Belgium	106.22		
1.70%	Denmark	158.81		
1.70%	Finland	117.28		
1.70%	France	103.14		
1.70%	Germany	90.38		
1.70%	Ireland	130.06		
1.70%	Italy	47.49		
1.70%	Netherlands	136.78		
1.70%	Norway	134.44		
1.70%	Spain	83.22		
1.70%	Sweden	145.76		
1.70%	Switzerland	104.18		
1.70%	United Kingdom	122.87		
3.75%	Australia	108.24		
3.75%	Hong Kong	205.68		
3.75%	Japan	98.98		
3.75%	Malaysia	302.32		
3.75%	New Zealand	44.43		
3.75%	Singapore	235.26		
30.00%	Emerging Markets	193.86		
100%		100		

Source: The Outside Analyst   1 January 1995 = 100

Table 10.6 Melton's equal global index (MEG) – DM

Weight	Country	Index 1 Jan 1995	Index Today	MEG Benchmark
3.70%	Canada	104.27		
20.00%	United States	151.30		
1.70%	Austria	147.26		
1.70%	Belgium	135.73		
1.70%`	Denmark	202.91		
1.70%	Finland	149.85		
1.70%	France	131.79		
1.70%	Germany	115.48		
1.70%	Ireland	166.19		
1.70%	Italy	60.68		
1.70%	Netherlands	174.77		
1.70%	Norway	171.77		
1.70%	Spain	106.33		
1.70%	Sweden	186.24		
1.70%	Switzerland	133.11		
1.70%	United Kingdom	157.00		
3.75%	Australia	138.31		
3.75%	Hong Kong	262.82		
3.75%	Japan	126.47		
3.75%	Malaysia	386.30		
3.75%	New Zealand	56.77		
3.75%	Singapore	300.61		
30.00%	Emerging Markets	247.71		
100%		100		

Source: The Outside Analyst   1 January 1995 = 100

BALANCING RISK AND REWARD

In 1945, in his allegory *Animal Farm*, George Orwell observed: "All animals are equal, but some animals are more equal than others." The same is true of country allocations. Though equal weighting is clearly the best point of departure, it by no means rules out further adjustments. Quite the contrary.

Once your allocation approach and related benchmark have been determined, ideally each country's part of the total score should be further attuned to risk and reward. There are two steps to doing this: first, adjusting your weightings to minimize the chance of correlated market movements, then tilting that mix towards the most promising markets and shares. The next two chapters cover these two steps. The first describes adjusting for *correlation*. The chapter thereafter will discuss adjusting your global portfolio country weights for *value*.

11

ASSURING VARIETY

"Though all things differ, all agree."
Alexander Pope, 1704

Which countries should you emphasize in allocating portfolio assets to minimize the chance of correlated market movements? We've seen you can best apply modern portfolio theory to your own investments by assembling a worldwide collection – from various industries – of some 25 attractive equities or equivalents, whose market movements relate as little as possible. You don't really need more than 25 equities when you invest globally in this way. That's because such an approach gives you a highly varied portfolio – and the more unlike your holdings, the fewer positions you need to be adequately diversified. Conversely, limiting your holdings to only 25 equities – or equivalents – means that for the sake of safety your portfolio has to be as diverse as you can make it.

Conclusion: *The markets to emphasize are the ones most unlike your own.*

DEVELOPED MARKETS

What is a developed market? One definition is the Group of Seven: the United States, Britain, France, Japan, Italy, Germany and Canada. These may have been the economic engines of the 1970s, when the G-7 was formed, but not all fill that role today. So let's add Belgium,

Denmark, Finland, t he Netherlands, Norway, Sweden, Switzerland, Spain, Australia, Hong Kong and Singapore – all recognizable nowadays as developed markets.

ADJUSTING FOR COUNTRY CORRELATION

You can identify those bourses most unlike your own by examining each country's correlation to your domestic market. Correlation in this context measures how far movements of two stock markets coincide or diverge. Correlation can range from +1, perfect synchronization, to –1, signifying movements that are perfectly opposed. If, say, the Umbrellastan stock market had a 1.0 correlation with the British FT100, then every time the Footsie went up 10 percent, the Umbrellastan stock index would also rise 10 percent. If, on the other hand, the correlation were –1.0, every time UK shares went up 10 percent, Umbrellastan shares would go down 10 percent. Correlation is important because it also measures diversification value – and diversification is the whole point of the allocation exercise. Like Goldilocks, you want your porridge just right. Not too hot or too cold, but just the right combination so when one stock chills out, the portfolio losses that would otherwise ensue are offset by another stock's sizzling advance.

Developed stock market correlations worldwide

Figure 11.1 shows the correlations of the US stock market with other major markets from 1980 through 1990.

The chart shows that if you live in the United States, your best choices among major markets to offset the risk of a domestic portfolio are Japan, Italy, Spain, Denmark and Germany.

The more effectively diversified your portfolio, the lower – or more negative – the correlation among your various holdings. Correlation coefficients vary somewhat across countries. They are less than 0.4 for Japan and Germany and a much higher 0.6 for the United Kingdom and the Netherlands.

Of course, the correlations of equity markets are larger between countries with strong economic and monetary ties, such as Canada and the United States, or Germany and the Netherlands. The United Kingdom, by the way, clearly dominates European equity markets, both with respect to market capitalization and the number of listed stocks. Three

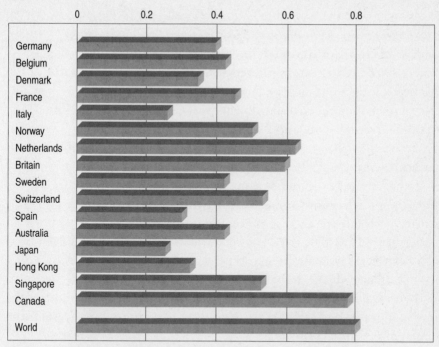

Fig 11.1 Correlations of US stocks (1980–1990), based on returns in US dollars

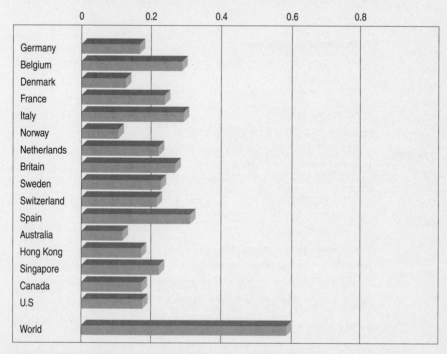

Fig 11.2 Correlations of Japanese stocks (1980–1990), based on returns in yen

major markets, the United Kingdom, Germany and France, constitute more than 60 percent of total European market capitalization. European markets are often also dominated by a few large multinationals. As I mentioned, Switzerland's top ten account for a hefty 68 percent of the country's total equity market, slightly more than Holland's 67 percent. Altogether, though, correlations are surprisingly low and explain the desirable risk-diversification benefits of investing abroad. Figures 11.2, 11.3 and 11.4 show major equity market correlations from the viewpoints of German, British and Japanese investors.

If you live in Japan, the best major countries in which to seek attractive stocks to offset domestic portfolio risk are clearly Norway, Australia, Denmark and Germany (Figure 11.2).

Figure 11.3 reveals that, if you reside in the United Kingdom, you can best offset your home market risk in the major markets by going into Denmark, Japan, Italy and Spain.

If you live in Germany, the best major markets in which to offset the risk of a domestic portfolio are obviously Singapore, Japan, Australia and Spain (Figure. 11.4).

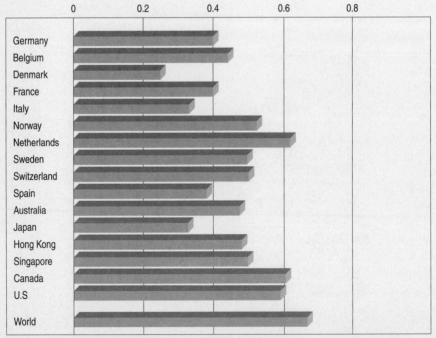

Fig 11.3 Correlations of British stocks (1980–1990), based on returns in Sterling

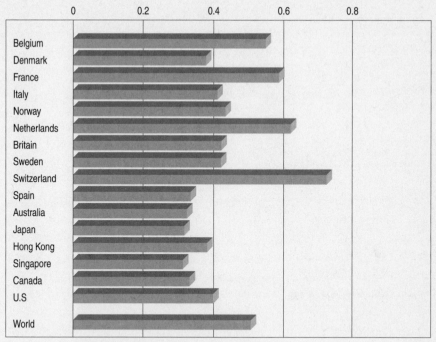

Fig 11.4 Correlations of German stocks (1980–1990), based on returns in Deutschmarks

The four preceding charts are based on data in Odier and Solnik's "Lessons for International Asset Allocation," in the *Financial Analysts Journal* of March/April 1993.

How to diversify within Europe

Earlier studies, particularly Bruno Solnik's *International Investments* (Addison Wesley, 1991), revealed that diversifying across European markets offers substantial risk reduction – despite the integration of Europe's economies. "Anatomy of the World Markets," a ranking published by Goldman Sachs & Co. in 1989, showed that from January 1986 through November 1989, correlations between European markets ranged from a high of 0.71 between Switzerland and Germany to a low of 0.09 between Austria and the United Kingdom. Figure 11.5 shows a useful way of viewing these relationships, called a dendogram.

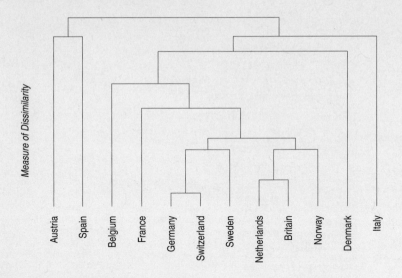

Fig 11.5 Cluster analysis of European markets, based on daily index returns, January 1986 – November 1989.

This dendogram groups the European markets into clusters according to their similarity. The shorter the vertical line, the more similar the two markets. Conversely, the higher the vertical line, the more the market movements differ. Austria and Spain, for instance, are quite dissimilar, as are Denmark and Italy. Such pairs are good candidates for a global portfolio. Pairing Germany with Italy is also clearly an attractive choice for a global portfolio.

The lowest cluster, as you might expect, links highly-correlated Germany and Switzerland. The Netherlands and the UK form the second lowest group. These two clusters are subsequently linked to Norway, Sweden, France and Belgium to form a rather homogeneous group. There is thus little benefit in diversifying equities among these countries.

In contrast, smaller markets such as Austria, Spain, Denmark and Italy behave quite differently from each other and from the remaining stock markets. These smaller markets thus provide good opportunities to diversify within Europe – especially for the individual investor, who, unlike an institutional heavyweight, need not be deterred by their relatively low capitalization and liquidity.

Aren't major stock market correlations on the rise?

No. In "Beating the Equity Benchmarks," in the July/August 1994 *Financial Analysts Journal*, Gary Gastineau reported that an examination of stock market movements in the United States, United Kingdom, Germany, France and Japan from July 1988 through January 1994 reveals that "correlations between the US equity market and other markets show no signs of increasing."

Indeed, other "evidence suggests that US equity market correlations with the other G-7 countries have generally declined in recent years," according to Erb, Harvey and Viskanta in "Forecasting International Equity Correlations."

At first glance, this is somewhat surprising. The increased globalization of capital markets during the past decade would suggest higher, rather than lower, correlations. But more globalization does not automatically mean more correlation between equity markets. For even when investors in two particular countries can trade freely in each other's stock markets, industry mixes within each country may differ sufficiently to cause low correlations of those markets.

Forecasting correlations from the business cycle

Correlation is tied to the business cycle because expected stock returns are tied to the business cycle. The Erb, Harvey, Viskanta study shows that correlations are highest when any two countries are in a common recession. They are lower during recoveries and lowest of all when the business cycles in the two countries are out of phase.

The United States, for instance, fell into recession in 1990, with European countries following in 1991 and 1992. A drop in the US market correlation with that of Canada seemingly came about due to Canada's entering a prolonged recession in 1989 and barely emerging by the end of 1993. In contrast, the official length of the US recession, according to the National Bureau of Economic Research, was only five quarters. So the business cycles of the United States and both Canada and the European countries got out of phase by at least a year. This accounts for the lower equity market correlations then between the US and Canada and between the US and Europe.

Conclusion: It is wise to diversify into countries in another phase of the economic cycle, especially if your home country is in recession.

Correlations also tend to be higher when two countries are both in a bear market than when they are both in a bull market, even ignoring the 1987 crash. This increased correlation of course reduces the benefit you gain from portfolio diversification. That's unfortunate, because a bear market is just when you especially need that edge. If you assemble your portfolio on the basis of average correlations, in a bear market your investments could well perform worse than you expect.

Conclusion: It makes more sense to assemble a portfolio on the basis of expected correlations rather than on past averages.

Table 11.1 Equity correlation forecasts for the G–7 stock markets: January 1994 through December 1998

Country	U.S.A.	Canada	France	Germany	Italy	Japan
Canada	86%					
France	49	49%				
Germany	25	46	69%			
Italy	27	34	47%	18%		
Japan	23	41	31%	28	49%	
Britain	60	64	44%	44	49	27%

To help you do just that, Table 11.1 shows the expected correlations of the world's major equity markets (or in any case the G-7) from January 1994 through December 1998.

These forecasts, from the Erb, Harvey and Viskanta study cited above, are derived from a statistical technique called regression analysis, based on Dalton's principle that events tend to return to their mean.

For France, the US return correlation is projected to remain stable at about 0.49, expressed in the table as 49 percent. The Germany–United States correlation is expected to decline from the present level of 36 percent to 25 percent. The United States–Italy correlation is forecast to increase from 24 percent to 27 percent over the time period. The Japanese–United States correlation will drop slightly from 26 percent to 23 percent. The correlation between the United Kingdom and the United States will remain steady at 60 percent. According to the forecasting model, Canadian correlations will rise to normal levels over the next five years. The correlation between Canada and the United States which fell sharply during 1992 and 1993, will rise from its present 64 percent to 86 percent.

Summary

The markets to emphasize are the ones most unlike your own. It is wise to diversify into countries in another phase of the economic cycle, especially if your home country is in recession. It makes more sense to assemble a portfolio on the basis of expected correlations rather than on past averages.

Over the years to December 1998, diversification into British shares will be most attractive to Japanese investors and least attractive to investors based in North America. Diversification into the United States will be most attractive to German, Japanese and Italian investors and least attractive to Canadians.

Similarly, among major markets, US investors can best diversify into Germany, Italy and Japan, while avoiding Canada. And pairing Germany with Italy will become an increasingly attractive choice for a global portfolio.

EMERGING MARKETS

Emerging markets plainly belong in a global portfolio. But following investments in such markets is notoriously difficult. Local stock markets compile indexes in widely different ways, making it almost impossible to make an "apples with apples" comparison of investments in Jordan with, say, those in Peru. External indicators, however, can provide a uniform basis of comparison among emerging markets. A leading compiler of such indexes is the International Finance Corporation, or IFC, based in Washington, DC. This arm of the World Bank has composite and regional indexes covering from 60 percent to 75 percent of the market capitalization of each country reviewed.

Not every market is going to emerge. Nevertheless, the IFC defines an emerging market as *any* in a developing economy. IFC also follows the criteria of the World Bank in classifying economies as low income, middle income or high income. Essentially, according to the IFC *Emerging Markets Factbook 1995*, an emerging market is one that in 1993 had a lower GNP per capita than $8,626, the IFC's dividing line between its middle- and high-income categories.

From January 1989 to January 1995, the IFC Global Composite Index rose more than 93 percent in dollar terms versus a rise of less than 24 percent for the *Financial Times* "A" world index. Even more impressive, Table 11.2 shows the total average US dollar returns you would have achieved by investing $1,000 in various emerging markets over the decade ended January 1995.

rformance of emerging equity markets: January 1985 – January 1995

	Percentage change on January 1985	Value of Initial $1,000
Chile	6,370.7	$64,707
Philippines	4,702.3	$48,023
Colombia	3,670.7	$37,707
Mexico	2,220.9	$23,209
Argentina	1,561.4	$16,614
Thailand	1,521.2	$16,212
Zimbabwe	1,103.2	$12,032
Taiwan, China	1,066.2	$11,662
IFCG Latin America	930.9	$10,309
Korea	646.6	$ 7,466
Greece	568.6	$ 6,686
Pakistan	550.3	$ 6,503
IFCG Composite	452.2	$ 5,522
IFCG Asia	445.9	$ 5,459
Brazil	438.2	$ 5,382
India	430.7	$ 5,307
Turkey	349.7	$ 4,497
Venezuela	262.2	$ 3,622
Malaysia	261.3	$ 3,613
Jordan	103.7	$ 2,037
Nigeria	65.8	$ 1,658
S & P 500	281.8	$ 3,818
FT "A" EuroPac	421.0	$ 5,210

Source: The Outside Analyst
IFC Global Indexes – Total Return in US$ terms January 1985 = 100

Over the decade, only four emerging markets had a lower return than the Standard & Poor's 500, and only five had a lower return than the *Financial Times* "A" World Index.

Quite apart from these superior past returns, there are five solid reasons for new investment in such emerging countries:

- The *biggest* differences in share price movements are those between developed and emerging markets. You get genuine diversification of risk.
- Emerging markets also have the most room for growth. They account for 5 of the world's 15 largest economies, 20 percent of the world's GNP and 85 percent of the world's population, according to the *World Bank Atlas 1995*, but still less than 13 percent of total world stock market capitalization.
- Moreover, emerging economies are growing much faster than those in developed countries. With low labour costs, deriving from young

and ever better educated populations, emerging countries challenge the industrialized world.

- As emerging markets grow, many are opening up to the private sector and overseas investors, who can buy shares with increasing confidence of being able to repatriate dividends and initial capital.
- Finally, emerging markets are less "efficient" than stock markets in developed economies. The less information available, the less quoted prices reflect true value. Good information can thus give you stunning profit opportunities.

Profiting from inefficiencies

The general inefficiency of emerging markets is illustrated by Table 11.3, where one year's best or worst performing stock market appears at the opposite extreme the next year on six occasions.

Table 11.3 Best and worst emerging stock market performers

Year	Best	Change in %	Worst	Change in %
1985	Zimbabwe	153.8	Venezuela	−26.6
1986	Philippines	382.6	Nigeria	−56.7
1987	Turkey	262.2	Brazil	−63.1
1988	Brazil	125.6	Turkey	−61.1
1989	Turkey	502.4	Venezuela	−33.1
1990	Venezuela	601.6	Brazil	−65.7
1991	Argentina	396.9	Zimbabwe	−52.3
1992	Thailand	40.3	Zimbabwe	−59.8
1993	Turkey	234.3	Nigeria	−11.6
1994	Nigeria	190.9	Turkey	−40.7

Source: The Outside Analyst
Statistics from International Finance Corporation, total returns in US dollars

As the table demonstrates, moves in these markets are huge. It is relatively common for a stock index to double or to halve.

Conclusion: *To alleviate recurrent wide swings, a global portfolio should not be concentrated too heavily in any one emerging market.*

Weighting emerging markets

A 1994 study by London brokerage Kleinwort Benson revealed that the best approach to asset allocation in emerging markets is also to weight all such markets equally. This method of asset allocation not only delivers the best performance, but gives you a portfolio more stable than weighting by market size. The low volatility is no surprise, because the equal weighting automatically assembles a highly diversified portfolio in markets that are largely uncorrelated. This strategy's superior returns stem from two factors. First, the equal weighting gives you more exposure to new markets. Secondly, the fixed weights in effect force you to take profits in the good-performing markets and invest in the lagging markets. In inefficient markets, this kind of rebalancing is a powerful way of generating excess returns. It requires rebalancing the emerging market segment of your global portfolio roughly once a year.

Just how risky are emerging markets?

Granted, the *national* risk for emerging markets is high. As you can see, their shares do tend to bounce up and down together over greater price ranges than those of New York or London. The key point, however, is that emerging market stocks behave much differently than developed market stocks. So as a group, emerging markets, despite their high individual market volatility, add but little risk to a global portfolio.

Though free lunches are notoriously hard to find, you do get something for nothing by diversifying into emerging markets. In the previous chapter, I noted you get optimum investment performance at lowest risk by putting 30 percent of your portfolio into emerging markets. This is readily illustrated. Assume you're a UK investor with a purely domestic portfolio. Over the five years to the end of 1993, the annual return from the All-Share index of UK shares averaged 6 percent and the standard deviation – how much each year's return varied from the average – exceeded 18 percent. In contrast, the IFCI index of emerging markets yielded returns of some 22 percent a year, but had a standard deviation of over 23 percent. The emerging markets were clearly a more volatile investment. But they paid a higher return.

So what should you have done to minimize your risk? Stay just in the UK? No. A far lower risk strategy would have been to invest about three-quarters of your money in the UK and the remainder in emerging markets. This would have had a standard deviation of just 16.5 percent. But better still (that free lunch), the combined portfolio was not only less volatile than the All-Share, it also posted a higher return: over 10 percent a year. (Obviously, you would further have improved your risk/reward ratio by adding other developed markets.) In the aggregate, emerging markets are less risky than any one OECD country. At no point in this century have the emerging markets all collapsed or risen simultaneously. But on two distinct occasions – the First and Second World Wars – the European markets and Japan literally crashed and burned. The volatility of return in emerging markets on a five and ten-year time frame is less than in France, Germany and Japan and only slightly higher than in the UK.

Building a more stable portfolio

As we've discussed, to smooth the ups and downs in your portfolio you want markets whose share prices move most differently from those at home. If, like me, you live and invest in a developed country, you *need* shares from emerging markets simply because these markets move most counter to your own. They tend, therefore, to make your portfolio more stable. This seems to fly in the face of conventional wisdom, which holds that the smaller bourses, especially those of the third world, are highly volatile and hence unsafe. But the contradiction is more apparent than real. That's because emerging markets are largely uncorrelated, so their swings and roundabouts tend to nullify each other. Nor do emerging markets tend to mirror movements of developed markets. Seven emerging markets show negative correlation with Wall Street, generally plunging when it rises and soaring when it tumbles: Brazil, India, Jordan, Venezuela, Argentina, Pakistan and Zimbabwe. If Wall Street sneezes, Zimbabwe does not automatically catch a cold – and vice versa.

Conclusion: Investing in generally countercyclical markets that offer the possibility of spectacular growth can improve returns without raising risk.

As a group, emerging markets have frequently outperformed world averages. In 1994, if we consider Finland a developed market as the IFC does, nine of the top 10 dollar performers were emerging markets (Table 11.4).

Table 11.4 Top ten world stock market performers in 1994
(in US dollar terms)

Kenya	179%
Nigeria	169%
Egypt	167%
Bangladesh	117%
Tunisia	114%
Ghana	69%
Brazil	68%
Mauritius	56%
Peru	52%
Finland	51%

Source: The Outside Analyst

Naturally, the fact that emerging markets as a group have often beaten world averages does not guarantee that they will *always* do so. In 1994, though seven emerging markets were the only countries with US dollar returns exceeding 60 percent, emerging markets as a *group* lost 2.2 percent of their market value versus a world average gain of 3.4 percent. Devaluation of the Mexican peso had kicked off an indiscriminate capital flight from the emerging markets, depressing share prices – and creating unique buying opportunities. But the worst dollar performer in 1994 was not Mexico, down 41.6 percent, but Turkey, which fell 43.3 percent. Still, as Turkey had risen 214 percent in 1993, it retained a 78 percent gain in dollar terms over the two-year period. Granted, the world's emerging markets fared badly in 1995. In dollar terms, the IFC index of emerging markets fell by 17 percent while Morgan Stanley's world index of stock markets rose by 18.7 percent. Rich-country investors, emerging-market skeptics jeer, not only burnt their fingers but missed the chance to make more money at home. The S&P 500, for instance, was up 35.36 percent. Yet, paradoxically, the poor performance of emerging markets in 1995 was somewhat reassuring. Like 1993, when emerging markets outperformed mature ones, it provided more evidence that emerging and mature markets continue to move in opposite directions, thus strengthening the case for spreading an equity portfolio between them.

Here are the book's major conclusions up to this point.

Summary

- *Just as you can diversify away specific risk by holding variou. of shares, so too you can substantially reduce market risk by hold-ing investments in uncorrelated markets.*
- *For optimal global equity diversification, it makes sense to select some 25 stocks, or their equivalents, from different countries and industries, emphasizing country diversification over industry diver-sification.*
- *Country weightings largely determine the performance and risk of a global equity portfolio. The most practical approach is to assign the major markets equal weights, then overweight the markets most unlike your own.*
- *It is also wise to emphasize countries in another phase of the eco-nomic cycle, especially if your home country is in a recession.*
- *It makes more sense to assemble a portfolio based on expected correla-tions than on past averages. On this basis, diversification into British shares is most attractive to Japanese investors and least attractive to investors based in North America. Diversification into the United States is most attractive to German, Japanese and Italian investors and least to Canadians. Similarly, among major markets, US investors can best diversify into Germany, Italy and Japan rather than Canada. Pair-ing Germany with Italy is a good tactic for a global portfolio.*
- *Well-diversified shares drawn from no less than 10 emerging coun-tries should comprise roughly 30 percent of a global portfolio. But to alleviate recurrent wide swings, a global portfolio should not be concentrated too heavily in any single emerging market. Brazil, India, Jordan, Venezuela, Argentina, Zimbabwe and Pakistan are the emerging markets least correlated with the US and Canada. For the best balance of risk and reward, an optimum global equity fund will track the MEG Index.*

You now have the information needed to apportion your investment funds between home and abroad, selecting the countries whose stock markets move most counter to your own. Before moving on to review-ing your allocations in terms of *value*, let's briefly consider the question of currency risk.

12

HANDLING CURRENCY RISK

*"The Owl and the Pussy-cat went to sea
In a beautiful pea-green boat,
They took some honey, and plenty of money,
Wrapped up in a five-pound note."*
Edward Lear (1812–1888), *Nonsense Songs*

When the verse above was first published in 1871, the joke was, of course, that a five-pound note was also money. Today, the money is probably Japanese yen, while the five-pound note, like the US dollar, has indeed largely been reduced to wrapping paper. What to do about currency risk?

Suppose you live in the UK and put £10,000 into US equities when $2 is equal to £1. Your £10,000 investment buys $20,000 worth of US shares. Let's assume your US positions soar by an average 25 percent but the dollar tumbles by 20 percent against sterling, so it stands at $2.40 to the pound. Thanks to the market rise, your shares are now worth $25,000. Alas, that translates into only £10,417 in sterling, due to the dollar's fall. The currency movement has wiped out most of your stock market gain.

Japan provided a classic illustration of currency risk in 1995. While the Nikkei Dow zoomed some 35 percent from July 1995, the yen slid 15 percent against sterling in the same period. The average UK investor in Japanese equities who did not do currency deals to protect those assets against the fall forfeited half the stock market gain.

In theory, you can get around currency risk by hedging – either borrowing currency or using futures or options: taking on a contract or option to buy or sell a currency at a given price on a fixed date. But either strategy can be expensive. And, alas, when you protect your portfolio against falls in the value of a currency, you also miss out on any rise in that currency.

Portfolio managers who hedge are generally loath to do so unless they have an extremely strong view about which way a currency is moving. No wonder. Not only is hedging expensive, but getting a hedge wrong can cripple your result.

Save & Prosper's Japan unit trust hedged against a fall in the yen in early 1995, but the yen kept rising. In the summer, the manager then unwound the hedge just before the yen fell. In consequence, his fund's performance plummeted like a stone.

Just as the specific risks of individual stocks tend to nullify each other, Chapter 5 concluded, so the currency risks of different markets can be reasonably counterbalanced. Effectively, this would imply that no currency hedging is required for a properly diversified global portfolio. Still, there is an ongoing debate about the value of hedging currencies.

André Perold and Evan Shulman hold that any exposure to foreign currencies is an active investment decision. Failure to hedge, they imply, does not enhance long-term returns. At the other extreme, Kenneth Froot's study of a 200-year period (with special attention to the past 20 years) shows that the value of hedging virtually disappears over any eight-year period. Froot argues that hedging currency over the long term merely adds to costs. Fischer Black, who died while I was writing this book, would, I believe, have eventually won the Nobel Prize for his economic perceptions. "Investors in different countries," he wrote in 1989, "can all add to their expected returns by taking some currency risk in their portfolios." Barring specific information or conviction to the contrary, Black suggests 30 to 77 percent of foreign currency exposure be hedged.

In the absence of a compelling case for any other ratio, Gary Gastineau, to whom I'm indebted for outlining the nuances of the hedging debate, suggests a middle course: half hedged and half not.

However, for the true global investor, diversified both in time and space, I believe currency hedging makes little sense. Here's why.

IN DEVELOPED MARKETS

Chapter 10 mentioned that you get optimum performance at lowest risk with 30 percent of your portfolio invested in emerging markets and the rest in developed markets. Is there any benefit in hedging currencies in the 70 percent allocation to developed markets? To answer that question, let's see how much currency risk those markets involve.

If you weight your global portfolio more or less equally in conformity with the MEG benchmark outlined in Chapter 10, you'll find that the developed markets embody almost no currency risk at all. A recent study by Mark Kritzman, "The Minimum-Risk Currency Hedge Ratio and Foreign Asset Exposure," proves "it is more relevant to hedge currency risk for small allocations to foreign assets than for large allocations." With the equal weightings I've suggested, your foreign allocations to developed markets will be quite large: at least 66 percent of your total portfolio – unless you live in the United States, in which case they will be 50 percent (70 percent minus the 20 percent US allocation). Foreign equities will weigh even heavier *within* the developed market part of your portfolio. That works out as follows. Of your total portfolio, 20 percent is in the United States. That US slice represents some 29 percent of the 70 percent allocation to developed markets (0.20 divided by 0.70), with the other 71 percent in non-US developed markets. No other country has asset allocation greater than 3.75 percent. So any country other than the US gets less than 6 percent of the total allocation to developed markets (0.0375 divided by 0.70), with the remaining 94 percent apportioned among other developed markets. No matter where you live, in other words, at least 71 percent to 94 percent of your allocation to developed markets will involve foreign equities. And if you live in Europe, where your home market gets only 1.70 percent of the total, over 97 percent of your allocation to developed markets will involve foreign equities.

Naturally, the more you depart from equal weighting, the more attention currency risk will demand. However, currencies in developed markets tend to move in tandem with either the Euro, the dollar or the yen. Therefore, so long as your developed-market holdings are more or less equally divided between these three currency blocks, your currency risk is not excessive. Granted, currency translation can have a sizable effect on total equity returns in the short run – upside or down.

But over longer periods, these effects have tended to cancel out. The dominant long-term influences on equity prices are the track record of each individual company and local stock market performance. With equities, you're buying productive capacity, not pesos, francs or yen. Over time, price gains in those equities will tend to compensate for changes in currency values.

On the other hand, currencies can be muscular or flabby. Given two equally promising companies, one denominated in a weak and the other in a strong currency, the latter is likely to produce better returns when translated into your home currency. The strong foreign currency provides an extra boost. The next chapter cites a study proving that countries with strong currencies generally tend to have stronger economic growth, lower inflation and lower interest rates than countries with weak currencies.

Conclusion: Currency effects tend to cancel out over the long term. What ultimately matters is local stock market performance and the track record of each individual company. With equal weighting of countries or the three major currency blocks, hedging developed-market currencies is not essential. A strong foreign currency tends to boost portfolio performance. If your developed-market portfolio becomes heavily tilted towards weak-currency countries, rebalance it. The final decision of whether or not to hedge a portfolio's currency risk should reflect a realistic assessment of the costs of hedging this risk.

IN EMERGING MARKETS

A study entitled "Further Evidence on the Benefits of Portfolio Investments in Emerging Markets" supports the notion that overall risk can be substantially *reduced* by including emerging markets in global portfolios. The paper, by Viha Errunza of McGill University and Prasad Padmanabhan of Vanderbilt University, appeared in the July–August 1988 *Financial Analysts Journal*. (Errunza had previously published a seminal article on this subject in the September/October 1983 issue: "Emerging Markets: A New Opportunity for Improving Global Portfolio Performance." The 1983 study supplied the first evidence of a rationale for including emerging markets in global portfolios.)

The two finance professors also examined how currency fluctuations affect the relative returns of developed and emerging markets. Their conclusions are reassuring. They demonstrate that in the late

1970s and early 1980s the benefits of diversifying into the emerging markets actually increased. What's more, during the same period, exchange-rate fluctuations had a negligible effect upon returns in emerging markets as compared with US returns, whether measured in dollars or in local currencies.

In professional jargon, "return correlations between emerging market and US securities in local currency terms were generally negative or not significantly different from zero." The return correlations were, in fact, quite similar to those based on dollars. Put simply, as investments in emerging economies are long-term and any global portfolio would invest reasonably small amounts in low-volume bourses, currency fluctuations in emerging markets have little or no effect upon overall portfolio diversification.

Conclusion: Assuming a well-diversified 30 percent allocation to emerging markets, hedging their currency risk is unnecessary.

Summary

A strong foreign currency tends to boost portfolio performance. If your developed-market allocation becomes heavily tilted towards weak-currency countries, rebalance it. For the global investor, however, currency risk, whether in developed or emerging markets, is largely irrelevant for the long term. You're buying productive capacity, not pesos, marks or yen. Over time, price gains in equities will tend to compensate for changes in currency values.

Once you have decided where you want to invest in terms of correlation – or, rather, the lack of it – the next step, as I've said, is to review your country and share allocations in terms of *value*. To help in that task, the next chapter describes how to find the world's best bargains.

13

THE WORLD'S BEST
BARGAINS

*"Let us not go over the old ground, let us rather
prepare for what is to come."*
Marcus Tullius Cicero (106–43 BC)

Tilting your global portfolio towards the most promising markets
and shares of course involves value judgments and implies some
ability to predict returns.

THE BARGAIN EQUITIES

What's a firm worth? This question – for most investors the only
important one – keeps thousands of analysts all over the world in full-
time employment. In New York, Paris, London, Amsterdam,
Frankfurt, Zürich and Hong Kong these investment professionals are
tracking which shares will show the most powerful earnings growth
well into the next century. The number-crunching involved in sifting
all earnings forecasts for all quoted companies is staggering.

Take the London market alone. Roughly 1,100 London-listed companies are researched by analysts. Multiply that by the number of
brokers who follow each stock. Let's say six. Multiply the result by
two (every company reports results twice a year, when forecasts usually change) – then factor in another small multiple, say 1.3, to take

account of forecasts being revised up or down between results announcements. The answer – 17,160 – is a very approximate figure for the number of analysts' forecasts swimming around the London market each year.

Monitoring such vast numbers is a formidable task. All the same, a major industry has arisen around gathering, logging and combining earnings forecasts in all the major markets, then disseminating the information.

Expectations drive equity markets

As Nobel Prize-winner William Sharpe notes in the fifth edition of the classic text *Investments:* "Earnings expectations are the most important determinant of stock prices." The share price of any company is determined by the market's view of that company's future earnings. The best way to approximate this market view is to poll the maximum number of qualified analysts of the security and take the average (or consensus) of their forecasts. As share prices move to reflect the current level of analyst earnings forecasts, this consensus becomes embedded in the current price of the stock. So the future price of a share is largely determined by what professionals now think it will earn.

Some investors believe that extrapolation of the past is a much more reliable guide to future share prices than analyst "guesstimates" of future earnings. Simply extrapolating from the past, however, can mean gaping into the rear-view mirror as you drive into a wall. Naturally, a company's past history is important, but any decent analyst has already factored it into the earnings estimate.

Two monthly publications list brokers' forecasts for UK stocks. The *Estimate Directory* is published by Edinburgh Financial Publishing (tel: + 44–31–220–0468) at £275 a year and the *Earnings Guide* (tel: + 44–403–791155) costs £202 a year. The *Earnings Guide* also contains forecasts for several European markets and is available on diskette for downloading onto personal computers (subscription £1,410 a year). The *Estimate Directory*, however, is more user-friendly and is presented alphabetically by industry sector with useful background information about each company. Both publications have sections devoted to brokers' revised profits estimates – one of the most important parts of the process.

US analysts have a far bigger universe. They follow some 4,200 listed firms, which report four times rather than twice a year. Applying the same formula, there are roughly 131,040 different annual US earnings forecasts. The 80-page *Earnings Outlook*, at $240 a year from Nelson Publications (tel: + 1–914–937–8400), carries earnings estimates each month on about 3,800 US stocks.

Coverage of earnings estimates by all 185 US brokerage firms is available from Zacks Investment Research, 155 North Wacker Drive, Chicago, IL 60606; Tel: 1–312–630–9880. Zack's 40-page bi-weekly *Analyst Watch*, at $249 a year, provides performance ratings on some 4,000 US stocks.

First Call, a unit of Thomson Financial Services (tel: + 44–171–369–7000), reports earnings estimates from about 150 brokerage firms worldwide on some 15,000 equities: 10,000 outside the US and 5,000 in the US, including about 1,000 ADRs. First Call provides estimates, corporate data and broker research in various forms, including print, fax, electronic feed and via the Internet through America Online, which you can access via the keyword "earnings." Its World Equities Windows database, updated weekly by CD ROM, covers some 7,000 companies in about 30 countries.

The Institutional Brokers Estimate System

The veteran global tracker of monthly changes in earnings estimates is the Institutional Brokers Estimate System, better known as IBES (tel: + 1–212–647–5700). Subscribers (who pay an average $15,000 per year) are brokers who want to know what their competitors are doing and – more importantly – what institutional investors are doing.

Before IBES set up shop in 1971 as the first database of analysts' earnings estimates, there was no way to prove the relationship between stock prices and earnings expectations. Since then, over 200 published studies have confirmed that this relationship exists worldwide. More and more evidence supports the hypothesis that earnings expectation works in similar ways from the US to the UK, on through Hong Kong and Sri Lanka. A recent study by Erickson and Cunniff, for instance, examined IBES estimate revisions for the US and ten markets in Europe and Asia from end-1988 through 1993. Earnings revisions correlated positively with stock returns in all the markets studied.

Today the IBES database is a superb treasury of statistics on earnings estimates, comprising detailed profit forecasts updated monthly from over 7,000 top financial analysts around the globe. Employed by the world's leading investment houses, these analysts research shares for major banks, insurance companies and pension funds. Every leading institutional broker in the world is represented. All the most respected analysts contribute, as do many regional firms and boutiques.

The Outside Analyst

The Outside Analyst (tel: + 1–510–596–9300; $390 a year) is the only newsletter that compares stocks globally and gives subscribers the benefit of such forecasts. I'm the editor. Each month, sifting all major analyst earnings estimates for over 15,000 firms in more than 40 countries, *The Outside Analyst* reveals which shares professionals now consider most attractive, supplying fundamental research on each. In theory, a share's quoted price should reflect its future value. Fortunately, though, that is not always the case. For this reason, disciplined coverage of brokers' forecasts can pinpoint the world's bargain equities.

The efficient market theory

Skeptics claim this is a futile exercise. As a rule, these critics subscribe to the "efficient market" hypothesis, an academic theory which holds that share prices react so swiftly to information that no one can pick shares that will outperform the market over the long haul. The stock market – any stock market – is deemed to be "efficient," meaning that all new information is swiftly absorbed in its entirety and reflected in share prices. Share prices, the theory holds, reflect fundamental information and change only if that information changes, not in response to the whims of fickle investors.

Efficient market proponents scoff at the predictive ability of stock analysts, maintaining that all publicly available information about a company is already reflected in its share price. But a 1995 study by Kent Womack, a financial economist at Dartmouth College, seems to give the last laugh to the analysts – at least the good ones. Womack examined the stock selections of analysts from the 14 top US stockbrokers, as ranked in an annual survey by the magazine *Institutional Investor*. Using data from First Call, he looked at market reactions to more than 1,500 buy-and-sell recommendations over a three-year period.

He found that, on the day a stock was recommended, its price jumped by an average 3 percent over and above any change in the market as a whole. Sell recommendations had an even bigger impact, triggering an average 4.7 percent drop in price. Moreover, in the following days and weeks a stock price continued in the same direction. In the wake of a "buy" advice, a share's price rose an average additional 2.4 percent during the next month – and still held the gains a year later. The long-term reaction to a "sell" was even more striking: following the initial plunge, the share price continued to fall steadily. Womack calculated that equities lose an average 13.8 percent of their value during the first six months of appearing on a sell list.

Conclusion: *The best analysts have a knack for finding shares that are mispriced – and the market knows it.*

The efficient market hypothesis further contends it is impossible to beat the market because competition among professional investors makes prices roughly what they should be. But just as the theory holds that even professionals cannot do better than the market over time, it also holds that they cannot do substantially worse. After all, it is their decisions that keep prices at the proper level in the first place.

Normal distribution, I noted earlier, suggests that, if a coin has just landed heads, chances are higher the next toss will come up tails. But a coin has no memory, so in fact the chances of heads or tails remain 50:50 no matter how many times you toss it. If you studied chemistry in secondary school, you may recall how particles under a microscope wander in a seemingly random way. This phenomenon, known as the Law of Brownian Motion, underlies the efficient market hypothesis, born in 1953 when Maurice Kendall, a British statistician, found that stock prices seemed to behave in a manner similar to a roulette wheel, i.e. the past had no impact on the future and could not be used to predict it. If a roulette wheel is fair, then knowledge of recent outcomes will not be of any value in predicting the result of its next spin. Similarly, Kendallan and other University researchers found through a series of statistical tests that past price changes in securities provide no clues as to future movements. Stock prices, like a coin, they concluded, have no memory. Despite understandable skepticism from the brokerage industry, this theory – then called the Random Walk Hypothesis – began gaining some credence. In the late 1960s, the random walk notion was amplified into the efficient market hypothesis, which held that returns should be independent and identically distributed. All information was supposed to be discounted immediately, or at least very quickly. Large movements were supposed to occur by way of a series of small movements. Any process of this type will exhibit a normal distribution of returns. But does that sound like any stock market you've ever experienced? Over the years, the "efficient" market has repeatedly been refuted, then redefined. Here are the current major definitions.

The weak form of "efficiency"

This is a slightly modified version of the random walk. It presumes that share prices fully reflect all *past* information. Stated another way, analysis of the past cannot provide a profitable trading strategy. Technical analysts, who extrapolate squiggles on price charts, hate this version.

The semi-strong form of "efficiency"

This version claims that share prices fully reflect all available public information, including that found in published financial reports. Fundamental analysts, who pore over such reports, hate this version.

The strong form of "efficiency"

This version states that share prices fully reflect *all* available information, including insider information. The strong version is hated by technical and fundamental analysts alike.

This is the traditional order of presentation, suggesting that the efficient market theory evolved from the weak form to the strong. Actually, it was the other way round. I call the efficient market theory the Creature because, every time someone shoots a hole in it, another Doctor tapes a neat bandage over the wound. Each bandage simply modifies the definition of efficiency in the face of overwhelming evidence to the contrary. Today, the Creature, though seemingly immortal, is more gauze than flesh. Gauze so thin, fortunately, that it does not block the light.

On the other hand, champions of the efficient market theory do cite numerous studies showing that most professional money managers, stockbrokers and investment advisers are unable to beat the market averages – or even to outperform a portfolio of stocks picked at random.

The random walk approach

Given this pessimistic view, the best alternative might indeed be to select stocks on a random basis. Mind you, random walk advocates do not suggest that you avoid the stock market. Rather, they recommend that you adopt a "buy-and-hold" strategy because stock prices on the whole trend upwards. Studies indicate that over the past 60 years, the general US stock market, measured by the S&P, rose at an average compounded rate of 10 percent a year. The most popular book on the subject is *A Random Walk Down Wall Street*, by Burton G. Malkiel – the same Burton Malkiel who says the dispersion of analysts' forecasts serves as a good proxy for systematic risk. In that 1973 book, Malkiel, erstwhile dean of management at Yale University and now Professor of Economics at Princeton University, defines "random walk" this way:

> A random walk . . . means that short-run changes in stock prices cannot be predicted. Investment advisory services, earnings predictions, and complicated chart patterns are useless . . . Taken to its logical extreme, it means that a blindfolded monkey throwing darts at a newspaper's financial pages could select a portfolio that would do just as well as one carefully selected by the experts.

Every six months, *The Wall Street Journal Europe* conducts a lighthearted test of the random walk theory, simply replacing the monkey with a staff reporter. Since the game began in January 1992, the portfolio selected by investment professionals has won slightly more often than the random portfolio. And the monkey. But when the monkey loses, he loses heavily – so his aggregate gain badly lags that of the professionals.

Market inefficiencies

The efficient market theory has five major flaws. First, though most professional money managers and investment advisers fail to beat the averages, a minority have had outstanding market performance over the long run. Warren Buffett began an investment partnership in 1956, with $105,000 supplied mostly by uncles, aunts and other assorted relatives. That partnership ended in 1969 with $105 million and a compounded growth rate of 31 percent. A thousand dollars invested in it in 1957 would have grown to $26,000 in 12 years. The partnership did not have a single losing year, and gained in years of severe market decline, including 1962 and 1966. A thousand dollars invested in 1934 with T. Rowe Price would have compounded by 16.4 percent a year to become $271,000 by 1971. A thousand dollars placed in 1954 in Sir John Templeton's Templeton Growth Fund would have grown to $218,000 by the end of 1993. The same amount invested in

1964 in Berkshire Hathaway, Warren Buffett's corporate vehicle, would have become $434,000 by the start of 1994, having compounded at over 23 percent a year. And $10,000 entrusted to Fidelity's Magellan fund in 1977, when its management was taken over by Peter Lynch, would have become $281,000 when he retired in 1990.

Magellan, which also beat the market over the period of Jeffrey Vinik's watch from mid-1992 to mid-1996, Malkiel gloomily admits, is "one of the problems" for theorists like himself. So, I suppose, is George Soros; an investor who put $10,000 in his Quantum Fund in 1969 would have had about $21 million at the end of 1994.

In Britain, such people as James Goldsmith, Christopher Moran, Jacob Rogers, Jim Slater and Sir John Woolf also have long-term track records superior to the market.

Other investors who have beaten the averages over the long term include Thomas Knapp of Tweedy Browne and William Ruane of the Sequoia Fund, as well as former theatrical producer Arnold Bernhard, founder of the *Value Line Investment Survey* (tel: + 1–212–687–3965), and at least four other US newsletter publishers: Charles Allmon of *Growth Stock Outlook* (tel: + 1–301–654–5205), Al Frank of *The Prudent Speculator* (tel: + 1–505–983–0412), Norman Fosback of *Market Logic* (tel: + 1–305–421–1000) and Martin Zweig of the *Zweig Forecast* (tel: + 1–800–535–9649).

Forbes' yearly survey of mutual funds lists a number of money managers who have also outperformed the market averages over long periods, appearing regularly in the magazine's honour roll. In rebuttal, efficient market supporters say that such repeat winners are largely the result of statistical chance. "If you have 5,000 people in a room tossing coins," Malkiel argues, "there are going to be some that got 10 heads in a row."

But steady market performers neither flip coins nor imitate the blind choices of Malkiel's monkey – and their record has been consistent for three decades or longer. Scoring outstanding returns year-in year-out has nothing to do with luck. It involves hundreds of decisions a year. You can no more pile up a superlative investment record by accident than you can win a chess tournament by accident.

Second, a study by Pratt and DeVere in 1968 and one by Jaffee in 1974 showed that the officers and directors of listed US companies do much better than the public at trading shares of their own companies. Insider buys outperform insider sells. That's partly because the insiders exploit knowledge most other investors lack and partly because minimum holding periods set by law compel insiders to take a long-term view of the market. (In the late 1980s, however, investment newsletters that tracked insider transactions badly lagged the market, possibly because insiders favour low P/E stocks with smaller capitalizations and that style of investment was no longer in favor.)

Third, the efficient market theory holds that at any given moment most market parties have obtained and absorbed complete up-to-the-minute data on corporate earnings and the like – and then act on this basis. That notion becomes especially hard to swallow in a financial crisis. If the markets are so very efficient, how can shares be worth some 10 percent less on a Monday than on a Friday? Mike Royko made this point neatly in his column in *The Chicago Tribune* on 16 October 1989:

> It baffles me that one day a big corporation can be worth $10 billion. But a day or two later, it is suddenly worth only $8 billion. It is still making the same products that are selling for the same price in the same quantity. The same people are coming to work and getting the same paychecks. Yet, on paper, the company is worth far less today than it was yesterday.

The October 1987 US stock market debacle shook the foundations of the efficient market theory because it revealed that prior to the crash, the market did *not* obtain and incorporate all the essential information.

Fourth, as noted, the efficient market theory holds that over time professionals cannot do substantially worse than the market. But massive underperformance by the mass of investment professionals in both up and down markets reveals that this crucial assumption also fails to jibe with the facts. Surveys mentioned in the next chapter, which explains these dismal results, present a far different picture than that portrayed by the theorists.

The last flaw in the efficient market theory is that certain *methods* of investing consistently outperform the averages. Proponents of the theory claim professional traders will eradicate such "anomalies" over time, but that has yet to happen. Though it is well known that stocks generally rise more consistently in January than any other month, investors still don't buy more heavily in December.

Conversely, share prices fall in September far more often than they rise. Jeremy Siegel notes in "Calendar Anomalies," Chapter 17 of *Stocks for the Long Run*, that from 1890 through 1994 the Dow Jones industrial average or its predecessor fell in 63 Septembers, rising in only 41. September was in fact the only month with a losing record over the 104 years – and also the only month with a negative total return, i.e. including dividends. Records for the markets outside the United States are shorter and sketchier, but Siegel found that from 1970 through 1994, September was a loser in local currencies in all 20 markets he studied. Avoiding September clearly seems to be a trading method that improves returns. Buying and holding the Dow for 104 years would have turned $1 into $101. But an incompetent market timer who bought at the end of August each year and sold a month later would have seen that dollar dwindle to less than 25 cents. On the other hand, a timer astute enough to sell each year at the end of August and buy the shares back a month later would have racked up nearly $410, more than four times the gain posted by the buy-and-hold approach. Despite this well-documented September effect, no stock market as yet shows signs of significant selling at the end of August.

Even the major argument for the efficient market hypothesis has a logical flaw. The theory, we've seen, is based on the Brownian notion of a random walk, which holds that a share's future price is no more predictable than the path of a dust mote dancing in the rays of the sun. When statistical tests produced no evidence that past price changes in equities gave clues to future movements, researchers concluded that changes in equity prices are independent of each other. But the reasoning is defective. Failure to find a link between past and future equity prices by no means rules out the possibility that such links exist. These links are, in fact, visible both in market cycles and in the recurring concentration of large gains in short periods. More on this in a moment. As you can see, the gloomy notion of efficient markets has been shot full of holes, each admitting light.

How to find tomorrow's global winners

My criteria for selecting tomorrow's winners in the global equity sweepstakes are based upon twelve tried and tested exceptions to the "efficient market" theory:

- The investment return on small firms consistently outstrips the return on big ones.
- Stocks whose price is low relative to earnings tend to outperform stocks whose price-earnings ratio is high. (This criterion, oddly enough, works best for large firms.)

- A stock's price tends to rise after insider buying has been reported.
- Less-researched firms, no matter what their size, tend to produce higher returns.
- Emerging stock markets are especially inefficient in pricing securities, and so frequently offer superior profit potential.
- Stocks held primarily by individuals outperform those held mostly by institutions.
- A stock's price tends to rise if analysts jack up their consensus earnings estimate.
- The best-performing stocks are those which earn more than analysts expect.
- In seeking tomorrow's global winners, small size in a firm is more important than a low earnings multiple.
- In choosing companies whose shares are likely to produce superior returns, institutional neglect is even more important than small size.
- A stock priced at two-thirds or less of market net asset value per share tends to outperform its market.
- Closed-end mutual funds or investment trusts – those with a fixed number of shares – usually trade at a lower price than the underlying value of the shares they own. Buying deeply discounted closed-end funds would have yielded above-average results since World War II.

Have I now totally demolished the efficient market theory? I would hope not; for that would mean embracing the outdated notion that something is always either true or false. As Chapter 9 demonstrated, this Aristotelian logic is a clumsy tool in a world of half-truths.

Moreover, the notion of an efficient market itself embodies a paradox. In order for the theory to be true, investors have to go on trying to beat the market. And analysts by and large, despite evidence to the contrary, have to continue believing they can accurately forecast earnings. Market prices can promptly and fully reflect what is knowable about firms whose shares are traded only if investors seek to earn superior returns, steadily making honest and capable efforts to learn about those firms. If those efforts were abandoned, the whole house of cards would collapse. Quarrel with the efficient market hypothesis is thus a precondition for its survival. The efficient market theory intrinsically predicts that the majority of the investment community will disagree with its academic champions.

Not all the "inefficiencies" enumerated above will keep outperforming the averages. That's the big problem with basing decisions on past events: trends work in some years and not in others. In London, May is reputed to be a terrible month to invest. An adage in the City warns: "sell in May, don't come back till St Ledger's Day" – which, in the British horse-racing calendar, falls in September. Investors who still obey this 19th century adage, however, miss out on August: one of the best months for stocks in the UK since the end of World War I. Statistician David Schwartz, author of the *Schwartz Stock Market Handbook*, reports that from 1919 through 1994, August prices on the *Financial Times* 30 index rose 64 percent of the time. Further, if you had decided to follow historical price patterns and sell your UK shares at the beginning of May 1995, you would have missed out on a sharp market rise.

Technical and fundamental analysis

The two basic approaches to forecasting stock prices – technical and fundamental – have more in common than some of their adherents realize. Both schools of thought hold that the future is uncertain in a predictable way. Technical analysts, assuming history tends to repeat itself, chart market and stock-price movements, while fundamental analysts assume that at any given moment a share has an intrinsic value (based on its earnings potential) toward which it will eventually move.

In dealing with the future, as Mark Skousen notes in *Economics on Trial*, investors seem to fall into three categories. The first group believes perfect knowledge of the future is an attainable goal. These are often the technical analysts who believe stock markets are wholly rational, predictable and deterministic. They are convinced that recent trends, volume, momentum and other investment data reveal the precise future of stock prices, especially in the short run. Technical analysts may also rely on previous cycles or wave analysis to plot the future direction of prices. Some even go so far as to predict exact dates for economic events, such as the next depression, and specific price targets for equities. They strongly believe there is a direct correlation between markets and movements in such things as interest rates and the money supply. Technical analysts often have a background in physical sciences such as engineering, physics or mathematics, impelling them to hunt for mechanistic formulas. Today's cornucopia of computing power has made technical analysis more popular. Though not everyone can read a balance sheet, most investors can understand a chart.

The second group of investors, at the other extreme, considers markets totally irrational and unpredictable, both near and long term. These investors contend that knowledge of the future is totally unattainable. They believe the market knows and instantly discounts everything, while the individual knows nothing and is driven by popular manias. Random walk and efficient market advocates usually take this view.

Like Mark, I belong to a third group, which believes the truth is in the middle, somewhere between the extremes of perfect knowledge and no knowledge. Our knowledge of the markets and the future is by no means perfect. Neither is it totally imperfect. Though stock prices are not always predictable, sometimes they are quite predictable. Markets are neither totally efficient nor inefficient.

Conclusion: *Though equity markets are mostly efficient most of the time, they are also rife with "anomalies" offering opportunities to outperform the averages.*

Nonlinear models

Is there any approach that can help you find such "anomalies"? Yes. You can improve your chances of uncovering profitable "anomalies" by recognizing that the efficient market theory is sometimes true and sometimes false. The world's equity markets are efficient when relatively stable, which they are most of the time. Analysis of the Dow Jones index over a period of 90 years shows that, aside from the four days around the turn of each month when returns are abnormally large, the index generally falls. Such normal daily adjustments can be estimated by so-called linear models, in which a particular cause has only one effect. The Capital Asset Pricing Model (CAPM) discussed in Chapter 5, for example, relies on linear mathematics.

Linear relationships are simply the sum of their components, but social phenomena such as a stock market are vastly more complex. Abnormally large returns are clumped within the space of a few days in most stock markets, not just in New York. Though such market cycles clearly exist, their irregularity makes them invisible to the standard statistical techniques that do such a good job of describing a market's normal daily adjustments. The *significant* moves in markets – those crucial four days for instance – are *nonlinear*, with feedback loops between the various components, causing the whole to be more than the sum of its parts. *Then* the world's equity markets are inefficient.

Conclusion: *The significant moves in equity markets are non-linear.*

Alas, you can't know in advance whether the linear or non-linear model will apply. American humorist Will Rogers put this conundrum in a nutshell: "Don't gamble; take all your savings and buy some good stock, and hold it till it goes up, then sell it. If it don't go up, don't buy it."

Chaos theory

Figure 13.1 shows how deducting the returns produced in the best month in a five-year period for the S&P 500 reduces the annual return by 2.2 percent a year. Curiously, if this exercise is repeated by taking out the best three months annually in a run of 15 years, the reduction in annual return is 2.4 percent, and if the best six months annually are subtracted from a 30-year series, then the reduction is one of 2.6 percent a year.

This so-called "self-similarity" over different time periods is also found in other financial markets. It cannot be explained by the efficient market hypothesis, but is characteristic of a branch of nonlinear mathematics called chaos theory, where the recurrent pattern is known as a fractal. Fractal systems, such as the coastline of a country or the leaf of a fern, show similar patterns when examined at different scales. Researchers have also uncovered fractal patterns in the volatility of

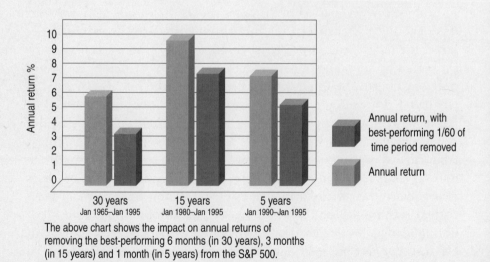

The above chart shows the impact on annual returns of removing the best-performing 6 months (in 30 years), 3 months (in 15 years) and 1 month (in 5 years) from the S&P 500.

Fig 13.1 Comparision of annual returns, Standard and Poor's 500

the foreign exchange market over different periods of time. The pattern of volatility over ten minutes is similar to the pattern across an hour, and similar again across a day. This fractal scaling has been shown to hold for periods up to two months and beyond.

Chaos theory, or "complexity theory," has thus become a popular buzz phrase. The theory states that in a complicated situation, with many inter-related variables, even if the causal link between these relationships is known and precisely defined, chaotic or random changes can still take place. Even if a previous situation seems to be repeating itself exactly, a tiny alteration of one variable can lead to a dramatically different outcome. In the 1960s, while running standard non-linear mathematical models of the atmosphere on his computer, meteorologist Edward N. Lorenz discovered that the output (a weather prediction) was wholly altered by minuscule changes of input data. These were equivalent to temperature differences of less than a thousandth of a degree or pressure variations like that produced by a single puff of air. This is known as the "butterfly effect," because the usual poetic example is that the flutter of a butterfly in Bolivia can cause a tornado in Tokyo.

Chaos theory has already had at least one useful by-product. It has introduced the financial world to nonlinearity – a broader term than chaos: the idea that in the real world events change not according to some predetermined formula, but in fits and starts under the impact of many different factors. The next chapter shows how nonlinear thinking can help you uncover profitable deviations from efficiency in the world's equity markets.

The theory of rational expectations

Random walk fatalists ignore the fundamental role of expectations in economic behaviour. Until the 1970s, economists, in a similar error, issued projections based on the past, in the belief tomorrow would be much like today. Next year's expected inflation rate might be a weighted average of current and past rates.

Here's an example of the pitfalls in extrapolating such trend lines: In 1960, there were 216 Elvis impersonators by unofficial count. In 1970, there were 2,400. By 1980, there were an estimated 6,300 Elvises. Assuming continuation of the trend, by the year 2010 one in four people will be an Elvis impersonator.

Economic behaviour is based on expectations. Economic projections based on trend lines presume people will go on behaving in the same way, believing what they know to be false. But when policies change, so do our expectations. Pointing this out in *Rational Expectations and Econometric Practice* won Robert Lucas the 1995 Nobel Prize.

Up until then, conventional economic models did not describe investors' behavior. Now, however, in "Asset Prices with Rational Beliefs," Professor Mordecai Kurz of Stanford University has devised an important new theory of asset pricing that neatly resolves many such discrepancies and conflicts. Just as Robert Lucas developed a theory of rational expectations for macroeconomic models, Kurz has created a theory of rational expectations for equities.

The crux of both theories is that people will maximize their own interests in the face of change, whether that change is in government policies or in the stock market. Unlike the random walk and efficient market advocates, Kurz does not need to assume irrational behavior by any market participants. He starts off by replacing the classical CAPM assumption that all investors possess the same beliefs about the future with the much more realistic assumption that their beliefs differ. The only restriction Kurz places on these beliefs is that they be "rational:" in harmony with available economic data. Given this assumption of diverse-yet-rational beliefs, Kurz argues that most stocks will generally be mispriced by the market. That's mainly because the market price reflects the interaction, or feedback, between investors, most of whose mental models about how the economy works – the notions underlying their differing forecasts – are wrong. The next chapter, "Mind over Market," explains why investors continue to cherish such invalid notions. It also provides several useful tips on how to identify and counter your own emotional bias.

Analysts' forecasts, by the way, are not nearly as wrong as they used to be. In the 1980s and early 1990s, analysts were inveterate optimists and you could count on them to whittle down their forecasts on US company earnings by about 1 percent each month. In the last few years, however, something has changed. Optimism has vanished, and accuracy has been uncanny. Since July 1 1993, the average monthly cut in forecasts for S&P 500 firms has been less than 0.1 percent. In 1994, forecasts remained unchanged on average from the beginning of January to the end of December. On a quarterly basis, analysts have become consistent pessimists. As I write, actual earnings have beaten expectations for 11 straight quarters by an average 4 percent.

Have analysts become more rational?

No. Companies have. Adapting to change, they've reversed their pressure on analysts. Rather than talk up quarterly forecasts, as the firms used to, they now often talk them down because of the impact of earnings surprise strategies. Companies have learned that beating per share earnings forecasts by a few cents helps their stock. Conversely, falling short by a few cents hurts. So companies now try to lower expectations. The analysts have simply remained pliable.

Conclusion: No system works all the time. Any technique that uncovers profit opportunities in equities – so-called "anomalies" in the efficient market – is likely to be ephemeral. As more people recognize that a technique is profitable, more will use it. More accurate and extensive research will be done on the "anomaly" until it vanishes. History is a guide, not a template.

Barring a change in the economic environment, the trend towards more accurate estimates seems likely to continue. "Accounting Valuation, Market Expectation, and the Book-to-Market Effect," a recent IBES study by Frankel and Lee, shows that analysts' predictable optimism helped explain the better performance of value stocks from 1975 to 1993.

But adjoining both sides of the millenium, as expectations become more conservative, growth should do well relative to value. Therefore, a moderate shift to growth stocks is now somewhat more acceptable. But not the growth stocks everyone else is buying. Remember Templeton's estimable maxim: "If you buy the same securities as other people, you will have the same results as other people." More on Sir John in a moment.

Growth versus value

Benjamin Graham advised buying stocks for no more than a third more than their tangible asset value. Each stock, he said, should also have a reasonable P/E ratio, a sufficiently strong financial position and the prospect that earnings will at least be maintained in coming years. Investors willing to forego brilliant prospects – i.e. better than average expected growth – should have no difficulty, Graham declared, in finding a wide selection of stocks meeting this definition of value.

While a "value" investor, as Chapter 8 noted, seeks stocks that are low-priced in terms of a firm's assets or ability to make money, a "growth" investor typically buys higher P/E stocks with earnings in a strong uptrend. Graham defined a growth stock as one which has increased its per-share earnings in the past at well above the average rate for stocks generally, and is expected to continue doing so in future. Such equities are obviously attractive to buy and retain – if you can get them at a decent price. Alas, growth stocks usually sell at steep, even excessive, earnings multiples.

"International Value and Growth Stock Returns," a study by Capaul, Rowley and Sharpe, examined the returns on growth stocks (with high price to book ratios) and on value stocks (with low price to book ratios) in six markets from January 1981 through June 1992. In all these countries – France, Germany, Switzerland, the UK, Japan and the US – value stocks, the so-called "dogs," did better on average than growth stocks. More on such contrarian strategies in the next chapter.

If you manage a pension fund *anywhere*, however, you may find your trustees look askance at an equity portfolio stuffed with unpopular value stocks bumping along the bottom of the market. Still, that's where the big potential gains lie, not in the growth or glamour stocks of the day.

Okay. We've established that stocks whose price is low relative to earnings tend to outperform stocks whose price-earnings ratio is high. Yet somehow stocks trading at stratospheric earnings multiples are often deemed "safe" representatives of "growth." Let's examine this common fallacy.

What would happen if, year after year for a dozen years, you bought and held the hottest stock on the New York Stock Exchange? Simple. You would get burned. Take the stocks with the highest P/E ratios on the New York Stock Exchange in April of each year from 1982 to 1994. As a whole, these equities, widely praised at the time and eagerly bought by seasoned investors and novices alike, lost 32 percent of their value even in a strongly rising market. Over the same period, the average stock in the S&P 500 rose 95 percent.

Do growth stocks eventually justify their high prices? This question was addressed in 1995 by Professor Jeremy J. Siegel of the Wharton School of Philadelphia in the *Journal of Portfolio Management*. He studied the previous era of high P/E ratios, the early 1970s, when issues like IBM, Polaroid and McDonald' were called "one-decision" stocks, because the only rational investment decision you would ever have to make was to buy them. Selling them was out of the question.

Siegel based his research on a list of 50 such stocks compiled by Morgan Guaranty Trust Co. in the mid-1970s that also included such household names as Disney, Xerox, Gillette and Coca-Cola. On average, the 50 stocks traded at 42 times earnings at the market top at the end of 1972. Over the next two years, the Dow Jones industrial average plunged 45 percent but the Nifty Fifty glamor stocks plummeted much further and continued to languish through the rest of the decade. Given the extraordinary magnitude of the 1973–1974 losses and the failure of these issues to rebound during the rest of the 1970s, it is unlikely that many of them proved to be "one-decision" investments. Most investors probably dumped them.

Nearly a quarter of a century later, Siegel, in the painless role of academic historian, examined how the game ultimately played out. He concluded that most of the stocks eventually justified the lofty P/E ratios paid for them in late-1972. From December 1972 through May 1995, the Nifty Fifty gave their investors an annualized total return of 10 percent, just 1 percent less than the total return of all NYSE, Amex and Nasdaq stocks. Of course, any investor who held on for that quarter of a century incurred more risk than the market and suffered below-average returns. Not to mention sleepless nights. In the "short" term, bourses have a wicked way of correcting – even overcorrecting – those stocks priced far above average.

Ultimately, P/E ratios must be justified by future earnings growth – a fact to bear firmly in mind when you contemplate buying so-called growth issues selling like hot cakes at 30 to 60 times earnings. The trap in the growth approach is its lack of any visible ceiling on share prices. An increase of 1 or 2 percent in long-term growth assumptions can readily justify a 20 percent rise in price. While a market priced on value criteria is restrained by historical levels of, say, yield or price/book ratio, growth managers – given enough liquidity – can soar into the stratosphere more or less at will. Thus, with the US market recently above 5,000 on the Dow, dividend yield has been eliminated as an investment consideration. Coca-Cola, for instance, yields little more than 1 percent.

Conclusion: A portfolio with an investment horizon of less than a quarter of a century should avoid equities selling at the highest earnings multiples, no matter how attractive they may seem.

The value approach now also has a trap. Today's investment community simply divides the universe of stocks into two equal camps – growth and value. Standard & Poor's maintains two indexes to track growth and value stocks. It defines growth stocks as those in the S&P 500 with the greatest price and earnings momentum. The value half is everything else. "This," as Mark Hulbert observed recently in *Forbes*, "is a travesty of Graham's approach. It simply assumes that half of the stock market always will satisfy the definition of value." Obviously, you're better off defining value yourself.

Conclusion: Potential gains are higher in unpopular "value" stocks than in the more popular "growth" or glamour stocks of the day.

The danger in estimates

Just as the Hindu goddess Kali both destroys life and gives it, the focus on earnings estimates is a doubled-edged sword. In the past, as Graham observed in a 1958 talk at the University of California in Los Angeles, the speculative elements of a stock resided almost exclusively in the company itself: uncertainties or weakness in the sector or the firm. Such speculative factors still exist today of course, but they've been tempered by the contemporary preference for capital appreciation.

In reprisal, however, a new and major element of speculation has been introduced into the equation: today's heavy emphasis on future expectations. Old-time equity investors did not care a fig for capital gains. They bought almost entirely for safety and income, and let speculators worry about price appreciation. Today, however, the shrewd and experienced investor pays less attention to dividend return and more to long-term gain. "Yet one might argue," said Graham in his speech, "that precisely because the old-time investor did not concentrate on future capital appreciation he was virtually guaranteeing to himself that he would have it, at least in the field of industrial stocks. And, conversely, today's investor is so concerned with anticipating the future that he is already paying handsomely for it in advance." The danger, Graham went on to say, is that even an accurate earnings estimate may not bring today's investor any profit, while one that falls short may well bring a loss.

Detecting hidden worth

In this environment, I believe a prudent investor should devote part of a portfolio to equities that have managed to avoid the impact of earnings estimates. Neglected shares are less subject to exaggerated expectations concerning their price. By seeking hidden worth, you can often buy good prospects at a discount. That, in a nutshell, is the logic underlying one of this book's major conclusions: namely that shares and countries ignored by institutions can provide individual investors with superior returns. It's also why I urge you to seek value among the "wallflowers:" those stocks throughout the world followed by few analysts and owned by few institutions.

Waltzing the wallflowers

You can benefit both from the analysts' neglect of certain securities and from their positive bias towards others. Wallflowers, the shares neglected by analysts, generally outperform those whose dance cards are full. Waltzing the wallflowers can in fact be highly profitable. In the 1970–1979 decade, neglected firms paid off far more lavishly than those that were highly researched. The most poorly followed shares in the S&P 500 Index had a yearly return, with dividends, of 16.4 percent, versus only 9.4 percent for the favourites. This pattern, enumerated by Arbel and Strebel in the Winter 1983 issue of *The Journal of Portfolio Management*, was reaffirmed from 1971 to 1981, when institutionally neglected shares in the S&P 500 had a total yearly return of 20.84 percent, versus 10.36 percent for the favourites. The latter study, by Arbel, Carvell and Strebel, appeared in the May/June 1983 issue of the *Financial Analysts Journal*. These findings should encourage you to check out any wallflowers that fit within the constraints and parameters of your own portfolio.

When a wallflower demonstrates a persistent high growth rate and also sells for a low multiple of estimated earnings, both one and two years out, I recommend it. Obviously, therefore, I too emphasize future earnings. But I do not share the belief – common these days – that promising companies automatically sell at high price-earnings ratios.

Conclusion: Wallflowers, the shares neglected by analysts, generally outperform those whose dance cards are full. To combine the growth and value styles, buy highly profitable companies selling at a discount. That will provide strong earnings growth at a bargain price.

Evaluating profitability

How to measure earnings? When two equities are listed in different countries, it can be hard to tell a golden goose from a dead duck. The

1993 US annual report of Daimler–Benz, one of the few German companies to adhere to US accounting standards (because it was forced to raise money in the US) showed a $1.06 billion annual loss (DM 1.8 billion). But under German accounting rules, Daimler reported a $354 million profit (DM 615 million).

Reporting frameworks governing the definition of earnings remain stubbornly nationalistic. To an accountant, "earnings" is merely a word, which as Humpty Dumpty explains in *Through the Looking Glass*, "means just what I choose it to mean – neither more nor less."

A character in William Saroyan's prize-winning play, *The Time of Your Life*, sits at a table muttering: "No foundation – all the way down the line." That's an apt description of global bookkeeping. The term "commonly accepted accounting standards," generic to annual reports, is a flagrant oxymoron. A survey by Vinod Bavishi, published at the end of 1995 by the US-based Center for International Financial Analysis and Research (CIFAR), solemnly concluded: "In spite of worldwide efforts...to harmonize financial reporting practices, the form and substance of published annual reports varies significantly." Even in Europe, with the deadline for a unified market long past, standardized financial reporting remains mostly a pious hope.

Do accounting standards matter? Of course. In theory, you as an investor buy equity to share in a firm's earnings. A company either passes these on in the form of dividends, or, if it retains profits to invest in new projects, you take your reward indirectly in the form of capital gains. Your challenge is to find out what a firm is really earning.

That's no easy task. Japanese and German companies tend to understate profits to escape taxes. On the other hand, British and US firms are sufficiently nervous of their shareholders to prefer the opposite approach. British firms generally report higher profits than companies in other European countries, purely as a result of different accounting practices.

Cost of sales

There are, for instance, two basic methods of measuring the cost of sales: Fifo (first-in-first-out) and Lifo (last-in-first-out). If prices of inputs and outputs are constant, Lifo and Fifo give the same results. But here in the real world, where prices rise continually, Fifo produces higher profits for a given level of sales than Lifo. British companies must use Fifo.

Inventory

Then there's inventory, which can be valued either at cost or at current value. Valued at cost, its worth is understated in the balance sheet. (I assume here that most companies are enterprising enough eventually to sell inventory for more than its cost.) But inventory written up to current value raises the cost of stocks taken into next year's profit and loss account, and so lowers profit. British companies normally value inventory at cost, thus generally understating its value.

Depreciation

German firms follow unique depreciation rules that let them dramatically undervalue assets, thus building up hidden reserves and lowering stated profits. British firms, on the other hand, generally set aside less through depreciation and other discretionary provisions than do companies on the continent.

The lower UK write-offs also tend to raise stated profits. Whether these accounting practices are used to make profits look higher or lower depends on a firm's circumstances. Germans, for instance, save more of their income than most other Europeans. Because of that huge pool of savings, German firms do not have to compete so keenly for investment funds so there is less pressure to produce high returns. German firms can thus make their profits look lower and flatten out cyclical trends. In Britain, by contrast, fierce competition for savings puts a heavy burden on firms to deliver the kind of performance that attracts investors.

Goodwill

The treatment of goodwill is another clear example of the potential impact of differences in accounting principles. In an acquisition accounted for as a purchase, any difference between the price paid for the net assets and their fair value is usually recognized as an intangible asset called goodwill. In the US, this merger premium must be amortized as an expense over a period not to exceed 40 years. The result is an ongoing drain on reported earnings. In the UK, the preferred accounting treatment is to write off goodwill directly to reserves, leaving reported earnings virtually unscathed. This accounting difference can give UK firms an edge over US firms in bidding for acquisitions.

Deferred taxes

Other disparities in accounting principles can also impact the bottom line in opposite ways across borders. Recognition of deferred taxes as a current expense item is permitted in the US and the UK, but disallowed in Germany, Sweden and Switzerland. Earnings in the latter countries may thus be biased upward by such taxes.

Reserves

Another disparity: general purpose, or purely discretionary, reserves are not allowed in the US or the UK, but are commonplace in Germany, Switzerland, Japan and elsewhere. Reported earnings in countries that allow such reserves may tend to be understated. What is more, many leading banks in Europe and Asia shift money in and out of secret reserves without accounting for them. German banks are prime offenders.

Disclosure

The US is alone in requiring quarterly reports of its large, publicly traded firms. Most of the rest of the world requires only semiannual or annual reporting. As a result, comparisons of first, second and third-quarter reports between US firms and other firms are basically ruled out.

Audiences

Accounts in different countries are meant for different audiences. In Britain, the aim is to provide a "true and fair view" for investors. The US has no less than *three* sets of accounting rules: one for external reporting, one for regulatory agencies and one for figuring taxes. In Germany, Italy and Japan, accounting principles are said to be "tax-driven," as there is no distinction between the three principles. Firms that have this tradition of supplying only one "correct" accounting statement naturally resist preparing a second and potentially confusing one.

Emerging markets

In emerging markets, the big problem is lax standards rather than differences in approach. Although countries such as Chile have stiffer rules on disclosure of financial information than the US, others, such as South Korea, are notably casual. Korean firms do not have to consolidate results of subsidiaries, so there is room for creative bookkeeping. Foreigners, hoping Korea will be the new Japan, have put up with standards of disclosure that would not have been tolerated in Japan in the sixties and seventies, when consolidated accounting was not required there.

Adjusting P/E ratios

In 1992, investment firm Morgan Stanley worked out how much cheaper European stocks would appear if the firms prepared their accounts according to British rules. The stocks would appear cheaper because their stated profits would tend to be larger. For instance, if German firms used British accounting practices, the German stock market's price/earnings ratio would sink from 14.8 to 9.87. Table 13.1 shows other examples from Morgan Stanley's study.

Table 13.1 Two ledgers for price/earnings ratios

	Unadjusted	Adjusted
Britain	14.40	14.40
Belgium	11.10	7.68
France	12.10	9.68
Germany	14.80	9.87
Holland	13.60	9.52
Italy	14.00	13.00
Spain	9.10	6.25
Sweden	14.70	9.78
Switzerland	15.40	9.90

Real prospective price/earnings ratios 1992, before and after adjustment to British accounting standards.

As "Adam Smith" says in *Supermoney*: "The numbers may or may not mean what they say."

Conclusion: *Earnings reports should be taken with a grain or more of salt, especially when trying to compare firms across national borders.*

Comparing firms across borders

Is the company that makes the most money the most profitable? By this yardstick, according to Evan Davis and John Kay in *"Assessing Corporate Performance,"* Royal Dutch was the world's most successful concern in 1989.

Or is the world's most successful concern the one with the highest profits as a proportion of sales and assets? That would put Brazilian mining company Vale do Rio Doce at the top of the list. US oil firm Lyondell Petrochemical, which racked up the most profits per employee and the highest return on equity, might also claim the title.

All these definitions of profitability have drawbacks. Though giant Royal Dutch made the most money, its profits relative to sales were only one-sixth of those posted by Rio Doce. Measuring profit as a percentage of sales discriminates against businesses with high turnovers and low margins. Supermarkets and large retailers, no matter how successful, will also do badly under this definition.

Using profits per employee is no more reliable. Resource industries, such as oil and mining, are much less labour-intensive than services and so will look more successful on this count.

Measuring profit as return on total net assets discriminates against banks, property firms and utilities, which are highly capital-intensive. Service and drug companies, on the other hand, have few assets and will usually score better on this measure of profitability.

Return on equity

Return on equity, which the lip-lazy call ROE, is a somewhat better measure of a company's underlying profitability. This percentage return on equity is calculated by dividing net income by shareholder equity. ROE tells you how much a company earns per dollar of equity that shareholders have contributed. Return on equity can be inflated with debt leverage, so you should look for companies with modest debt . . . or, better still, no debt at all. A return on equity above 15 percent, with little debt, traditionally indicates strong profitability and good management . . . especially when high ROE has been sustained for a number of years.

Here's a common oversight: simply investing in a company with a low P/E relative to growth in earnings per share. This approach ignores the *base* of those earnings. A firm earning 25 percent on its equity is plainly a better bargain than one earning only 1 percent. Also measuring profit as return on equity or net assets will set things aright.

But measuring profit relative to net equity or total assets has a pitfall too. Both net equity and total assets tend to be valued at historic cost rather than their current market price, and so can distort a firm's financial health. The belief that profit depends on capital employed is deeply ingrained. It was the abiding theme of Karl Marx's *Das Kapital*. But there is no more reason that profit should be expressed relative to capital than relative to any other input.

Fed up with this maze, leading institutions and fund managers are turning away from traditional measures of earnings and capital employed. Quite rightly, too. The only meaningful way to rank firms worldwide is balancing the books by the same set of accounting rules. Here is a practical and increasingly popular cross-border method of separating well-managed and highly profitable companies from all the chaff.

Cash flow

When you compare a firm's price per share to an estimate of its free cash flow per share, it matters little how national accountants handle such non-cash items as goodwill or deferred tax. For the global investor, therefore, cash flow is one of the best measures of a firm's profitability. To determine it, you need the cash flow statement from a recent annual report, such as that of Philips (see Figure 13.2). Now you simply add net income, depreciation and amortization and subtract total dividends, capital expenditures and payments on long-term debt.

The consolidated statements of cash flow tell you that in 1994 Philips had net after-tax income of 2,125 million guilders, conventionally written f2,125 million because the guilder used to be called a florin. Depreciation and amortization came to f3,231 million. These two figures add up to f5,356 million, with net adjustments of f327 million bringing net cash generated by operating activities down to f5,029.

Dividends paid totalled f164 million and capital expenditures f3,541 million. Payments on long-term debt were f4,222 million, but as f3,325 of new long-term debt was issued, net retirement of long-term debt amounted to only f897 million. Dividends, capital expenditures and net payment on long-term debt add up to f4,602 million. Adjustments of f167 million arising from the net balance of divestments and other purchases reduce the cash used for financing activities to f4,435. Deducting this net amount from f5,029 gives us a total cash flow of f594 million.

At the end of 1994, according to the annual report, Philips had 338.5 million shares outstanding, so cash flow came to f1.75 per share. The shares were trading at f50, putting the ratio of price to cash flow at 28.6: a figure you can easily compare across borders. This

	1994	1993
Consolidated statements of cash flows of the Philips group in 1994		
in millions of Dutch guilders		
Cash flows from operating activities:		
Net income	2,125	1,965
Adjustments to reconcile net income to net cash generated by operating activities:		
Depreciation and amortization of (in)tangible fixed assets	3,321	3,203
Net gain on divestments	(235)	(1,593)
(Increase) decrease in working capital	(480)	2,269
Increase (decrease) in provisions	234	(316)
Income of unconsolidated companies (net of dividends)	(285)	(3)
Income of other group equity (net dividends)	253	134
Other adjustments	186	75
Net cash generated by operating activities	5,029	5,734
Cash flows from investing activities:		
Purchase of intangible fixed assets	(54)	(96)
Capital expenditures	(3,541)	(2,576)
Proceeds from disposal of (in)tangible fixed assets	544	689
Purchase of other non-current financial assets	(301)	(187)
Proceeds from other non-current financial assets	579	282
Purchase of interests in businesses	(553)	(1,173)
Proceeds from sale of interests in businesses	206	3,939
Net cash (required for) generated by investing activities	(3,120)	878
Financing surplus before financing activities	1,900	6,612
Cash flows from financing activities:		
Decrease in short-term debt	(392)	(4,803)
Payments of long-term debt	(4,222)	(3,037)
Proceeds from issuance of long-term debt	3,325	1,803
Payments of conversion certificates	-	(554)
Effect of other financial transactions	-	599
Share issue and treasury stock transactions	138	27
Dividends paid	(164)	-
Net cash used for financing activities	(1,315)	(5,965)
Cash flow	594	647
Effect of changes in exchange rates and consolidations on cash positions	(92)	17
Cash and cash equivalents at beginning of year	2,322	1,658
Cash and cash equivalents at end of year	2,824	2,322

Fig. 13.2 Consolidated statements of cash flows of the Philips group in 1994.

method enables you to rank firms worldwide in terms of their capacity to generate long-term cash flow in excess of the costs of capital.

The notion behind cash-flow analysis is that net inflow and outflow of real money – not some accountant's abstraction called earnings – is the best measure of corporate profitability. The key point is not stated profits, but actual profitability. Instead of thinking of cash flow as net income plus depreciation, it is more useful to think of it as a net flow figure coming from customers, after allowing for cash expenses including taxes. Positive cash flow tells you that a company is living within its means, with money left over after paying the bills.

The lower the cash-flow multiple, the more earnings power you get for your money. Alas, the cash-flow multiple doesn't tell you how effectively that power is being used. A firm can generate good cash flow year after year, yet remain in the red. Its earnings power can be misapplied or diverted. Ambitious acquisitions may fail to pay off. Technological changes may demand heavy capital investment. The company may have to defend itself against protracted and expensive product liability suits.

This reveals a weakness in cash-flow analysis: depreciation – the big gap between cash flow and earnings – is often a legitimate charge, reflecting expenditures that will ultimately be necessary to replace capital assets such as plant and equipment. In a going concern, the bulk of the cash flow must be used to keep the company going, including paying off debt. For these reasons, cash flow per share is a tool in many ways inferior to net earnings per share. You can use earnings per share as a measure of your return on the price you paid for a stock. You can relate earnings per share to the share's current price to see how the market values the stock, either in terms of earnings multiple or current return. You can relate net earnings per share to dividends per share to see quickly what portion of current earnings has been paid out and what portion retained in the business.

Though cash flow will tell you none of these things, it nevertheless remains a handy tool for cross-border profitability comparison.

The information needed for cash flow computations on individual stocks is all available in annual reports, as well as in most comprehensive stock services, which in the US include *Value Line* and *Standard & Poor's*.

Conclusion: *The ratio of a stock's price to cash flow measures profitability across borders better than do price/earnings or price/sales ratios and the ratio of earnings to a firm's total assets or shareholders'* *equity. But cash flow ignores such expenses as depreciation, amortization and debt retirement that are needed to keep a company going.*

The bottom line

How good is cash flow in selecting winning equities? A study by Kenneth Hackel, Joshua Livnat and Atul Rai in the *Financial Analysts Journal* found it to be an excellent predictive tool that combines the benefits of growth and value investing. The three researchers devised a stock-selection system based on cash flow and applied it to all NYSE, Amex and OTC stocks for the 14 years from 1978 through 1991.

Stocks were included in the simulated portfolio at the end of each year if they met five criteria:

- Market capitalization between $50 million and $2 billion. This focuses on small and medium-size firms, eliminating both the big oaks and little acorns.
- Positive four-year average cash flow. This identifies firms that have steadily been able to generate cash to finance growth.
- A growth rate higher than 5 percent in cash flow over the past four years. This identifies growth companies.
- Total debt, both short and long term, of less than ten times average cash flow over the last four years. This eliminates firms heavy with debt, assuring there is an adequate margin of borrowing resources in reserve to finance growth.
- Current stock price between 5 and 20 times average cash flow over the last four years. This is a strange criterion. Excluding stocks with price/cash flow ratios above 20 obviously eliminates high-priced equities in much the same way that excluding high P/E ratios eliminates overvalued equities. But eliminating firms with price/cash flow multiples under 5 appears also to eliminate extremely undervalued equities with high potential returns.

Be that as it may, the average annual compound return on the stocks that passed this screening was 22.7 percent. That's about 40 percent better than the US market, which over this period rose at a well above-average rate.

Allowing for 2 percent commissions to buy and 2 percent commissions to sell, the cumulative 14-year return would have totalled 995 percent, or 18.6 percent a year. At that rate, $10,000 grows to

$109,495 in 14 years. The researchers found that this strategy works for a global portfolio as well, producing "superior returns on a portfolio of small firms with stable free cash flows, low debt and low free cash flow multiples."

THE BARGAIN MARKETS

Adjusting for value

Once you've selected countries in terms of correlation, as set out in Chapter 11, you naturally want to tilt your portfolio towards the most promising markets and shares. In other words, adjust your weightings for *value*. To accomplish this next step in asset allocation, global equity managers usually follow one of three methods: top-down, bottom-up – or a combination of both.

Bottom-up

A bottom-up investor believes superior stock selection – not market selection – is the key to superior returns in all the world's stock markets. The bottom-up investor picks promising shares, without regard to the allocation between industry or country. After assembling the initial equity portfolio, this investor may optimize it to reflect benchmark weightings and other factors.

The bottom-up approach places a relatively low priority on the analysis of macroeconomic factors, such as political and currency risk or government monetary policies, whose significance may only become apparent when the equities are aggregated into country portfolios. A true bottom-up investor believes that superior stock selection, and not market selection, is the key to superior returns in all the world's stock markets. A number of subjects treated in this book, including beta, the Capital Asset Pricing Model, country correlations and covariance in return among securities, are largely ignored by bottom-up investors, who tend simply to focus on two variables: price and value. One highly successful such investor is Sir John Templeton.

In 1939, just after war had broken out in Europe, a young man who had partly financed his Yale education from poker winnings borrowed

$10,000 to invest in small capitalization stocks, allocating an equal amount to each holding. He told his broker to buy $100 worth of every single stock on the New York and American exchanges selling for no more than a dollar a share.

Later, Sir John Templeton, older and wiser, refused to invest with borrowed money. Today, moreover, the asset allocation of his fund family is determined not by equal weights but by the location of bargains, while the funds themselves have grown so huge that they are compelled to invest only in larger companies.

The stock selection process at the organization bearing Sir John's name is in fact a perfect example of the bottom-up approach. At its Edinburgh headquarters, the Templeton group screens a global universe of roughly 15,000 equities. Between 800 and 1,000 of these are then taken up in its global research database, after which the portfolio managers identify those stocks meeting the firm's investment criteria on value and price. The value analysis involves an earnings forecast, based on sales growth, margin analysis and currency impact, and study of the balance sheet, any restructuring and adjusted asset value. The price analysis determines if the stock is cheap relative to its historic price, its industry globally, other stocks in the global database and other stocks in its own market. From the database, managers select the 70 or 80 companies with the most potential for the portfolio. Equities are sold if they approach their target price, or their fundamentals deteriorate, or there is substantially greater value in another name on the "bargain" list.

The Templeton group does not try to forecast market movements by means of an economic model. Its managers compare industries worldwide, rather than countries, and buy cheap stocks with no reference to asset allocation among markets, currencies or industries. No effort is made to time markets or to hedge currencies. Nor is there any predetermined allocation to cash; the cash levels rise automatically when there are fewer bargains.

In its purest form, bottom-up investment assumes that a large enough basket of stocks will be diverse enough to minimize the risks of individual markets. But this is not always the case. Let's say you screen 4,000 stocks so as to create a portfolio with a probable annual return of 20 percent over the next five years. This methodology might well create a portfolio concentrated in only four or five countries, thus exposing you to excessive political and economic risk.

Top-down

In contrast, a top-down investor views market selection – not stock selection – as the key to superior returns. The top-down investor believes nations with prospects of the strongest economic growth will have the strongest stock market performance and chooses shares largely in those markets. A rising tide lifts all the boats, so the top-down investor zeros in on those countries whose economic tide promises to rise most rapidly. The top-down investor (or investment committee) starts with aggregate macroeconomic data, such as fore-cast GNP/GDP growth, currency exchange rates, interest rates and money supply growth, to forecast the return for each stock market over a given period. The top-down investor then overweights stock markets with the highest expected rate of return and underweights stock markets that are forecast to perform poorly.

A good example of the top-down approach is the asset allocation process at investment managers Foreign & Colonial. Each month, its country fund managers write an analysis of the local economic, politi-cal and market scene. An investment team in London then reviews these analyses and produces a global asset allocation, based on over-weight, underweight and neutral positions with regard to the relevant benchmark. The fund managers then implement the asset allocation decisions in their individual markets, working from a selected list of equities that have been analyzed and visited by members of the team.

Another top-down method merely emphasizes countries that combine relatively strong economic growth with a strong currency. This decidedly simple method is currently popular in the Netherlands, which has repeat-edly met these two criteria in recent years. "Reflections of Reality," a study by Ned Davis Research, shows the validity of this technique: from 31 January 1967 through 31 January 1994 the G-7 countries with the strongest currencies had stronger economic growth, lower inflation and lower interest rates than those countries with the weakest currencies.

Still another top-down method exploits a fact noted in Chapter 8: countries with the most vigourous economic growth often include those freeing their economies from state control. Essentially, economic freedom concerns property rights and choice. The best attempt to date to define and measure it, *Economic Freedom of the World: 1975–1995*, by Walter Block, James Gwartney and Robert Lawson, produced strong evidence that economic freedom helps a country grow more quickly. Their research into 102 countries over two decades showed that the more economic freedom a country had in that period, the more prosperous it became.

The chief advantages of the top-down approach are that adequate country diversification can be assured and currency and political risks properly monitored. The chief disadvantage is that very little research shows any correlation at all between market performance and changes in GDP/GNP in the world's stock markets. Though the stock market is well known as the best leading indicator of an economy, top-down investors turn reality on its head by trying to use past statistics on the economy as the leading indicator of a stock market. Moreover, the world's stock markets are not a simple mirror of macroeconomic projections. A 1994 study by Dropsy and Nazarian-Ibrahimi in the *International Review of Economics and Finance* shows that anticipated economic policies in 11 industrialized countries failed to predict real equity returns for more than two decades.

A second disadvantage of the top-down approach is its implicit assumption that monitoring country exposure automatically assures adequate diversification across industries, which is not always the case. Moreover, most GDP/GNP projections have to be taken with a grain of salt. The figures ignore much of the real world, such as volunteer work, child care and other work at home, while including the cost of creating pollution, building prisons and the fees of divorce lawyers: items that seem more to reflect social breakdown than economic progress. National income statistics were not originally intended in fact as a yardstick of economic progress. They were pioneered in Britain and France in the late 17th century to gauge the scope for raising taxes. The precise numbers that emerge are arbitrary and almost meaningless. In December 1996, for instance, the US is to change its basis of statistics, rewriting economic history at a stroke. Over the past five years, US GDP has grown by 3.1 percent – or maybe by 2.6 percent, depending on which system you use.

Ideally, official statistics should be timely, accurate, and comprehensive. But those put out by some emerging markets are nothing of the kind. In early December 1994, just before Mexico devalued its peso, the latest published foreign reserve figures were those for June, suggesting that Mexico had a comfortable cushion of $17 billion. In fact, by December those reserves had already dwindled to $6 billion. Also in December 1994, Brazil's preliminary statistics put its trade deficit at

$47 million, but within a few weeks this was revised to a massive $900 million. Some countries seem to fiddle their trade figures deliberately. In March 1995, China's official 12-month inflation rate had supposedly fallen from October 1994, yet, added together, the monthly changes over the same period showed inflation had not dropped.

The final flaw is in the forecasts themselves: economic growth generally falls short of projections while inflation tends to exceed projections. The OECD admits that random walk forecasts were superior to its *World Economic Outlook* projections of both growth and inflation from 1971 through 1991. From 1980 through 1994, GDP estimates of the US Federal Reserve Board Open Market Committee, which is in the unique position of being able to use monetary policy to influence the events it projects, were roughly on the mark only a third of the time. And that was no worse than the leading private forecasters as a group. Perhaps economists state economic growth projections to the nearest percentage point merely to prove they have a sense of humor.

Combination methods

Some investors combine the top-down and bottom-up approaches, using economic data to identify promising countries, but emphasizing individual stock selection within each market.

IDENTIFYING THE RIGHT COUNTRIES

Rapid economic growth

As the rate of growth in gross domestic product – total output of goods and services – reflects a country's economic strength, albeit imperfectly, it generally moves in the same direction as corporate earnings. As we've seen, however, a rising GDP does not always herald a rising stock market. (I'll come back to the relationship between the economy and the stock market in a moment.)

All forecasts should carry a government health warning, but some are less dangerous than others. Among the less dangerous, despite their inferiority to random walk forecasts, are the GDP projections provided in June and December by the *OECD Economic Outlook*. These are reported in the press, and monthly by *The Economist*, whose own September 1995 poll of forecasters projected these percentage changes in real GDP for 1996 (Table 13.2).

Table 13.2 GDP Projections for 1996 from a poll by *The Economist*

Australia	3.0
Austria	2.5
Belgium	2.4
Britain	2.8
Canada	2.5
Denmark	2.9
France	2.8
Germany	2.5
Holland	2.6
Italy	2.9
Japan	1.8
Spain	3.2
Sweden	2.3
Switzerland	2.3
USA	2.4

Ratio of valuation to growth

One combination method of identifying promising countries is to examine how next year's estimated P/E for a country compares to that market's projected growth rate. In other words, how expensive are stocks considering the growth expected? Economic growth can be forecast in terms of GDP or in terms of corporate earnings. Despite shortcomings, either growth projection can be useful in identifying attractive markets.

To use a GDP projection to identify promising markets, just divide it into the forward P/E ratio of that country's average stock. A forward price/earnings ratio compares current stock prices to anticipated corporate earnings for the coming 12 months. The forward price/earnings ratio of numerous countries is supplied by such services as First Call and the Institutional Brokers System (IBES), whose August 1995 issue projected these price/earnings ratios for 1996 (Table 13.3).

Using GDP growth

Dividing the forward price/earnings ratio of the average stock by a country's expected GDP growth gives you one version of what can be called a Value/Growth Index. The lower the ratio between a country's forward P/E ratio and its expected GDP growth, the more its stock market seems a bargain (Table 13.4).

Table 13.3 P/E Projections for 1996 from IBES

Australia	12.1
Austria	12.8
Belgium	9.8
Britain	12.4
Canada	11.2
Denmark	11.6
France	13.0
Germany	17.3
Holland	11.0
Italy	15.7
Japan	42.0
Spain	10.6
Sweden	8.8
Switzerland	13.4
USA	13.0

Table 13.4 Value/growth index for 1996, based on GDP projections

Spain	3.31
Denmark	4.00
Australia	4.03
Belgium	4.08
Holland	4.23
Britain	4.43
Canada	4.48
France	4.64
Austria	5.12
USA	5.42
Sweden	5.83
Italy	6.04
Germany	6.92
Switzerland	6.96
Japan	23.33

In countries nearer the top of the above list, high growth is being bought for a lesser price. Other things being equal, investments in these countries should show a better long-term return than those nearer the bottom. Similar rankings for other markets as shown (Table 13.5).

This system is used by David Muller in *Foreign Markets Advisory*. Though his sources of raw data are sometimes unclear (perhaps because he once worked for the CIA), I often agree with Muller's opinion of which markets are most attractive.

Table 13.5 Value/growth index for 1996, based on GDP projections

Turkey	0.29
Poland	1.12
South Korea	1.34
Hong Kong	1.63
Brazil	1.83
Indonesia	1.84
Thailand	1.89
Taiwan	1.94
Malaysia	2.01
Singapore	2.04
Chile	2.21
India	2.22
Czechia	2.41
Israel	3.00
Hungary	3.00
Philippines	3.57
South Africa	3.59
Argentina	4.08
Greece	10.60
Portugal	103.00
Mexico	negative
Russia	negative
China	nmf
Venezuela	nmf

Using aggregated earnings growth

Sifting statistics on national income, consumption and investment is a laborious process: part of the study called macroeconomics. Much of orthodox macroeconomics, a model of linear thinking, amounts to little more than finding statistics and adding them up. Traditional macro-economists count up private consumption, construction outlays, foreign trade, stockbuilding, retail sales and industrial output to arrive at a GDP estimate. But there is a much easier method, one with fewer defects, to discover which economies are likely to show the highest growth rates with low inflation. A country's aggregate earnings growth forecast *already* factors in these statistics. The right regions simply have more bargain equities. Recent studies show in fact that company earnings forecasts, when lumped together, are a reliable barometer of future stock market performance within a country. Therefore, another useful tool to find the right regions is the earnings growth predicted by analysts for each market. Such aggregated corporate growth estimates are a good proxy for a country's projected economic growth. Instead of dividing the market's forward P/E ratio by forecast GDP, you divide the P/E by estimated corporate earnings growth. I use this system, based mostly on IBES data, in *The Outside Analyst*.

Granted, these simplistic rankings, whether based on GDP projections or on aggregated corporate earnings estimates, largely ignore such key factors as currency strength and prospective recovery from recession. Pegging market cycles, a subject covered at the end of this chapter, can bring you up to speed here. Bearing that caveat in mind, let's examine the minor as well as the major markets. The highest corporate profit growth between 1995 and 1996 is anticipated in Turkey (69 percent), Brazil (46 percent), Mexico (37 percent), Japan (34 percent), Finland (33 percent), Hungary (28 percent), Italy (28 percent), France (27 percent), South Africa (26 percent), India (25 percent) and Pakistan (25 percent). Of these markets, Turkey, Mexico, Finland, Hungary and Pakistan sell at an average of less than 10 times their estimated 1996 earnings. The smaller stock markets, as you can see, are clearly worth your attention. Emerging markets are by definition neglected. This, as we've seen, makes them notably inefficient in pricing securities, so they often provide superior long-term growth potential.

Using estimate revisions

A new method of finding the right regions takes still another tack, based on this intriguing fact: changes in earnings estimates foreshadow the movement of stock prices. An extensive body of studies has proven this relationship. In 1981, Elton, Gruber and Gultekin showed that investors in the US could post higher returns more readily by correctly guessing analysts' earnings per share (EPS) forecasts than by correctly guessing the firms' actual EPS. Revisions of earnings estimates, in other words, were even more important than the estimates themselves. In 1984, Hawkins, Chamberlin and Daniel showed how excess returns of 14.2 percent a year could have been realized in the US from 1975 through 1980 by investing in companies with positive earnings-estimate revisions.

Until the early 1990s, all the research done into the relationship between earnings estimates and stock prices focused on individual stock selection. But, as I've mentioned, recent studies by some of the top analysts at the Institutional Brokers Estimate System demonstrate that individual earnings forecasts, when lumped together, are a reliable barometer of the future performance of equities within a country. The incidence of bargain stocks reveals the bargain countries. Similarly, changes in the aggregate consensus earnings estimate foreshadow the movement of stock prices.

IBES calls its aggregate measure of changes in analysts' earnings forecasts the earnings-estimate revision ratio. This ratio measures both the direction and the degree of changes in the consensus forecast. A country's one-month earnings-estimate revision ratio for the current year, for instance, is calculated by taking the total number of current fiscal year estimates raised during the past month and dividing it by the total number of current fiscal year estimates lowered during the month. If no estimates are raised during the month but some are lowered, the revision ratio is 0.0. If nine estimates are raised for each estimate lowered, the revision ratio is 9.0. If one estimate is raised for each one lowered, the revision ratio is 1.0, revealing that analysts are neither overly bullish nor bearish on that country.

Does this approach work outside the US? Absolutely. In 1994, Joseph Emanuelli and Randall Pearson, in "Using Earnings Estimates for Global Asset Allocation," showed that, from September 1987 through December 1991, investing in countries with the highest earnings-estimate revision ratios gave returns 10 percentage points higher than Morgan Stanley's market-weighted Global Index, denominated in dollars. The study included IBES data for 24 countries: Australia, Austria, Belgium, Canada, Denmark, Finland, France, Germany, Hong Kong, Ireland, Italy, Japan, Malaysia, the Netherlands, New Zealand, Norway, the Philippines, Singapore, Spain, Sweden, Switzerland, Thailand, the United Kingdom and the United States.

This new and innovative method of asset allocation steadily beat the averages by a wide margin – with no increase in risk. Incidentally, three emerging markets – Malaysia, Singapore and Thailand – appeared in the top-performing portfolio more often than any developed market did. The other two emerging markets – Hong Kong and the Philippines – were also among the better performers.

Conclusion: *The trend of revisions in analyst earnings estimates is a highly useful tool in finding the bargain markets. Revisions of earnings estimates in fact are often more important than the estimates themselves.*

That makes sense. After all, as we'll see in the next chapter, the average analyst's earnings estimate has been off 45 percent annually over the last

17 years. Let's have a look at the trend of revisions in current earnings estimates for the world's stock markets. Though the French bourse does seem cheap from an historic perspective, each analyst who recently raised 1996 earnings estimates for French firms is contradicted by two analysts who lowered them. In Sweden, on the other hand, the current ratio of optimists to pessimists is precisely the reverse.

At present, the earnings revisions of Austria, Chile, Colombia, Finland, Greece, Hungary, Indonesia, Ireland, Mexico, the Netherlands, Norway, Peru, Spain, Sweden and Turkey all show a rising trend. Of these countries, Colombia, Finland, Greece, Hungary, Ireland, Mexico, Norway, Sweden and Turkey sell at an average of less than ten times their estimated 1996 earnings. Based on the foregoing yardsticks, promising growth areas in the Americas to the turn of the century and after include Brazil, Canada, Chile, Colombia and Mexico. Western Europe's growth regions are Belgium, Denmark, Greece, Ireland, the Netherlands, Norway, Spain, Sweden, Turkey and the United Kingdom. The growth markets in Eastern Europe include Czechia, Finland, Hungary and Poland. South Africa also seems to have good potential as, in the Far East, do Australia, Hong Kong, Indonesia, Malaysia, the Philippines, South Korea, Singapore, Taiwan and Thailand. India, Israel and Pakistan are among promising markets in the Middle East, while Jordan and Egypt, also seem attractive. You can pare this list down by eliminating all emerging markets with a Value/Growth Index exceeding 2.00 and all developed markets with a Value/Growth index exceeding 5.00 – or use tighter parameters, if you prefer, in order to meet your asset allocation targets.

When to buy and sell

Attempts to time short-term market movements are mostly futile. William Sharpe put it this way: "Unless a manager can predict whether a market will be good or bad each year with considerable accuracy (e.g. be right at least seven times out of ten), he should probably avoid attempts to time the market altogether." That predictive accuracy of 70 percent is clearly beyond most of us. And there are sharks in these waters. A study by Robert Jeffrey in the *Harvard Business Review* showed that while perfect timing from 1975 through 1982 would have improved the annual real return in the US market by 10.2 percent, totally imperfect timing would have *slashed* that return by 17.6 percent. A study by Sanford Bernstein and Company also has dismaying news for would-be market timers: Over the 1980s as a whole, the S&P 500 produced an average annual rate of return of 17.5 percent, but investors who missed the 40 best days of the decade – only 1.6 percent of the decade – would have earned a mere 4.5 percent. A $1 portfolio fully invested in the Dow Jones industrial average in January 1946, Gary Shilling reports in *Market Timing*, was worth $116 at the end of 1991, including reinvestment of dividends but no deduction for taxes. That's an 11.2 percent compound gain. But if the investor had missed the 50 strongest months for stocks, the annual gain would have fallen to only 4.0 percent. As I mentioned in illustrating market inefficiencies, buying and holding the Dow for 104 years would have turned $1 into $101. But a maladroit market timer who bought at the end of August each year and sold a month later would have seen that dollar dwindle to less than 25 cents.

Conclusion: *Short-term market timing is generally unprofitable. Take the long view.*

Pegging market cycles

Over the long term, there are many reliable signs of roughly when to enter and when to leave a specific market – or, in our global context, when to overweight a country and when not.

As we have seen, diversifying into uncorrelated markets smooths their swings and roundabouts, stabilizing your portfolio. Global investing thus frees you from the burden of following regional economic cycles. (It also frees you from the dangers of being a market timer.)

You're engaged here, however, in adjusting your global weightings for value. In this process, awareness of cycles is highly useful in tilting your portfolio towards the world's most promising markets, thus adding to your bottom line. Moreover, as Chapter 11 established, it is wise to diversify into countries in another phase of the economic cycle, especially if your home country is in recession. Though as a global player you're no longer compelled to peg market cycles, you do have the option.

In Eugene O'Neill's *Moon for the Misbegotten*, Jim Tyrone wails: "There's no present or future, only the past happening over and over again." The investment clock below, based on more intricate diagrams by James McWilliams in *The Journal of Portfolio Management*, shows that the economic and investment cycles are equally inexorable. The outer circle denotes the various monetary stages of the investment cycle, as it moves from boom to bust to boom: from monetary inflation to price inflation to recession and back again. The inner circle describes the economic changes that usually accompany the business cycle. Though depicting the cycles as a clock is a handy metaphor, it is somewhat misleading. Cycle time, in contrast to clock time, is not uniform. The up phase of the economic cycle, from 7 to 11 o'clock, almost always takes many more months than the down phase, from 1 to 5 o'clock. Moreover, the time it takes to complete a cycle is not exact. Cycles do not keep to a regular schedule.

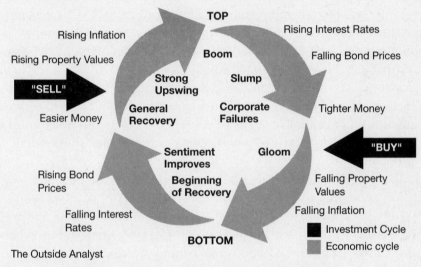

Fig 13.3 Wheels within wheels: the economic and investment cycle

Economists are still debating what causes the business cycle. Some say it is related to the money supply. Some say it is caused by excesses in the business community and others see government as the villain. A few argue that it is a sociological phenomenon, while others proclaim deep-seated biological forces the underlying cause. My purpose is not to join in this threadbare debate, but simply to provide a good tool to help you define where an economy is positioned in the business cycle – and what events are likely to happen, in what sequence, in the months ahead.

A "boom" is found at 12 o'clock and a "recession" at 6 o'clock. The boom always plants the seeds of its own demise. During the boom, interest rates increase due to higher demand for investible funds by companies to finance expansion. Competitive firms keep expanding as fast as possible until they eventually overinvest. The business cycle cannot be fully eliminated because nobody can predict economic turning points sufficiently far in advance. Economists usually fail to spot a recession until it has actually begun – by which time it is too late for any countermeasures to take effect.

As the hour hand goes round, each phase of the investment clock represents monetary and economic conditions at a given moment. These phases generally also represent the current monetary policy of a country's central bank. The US Federal Reserve Board, for instance, uses its key interest rates, the discount rate and Federal funds rate, to shape monetary policy. When the Fed wants to kick-start the US economy, it lowers interest rates, thus creating easier money. This generally boosts US share prices. When interest rates have been left too low for too long, price inflation usually follows and the Fed tightens the monetary spigot, which can hammer down US shares.

Scattered around the clock are 18 short statements describing the things you should observe to establish an economy's place in the cycle. A stock market generally peaks at about 10 o'clock and bottoms out at about 4 o'clock. When economic events suggest that an economy is approaching the area of 10 o'clock, it has generally been wise to cut back on equities. Conversely, the area around 4 o'clock usually indicates a good buying opportunity. Bear markets have always been temporary. Share prices turn upward from one to twelve months before the bottom of the business cycle. Here are some other events likely to take place in the "buy" area around 4 o'clock.

- The mood of popular magazine covers is bleak.
- The money supply – the amount of money in circulation – shrinks in the wake of the central bank's policy of restraint.
- Bankruptcies are at a high level.
- Bank write-offs are high.
- Bank loans are shrinking.
- Union negotiations concentrate on job security.

Here are some additional factors likely to be present in the "sell" area around 10 o'clock.

- The prime rate is up sharply from its lows.
- Corporate capital expansion and improvement projects are started.
- Volume is up in the commercial bond market.
- There are substantial reports of poor vendor performance.

Though not all of these events will always be visible, a recognizable pattern should be evident.

Conclusion: Taking careful note of a country's place in the economic and investment cycles enables you to decide when investment there is opportune. The time of maximum pessimism is the best time to buy, and the time of maximum optimism is the best time to sell. In the world's equity markets, the only way to get a bargain is to buy what most investors are selling.

Summary

The best analysts have a knack for finding shares that are mispriced – and the market knows it. Though equity markets are mostly efficient most of the time, they are also rife with so-called "anomalies" offering opportunities to outperform the averages. Some major examples:

The investment return on small firms consistently outstrips the return on big ones.

Stocks whose price is low relative to earnings tend to outperform stocks whose price-earnings ratio is high. A stock priced at two-thirds or less of market net asset value per share tends to outperform its market.

A portfolio with an investment horizon of less than a quarter of a century should avoid equities selling at the highest earnings multiples, no matter how attractive they may seem. Potential gains are higher in unpopular "value" stocks than in the more popular "growth" or glamour stocks of the day. Neglected shares are less subject to exaggerated expectations inflating their price, so less-researched firms, no matter what their size, tend to produce higher returns. To combine the growth and value styles, buy highly profitable companies selling at a discount. That will provide strong earnings growth at a bargain price.

Emerging stock markets are especially inefficient in pricing securities, and so frequently offer superior profit potential. Stocks held primarily by individuals outperform those held mostly by institutions.

A stock's price tends to rise after insider buying has been reported. A stock's price tends to rise if analysts jack up their consensus earnings estimate. The best-performing stocks are those which earn more than analysts expect.

In seeking tomorrow's global winners, small size in a firm is more important than a low earnings multiple.

In choosing companies whose shares are likely to produce superior returns, institutional neglect is even more important than small size. Potential gains are higher in unpopular "value" stocks than in the more popular "growth" or glamour stocks of the day.

Closed-end mutual funds or investment trusts – those with a fixed number of shares – usually trade at a lower price than the underlying value of the shares they own. Buying deeply discounted closed-end funds would have yielded above-average results since World War II.

Earnings reports should be taken with a grain or more of salt, especially when trying to compare firms across borders. The ratio of a stock's price to cash flow measures profitability across borders better than do price/earnings or price/sales ratios and the ratio of earnings to a firm's total assets or shareholders' equity. But cash flow ignores such items as depreciation, amortization and debt retirement that are needed to keep a company going.

The significant moves in equity markets are nonlinear.

Aggregated bottom-up data on individual companies provides an accurate guide for a top-down investor, especially in the emerging markets. The trend of revisions in analyst earnings estimates is a highly useful tool in finding the bargain markets. Investing in those stock markets on which analysts as a group are increasingly bullish tends to produce above-average returns with no increase in risk. Revisions of earnings estimates in fact are often more important than the estimates themselves.

Short-term market timing is generally unprofitable. Taking careful note of a country's place in the long-term economic and investment cycles enables you to decide when investment there is opportune. The time of maximum pessimism is the best time to buy, and the time of maximum optimism is the best time to sell. In the world's equity markets, the only way to get a bargain is to buy what most investors are selling.

No system works all the time. Any technique that uncovers profit opportunities is likely to be ephemeral. As more people recognize that a technique is profitable, more will use it. More accurate and extensive research will be done on the "anomaly" until it vanishes. History is a guide, not a template.

Why price inefficiencies persist

A market may indeed have all the information it needs to establish correct share prices, but that doesn't mean the prices it actually sets are in fact correct. Market prices are also set to a considerable degree by emotion and flawed perceptions.

That brings us to the subject of market psychology: how you and other investors react. Your mind set, by and large, will be the same,

14

MIND OVER MARKET

"When a man does not know what harbour he is making for, no wind is the right wind."

Lucius Annaeus Seneca (4 BC–AD 65)

There are global investment strategies to suit all tastes and pocket-books. The key is to decide which approach best suits your circumstances, special skills, unique sources and, above all, your character. Have an investment method, hone it, then stick to it. Obviously, not everyone can outperform the averages. The crowd cannot go against the crowd. But looking *outside* your home market decidedly improves your odds. The habit of non-linear thinking can improve those odds even further.

As noted in the previous chapter, non-linearity recognizes that events in the real world unfold in fits and starts under the impact of many different factors. One such factor, irrationality, creates many potentially profitable deviations from efficiency in the world's equity markets. Literally hundreds of such investment opportunities arise each year around the world. And the more places you look, the more bargains you can find.

BEHAVIORAL FINANCE

Though chaos theory has so far failed to show that securities prices deviate from true value in a predictable manner, findings from behavioral finance – another form of non-linear thinking – can help you exploit these common events to make steady profits.

How do investors normally pick shares and run portfolios? The facile way to get a fix on their usual conduct is to ask investors themselves, as Nagy and Obenberger did in 1994. "Factors Influencing Individual Investor Behavior," their study of 137 completed questionnaires (of 500 they had mailed), diligently reported that investors base decisions mostly on expected earnings, diversification needs, a firm's products and services and its financial statements.

If the conclusions of this naive survey are valid, then the world's equity markets are always both rational and efficient. But we've seen plainly that they are often neither. Evidently investors are not the most reliable guides to their own behavior.

Let's try another tack. Though most people do worse than the market in picking shares and running portfolios, a select few manage consistently to score outstanding returns. As some investors win *consistently*, other factors than the questionable notion of statistical chance must cause most of us to lag the averages. What traps and snares might hinder you from joining this winning circle?

Another mystery: Why do share prices frequently diverge substantially and for protracted periods from their "correct" levels?

And finally, why are investment "experts" so often wrong?

The previous chapter's discussion of the theory of rational expectations provides a partial answer to all three questions. The theory, you'll recall, posits that shares are generally mispriced because investment expectations are largely based on invalid notions of how an economy works. Such misconceptions also seem to explain the poor record of most investors – and of the experts. But why do people *continue* cherishing misconceptions? Psychology and physiology both provide explanations. You can in fact vastly improve your chances of consistently outperforming an investment benchmark by learning how to identify and offset your own quota of certain inherent human shortcomings. These shortcomings can readily distort your mental models of the global investment environment.

LIMITS OF THE BRAIN

Human beings cannot process a great deal of information – let alone convert it into action. Sometimes, indeed, when trying to process information, the human brain essentially grinds to a halt. Herbert

Simon, who won the Nobel Prize in 1987, studied humankind's abilities and limitations in this regard for over more than four decades. In a study published in the *Journal of Economics*, he demonstrated that the human mind can digest only five to seven different things at once.

Conclusion: *We react consciously to only a fragment of the data being thrown at us.*

Interactive reasoning

Granted, we can handle information reliably in a linear fashion: moving from one point to the next in a logical sequence. That has enabled the human race to put a man on the moon, splice genes and make movies with computer-generated dinosaurs more believable than the actors. Even with such complex technology, each step is linked to the previous one and will be linked to the next until the job is done.

But the kind of problem we face as investors is of quite another order. Though linear relationships are simply the sum of their components, social organisms such as equity markets are vastly more complex. The problem we face as investors seems to require configural, or interactive, rather than linear reasoning. In a configural problem, your interpretation of any bit of information depends on how you evaluate many other bits.

Two companies, each with annual earnings growth of 15 percent over the past five years, may not be equally attractive purchase candidates. Perhaps one runs hospitals in Munich while the other builds dredging vessels in Hong Kong. One could have heavy debt and the other virtually none. One might pay out two-thirds of earnings in dividends, while the other plows earnings into new plant and equipment. One could have a much narrower profit margin and return on capital. You can continue in this vein for days, weeks, even months, poring over reams of analytical data gleaned from company reports.

Other factors will of course also play a role. What about quality of management? Prospects for the sector? The company's expansion plans? The quality of its accounting?

Your configural analysis is by no means yet complete. What about the local economy? The level of interest rates? Unemployment? Inflation? Industrial production? Capital spending? The competitive environment? What revisions are likely in all of the above? And how should you weight these many factors?

This rocky road to investment success obviously demands top-notch configural processing skills, as a change in any one factor may well require radical revamping of the entire estimate.

Curious to see if investment professionals matched this theoretical profile, researcher Paul Slovic devised a test to see how important configural (or interactive) reasoning was in their decisions. His report in the *Journal of Applied Psychology* concluded that on average such reasoning accounted for a mere 4 percent of the decisions made.

No wonder. The amount of information an investment professional is expected to process is mind-boggling. Moreover, much of it is qualitative and tricky to pin down, so a money manager or analyst has to use judgment repeatedly along the way. In theory, an investment analyst needs information-processing capacities akin to those of a state-of-the-art computer. Plus a central storage file for the extensive political, economic, industry, market and company data needed. Not to mention an ability to update and cross-reference the whole works instantly as new and contradictory developments occur. Star Trek's engaging android, Commander Data, might be up to this task, but certainly not us mere mortals. A study by David Dreman and Michal Berry reveals that the average analyst's earnings estimate has been off 45 percent annually over the last 17 years.

Research into configural, or interactive, reasoning shows in fact that experts not only fail to analyze information correctly but can also find relationships that are not there – what psychologists call "illusionary correlation." The technical analyst's head and shoulders formation on the chart cuts through thousands of disparate facts no one can interpret. Concentrating purely on growth stocks simplifies a bewildering range of investment alternatives. The 50-year recurrence of the Kondratieff wave clarifies complex economic activity. Such mental shortcuts, which seem to have worked in the past, are pervasive in the marketplace. Alas, some of the correlations are illusory and others are chance. Trusting in them begets error. One technical analyst sighed: "If I hadn't made money every so often, I would have grown wise much sooner."

Information overload

Under conditions of complexity and uncertainty, experts demand as much information as possible to help them make decisions. But research indicates that more data does not automatically mean better judgment.

A study of people who bet on horse races, for instance, shows that more information merely increases their confidence in the wagers, but does nothing to increase their accuracy. In the field of investment, the more detailed an analyst's knowledge, the more that individual is presumed an expert. In fact, however, ingesting large amounts of investment information can lead to making worse rather than better decisions. A couple of decades ago, in *Institutional Investor*, Reba White described a US analyst so knowledgeable about Clorox "that he could recite bleach share by brand in every small town in the Southwest. . . . But somehow when the company began to develop massive problems he missed the signs." The volume of information had little to do with the outcome. The stock fell from a high of 53 to 11.

Conclusion: *We tend to become more confident and less accurate as we process increasing amounts of information.*

STRENGTH IN SIMPLICITY

These psychological findings remain unknown – or at least widely ignored – in the global investment community, where experts remain convinced that major problems can be solved if only more facts can be uncovered. Analysts and money managers thus tend to overload themselves with information, which instead of improving their decisions tends only to make them more confident and prone to error.

The great golfer Tommy Armour observed: "Simplicity, concentration, and economy of time and effort have been the distinguishing features of the great players' methods, while others lost their way to glory by wandering in a maze of details."

Over Benjamin Graham's 50 years as an active investor, his basic approach was simply to buy a stock at less than two-thirds of its net quick assets (working capital minus all debt) and sell it at 100 percent of the net quick assets. (More on Graham's criteria in the next chapter.)

Less is more. In place of a glut of facts, I prefer to recall this variant on a Quaker hymn:

'Tis the gift to be simple, 'tis the gift to be free, 'tis the gift to wind up where you want to be.

Garfield Drew, a famous US market theorist of Graham's era, saw that clearly. In 1941, he wrote:

Simplicity and singleness of approach is a greatly underestimated factor of market success. As soon as the attempt is made to watch a multiplicity of factors, even though each has some element to justify it, one is only too likely to become lost in a maze of contradictory implications (and)...the various factors involved may be so conflicting that the conclusion finally drawn is no better than a snap judgment would have been.

I'm by no means recommending snap judgment. But if you, like most people, can handle a maximum of only seven pieces of information at once, it would seem to make sense to delimit your stock-selection criteria to that number. That is in fact just what one successful US fund manager has done, insisting that each equity in his unique portfolio meet these unusually stringent criteria:

- The firm does not defer operating expenses or realize revenues prematurely, and its auditor's report is unqualified in all material aspects.
- The firm has shown at least 10 percent growth in adjusted pre-tax income in each of the last six years.
- Adjusted pre-tax income, exclusive of acquisitions and divestments, has grown at an annual compound rate of at least 20 percent over the last six years.
- Working capital meets one of three conditions: 2 : 1 or better current ratio (i.e. current assets divided by current liabilities); 1 : 1 or better quick asset ratio (this simply means that current assets minus inventory at least equal current liabilities); or a working capital greater than market valuation.
- Long-term debt is covered by either working capital, cash and equivalents or latest 12-month cash flow.
- Investment firms own less than 10 percent of the total shares.
- The shares sell for less than ten times estimated current earnings.

These impressive criteria were developed by Barry Ziskin, manager of the nonconformist Z-Seven Fund, which over the ten years ended 31 December 1995 outperformed 90 percent of US–listed closed-end funds. You can use them – or assemble your own list. Just to start you off, here are the two criteria used by Mark Mobius, managing director of Templeton Investment Management in Hong Kong:

- A stock must be a bargain in terms of its ability to generate earnings over the next five years so that it will be cheap relative to its own history, other stocks in its market and other stocks around the world in its industry.

- A stock must have good prospects, with a high growth rate over the next five years.

Mobius follows Templeton's rule of selling if he can find something roughly 50 percent cheaper than what he already owns.

Conclusion: As most people can handle no more than seven pieces of information at once, it is wise to employ no more than seven criteria for choosing each stock.

DEALING WITH CHANGE

David Dreman's book *Contrarian Investment Strategy* cites a number of studies revealing that the favorite stocks and industries of large groups of professional investors, chosen by interactive reasoning, did far worse than the averages over nearly half a century: from 1929 through 1976. From 1963 to 1978, the Becker Survey discovered that 87 percent of US money managers lagged the market averages, while SEI Funds Evaluation found they consistently lagged the market averages from 1962 through 1987. And, as noted in Chapter 8, from 1984 through 1994, the annual return of US stock funds was an appalling 15 percent below the return of the S&P 500. Benjamin Graham alluded to this disheartening pattern in *The Intelligent Investor*:

> In an astonishingly large proportion of the trading in common stocks, those engaged therein don't appear to know – in polite terms – one part of their anatomy from another.

Anatomical aspects

Let's review some anatomy to see why, with the best guns and ammunition available, money managers so often miss the target. Throughout her long career, Katherine Hepburn got "butterflies" in the stomach before going onstage. Similarly, an impending job interview can cause an attack of intestinal cramp. And anti-depressants meant for the brain cause nausea or abdominal upset in millions of people who take them. The reason, say scientists, is that human beings actually have two brains: one in the skull and one in the gut. The two brains are linked: when one gets upset, so does the other.

The gut's brain, a single entity known as the enteric nervous system, is found in tissue casings that line the esophagus, stomach, small intestine and colon. Like the brain in the skull, it has support cells, neurons, neurotransmitters and proteins that send messages between neurons. It also has a complex circuitry enabling it to act independently, learn, remember and produce gut feelings.

Though the brain in the gut plays a major role in human happiness and misery, few people know it exists. For years, people who had ulcers, or trouble swallowing, or persistent abdominal pain were told their problems were emotional or imaginary. Doctors were right in ascribing these problems to the brain, but they blamed the wrong one.

In recent years, however, details of how the enteric nervous system mirrors the central nervous system have been emerging. Nearly every substance that helps run and control the brain in the skull has turned up in the one in the gut. The two brains are connected shortly before birth by the vagus nerve. As this circuitry becomes more clear, researchers are beginning to understand why we feel the way we do. When the brain in the gut perceives a threat, it releases stress hormones that prepare the body to fight or flee. The stomach contains sensory nerves that are stimulated by this chemical surge. Hence Hepburn's "butterflies." But fear also causes the vagus nerve to turn up the volume on serotonin circuits in the gut. This overstimulation results in diarrhea. Similarly, people are sometimes "choked with emotion." When nerves in the esophagus are highly stimulated, we have trouble swallowing. Stress signals from the brain in the skull can also alter nerve function between the stomach and esophagus, resulting in heartburn.

The more familiar brain in the skull has two parts, called the left and right hemispheres. Each of us is dominated by one side or the other. The left hemisphere reasons logically, step for step, and is the centre of speech. This linear thinking is the chief beneficiary of the Western world's highly analytical educational process. Computers can duplicate many left-brain functions. (I recently programmed a computer to carry on a plausible conversation.)

In contrast, the right hemisphere is intuitive and unique. It does not operate step-by-step, but by leaps of association. It is artistic, has feelings and sees the forest better than the trees. As the right hemisphere is non-verbal, you can tap into it only through dreams and gut reactions. It blends all your collective experience and generates enormous input – far more than you can articulate.

This anatomical structure may explain why risk has always had two components: gut feeling and attempts at measurement.

Logic versus intuition

Which half of the skull holds the investment brain? Though there is little or no research on how portfolio managers tick, some studies do shed light on the decision-making process of top managers. By observing many chief executive officers in action, Professor Henry Mintzberg of Canada's McGill University discovered they do not run things as taught at the Harvard Business School. Top executives, he found, show a dislike for written memos and long, step-by-step tasks. They thrive on disorder, ambiguity and frequent interruptions. In short, top executives are intuitive, right-brain types.

That's exactly the sort of approach equity investment demands. Here's why. An initial change in the economy or the fortunes of a specific company has no numbers. The numbers that quantify a change can only become available after it has happened. As noted in the previous chapter, economists usually fail to spot a recession until it has actually begun. Nor can whether a market is in a bull or bear phase ever be established beyond reasonable doubt until the trend is well advanced. No amount of information can remove all uncertainty. To deal with change, therefore, you have to rely on your intuitive skills.

Running an equity portfolio is not purely an exercise in numbers, but more like playing golf or riding a horse: a melding of experience and intuition. A violin is just a construction of wood and strings. It takes an artist to play it. Any facts you assemble, whether fundamental or technical, are nothing but wood and strings: no good without the player.

Conclusion: *As ongoing changes cannot be quantified, intuitive skills are generally much more useful than interactive reasoning in managing an equity portfolio.*

HANDLING UNCERTAINTY

As a portfolio manager, you need to identify change early, before every Tom, Dick and Harry can measure it. You need the guts to make decisions with only partial information.

Alas, that's the very moment at which emotional bias can tug the rug out from under you. Studies in behavioral psychology reveal that we all have specific glitches in our thinking patterns that come to the fore in complex, ambiguous situations, or during periods of anxiety or uncertainty. At such moments, a stock market becomes a gigantic Rorschach test, allowing us to see anything we wish. Our shared leanings to emotional bias, as Robert Prechter argues in *At the Crest of the Tidal Wave*, are why investor behavior follows set patterns.

The set patterns of investor behavior are visible in the markets as fashions or manias and in individuals as perceptual distortions.

Conclusion: *The uncertainty involved in making decisions with only partial information causes investors to behave in set patterns.*

MARKET MANIAS

The theory of balance

Conventional economic models do not describe the actual behavior of investors. One reason for this deficiency is that orthodox economic theory is based on the dubious assumption that investors make rational choices. Price, John Maynard Keynes asserted, is determined by a balance between supply and demand. The market mechanism, according to this theory of balance, assures that the price of an object is a fair reflection of its true value. Economists label the square pegs that don't fit into this round hole "anomalies." Cognitive psychologists have been sniping at the theory of balance for years; for empirical research shows that markets do *not* always behave rationally. That's logical because markets after all are made up of people.

The herd instinct

As I mentioned in "Allocating Assets," the stock market – any stock market – is a moving target. At a given moment, some markets seem priced at about twice their value and others at about half. A market is a scale that simply reflects the weight of belief. So markets always swing from periods of being overvalued to periods of being undervalued. Such discrepancies – or "inefficiencies" – are transitory, providing great opportunity. Nonlinear thinking can help you uncover such profitable deviations from efficiency.

Academics keep insisting markets are "efficient" in setting prices, adjusting them almost instaneously in the light of new developments. True, the world's equity markets do absorb information with amazing speed. Within seconds after a firm releases a poor earnings report, the price of its stock can plummet by 30 percent. However, while a market may know everything that *has* happened, it does not know everything that is *going* to happen. Prices are pinned to nothing more palpable than expectation of what prices will be tomorow. The price you pay for Microsoft reflects the market's expectations about the stock's future value, based on historical information. But emotion always colours such expectations because economic value depends on the subjective opinions of people. Nobody has a magic formula that proves conclusively what Microsoft or anything else is worth. The market has a good record of anticipating short-term economic developments, not long-term ones. The longer the time horizon, the more likely the market will err. But ironically, though the long run is inherently unpredictable, the market's *long-term* expectations determine most of the price you pay for any equity. When you pay $85 for a share of Microsoft, you're buying a claim on the firm's assets, earnings and dividends for as long as it remains in business. Only a small part of your purchase price reflects the concern's immediate prospects. Most of the $85 is for a piece of the company's growth in the distant future.

But if no one has the foggiest notion what Microsoft will be worth in the distant future, how can the market put a rational price on the share? The obvious answer – the painful truth academics hate to admit – is that the market cannot price an equity rationally. Part of the price you pay for a share of Microsoft is rational and part is emotional. The short-term component is somewhat more rational because investors know pretty much what Microsoft's earnings will be for the next quarter or two, perhaps even the next year or two. But the long-term component, which has by far the greater weight, depends almost entirely on investor psychology. Share prices change not only when fundamental information changes but also in response to the whims of investors, thus once more partially refuting the efficient market theory.

Eventually of course the market is generally right – but, as Chapter 7 noted, the market is dead wrong when gripped by fears or fads. Just as extreme optimism pumps up share prices, extreme pessimism hammers share prices down. How, other than psychology, is one to explain the fact that overall share prices sometimes plummet or recover more than 10 percent within a couple of days? From 1987 to 1992, the world share markets made three screeching U-turns on the financial highway. All three times, it was evident in retrospect that the panic reaction was unnecessary. The thousands of individuals who jointly determine demand and supply in the capital markets are strongly influenced in their perception of value by feelings which sometimes border on mass hysteria. "I can calculate the motions of heavenly bodies," Sir Isaac Newton said, "but not the madness of crowds."

Most investors are bright, sophisticated, well educated and well informed. Why, then, do fears and fads, these so-called "anomalies," so often move the markets?

Simple. Aberrations are a normal part of human behavior.

The naked investor

Here's one normal aberration. Seven people are sitting in a doctor's office. When an eighth person walks in, the seven get up and start removing their clothes.

And the eighth? University research projects show that after a moment's hesitation, he or she is also likely to undress. Scientists have found similar behavior in the animal world. Studies of guppies show that when a female guppy shows sexual interest in a male, her attention attracts other female guppies. So male guppies either get lavish attention from the ladies or none at all.

Psychologists believe this behavior gives some insight into how stock markets work. When people see others buying a stock or mutual fund, they follow suit. Useful information such as cash flow or debt-to-equity ratio is ignored as the herd instinct takes over.

Conclusion: Remember Templeton's maxim: If you buy the same securities as other people, you will have the same results as other people.

The tulip craze

History is rife with examples of herd behavior demonstrating the huge irrational component in market movements. Holland once went literally mad for tulips. Introduced to Western Europe in the middle of the 16th century, the flower became a status symbol within a decade. Wealthy burghers in Amsterdam sent directly to Constantinople for the bulbs, paying extravagant prices, especially for those infected with a virus that produced flowers of variegated hues. In the next century, the rage for collecting tulips spread to the middle class, then, as now, eager to mimic the rich. By 1634, the Dutch were so taken by tulips that the daily affairs of the country were neglected: nearly everyone was too busy speculating in the exotic flowers. As the mania increased, so did prices – until finally a single diseased tulip was worth ten fat oxen, sixteen fat swine, twelve fat sheep, two hogsheads of wine, four casks of beer, two tubs of butter, a thousand pounds of cheese, a complete bed, a suit of clothes – and a silver drinking cup.

By 1636, the demand for rare tulips had grown so frenzied that regular markets in tulip derivatives were operating in Rotterdam, Haarlem, Leyden and Alkmaar. Market makers created swings in the price, making large profits by buying when it fell and selling out when it rose. The public swarmed to the tulip markets like flies to honey. Nobles, citizens, farmers, mechanics, seamen, footmen, maid-servants, even chimney sweeps – all dabbled in tulips. Land and houses were unloaded at fire-sale prices or attached to pay for tulip trades. Foreigners caught the craze – and money rolled in from every side.

Then inflation took hold. Food and shelter became more expensive. The more prudent began to see that tulipomania couldn't last forever. It became obvious that someone was going to lose badly. As this conviction spread, tulip prices plummeted, never to rise again. Confidence was shattered, panic seized the dealers – and money was suddenly scarce.

Portfolio insurance

Similar irrationality also triggered the US stock market crash of 1987. Institutional investors behaved like lemmings in breeding season, selling into a sagging market to delimit downside risk in case stocks slid further. These blue-chip fire sales were exacerbated by computer-generated trading. In this approach, portfolio managers surrender decisions to an idiot savant: the computer, which triggers automatic sell signals when certain parameters are reached. US megabuck men call this suicidal "monkey see, monkey do" behavior, believe it or not, "portfolio insurance."

Of course, it's just another market mania. Traditionally, successful investing has meant buying shares as prices fall and selling when prices rise, as the tulip market makers did. But now portfolio "insurers" use formulas that require them to buy shares as prices rise and dump them as prices fall. The result in 1987 was exactly what you might expect: unstable markets leading to panic, just as in the 17th century.

Many observers, including myself, had fingered program trading as the culprit for the Dow's historic 36.1 percent drop on October 19th, so President Reagan appointed a Presidential Task Force on Market Mechanisms, headed by Nicholas F. Brady, to look into the matter. The Brady Report supported the charge in these words: "The ability of the equity market to absorb the huge selling pressure to which it was subjected in mid-October depended on its liquidity. But liquidity sufficient to absorb the limited selling demands of investors became an *illusion* of liquidity when confronted by massive selling, as everyone showed up on the same side of the market at once. Ironically, it was this illusion of liquidity which led certain similarly motivated investors, such as portfolio managers, to adopt strategies which call for liquidity far in excess of what the market could supply."

In other words, portfolio managers, despite their good intentions, had increased risk rather than averting it.

Recent bubbles

Human irrationality is ever-resourceful. That is why bubbles are an inevitable and recurring feature of financial markets. One bubble took place in US stocks in the late 1920s and one in Japanese stocks in the late 1980s. In 1980, people were eagerly buying gold at $850 an ounce, while in 1995 they were largely indifferent to it at $380. Another bubble was visible in biotechnology in 1990 and 1991, and yet another in emerging markets from 1993 to 1994. Hong Kong and Japanese land price bubbles then gave way to high-tech and Internet crazes. In early 1996, at $130 a share, Netscape Communications Corp., which makes software for browsing the Internet, had a higher market capitalization (stock price times outstanding shares) than 100-year old leviathans like Union Carbide and Westinghouse. Netscape's market capitalization worked out to $5.27 billion, some $300 million more than the combined market valuation of UAL Corp. (parent of United Airlines) and the New York Times Co. (which also owns other newspapers, including the *Boston Globe*, as well as magazines and broadcasting stations). At the time, Netscape's 1997 profit was estimated at a paltry $10 to $15 million, while UAL and the New York Times Co. were expected to earn $400 million.

The bigger fool theory

Devotees of pure market theory would of course argue that if you can find a buyer for your tulip, Tokyo lot or Netscape stock, that asset is not overvalued. Cynics refer to this line of thought as the "Bigger Fool Theory," under which prices keep rising until no one can be found to buy. The biggest fool, who buys at the highest price, is left holding the bag.

INDIVIDUAL BIAS

As investors, we all have perceptual distortions. Fortunately, many of our shared leanings to emotional bias, the various irrational glitches, can be measured and form predictable trends. And once these forces are understood, we as individuals can find routes to skirt the pitfalls. Let's examine some of our most dangerous common propensities in the field of investment.

Ritual

One reason for the set patterns of investor behaviour is mindless routine. The American Plains Indians were convinced the buffalo returned each year in response to the ritual buffalo dance. Of course, the Indians simply kept dancing until the buffalo came back.

Investment can also become ritual. Many investors place their bets and feel when the chips come their way that their persistence has been rewarded. They accept any evidence that confirms this view and dismiss any that negates it. Psychologists call this "cognitive dissonance." Die-hard US doomsayers of the 1960s and 1970s are still waiting for the buffalo. Many have been predicting a bear market for decades. One top portfolio manager was mostly in cash from 1986 to 1996, missing the biggest bull market in US history. Naturally, just as a stopped clock tells the right time twice in any 24-hour period, one day these pessimists will inevitably be right. Roger Babson regularly predicted a Wall Street crash from 1926 on. He did this every six months in his newsletter until September 1929, with the Dow at its peak of 380, when he again said that someday there would be a great crash. The "prediction" was picked up by a wire service and made him famous. Many of his subscribers cancelled, however, because Babson hadn't warned them the crash was imminent.

Conclusion: One individual's faith will not move a market.

Self-deception

Investors also seem to behave in set patterns due to self-deception: an unfounded belief that they are able to "outsmart" the market. In this context, one attitude survey is especially relevant. A random sample of adult males were asked to rate themselves on a number of parameters: First was ability to get along with others. Every single man ranked himself in the top 10 percent of the population on this score; and a full 25 percent put themselves in the top 1 percent. Similarly, 70 percent rated themselves in the top quintile in leadership ability. Only 2 percent felt that they were below-average leaders. Finally, in an area where self-deception should be particularly tough, 60 percent said they were in the top quintile in athletic ability and only 6 percent said they were below average.

Similarly, people active in equity markets tend to confuse market gains with trading gains. As I explained in Chapter 3, it is possible to diversify a portfolio enough so that essentially only market risk remains: uncertainty as to whether the overall market will rise or fall. If the market moves up, investors in general will benefit, whether trading stocks or merely holding them. But if you're trading while the market moves up, the all too human tendency is to attribute the increase in wealth to your trading rather than the market rise. Portfolios invested in small and highly leveraged stocks are often so sensitive to market movements that a 10 percent rise in the general market causes a 20 percent rise in the value of the portfolio. Investors who manage this kind of portfolio in a rising market can find it easy to convince themselves and others that they are brilliant.

Conclusion: An investor is wise to cultivate humility. It's what you learn after you know it all that counts.

Myopia

Every investment market, be it ever so rational, suffers from incurable myopia: an inability to focus promptly on the long term. US stock prices had been falling for almost two years when the Dow plunged to a low of 777 in August 1982. Slumping stock prices were saying that the market expected the economy to weaken. And the market was correct. The recession that began in late 1981 continued to deepen for four months after the market had bottomed. But for any investor with a longer perspective, the Dow was absurdly undervalued. The market was right about the immediate outlook, but dead wrong about what was further down the track. What the market failed to see in the summer of 1982 was that the Federal Reserve was to embark on an easy money policy, sparking the longest peacetime economic upswing of the 20th century. The market, of course, quickly shifted focus as the recovery became visible in statistics writ large enough for nearsighted Mr Magoo. By June 1983, a mere ten months after the lows, the Dow had soared 61 percent.

People make markets – and people follow trends.

Studies have uncovered a number of factors other than our "monkey see, monkey do" instinct that make us trend followers. One, says Richard Thaler, economics professor at the University of Chicago, is precisely the propensity to myopia: we focus too much on recent data, and not enough on long-run averages or statistical odds. Perceived risk and actual risk simply do not coincide. Thaler and a colleague, Werner F.M. De Bondt of the University of Wisconsin, found a 25 percent higher return in stocks that were winners in the preceding period than in stocks that previously performed poorly. The persistent bias is not explained by risk, the researchers concluded, but by the human tendency to overweight recent data. Thaler and De Bondt also examined whether each year's "worst" stock would offer superior returns over a *longer* period. They pored over decades of Big Board stock prices to find the real dogs. Some were chronic money-losers, often on the verge of bankruptcy. Some had simply racked up a highly volatile earnings history. Then the researchers created theoretical portfolios of the 35 worst-performing stocks.

Their conclusions may startle you: Three years later, the "worst" stock portfolios proved to be the big winners. What's more, during the same period portfolios made up of the "best-performing" stocks faltered, trailing the market by 5 percent. These findings imply there can be considerable rewards in swimming against the current.

The findings also show that investors need patience; for most of the excess gain in the "worst" stock portfolios occurred in the second and third years of the test periods.

Another example of myopia: just as some investors confuse market gains with trading gains, others attribute transitory market losses to poor stock choices.

Conclusion: *It is advisable to focus on the long-run odds, then stay cool as the markets gyrate. The wise investor does not attribute transi-*

tory market losses to poor portfolio choices. Though volatility is painful to experience, the compensation for living with it is high.

Misjudging probability

Errors in judging probability also create a number of severe and predictable tilts in our investment decision-making – as well as in the pricing of equities. We tend to misjudge probability in three ways. First of all, we overvalue certainty. Second, we overestimate the value of small chances of large gains or losses. Finally, we have a disproportionate aversion to losses. You can discover your own bias on this score by answering a few simple questions. Here's the first.

You receive a visit one day from a mysterious benefactor who offers you an outright gift of $70,000 or an opportunity to spin a wheel to win $100,000. Four of the five numbers on the wheel show $100,000. Only one displays a zero. So you have an 80 percent chance of winning the $100,000. Do you take the money or the risk?

If you seriously considered spinning the wheel, you have the makings of a shrewd risk-taker and sophisticated investor. Like most people, however, you probably chose the gift, meaning you feel the 80 percent chance of an extra $30,000 isn't worth the 20 percent risk of losing the certainty of $70,000. In this context, you're risk-averse.

Remember the discussion in Chapter 5 on choosing individual equities? As you may recall, the dispersion of analyst earnings estimates for any given equity is a good proxy for its market risk, and the wider such estimates are scattered the higher the return you can anticipate. Therefore, we established, in choosing individual holdings for a global portfolio it is wiser to *seek* market risk than to *avoid* it.

That of course goes against human instinct. We tend to shy away from risk, even when the odds advise otherwise. People will pay a premium, a lower return on their capital, for the greater certainty of preserving that capital. Offered the choice of $70,000 or a shot at $100,000, most of us will grab the sure thing. But an uninhibited mathematician would shout "Spin the wheel!" – because an 80 percent chance of winning $100,000 is a better bet than a certain $70,000.

Granted, if you had only one spin of the wheel, it might be wiser to take the gift and run. But you can make *many* investment decisions, spread over long periods of time, and choose among many opportunities. That's when playing the odds really starts to pay off.

Conclusion We tend to avoid the possibility of loss in favor of a sure win, even when the odds advise otherwise.

Utility of wealth

In *Exposition of a New Theory on the Measurement of Risk*, first published in 1738, Daniel Bernoulli declared: "the determination of the value of an item must not be based on its price, but rather on the utility it yields. . . . Thus there is no doubt that a gain of one thousand ducats is more significant to a pauper than to a rich man though both gain the same amount."

Would gaining two million dollars make you precisely twice as happy as gaining one million? Obviously not. People tend to feel less and less excited by additional increments of wealth, and so are willing to take less and less risk to increase that wealth. This set of relationships is described mathematically by another orthodox economic proposition, utility theory, which traditionally has played an important role in modeling short-term human behaviour and analyzing how investors make decisions.

Utility theory holds that each of our investment decisions is a trade-off between consumption now or consumption later. The theory says we weigh the benefits of spending funds today against the benefits of investing them so we can spend more in the future. This hypothesis, developed by Von Neumann and Morgenstern in *Theory of Games and Economic Behavior*, is based on four assumptions that by this point in our discussion are obviously rather shaky:

- Investors are completely rational.
- Investors can deal with complex choices.
- Investors are averse to risk.
- Investors will maximize wealth.

A fifth assumption makes the hypothesis even more suspect: utility theory itself seeks to define rationality.

Prospect theory

Now, however, new research, primarily by behavioral psychologists Daniel Kahneman of Princeton and Amos Tversky of Stanford, has shouldered the earlier approach aside. Their research, called prospect theory, outlined in *Judgment under Uncertainty*, suggests there are a number of areas where people's decisions are consistently out of whack with what would be predicted from utility theory.

Say you have a loose £300 rattling around and can elect one of two ways to increase it. You can accept a heads or tails deal, in which you either win an additional two hundred pounds or get absolutely nothing. Alternatively, you can simply accept £100, without having to do a thing. Which would you choose?

Now let's imagine instead that you have £500, and you have the choice between giving up £100 or tossing a coin. If your luck on the toss is bad you lose £200 and if it's good your initial £500 remains intact. Which do you choose now? Think it over carefully before you read on!

If in the first instance you chose for the coin and in the second for certainty, then you, like most people, are led more by emotion in money matters than by logic. Consistency would be to choose in both cases for certainty or in both cases for the gamble. Not that it matters much; for statistically the average outcome, in all cases, is £400. The problem is simply posed in a way that masks the actual choice.

When this test was performed in a study of irrational behavior among investors, it revealed that the majority of those who began with £300 opted for the certainty of £100 profit, while those who began with £500 and faced a loss chose for the most part to gamble.

Conclusion: *We tend to take on risk to avoid a sure loss, even when the odds advise otherwise.*

Now try this second question, suggested by Peter Carman in "The Psychology of Investment Decision-Making," General Crunch, though a canny military strategist, finds himself in a tight spot. He commands 600 troops, all now cornered. He has two choices. He can choose Strategy A and save 200 of his men or adopt Strategy B, risking a one-third chance that all of his troops will be saved and a two-thirds chance that all will die.

Which should he choose?

In studies of many groups, some who knew the mathematics of probability and some who didn't, the majority of people picked A. The certainty of saving 200 clearly outweighed the chance of saving all. The motivation? Probably a distaste for gambling with lives.

On the other hand, what about Doctor Dimbleby? He's been called in to treat 600 acutely ill people. He also has two choices: Therapy A will cause 400 of them to die. With Therapy B, there's a one-third chance everyone will be saved and a two-thirds chance no one will. What should he do?

Studies of people faced with these choices showed an overwhelming preference for Therapy B. Why? In this case, the certain death of 400 apparently made them reason: Why not gamble and try to save them all?

Of course the situations faced by the general and the doctor are perfectly comparable. Strategy A and Therapy A carry the same result: 400 deaths. Similarly, the objective result of Alternative B in both situations is identical. Yet when the problem is stated in terms of a certain gain (that is, lives saved) versus stating the problem in terms of a certain loss (i.e. lives lost), people react very differently.

Conclusion: We try to avoid regret, and so react quite differently to a problem depending on how it is framed.

Missing the big picture

The wish to avoid regret underlies a common investment mistake. Robert J. Shiller, a professor at Yale University's Cowles Foundation for Research in Economics, has conducted wide studies into investor behavior. One of his major conclusions: "People tend to single out individual stocks or investments rather than looking at a portfolio's overall success."

If you own two stocks worth £40, one of which you bought at £20 and the other at £50, you might not sell the latter, even if its price was falling. Quite understandable. You're trying to avoid pangs of regret. If, however, you frame the problem differently, thinking of the *combined* value of the two shares, you might be happy to sell both, thus producing a net gain. This helps explain the popularity of investment funds (which show only the combined effect of many transactions), even though the average fund lags its relevant index.

Conclusion: Focusing on single holdings is a common propensity global investors should especially avoid.

Odds and emotions

When making investment decisions in uncertain conditions, we normally require very high odds of winning to offset a relatively small probability of loss. Indeed, we're then roughly twice as sensitive to losses as to gains.

On average, we require a 65 percent chance of winning £100 to offset a 35 percent chance of losing £100. Traditionally, financial economists have treated upside and downside risk as identical. But prospect theory implies that we're more concerned with the downside.

What do you do with a stock that has fallen 20 percent from its purchase price? Sell? It might bounce back. On the other hand, it might fall further.

Normally investors do nothing. Experiments by Martin Weber, professor of banking and finance at Germany's Mannheim University, show convincingly just how difficult we find it to sell stocks, especially when we're sitting on a loss. A group of students was given fictional stocks in several firms. The prices of these shares were then changed randomly on 20 occasions and the students were encouraged to buy and sell.

The professor reported: "People who had made a profit were two times as likely to sell their stock than those who had made a loss."

Why do investors tend to hold on to losers for too long and sell winners too soon? Because it's hard for people to ignore recent history in practical everyday situations. You plan, for instance, to see a play. The ticket costs £25. You buy the ticket, but lose it five minutes later. What do you do? Buy another ticket – or go home and watch television?

Now let's say you lose your wallet containing £25 on the way to buy the theatre ticket. You retrace your steps and find the wallet with all your identification and credit cards, but the £25 is missing. Do you go to the bank for more money – or again abandon your theatre plans?

The rational answer depends on how much you want to see the play. If you're a New Yorker come to London to enjoy Shakespeare, in both cases you should arrange to see the play. But if you live in London and are not particularly keen on *Coriolanus*, in both cases you should probably go home.

Did you make different decisions in these two scenarios? If so, emotional factors heavily influence you. It might be wise for you then to consider an investment technique that takes the psychological content out of investing. One way is to set strict rules on when to sell.

Max Bowser, who runs a penny stock newsletter called *The Bowser Report* in the United States, recommends this approach. He sells half his holding in a stock when it doubles in value and the rest when the stock falls 25 percent from its peak. If a stock falls immediately on purchase, he sells it when it has fallen 25 percent from its purchase price. From 1985 through 1994, these rules helped Bowser turn an initial stake of $4,000 into $40,000. His parameters, suitable for highly volatile US penny stocks, may not be right for a global equity portfolio, but the principle is sound. You might peg your own mental "stop loss" at 10 or 15 percent. Other such techniques are discussed in the next chapter.

Conclusion: Investors tend to hold on to losers for too long and sell winners too soon. The rational approach is to ignore an equity's history in your portfolio. All that counts is the simple question: Would you be willing to buy it now? If not, then you should sell. Don't be afraid to take a loss. Mistakes are part of the game.

Remote chances

Let's turn to another question. You have a choice between:

- A. 1 percent chance of winning $6,000 or . . .
- B. 2 percent chance of winning $3,000.

Both are remote chances. If you picked A, in this context you're not averse to risk. In general, people go for A in a ratio of about 7 to 3. The bottom line here is that in the case of small chances of very large gains or losses, people turn into risk-seekers, even though that clearly violates utility theory.

This psychological truth underlies the popularity of lotteries. People pay to play because there's a big return for being right. They're willing to accept an almost certain loss for the remote possibility of a huge payoff, plus some fun in playing. It's been estimated that Massachusetts residents spend an average $106,000 per person to play the lottery over their collective lifetimes.

Hope springs eternal in the human breast. Jay Ritter, an economist at the University of Illinois, has found that initial public offerings earn lower returns than the stock market as a whole. Yet people keep buying new issues.

Conclusion: We tend to overreact to long shots in two ways: becoming risk-takers when contemplating large gains and risk-avoiders when contemplating large losses.

CORRECTIVE ACTION

Prospect theory teaches us two important things about managing our own portfolios. First, not to overvalue certainty. Overemphasizing earnings stability during recessions and consistency of earnings growth at all times can lead to the bad habit of buying stocks for more than their true value. That's a point to bear in mind when you're tempted to buy a "growth" stock at 30 to 60 times earnings. Just remember Benjamin Graham's warning, cited in the previous chapter: today's heavy emphasis on future expectations is a doubled-edged sword.

The second lesson is not to exaggerate tiny probabilities. As we've seen, investors become risk-takers when contemplating large gains and risk-avoiders when contemplating large losses. So counter this tendency by thinking twice before overpaying for the prospect of a promising new drug in early clinical trials, the potential of a big oil find or a technology firm's current rapid growth.

On the flip side, try to avoid what I call the Chicken Little syndrome. Investors often find reasons to fear exposure to sectors of an economy, a certain industry, region, country or individual companies. The Mexican peso crisis hammered down emerging market equities indiscriminately, even in the Far East. When the likelihood and size of a potential calamity are thus exaggerated, the areas in question will usually be undervalued.

Conclusion: We tend to overvalue certainty and to overestimate the chance of large gains or losses. Investors who can cut through such emotional blocks and weigh probabilities will, in time, beat the market averages.

Exploiting irrationality

Irrationality creates distortions in value, offering periodic opportunities for superior portfolio performance. George Soros, dean of hedge-fund managers, bases his investment strategy on an analysis of the psychological factors behind financial bubbles.

Benjamin Graham had an equally unflinching view of how to exploit such recurrent distortions. As Warren Buffet noted in the 1987 annual report of Berkshire Hathaway, Graham suggested that you imagine stock quotes as emanating from a certain Mr Market, who is your partner in a private business. This accommodating chap appears daily and names a price at which he will either buy your stake or sell you his. Your joint business may be economically stable, but Mr Market's quotations will be anything but. The poor fellow suffers from wide emotional swings. Worse, they are incurable. Sometimes, exhilarated, he sees only rosy prospects. In that mood, he names an exorbitant buy–sell price, fearing you will snap up his interest and rob him of imminent gains. At other times, he is despondent and sees nothing but trouble ahead. At such moments, he quotes a low-ball price, terrified you will unload your interest on him.

Graham, Buffet says, would then add: "Mr. Market has another endearing characteristic: He doesn't mind being ignored. If his quotation is uninteresting to you today, he will be back with a new one tomorrow. Transactions are strictly at your option. Under these conditions, the more manic-depressive his behavior, the better for you. But, like Cinderella at the ball, you must heed one warning or everything will turn into pumpkins and mice: Mr. Market is there to serve you, not to guide you."

In other words, if you can't understand and value stocks better than irrational Mr Market, you don't belong in the game.

Conclusion: *Aberrations are not anomalies, but a normal part of equity markets. Self-knowledge helps us profit from such aberrations.*

Contrarian implications

To exploit these common events for steady profit, consider swimming *against* the current. Oil tycoon J. Paul Getty advised: "Buy when everyone else is selling, and hold until everyone else is buying. This is more than just a catchy slogan. It is the very essence of successful investment."

A farmer in Texas made steady profits with this strategy during the 1960s. When he read in the papers that the market was hitting new lows and that experts were predicting it was sure to fall further, the farmer would pick around 30 stocks that had fallen below $10 – solid, unknown profit-makers like pecan growers or furniture makers, that paid dividends. He would come to Houston and buy a $25,000 package of them. Then, one, two, three or four years later, when the stock market was bubbling and gurus were enthusiastic, he would come to town and sell his whole package.

Buying stocks, he felt, was just like buying a truckload of pigs. The lower he could buy the pigs, when the pork market was depressed, the more profit he would make in the next seller's market. He preferred using this strategy on stocks because pigs didn't pay a dividend. You had to feed pigs.

Contrary thinking does not automatically assume the crowd is wrong. The crowd is often right, for months on end. Stocks can get trashed for very sound reasons. So blindly buying whatever is out of favor can cut you as painfully as catching a falling knife. Gerald Loeb put it this way in *The Battle for Investment Survival*: "It is a great mistake to think that what goes down must come back up."

An even bigger blunder, however, is to assume that what goes down will *not* come back up. The closer the crowd is to a consensus, the more likely it is hugely mistaken. In fact, it is *impossible* for a stock market to follow the path that an overwhelming majority expects it to take. If nearly everyone expects prices to go up (a consensus), who is left to sell? Only a small minority. If nearly everyone expects prices to fall, who is left to buy? Again, only a small minority. If investors are mainly ebullient or mainly glum, prices can only go in the opposite direction, just as a stone tossed high in the air must come to earth or a beach ball dunked under water must bob up again.

Behavioral factors underlie the long-term success of many contrarian investment strategies. In the previous chapter, for instance, I noted that unpopular "value" stocks tend to be more profitable than the more popular "growth" stocks of the day. I also mentioned that neglected shares are less subject to exaggerated expectations inflating their price.

Similarly, as a contrarian you can exploit two additional facts: large earnings surprises are common and investors overreact to such surprises. People generally believe the "best" stocks are those with high P/Es and the "worst" stocks those with low P/Es. In "Overreaction, Underreaction, and the Low-P/E Effect," David Dreman and Michael Berry found that positive earnings surprises have a marked favorable effect on low-P/E stocks and little or no impact on high-P/E stocks. Conversely, negative earnings surprises have a minimal effect on low-P/E stocks and a major impact on high-P/E stocks. There is little impact from earnings surprises on the stocks of firms with P/Es that fall between these two extremes.

Conclusion: *Contrarian strategies based on buying low-P/E stocks will continue to provide above-average returns.*

Going against the herd can be highly lucrative. Consider:

- In the autumn of 1990, many bank stocks were priced as if the entire industry was threatened with insolvency. The crowd was wrong. One share of Citicorp then: $11. One share of Citicorp in early 1996: $75.
- In June 1995, the crowd shunned major pharmaceuticals in the wake of a 30-month bear market triggered by upheavals in health care. The crowd was wrong. One share of Merck & Co. then: $29. In early 1996: $70.

Contrary thinking means blazing your own trail despite the pressures of the crowd. It works because of human nature. People love to be fashionable. Biotech stocks were "in" in 1993 and China funds in 1994. Alas, by chasing the crowd, most of us buy after prices have risen and sell after prices have fallen. We lose profits at both ends: buying too high and selling too low.

Granted, it is statistically impossible to peg exact market tops or bottoms. All the same, a contrary approach to the world's equity markets will capture a larger share of the profits to be made by any substantial market move. If you steadily buy into fear and sell into greed, you'll make money. It sounds easy. But people rarely do it. When everyone seems to fear a crash, we tend to be frightened too. When everyone seems to expect higher stock prices, the elation generally rubs off on us. Most of us hate to stand alone, clinging to an opinion everyone else seems to dismiss.

We also like to feel we have made prudent choices, but tend to confuse prudence with conformity. If we buy a share that subsequently plummets, the pain of the loss softens if we can view the investment as one that other sensible people would have made. This seems to explain why well-known blue chips such as General Motors remain popular with small investors despite generally dismal performance. It may also explain why so many portfolio managers seem more comfortable in failing conventionally than in succeeding unconventionally. Few after all have ever been fired for buying IBM.

More than brains, contrary investing demands self-discipline and courage. If you're a maverick or lone wolf or have a tendency to rock the boat, you probably have what it takes to be a successful contrarian.

Conclusion: Stick to a plan. Beware of fads and mindless conformity. Learning to recognize manic tops or panic bottoms will improve portfolio return.

How the bumblebee invests

Though aberrations are a normal part of human behavior, bees respond differently. If you've ever been attacked by an angry bee, the insect may have seemed impulsive to the point of kamikaze madness, willing to risk life and sting to protect its nest. But in its daily round of rummaging for nectar and pollen, the bumblebee, it turns out, is actually the epitome of conservatism: carefully weighing risk and reward in deciding which plants to visit. In an experiment designed to explore the bumblebee's thinking, a US researcher set out an artificial meadow of reliable blue flowers, each containing a small amount of nectar, and chancy yellow flowers, some containing nothing, some a jackpot of nectar.

Guess what? The bees quickly learned to avoid the chancy flower and home in on the known quantity. They clearly preferred steady small rewards to the chance of hitting it big. The researcher, Dr Leslie A. Real of the University of North Carolina in Chapel Hill, says this shows that bees make decisions in a way quite unlike human beings, who often rely on a subjective sense of luck, fate and intuition in choosing actions. The bees preferred blue flowers with reliable though meagre nectar to yellow flowers with a greater but inconsistent reward. When yellow flowers were made the steady source and blue flowers the fickle one, the bees switched from blue to yellow after sampling only three flowers. The quick switch conserves energy. Dr Real suggests that the conservative approach is of great benefit to the bee, and that a more daredevil style would probably doom it to extinction.

Rather than dismissing the bee as a stupid creature whose every action stems from a fixed reflex, Dr Real says that the bee uses its limited neurological capacity to good advantage, and that it reaches surprisingly sophisticated conclusions from a restricted sampling of its environment. "Bees ignore rare events and pay attention to common events," Dr Real explains. "Humans are optimists and they believe rare events will happen more frequently than they actually do." That's the sort of faith that keeps Las Vegas and lotteries in business.

Conclusion: Contrarian thinking helps you exploit common events for steady profit and is more rewarding than chasing improbabilities.

Summary

We react consciously to only a fragment of the data being thrown at us. We tend to become more confident and less accurate as we process increasing amounts of information. As most people can handle no more than seven pieces of information at once, it is wise to employ no more than seven criteria for choosing each stock.

As ongoing changes cannot be quantified, intuitive skills are generally much more useful than interactive reasoning in managing an equity portfolio.

The uncertainty involved in making decisions with only partial information causes investors to behave in set patterns.

If you buy the same securities as other people, you will have the same results as other people.

One individual's faith will not move a market. An investor is wise to cultivate humility. It's what you learn after you know it all that counts.

Regardless of the odds, we tend to avoid the possibility of loss in favor of a sure win and to take on risk to avoid a sure loss. We try to avoid regret, and so react quite differently to a problem depending on how it is framed.

Focusing on single holdings is a common propensity global investors should especially avoid.

Investors tend to hold on to losers for too long and sell winners too soon. The rational approach is to ignore an equity's portfolio history. All that counts is the simple question: Would you be willing to buy it now? If not, then you should sell. Don't be afraid to take a loss. Mistakes are part of the game.

We tend to overvalue certainty. We tend to overestimate the chance of large gains or losses, becoming risk-takers when pondering large gains and risk-avoiders when pondering large losses. Investors who can cut through such emotional blocks and weigh probabilities will, in time, beat the market averages. Aberrations are not anomalies, but a normal part of equity markets. Self-knowledge helps us profit from such aberrations. Identifying manic tops and panic bottoms improves portfolio return. It is therefore wise to focus on the long-run odds, staying cool as the markets gyrate. So stick to a plan – and beware of fads and mindless conformity. Contrarian strategies based on buying low-P/E stocks will continue to provide above-average returns. The wise investor does not attribute transitory market losses to poor port-

folio choices. Though volatility may be painful to experience, the compensation for living with it is high.

Contrarian thinking helps you exploit common events for recurring profit and is more rewarding than chasing improbabilities.

The next chapter describes some practical ways you can use probability to create steady profits.

15

PRODUCING STEADY PROFITS

"Keep probability in view."
John Gay, 1727

A disciplined approach that exploits probability is a true passport to profits. Playing the odds is typically more rewarding than trying to guess the future. Indeed, recognition of the key role of probability may well be what has led you to global investing. The bumblebee clearly believes with Publius that it is better to have a little than nothing. Which risks, he asks, reap dependable rewards? Let's pose the same reasonable question in our global context.

DEPENDABLE GAINS

From fundamental formulas

Unrivaled in uncovering risks that reap dependable rewards is the seminal work of Benjamin Graham, who never stopped questioning and trying to simplify. We've already examined the techniques used in the world's stock markets by some of Graham's most successful disciples, including John Templeton and Barry Ziskin. Just before Graham's death at his home in France in 1976, he had completed research going back 50 years (from 1925 to 1975), showing that using just a *few* of his investment criteria during that period would have outperformed the Dow by more than two to one. His last message to friend and collaborator James Rea, recorded in "Remembering Benjamin Graham," was: "Invest in financially sound companies whose earnings and dividend yields are high." By Graham's criteria, a company is financially sound when it owes less than its net worth; and its earnings and dividend yields are high when they are, respectively, twice and two-thirds the average AAA bond yield. One way of creating steady profits in any major market is to follow these proven criteria for stock selection:

Criterion 1

The company should owe less than it is worth. In other words, the ratio of debt, including preferred stock, to tangible equity should be less than 1. This criterion is combined with *either* of the following:

Criterion 2

The "earnings yield" (the reciprocal of the P/E ratio) should be twice the prevailing AAA bond yield. For example, if the average AAA bond yield were 8 percent, twice that would be 16. This means you want a P/E ratio (100 divided by 16) of 6.25 or less. If a stock sells for 12.5 times earnings, it has an 8 percent earnings yield. If it sells for 5 times earnings, it has a 20 percent earnings yield, and so on. The higher the bond yield, the lower your P/E prerequisite. Thus, if AAA bonds yield 10 percent, a stock must have an earnings yield of twice that, or no more than 5 times earnings. On the other hand, if AAA bonds yield 4 3/4 percent, you can afford to buy a stock at a 9.5 percent earnings yield (or 10.5 times earnings). Graham found that if you had used only this earnings criterion (in combination with criterion 1), the average compounded gain in the share price, going back 50 years, would have been 19.9 percent, excluding dividends and commissions, as against 3.5 percent for the Dow.

Criterion 3

The "dividend yield" should be at least two-thirds the average AAA bond yield. Thus, if AAA bonds yield 6 percent then a stock should yield at least 4 percent. If AAA bonds yield 9 percent, then the dividend should yield at least 6 percent. Graham found that this approach (in combination with criterion 1) was almost as rewarding as the earnings criterion, producing a 50-year compound return of 19.5 percent, excluding dividends and commissions, versus the Dow's 3.5 percent.

The three selling rules that Graham and Rea developed together were equally elegant:

- Sell after your stock has gone up 50 percent or after the first two years, whichever comes first.
- Sell if the dividend is omitted.
- Sell when earnings decline so far that the current market price is 50 percent higher than the price at which you would buy the stock based on the above P/E criteria. If AAA bonds yield 6 1/4 percent, a purchase candidate should have a P/E ratio under 8. With earnings of 5, the target purchase price is 40. If this stock trades at 60 (50 percent over the target buying price), it should be sold.

Graham, by the way, eventually concluded that diversity was more important than in-depth research. He wanted to invest in no less than 30 companies, and found following so many both impossible and unnecessary. This recalls one of our initial conclusions: For optimal global equity diversification, it makes sense to select some 25 stocks, or their equivalents, from different countries and industries, placing more emphasis on country diversification than on industry diversification.

What if you no longer can find any equities that meet the above criteria? In that case, Graham and Rea would invest in bonds, but you, as a global investor, have the option of moving on to equities in another country. Remember: there's always a bull market somewhere.

Conclusion: *Buying stocks in firms that owe less than net worth, with earnings and dividend yields, respectively, of twice and two-thirds the average AAA bond yield will reap dependable rewards. If no equities meet these criteria in a particular market, move on to another. Sell after a stock has gone up 50 percent or after the first two years, whichever comes first. Sell if the dividend is omitted, or if earnings decline so sharply that the stock sells 50 percent higher than its target purchase price.*

From market risk

The question of which risks reap rewards was also posed in *The Journal of Portfolio Management* by Robert Arnott, who concluded that certain market risks bring dependable gains. Perceived risk and actual risk, as you've seen, simply do not coincide. If markets were perfectly rational and efficient, returns would relate to the risk you cannot diversify away. But markets are people, and people are not perfectly rational. People expect greater return for greater perceived risk, and price an equity accordingly. Share prices fluctuate much more widely than values. Popular equities are often overvalued and unpopular ones undervalued. Hence, one way to create steady profits is to follow strategies that exploit these recurring discrepancies between the risk the crowd sees in an equity and its expected non-diversifiable risk. This echoes a major conclusion of Chapter 5: For individual stocks, the dispersion of analyst earnings estimates seems the best proxy for market risk, and the wider such estimates are scattered the higher the return you can anticipate. In choosing individual holdings for a global portfolio, it is thus wiser to seek market risk than avoid it. We did that in the first instance by opting for equities over bonds.

Let's examine the methods of a select few who have exploited such probabilities to create steady profits. *The Hulbert Financial Digest* tracks the specific investment advice of 162 other US newsletters, using a whimsical methodology that sometimes treats a "hold" recommendation as a "sell." When Mark Hulbert started in mid-1980, he tracked just three dozen such services, and 19 of these have survived 15 years of publication.

We'll begin with the top risk-seeker: Louis Navellier, whose *MPT Review* (tel: + 1–702–831–1396) achieved the most consistent returns of any stock advisory service Hulbert monitored from 1985 to 1996. Navellier seeks market risk by investing in equities with low market capitalization that are listed on the US over-the-counter market. This small-cap strategy is especially vulnerable when markets plummet. During the 1987 crash, his model portfolios fell 35 percent, a loss exceeded by only four other services. When the market turned round, however, Navellier's stocks bounced back strongly. From January 1985 until January 1996, after deduction of 2 percent estimated round-trip commissions, his 15 model portfolios racked up average compound growth of 24.5 percent.

Navellier attempts to discern which stocks are likely to grow and which are likely to shrink at times when other managers think they could go either way. He aims to get the most out of the often-volatile OTC stocks without taking on too much of the downside. Within this risky sphere of operations, he is highly risk-averse. Recognizing that the fundamentals impacting Wall Street or any other stock market are always shifting, he has developed 23 different fundamental ways of screening equities. Each screen reflects a different market factor, such as profit margin expansion, projected P/E ratio, sales growth, earnings consistency, low institutional ownership and – one of Navellier's favourites – earnings surprise. Of these initial 23, he uses seven, the same number as Barry Ziskin. But just which seven Navellier uses depends on what currently works. Ziskin uses a pencil, Navellier several computers. To minimize exposure to risk in the small-cap market, the computers churn that 6,000 over-the-counter stocks through a three-stage filter to arrive at a risk/reward rating.

- Navellier's primary risk yardstick is monthly standard deviation, which, you'll recall, represents the probable range of a stock's up or down movements, reflecting its unique volatility, or unsystematic risk. Unsystematic risk is of course diversifiable.
- Second, he measures a relative strength indicator called alpha: how much a stock's gains vary from the market, the way it zigs when the market zags. Alpha represents the excess monthly return above an equally weighted market index of all stocks in his database during the last 12 months. In other words, if his market index has a zero rate of return, alpha would indicate a stock's expected monthly return. If all stocks were efficiently priced, alpha would always equal zero. Navellier searches for high alpha, inefficiently-priced equities, believing alpha is the most important indicator of their potential return.
- The third thing he does is divide this figure by the stock's standard deviation to arrive at a risk/relative strength ratio. The equities on his buy list are sorted in order of attractiveness based on this ratio, thus identifying those that have had better than average characteristics of risk and return for the past 12 months. Navellier's policy of holding only stocks that rank high in terms of risk/relative strength automatically imposes a selling discipline that prevents him from holding on to stocks through protracted declines.

The more volatile a stock, the less Navellier typically holds. Most of the time, he emphasizes low-beta stocks. (Beta, you'll recall, measures an equity's overall sensitivity to the movement of its market.) Navellier concentrates on OTC stocks because they tend to be less efficiently priced than those on the big board, which usually do not appreciate as dramatically. Essentially, he is buying perceived risk that is diversifiable.

A strategy based on buying perceived risk that is diversifiable can backfire in only two ways. First, it will fail if a risk cannot in fact be diversified away. While such systematic risk is plausible in a single market such as Navellier's, the global approach largely precludes it. Second, if aversion to a particular sector or country grows, creating an imagined "flight to safety," the strategy will also fail. The setback will, however, be temporary and its impact weaker the more effectively you have diversified. In a single market of course, investors may stand aloof from a sector for several years. Managers who used a value-oriented price to book strategy had an unpleasant time in the US during its two-tier equity market of 1969 to 1972. So choose unpopular stocks – but diversify. This recalls a major conclusion of Chapter 9. Shares and countries ignored by institutions can provide individual investors with superior returns.

Conclusion: Avoiding popular equities and buying a well-diversified global package of those generally believed risky will achieve superior results in the long run. Typically the strategy will produce some spectacular flops more than offset by spectacular gains.

Though this may seem the antithesis of the bumblebee's approach, your "risky" yellow wallflowers will have a much higher probability of success. The bumblebee would envy you.

George Soros, one of the world's most successful investors, also regularly seeks risky equities. He zeroes in on a sector, and then takes a position in just two companies: the best and the worst in that business. "The worst quite clearly offers the biggest possible turnaround," Soros explains. "A change in industry fortunes will have the biggest impact there because the worst-off is likely to be the most leveraged. At the other end, the best will obviously benefit, because it is a market leader."

From undramatic growth

Another form of bumblebee investing can be used by value and growth managers alike. David Dreman, of Dreman Value Management in Jersey City, New Jersey, buys beaten-down "value" stocks, hoping for a rebound. Terence McLaughlin, of New York's Ashland Management, buys higher-multiple "growth" stocks that have racked up strong earnings performance. Yet both men rely on the same stock-picking approach: seeking firms that show dull and plodding profit growth with no sudden leaps or plunges. (Earnings consistency is also used by Navellier and Ziskin.) A company whose earnings grow 10 percent, then 11 percent, is a better bet than one with 25 percent growth one year and 3 percent the next.

Do steady growers really perform better over the long run than volatile ones? Research done in 1995 by James Floyd of Minneapolis-based Leuthod Group suggests they do. He analyzed the firms in the S&P 500 index as if he were investing in them a decade earlier. First, he used a statistical technique to compare their annual earnings growth over the previous decade: 1974 through 1984. Then he calculated stock-price growth for the decade through 1994. And lo, the most stable shares led all the rest, soaring 246 percent. Those with jittery earnings rose only 169 percent. Overall, the 500 stocks gained 229 percent.

Conclusion: Earnings stability is a useful tool for selecting equities likely to provide steady gains. Other things being equal, go for consistent earnings growth, avoiding the zigzag mode.

LIMITING LOSSES

The bumblebee avoids the chancy yellow flowers that often turn its efforts to naught. A related way of making steady profits is simply to limit losses. Here are some practical methods for limiting losses in a global portfolio.

Through low turnover

When investing, it is often useful to recall Yogi Berra's advice to a young baseball player: "**Don't make the wrong mistakes.**" Expert tennis is called a winner's game because the ultimate outcome is determined by the actions of the winner. Conversely, amateur tennis is determined by the actions of the loser, making it a loser's game. The amateur seldom beats his opponent, but he beats himself all the time. The victor gets a higher score because his opponent loses even more points. In a 1975 article, Charles Ellis suggested that most investment managers fail to beat the market because they are playing a loser's game.

Institutions now account for the bulk of trading activity in the world's equity markets. Competition between them (and their advisers) has generated vastly increased portfolio turnover and thus higher costs. A study of Nasdaq trading costs by Meeta Kothare and Paul

Laux showed the average spread rose from less than 3 percent in 1984 to almost 6 percent in 1992. Such costs are precisely what have made institutional investing a loser's game.

Let me demonstrate. Suppose we estimate that in most markets institutional investors incur spreads and commissions some 60 percent lower than those on Nasdaq, say 3.5 percent

If equities return an average annual 9 percent return, turnover averages 30 percent a year, and dealer spreads and commissions on institutional transactions (one way) average 3.5 percent of the assets involved, how much does a professional manager have to outperform a market to deliver net returns 20 percent above its index?

The answer boggles the mind: over 43 percent. And that ignores management and custody fees. Using the same estimates, the active manager must beat a market gross by 23 percent just to come out with the market net.

Conclusion: Bring turnover down as a deliberate, conscious practice. Think twice before doing anything, because chances are it is a mistake.

Through puts

If, like the bumblebee, you prefer the sure thing to the high-risk venture, you can limit your downside with puts. You can purchase these options to sell a stock, or basket of stocks, at a specific price and puts on a wide range of market proxies are available, among other places, in Tokyo, New York, London, Sydney, Frankfurt, Paris and Amsterdam. The seller, or "writer," of a put receives a certain sum of money, the option premium, from the put buyer. In return, the buyer gets the right to sell the put writer 100 shares of a stated common stock, or basket of stocks, at a fixed price: the striking price. This right can be exercised at any time prior to the expiration date of the option.

In Amsterdam, for instance, when the EOE index was at 510.60 in February 1996, you could have bought a put on that index for ƒ18.50, giving you the right to sell the EOE index at 510 until July 1996. You'd want one such contract for each ƒ51,060 in your Dutch portfolio. You of course wouldn't exercise that option unless the EOE index stayed below your striking price. If you held the option until July, you'd lose the entire ƒ1,850 premium you paid, unless at that point the EOE index was below 510. No problem. You've simply taken out insurance. But do it selectively. It's expensive, more than 3.6 percent for the five-month coverage in this example.

If your portfolio rises in value, sure, you've lost the insurance premium, but you have a profit on your stocks. If your portfolio falls in value instead, your puts – an appropriate number equal to the market value of your Amsterdam-listed shares – should rise in value by an equal amount. You've covered your assets.

Through stops

A much cheaper way to accomplish the same thing implements a key bit of advice in the previous chapter: don't be afraid to take a loss. This is the approach used by Martin Zweig, another of the select few who exploit probability to create steady profits. He uses "stop" points on every recommendation he makes, and the system seems to work. Since Hulbert began rating US investment advisory services, Zweig has never had a down year. Adjusted for risk, which Hulbert defines as volatility, Zweig outperformed the other 18 surviving services from 1980 through 1995.

In 1939, Jesse Livermore, who made and lost four fortunes in the stock market, wrote *How to Trade in Stocks*, offering this tip: **"Always sell what shows you a loss and keep what shows you a profit."** That's the purpose of a stop. If you buy a share at 40, you won't be too badly hurt if you stop yourself out at 34 for a 15 percent loss. You'll still have the bulk of your capital. A 20 percent drop should be your maximum, because you then need a 25 percent rebound to break even. If a share falls from 40 to 32, it's down 20 percent. A return trip from 32 back to 40 works out to a 25 percent rise. Difficult but not impossible. But if a share drops 50 percent, say from 40 to 20, it has to double for you to break even. And riding a stock down 90 percent, from 40 to 4, means you need an unlikely tenfold increase, a gain of 900 percent, just to get back your money. So it is sheer folly to let losses run wild.

Zweig normally sets his stops 10 to 20 percent below purchase price, with the precise level depending on his view of the trading pattern. Usually, he gives more room to volatile equities, such as those in the high-tech sector, and less room to conservative issues, such as utilities. He often tries to set a stop point just before a share's previous low. Or he may draw a trend line and set the stop just below it on the assumption that a break in the uptrend might lead to a downward reversal in the price.

Setting stops is more art than science. You may find yourself getting stopped out of a stock that then proceeds to soar, simply because you set your stop a tad too high. But we're discussing probabilities. Most of the time, you'll be stopped out as a stock breaks from its trading range and, after taking a tolerable loss, be able to watch as a bystander as the stock plummets further. (At times, however, a stop-loss approach is inferior to the selling discipline imposed by a risk/relative strength rating such as that used by Navellier. During a long bull market, sharp pullbacks along the way can trigger stop-loss sales of equities that continue to show powerful long-term strength relative to the market. By focusing on *relative* strength rather than *absolute* strength during adverse market environments, you can avoid these costly and unproductive stop-loss sales.)

A stop order can be placed directly with a specialist on the NYSE and many other stock exchanges through your broker. It tells the specialist to sell your stock "at the market" when it hits your stop point, or "trigger price." On markets where this is difficult or impossible, I suggest the mental "stop loss" mentioned in the previous chapter. You or your broker then have to follow the equity involved so the broker can sell it the moment it hits your mental stop. Price targets, however, like precise predictions, can be a source of false security. Neither a mental stop nor one placed with a specialist guarantee the price you will receive. They simply trigger a sell order, and a stock in free fall may be sold well below the floor you have set. When a stop is triggered, don't waste your time on regret, but focus on what to do with the proceeds. A limited loss, when realized, is simply a chance for profit elsewhere. It hands you the opportunity to turn a liability into an asset.

Conclusion: *In the long run, stops limit losses to reasonable size and let profits run.*

HOW TO LOCK IN PROFITS

A stop can be used not only to protect against loss, but also to lock in a profit. The idea is to place a "trailing stop" under a stock that's on the rise.

In the previous example, you placed a protective stop at 34, which was 15 percent under your purchase price of 40. The time to begin thinking about raising that stop is when your paper profit nears 20 percent. If the stock moved up to 47, you might move the stop up to 39 3/4, just under the purchase price, and if the stock continued to climb to, say, 54, you could raise your protective stop to 46, locking in a 15 percent profit. Should the stock advance further to 62, you might raise your stop to 53, locking in a gain of more than 32 percent.

Place stops where you feel most comfortable. Your aim is to separate random and normal short-term sell-offs from really bad news. Bear markets are a fact of life, so ultimately the local index will turn down and trigger your trailing stop, often letting you realize substantial profits.

Zweig refuses to hold equities through a bear market. "The pain would kill me," he explains. When prices seem badly to exceed underlying values, he buys put options and shorts stocks or index futures.

Conclusion: *Trailing stops can enable a global investor to realize gains in declining markets. When several stops are triggered in a single market, implying a major downturn, buying puts is likely to produce gains.*

TIME IS ON YOUR SIDE

Currency-cost averaging

Here is another way probability helps you create steady profits, especially in volatile markets. Currency-cost averaging, regularly investing the same amount of francs, marks, yen or dollars, is a system that makes anyone an expert market timer. It saves you from the danger of buying into a market at its peak: a tendency to which small investors are notably prone.

In the long run, currency-cost averaging reduces the average cost of an investment. You may not get all your money in at the cheapest point, but you won't be committing your whole wad at the top either.

Depending on market conditions, it can pay you handsomely to take the regular savings route rather than the lump-sum approach. The nub of currency-cost averaging is that by investing a fixed sum each month, the number of shares you acquire depends on the level of a market from month to month. If the market rises, the price of shares goes up and each investment buys fewer. But, if the market falls, the price of shares goes down and each investment buys more of them.

If you regularly invest a fixed amount over a number of market cycles, the larger number of low-cost shares in your portfolio will lower the average price. This system is especially useful in purchasing volatile country funds, such as those in emerging markets.

Table 15.1 illustrates the concept more clearly. Two different market scenarios are shown, in each of which you invest a total of $6,000.

Table 15.1 Currency-cost averaging in action

Period	Investment amount	Scenario 1 share price	Shares purchased	Scenario 2 share price	Shares purchased
1	$500	$10	50.0	$10	50.0
2	$500	$8	62.5	$11	45.4
3	$500	$7	71.4	$12	41.6
4	$500	$6	83.3	$13	38.4
5	$500	$4	125.0	$14	35.7
6	$500	$4	125.0	$15	33.3
7	$500	$6	83.3	$16	31.2
8	$500	$8	62.5	$17	28.4
9	$500	$10	50.0	$18	27.7
10	$500	$11	45.4	$19	26.3
11	$500	$12	41.6	$20	25.0
12	$500	$14	35.7	$21	23.8
Total shares purchased			835.7		407.8
Total return under scenario 1: 835.7 shares at $14 per share = $11,699.80					
Total return under scenario 2: 407.8 shares at $21 per share = $8,563.80					

In the first scenario, a market tumbles more than 50 percent, but then rises from the ashes to end 40 percent up from its start. In the second, the same market rises steadily, finishing more than 100 percent higher. Though in the second scenario the market has more than doubled, you would have seen a 37 percent higher return under scenario 1, where the market slumped and then soared. This is because when the market was down, each $500 monthly investment bought more shares, which were then worth more at the end of the period.

Naturally, the opposite is also true. A lump sum of $6,000 invested at the outset would have been worth 50 percent more under scenario 2 than under scenario 1. But this presumes you are a skilled market timer – and few investors are. (Not that successful timing is impossible: from 1952 to 1985, Martin Zweig's seasonal model realized 223 up days versus only 8 down.)

Conclusion: *Regularly and automatically investing a fixed sum removes any risk of buying into a market at its peak. In the long run, such currency-cost averaging will reduce the average cost of your global investments.*

The futility of long-term timing

Should you bypass a stock market that is racking up new highs? Absolutely not. First, trying to guess the high point of any market is an impossible task. Second, short-term market timing, as Chapter 13 demonstrated, is generally unprofitable. Third, long-term market timing is of little help to most people anyway. In May 1995, James Glassman of the *Washington Post* described an exercise by analysts at Capital Research and Management Co. They invented a gent known as "Louie the Loser," who each year put $5,000 into Investment Co. of America, an actual mutual fund managed by Capital Research that has closely tracked US market returns. Louie, alas, was a lousy timer. Each year, he chose the worst possible moment to invest his $5,000: the day the Dow hit its annual peak. Still, after 20 years, Louie's total investment of $100,000 had grown to $441,000 – an average annual return of 13 percent. Louie's opposite number, an imaginary perfect market timer we'll call Winnie the Winner, invested her $5,000 the day the market hit its low each year, scoring a return of 15 percent – not much of a difference.

Conclusion: Time, not timing, is what matters.

The two basic types of diversification

Though diversification is the cardinal rule of investing, there is more than one kind. The wise investor diversifies not merely in space (geographically), but also in time. Patience is the key. You get the chicken by hatching an egg – not by smashing it. Though equity markets have been called a huge casino, over time they are anything but. Gambling in a casino where the house takes, say, 20 percent of every pot is a loser's game. The players as a group lose money. In the world's equity markets, on the other hand, only short-term traders bear a serious risk of losing money. Long-term investors almost invariably come out winners, because they benefit from time diversification: the notion that investments held for a long period are inherently less risky than those held for a short one. Indeed, about the only long-term losers in equities are those that fail to diversify in the other direction: across securities. Obviously, many individual shares lose money in the long run. But a diversified equity portfolio, especially one mirroring various markets, will rise on the back of the long-term upward trend.

I mentioned in Chapter 4 that US stock returns over one-year periods since 1925 have zigzagged all over the map, from a 54 percent gain to a 43 percent loss. Over 20-year periods, however, according to Chicago consultancy Ibbotson Associates, compound annual US returns have been in a much narrower band: from 17 percent down to 3 percent. That still makes a huge difference in final dollar amounts: An initial $1,000, compounded for two decades at 17 percent, grows to $22,542, while at 3 percent an investor winds up with only $1,844. Though time narrows the range of percentage returns, it clearly magnifies dollar differences.

You sidestep this pitfall simply by investing in more than a single market.

Conclusion: Together, security diversification and time diversification make an unbeatable combination for minimizing your chances of loss and meeting your long-term expectations of gain.

The optimum holding period

Common sense supports the notion that investments held for a long period are less risky than those held for a short one, academic theorizing to the contrary. If stock market returns are independent from one year to the next, then good years will offset the bad ones, and the risk of holding equities over long periods will be less than the risk of holding them, say, for only a year. A study of time diversification by Steven Thorley in the *Financial Analysts Journal* of May/June 1995 proves that the chance of any loss at all drops sharply as time goes by. The longer your time horizon, the less likely you are even to fall short of your target rate of return. In Thorley's example, if the chance that a market index fund will underperform a money-market fund over a year is 31 percent, in 10 years that chance will have dropped to less than 6 percent. In 20 years, it will have dropped to an infinitesimal 1.3 percent, and the likelihood of a real disaster will have become negligible.

Nevertheless, some prominent financial economists contend that while you are less likely to lose money over a long period, the size of your potential losses rises as the period extends. The growing improbability of a loss, they say, is offset by the growing size of potential losses. Granted, in theory the range of possible returns includes both zero and infinity. But in the everyday world, the probability of such investment results is infinitely remote. And even if a portfolio winds up in the red, its *average annualized* loss is what matters.

Like Procrustes, the mythical giant of Attica, who seized travelers, tied them to a bedstead and stretched them or lopped off their legs to make them fit, skeptics of the time diversification benefit usually invoke utility theory to refute it, asserting that if you choose a "riskless" asset over a one-month period you should also choose it over 20 years. Ignoring the fundamental difference between predicting behavior and prescribing it, they will even offer mathematical "proof," based on utility theory's definition of rationality, that your investment horizon is irrelevant to your choice of risk. But, as the previous chapter demonstrated, our decisions are often out of whack with the rigid scenarios postulated by utility theory. When it comes to long-term human behavior, utility theory is a faulty model and an even worse yardstick. Rational and informed investors regularly make choices that contradict it. So the model is wrong, not the investors.

Though a developed market is little better than a 50/50 proposition over brief periods of time, its inexorable secular uptrend means that in the long run you make money far more often than you lose it. A simple real-world example from a recent issue of Norman Fosback's *Market Logic*: If you had owned an equal-dollar market basket of all NYSE stocks in any single month from 1971 through 1994, you would have had a 44 percent chance of losing money, because the market declined in 44 percent of all months. Your average loss in the down months would have been at an annualized rate of 33 percent.

But suppose you had been indifferent to month-to-month market swings and interested solely in your risk and return for ten-year holding periods? If you'd invested in any ten-year period during the 124 years, you would have had only a 1 percent chance of losing money. In 99 percent of all ten-year periods, the market rose on a total-return basis.

The one-month and ten-year holdings are but two elements of a much larger matrix of time-diversification results. Fosback had his computer show the time-diversification benefits of 298 more holding periods, ranging from two-month to 300-month (25-year) holdings. You can see these in Table 15.2 which shows that time diversification produces lower and lower risk as your time spectrum lengthens. While as 44 percent of all one-month holding periods since 1871 were losers, only 30 percent of all overlapping 12-month (one-year) periods produced losses. Five-year holdings were even more profitable: just 11 percent were losers. As already mentioned, a mere 1 percent of ten-year holdings wound up in the red. As for 25-year periods, from 1871 through 1994 not a single one turned up in the loss column!

Table 15.2 Time diversification: 124 years, 1871–1994

Holding period		Chance of loss	Average annualized loss
1 Month		44%	32.5%
3 Months		38%	23.4%
6 Months		35%	17.2%
12 Months	(1 Year)	30%	12.7%
24 Months	(2 Years)	23%	8.6%
36 Months	(3 Years)	16%	6.2%
48 Months	(4 Years)	15%	4.4%
60 Months	(5 Years)	11%	4.5%
72 Months	(6 Years)	8%	3.7%
84 Months	(7 Years)	4%	3.7%
96 Months	(8 Years)	3%	2.0%
108 Months	(9 Years)	2%	1.8%
120 Months	(10 Years)	1%	1.6%
132 Months	(11 Years)	0.2%	2.0%
144 Months	(12 Years)	0.4%	1.5%
156 Months	(13 Years)	0.3%	2.3%
168 Months	(14 Years)	0.2%	1.4%
180 Months	(15 Years)	0.2%	1.5%
192 Months	(16 Years)	0.2%	1.1%
204 Months	(17 Years)	0.2%	0.3%
216 Months	(18 Years)	0.1%	0.2%
228 Months	(19 Years)	0.1%	0.2%
240 Months	(20 Years)	0.2%	0.4%
252 Months	(21 Years)	0.2%	0.1%
264 Months	(22 Years)	0.0%	0.0%
276 Months	(23 Years)	0.0%	0.0%
288 Months	(24 Years)	0.0%	0.0%
300 Months	(25 Years)	0.0%	0.0%

The Institute for Econometric Research

Time not only lessens the chance of loss, but, again roundly contra-
dicting utility theory, also reduces the size of any loss in the
increasingly sparse periods when the market declines. In the few cases
that saw losses in ten-year periods (just 1 percent), the average annualized loss was a trivial 1.6 percent.

The "best" holding period? Within a single market, you get most of
the benefits of time diversification within ten years. At that point, the
risk of loss is so low that you cannot reduce it meaningfully by extend-
ing your holding period. To demonstrate this, Fosback sliced the
124-study period into two 62-year halves. To see whether more recent
NYSE market history would change the results, he just looked at the last

Table 15.3 Time diversification 62 years, 1933–1994

Holding period		Chance of loss	Average annualized loss
1 Month		37%	40.5%
3 Months		32%	27.8%
6 Months		29%	19.6%
12 Months	(1 Year)	24%	13.2%
24 Months	(2 Years)	15%	9.5%
36 Months	(3 Years)	12%	6.6%
48 Months	(4 Years)	11%	4.1%
60 Months	(5 Years)	7%	4.3%
72 Months	(6 Years)	7%	3.4%
84 Months	(7 Years)	4%	3.6%
96 Months	(8 Years)	4%	1.2%
108 Months	(9 Years)	2%	1.5%
120 Months	(10 Years)	1%	0.6%
132 Months	(11 Years)	0.0%	0.0%
144 Months	(12 Years)	0.0%	0.0%
156 Months	(13 Years)	0.0%	0.0%
168 Months	(14 Years)	0.0%	0.0%
180 Months	(15 Years)	0.0%	0.0%
192 Months	(16 Years)	0.0%	0.0%
204 Months	(17 Years)	0.0%	0.0%
216 Months	(18 Years)	0.0%	0.0%
228 Months	(19 Years)	0.0%	0.0%
240 Months	(20 Years)	0.0%	0.0%
252 Months	(21 Years)	0.0%	0.0%
264 Months	(22 Years)	0.0%	0.0%
276 Months	(23 Years)	0.0%	0.0%
288 Months	(24 Years)	0.0%	0.0%
300 Months	(25 Years)	0.0%	0.0%

The Institute for Econometric Research

62 years, starting in 1933. The result is shown by Table 15.3, in which you can see precisely the same pattern of lower and lower loss with longer and longer time periods. However, much shorter periods were needed to reduce risk to as good as zero. In fact, this second table shows that every period of 10 years or longer from 1932 through 1994 made money on a total-return basis with NYSE-listed stocks. There was not one single instance of a loss with a holding period of 10 1/2 years or more. Adding more markets should reduce this period even more.

Summary

Buying stocks in firms that owe less than net worth, with earnings and dividend yields, respectively, of twice and two-thirds the average AAA

*bond yield will reap dependable rewards. If no equities meet these cri-
teria in a particular market, move on to another. Sell after a stock has
gone up 50 percent or after the first two years, whichever comes first.
Sell if the dividend is omitted, or if earnings decline so sharply that the
stock sells 50 percent higher than its target purchase price.*

*Avoiding popular equities and buying a well-diversified global pack-
age of those generally believed risky will achieve superior results in the
long run. Typically the strategy will produce some spectacular flops
more than offset by spectacular gains.*

*Earnings stability is a useful tool for selecting equities likely to pro-
vide steady gains. Other things being equal, go for consistent earnings
growth, avoiding the zigzag mode. Bring turnover down as a deliberate, conscious practice. Think twice before doing anything, because
chances are it is a mistake. In the long run, stops limit losses to reasonable size and let profits run. Trailing stops can enable a global
investor to realize gains in declining markets. When several stops are
triggered in a single market, implying a major downturn, buying puts
is likely to produce gains.*

*Regularly and automatically investing a fixed sum removes any risk
of buying into a market at its peak. In the long run, such currency-cost
averaging will reduce the average cost of your global investments.*

*Time, not timing, is what matters. Together, security diversification and
time diversification make an unbeatable combination for minimizing your
chances of loss and meeting your long-term expectations of gain.*

*The longer you hold a well-diversified global equity portfolio, the
more likely you will experience a higher average annual return and a
lower level of risk. In most stock markets, the optimum holding
period to balance risk and reward is 10½ years.*

In addition to guidelines for managing a global portfolio, *Going
Global with Equities* has now provided you with specific tools and
techniques for finding promising shares, countries and funds. To sum
up, here are seven golden rules for global investing:

- Buy equities or their proxies.
- Diversify broadly abroad.
- Diversify in time.
- Avoid fads and panic.
- Use an equal-weighted benchmark.

- Adjust allocations for value, correlations and cycles.
- Hold down turnover and fees.

Inevitably, your home market will take a tumble. Nothing like that predicted in 1995 by Robert Prechter in *At the Crest of the Tidal Wave*: a Dow plunging to 1,000 or lower, followed by a worldwide depression. But certainly enough to demand some forethought. When asked what he had done during the Terror of the French Revolution, the Abbé Sieyès replied, "I survived." This guide to going global should help you to do likewise.

APPENDIX

Useful References

"Great floods have flown from simple sources."

William Shakespeare, *All's Well That Ends Well*

The decisions you make can be no better than the information you use to make them. The successful global investor assembles a few reliable sources, sifted from the sea of dross on which we normally drift. It is no coincidence that Warren Buffet can be found far from the madding crowd in low-key Omaha, Nebraska, Louis Navellier on a Nevada mountaintop, Barry Ziskin in the Arizona desert, Al Frank in New Mexico and John Templeton on a Caribbean island. A certain detachment is clearly invaluable in making investment decisions.

Superior information on what is happening in the world is not easily obtained. You won't find it in your junk mail. Indeed, assembling dependable sources can cost you considerable time and money. Much of that work, however, has been done for you here. This Appendix lists some of the most comprehensive and reliable global investment sources available in the English language. Though a few subscriptions are expensive, you may be able to split the cost with other investors. Several periodicals can moreover be found in a good library, and trial subscriptions are usually available.

In addition to selected publications relevant to global investing, both in print and electronic form, this Appendix provides emerging stock market addresses and phone numbers plus an extensive list of depositary receipts.

Periodicals

Newspapers

Far and away the best daily newspaper for the global investor is the *Financial Times* of London, with excellent coverage of the United Kingdom, the Far East, Africa and Latin America. It has frequent surveys on specific countries or sectors as well. Also printed and delivered in the United States, it costs about $350 a year. You can write to the US office at 14 East 60th Street, New

York, NY 10022. In the US, you can phone + 1–212–752–4500 and in Tokyo + 81–3295–1711. If you're in Europe, address subscription inquiries to Nibelungenplatz 3, D–60318 Frankfurt am Main, Germany; Tel: + 49–69–156–850.

The following newspapers also provide financial news, currency quotations, interest rates, money and banking statistics and price data for the most popular shares on the world's bourses:

The *Asian Wall Street Journal* covers Asian markets, with charts and information on companies and economic developments in specific countries. $225 per year; GPO Box 160, Hong Kong. US office: 200 Liberty Street, New York, NY 10281; Tel: + 1–212–416–2000.

Barron's: National Business and Financial Weekly, 200 Burnett Road, Chicopee, MA 01021; Tel: + 1–800–544–0422. $135 a year. Subscriptions: PO Box 2845, 6401 DH Heerlen, The Netherlands.

The *International Herald Tribune* is available at many newsstands in Europe and Asia, or you can phone the US office on + 1–212–752–3980.

Investors Daily, PO Box 24933, Los Angeles, CA 90024.

New York Times, 229 West 43rd Street, New York, NY 10036.

Wall Street Journal, 200 Liberty Street, New York, NY 10281; Tel: + 1–212–416–2000.

Wall Street Journal Europe, Boulevard Brand Whitlock 87, B–1200 Brussels, Belgium; Tel: + 32–2–741–1211.

Magazines

Two magazines, neither exclusively investment oriented, offer useful commentary on world events from, respectively, a British and a Swiss perspective. The best single source of general news, emphasizing events of economic significance, is the British weekly *The Economist*. With editorial offices in London, Bangkok, Berlin, Brussels, Hong Kong, Los Angeles, Moscow, New York, Paris, Tokyo and Washington, DC, *The Economist* comes closest to an objective and informed view of the world, including incisive reporting on the United States. The US office is at 10 Rockefeller Plaza, New York, NY 10020; Tel: + 1–800–456–6086.

The second valuable source of background data is the *Swiss Review of World Affairs*, published monthly in English by the *Neue Züricher Zeitung*, PO Box 660, CH–8021 Zurich, Switzerland. $48 per year. It provides general analysis of world political and economic trends.

Euromoney is a monthly publication providing well-written feature articles on financial markets and companies around the world. Its primary focus is world capital and money markets and it has supplements with some excellent in-depth material. Nestor House, Playhouse Yard, London EC4V 5EX; Tel: + 44–171–779–8610.

Investors Chronicle, a weekly publication, is chiefly useful for London-listed shares. £94 (UK); £118 (Europe); £142 elsewhere. Greystoke Place, Fetter Lane, London EC4A 1ND; Tel: + 44–171–405–6969.

The Far Eastern Economic Review, a long-established and highly respected weekly owned by Dow Jones & Co., provides in-depth reporting on economic trends and events in the Far East. It is a good source of information on the changes occurring both in China and Japan. Periodically it also covers personal investing. GPO Box 160, Hong Kong; Tel: + 852–2503–1533.

The Central European Economic Review, a publication Dow Jones began recently, covers stocks and mutual funds in Azerbaijan, Bulgaria, Croatia, Czechia, Estonia, Hungary, Latvia, Lithuania, Poland, Romania, Russia, Slovakia, Slovenia, Turkmenistan, the Ukraine and Uzbekistan. PO Box 2845, In de Cramer 37, 6401 DH Heerlen, The Netherlands; Tel: + 31–45–576–1222.

The yearly *Schwartz Stock Market Handbook* is a collection of statistics on UK stock market behaviour, month by month and week by week, that seemingly refutes the random walk theory and shows the best and worst times to buy or sell shares. £17.95. Burleigh Publishing Company; Tel: + 44–1453–731173.

Similar data on the US market can be found in the annual *Stock Trader's Almanac*, which in 1996 celebrated its 30th year. Editor Yale Hirsch describes market patterns ranging from the four–year election cycle, to which hours of the day and which days of the week are most and least favourable for trading stocks. The almanac's 160-page format is hard cover, with ring binding so it will lay flat on your desk. Another treasure-trove of "anomalies." $32.00. The Hirsch Organization, 184 Central Avenue, Old Tappan, NJ 07675; Tel: + 1–800–477–3400.

Newsletters

Established in 1961 and edited by Dr Anthony Boeckh, *The International Bank Credit Analyst* is the Aston Martin of independent advisory services. This weekly publication probably provides the most comprehensive analysis of the economic trends and investment climate in the major countries. Based in Montreal, Quebec, it has a global outlook. Its forecasts assume that an expanding base of liquidity and noninflationary credit creates a favorable environment for sustainable economic expansion and thus a healthy climate for equities. A wide range of economic statistics are presented in graphic form, presupposing some basic knowledge of economic principles. Boeckh and his colleagues began in late 1986 to warn of the danger of a US stock market crash. *The International Bank Credit Analyst* is highly respected within the world economic and investment community. $565 a year. 1002

Sherbrooke Street West, Suite 1600, Montreal, Quebec H3A 3L6, Canada; Tel: + 1–514–499–9706.

The Hulbert Financial Digest, published monthly, tracks the specific investment advice of some 160 US newsletters. $135 per year. 316 Commerce Street, Alexandria, VA 22314; Tel: + 1–703–683–5905.

Weekly newsletter the *Value Line Investment Survey* provides specific investment information and advice on dozens of non-US stocks and closed-end country funds. Over the 15 years through 1995, according to *Hulbert, Value Line* outperformed all other US advisory services, with a compound annual return of 17% as against 14.4% for the Wilshire 5000. On a risk-adjusted basis, *Value Line* came in second. Its approach is clearly worth studying. $495 a year. 711 Third Avenue, New York, NY 10017; Tel: + 1–212–687–3965.

Four other newsletters also have superb long-term track records largely within the US market. Their approaches, applicable to global investing, are also worth studying.

Over the 15-year period, according to *Hulbert, The Zweig Forecast* had a compound yearly return of 15.1%, but on a risk-adjusted basis this monthly newsletter took first prize. $265 a year. PO Box 360, Bellmore, NY 11710; Tel: + 1–800–535–9649.

Charles Allmon's *Growth Stock Outlook,* published twice monthly, also did well over the 15 years on a risk-adjusted basis. This is the only newsletter on growth stocks that has survived bull and bear markets for more than two decades. $195 a year. PO Box 15381, Chevy Chase, MD 20825; Tel: + 1–301–654–5205.

With a 15-year compound annual return of 15.7%, Al Frank's *The Prudent Speculator,* published monthly, was just a whisker behind *Growth Stock Outlook* on a risk-adjusted basis. PO Box 8970, Santa Fe, NM 87504–8970; Tel: + 1–505–983–0412.

Louis Navellier's *MPT Review,* as noted earlier, achieved the most consistent returns of any stock advisory service *Hulbert* monitored from 1985 to 1996. From January 1985 until January 1996, after deduction of 2% estimated round-trip commissions, his 15 model portfolios racked up average compound growth of 24.5%. $225 a year. PO Box 10012, Incline Village, NV 89450–1012; Tel: + 1–702–831–1396.

The Outside Analyst is the only newsletter that actually *compares* stocks globally. Each month, sifting all major analyst earnings estimates for over 15,000 firms in more than 40 countries, this publication reveals which shares professionals now consider most attractive and provides fundamental research. *The Outside Analyst* also identifies the most promising regions for current investment, listing relevant country funds. $390 a year. PO Box 70322, 1007 KH Amsterdam, The Netherlands; Tel: + 1–510–596–9300.

Fund data

The performance of US mutual (open-end) funds is regularly reported by major financial publications, including *Business Week*, *Forbes*, *Money* and *The Wall Street Journal*. Here are some other sources of this information:

Morningstar Mutual Funds (tel: + 1–800–876–5005; $375 a year). Reviews more than 1,500 funds biweekly. Also available on CD–ROM and diskette as well as America Online, this publication includes about 100 global and international stock funds.

Value Line Mutual Fund Survey (tel: + 1–800–284–7607; $295 a year). Similar in type and scope to the data provided by Morningstar.

Mutual Fund Profiles (tel: + 1–800–221–5277; $152 a year), published quarterly by Standard & Poor's, with Lipper Analytical. Covers 750 fund families.

CDA/Wiesenberger Mutual Funds Update (tel: + 1–800–232–2285; $295 a year). Covers over 5,400 funds and is updated monthly.

Morningstar No-Load Funds, introduced in 1994, covers some 600 funds sold directly to the public, most of which have no load. The few that do have loads of less than 3%. A subscription provides about 600 pages of current information, 13 updates over a year, a 50-page booklet on how to use the service and a toll-free service to answer any questions. Tel: + 1–800–876–5005.

You can get a list of all US no-load funds from the Investment Company Institute, 1600 M Street NW, Suite 600, Washington, DC 20036; Tel: + 1–202–293–7700.

Sheldon Jacobs' annual *Handbook for No-Load Fund Investors*, at $45, is the most comprehensive source of information on no-load funds, covering 1,304 no-load and low-load funds. Data is drawn from monthly newsletter *The No-Load Fund Investor*, PO Box 283, Hastings-on-Hudson, NY 10706; Tel: + 1–914–693–7420.

The best research to implement the polar bear strategy outlined in Chapter 8 for no-load funds is available from the newsletter *No-Load Fund*X* ($119 a year), published by DAL Investment Co., 235 Montgomery St., San Francisco CA 94104–2994; Tel: + 1–415–986–1595.

The Individual Investor's Guide to Low-Load Mutual Funds is published annually by the American Association of Individual Investors. It costs $24.75, but is supplied free of charge to members. Dues are $49 per year. The guide covers some 800 funds, including 77 international stock and bond funds. Up to 10 years of history is provided, including performance, volatility, expenses and portfolio characteristics. 625 North Michigan Avenue, Chicago, IL 60611; Tel: + 1–312–280–0170.

The No-Load Fund Analyst is a monthly newsletter covering international stock and bond funds. It is published by L/G Research Inc., named after two

California-based money managers. *The No-Load Fund Analyst* has model portfolios allocated up to half outside the US. It focuses on fund managers, showing their track records and monitoring current style and performance. You may find this a useful resource for managing a global portfolio made up of funds. Tel: + 1–510–245–9017.

The *International Herald Tribune* carries a daily advertisement reproducing figures provided by open-end offshore fund managers showing net asset values, together with some addresses and telephone numbers.

The *Wall Street Journal Europe* carries quotes on open-end funds around the world compiled by Lipper Analytical Services. The funds listed are not registered with the US Securities Exchange Commission and are not available for sale to US citizens or residents.

Three *Financial Times* publications provide monthly performance tables for open-end funds around the globe. Each is sent only to non-US addresses. For *Resident Abroad*, write to Garrard House, 2–6 Homesdale Road, Bromley BR2 9WL. For *Offshore Financial Review* or *The International*, write to Greystoke Place, Fetter Lane, London EC4A 1ND; Tel: + 44–171–405–6969.

For UK open-end funds, the Association of Unit Trusts and Investment Funds has two useful free booklets: "The Unit Trust Directory," a list of all its members with address, phone and fax numbers, and "Unit Trusts: A User's Handbook." You can write to the association at 65 Kingsway, London WC2B 6TD or phone them on + 44–171–831–0898.

The *Financial Times* carries quotes on British closed-end funds and their premium or discount under the heading "Investment trusts." It also quotes bid and offer price and initial charges on open-end UK and offshore unit trusts.

A free directory of British closed-end funds, known as investment trusts, is available from the Association of Investment Trust Company Services, Park House, 16 Finsbury Circus, London EC2M 7JJ; Tel: + 44–171–588–5347.

The *Investor's Guide to Closed-end Funds*, published by Thomas Herzfeld, covers those in the United States. $325 a year. PO Box 161465, Miami, FL 33116; Tel: + 1–305–271–1900. Other newsletters that cover US closed-end funds include: *Frank Cappiello's Closed-end Fund Digest* (+ 1–805–565–5651), *The Scott Letter: Closed-end Fund Report* (+ 1–800–356–3508) and *Morningstar Closed-End Funds* (+ 1–800–876–5005). *Foreign Markets Advisory* (+ 1–703–425–5961) lists foreign-equity closed-ends traded in the US. Any of these publications will send you a sample copy. Just mention this book.

Morningstar also offers a monthly computer diskette, "OnFloppy," with data on over 500 US closed-end funds. (tel: + 1–312–696–6000; $185 a year)

A free report on US-listed closed-end funds is available from the Institute for Econometric Research. The institute publishes Norman Fosback's *Market Logic*, which appears twice a month and is also among the newsletters that have racked up impressive returns in the US market. $200 a year (US, Canada & Mexico); $245 elsewhere. 2200 S. W. 10th Street, Deerfield Beach, FL 33442; Tel: + 1–442–9000.

Two British monthlies, *Emerging Markets Fund Monitor* and *Offshore Funds Performance Monitor*, are sold in the US by Micropal Ltd., 31 Milk Street, Suite 1002, Boston Mass. 02109; Tel: + 1–617–451–1585. Each costs £650 a year. In the UK, Commonwealth House, 2 Chalkhill Road, London W6 8DW; Tel: + 44–81–741–4100.

Lipper Analytical Services has three publications particularly relevant to global investing:

The Lipper International Closed-End Funds Service tracks 350 funds through a 1,200-page quarterly profile service and a monthly 20-page performance fax. *The Lipper Overseas Fund Table* supplies performance tables on 3,000 funds domiciled in Europe, Asia and the Caribbean. Both are available from Lipper Analytical Services International Corporation, 47 Maple Street, Summit, NJ 07901; Tel: + 1–908–273–2772.

The third Lipper publication, *European Fund Industry Directory*, provides market comparisons, industry analysis and charges on more than 7,000 open-end funds domiciled in Western Europe. It is used mainly by fund companies themselves. No performance tables. £695. Finsbury Business Centre, Room 18, Bowling Green Lane, London EC1R 0NE; Tel: + 44–171–415–7047.

The 800-page annual *Encyclopaedia of Luxembourg Investment Funds*, weighing in at some 5 kilos, provides a market analysis of more than 3,000 funds, supplying such data as assets under management, total expense ratio and market share, but no performance tables. Published in English, French and German, it is also used mainly by fund companies. £599. Fitzrovia International Ltd., 57 Wimpole Street, London W1M 7DF; Tel: + 44–171–224 –3284.

Electronic quotes

You can obtain quotes on foreign shares from various on-line services via a home computer. *CompuServe* (+ 1–800–848–8199) subscribers can tap into Citibank's "Global Report," which provides detailed information on global financial markets: real-time exchange rates; worldwide stock prices; company, sector and country profiles; plus political and financial news. But this globe-trotting has a high price tag: In addition to CompuServe's standard connect charge of $8 an hour, Global Report has a surcharge of $60 an hour from 8:00 AM to 7:00 PM and $30 at other times.

Dow Jones News Retrieval (+ 1–609–452–1511) comprises 70 databases, one of which is "Worldscope." Updated monthly, it gives you extensive financial profiles of 11,000 companies in some 45 countries. Report formats are consistent within an industry. The Dow Jones service costs $29.50 a year. Accessing Worldscope prime time (from 6:00 AM to 6:00 PM) is $1.95 per minute plus $1.14 per information unit (1,000 data characters). Company reports run an extra $9.00 each. Non-prime time, costs dwindle to 15 cents a minute, 30 cents per information unit and $3 per company report.

Bankers and brokers

Trading directly in foreign shares listed on their own exchanges generally means turning to a foreign bank or broker. The more adventurous global investor simply opens a trading account abroad. And some firms, such as Nomura Securities of Japan, will allow a nonresident client to trade securities listed on Japanese, Hong Kong, Australian and certain European exchanges. Nomura has a US office at 2 World Financial Center, New York, NY 10281–1198.

The Netherlands has a long tradition of foreign investment and most Dutch brokerage houses readily let you trade abroad, placing your order with an associate broker on each foreign bourse. One such house, a member of the Amsterdam Stock Exchange and the European Options Exchange, is Effectenbank Stroeve, founded in 1818. You can conduct your transactions there in English, French or German. Herengracht 130, 1015 BV Amsterdam; Tel: + 31–20–624–3075.

If you prefer, however, to trade *directly* through a foreign bank or brokerage, you can contact local branches of foreign banks or trade embassies for the names of reputable firms. Two annual surveys published by Euromoney can be useful in this context: *The GT Guide to World Equity Markets* at £140 ($255) and *The Brokers 1000* £170 ($290), a global directory of brokers in over 50 markets; Tel: + 44–171–779–8999. Alternatively, you can contact the major market stock exchanges listed in Chapter 7 or the following list of emerging market stock exchanges for the names of firms authorized to trade there:

Emerging market stock exchanges

Argentina
Buenos Aires Stock Exchange
25 de Mayo, Buenos Aires 1002
Phone: (54–1) 313–4522 Fax: (54–1) 313–4472

Bolsa de Commercio de Rosario
Cordoba Esquina Corrientes, Rosario AR–2000
Phone: (54–1) 213–470 Fax: (54–1) 241–091

Brazil
Sao Paolo Stock Exchange
XV de Novembro 275, Sao Paolo 01013.001
Phone: (55–11) 258–7222 Fax: (55–11) 36–0871

Bolsa de Valores do Rio de Janeiro
Praca XV de Novembro 20, Rio de Janeiro 20010–010
Phone: (55–21) 271–1001

Chile
Bolsa de Comercio de Santiago
La Bolsa, 64, Santiago
Phone: (56–2) 6982001, 6958077 Fax: (56–2) 6728046

China
Shanghai Securities Exchange
15 Hang Pu Road, Shanghai 200080
Phone: (86–21) 306–3195 Fax: (86–21) 306–3076

ShenZhen Stock Exchange
15/F International Trust & Investment Bldg, HongLing Zhong Rd, ShenZhen
518001 PR
Phone: (86–755) 5583927 Fax: (86–755) 5583931

Colombia
Bolsa de Bogota SA
Carrera 8A, No. 31–82, 8, Apartado Aereo 3584, Bogota
Phone: (57–1) 243–65–01 Fax: (57–1) 281–3170

Bolsa de Occidente
Calle 10 #4–40 pisos 13 & 14, Cali
Phone: (572) 381–7022/381–7028 Fax: (572) 816–720/812–526

Medellin Stock Exchange
Carrera 50, No. 50–48, Piso 2, Apartado Aereo 3535, Medellin
Phone: (57–4) 2603000 Fax: (57–4) 2511981

Croatia
Zagreb Stock Exchange
saver 208, Zagreb 41000
Phone: (38–41) 42–8455 Fax: (38–41) 42–0293

Czech Republic
Stock Exchange of Prague
Na Mustku 3, Praha 1 110 00
Phone: (42–2) 268–391, 268392 Fax: (42–2) 23–55–233

Greece
Athens Stock Exchange
10 Sophocleous Street, Athens 105 59
Phone: (30–1) 3211301 Fax: (30–1) 3213938

Hungary
Budapest Stock Exchange
Dea Ferenc Utca 5, Budapest H–1052
Phone: (36–1) 1175–226 Fax: (36–1) 1181–737

India
Bangalore Stock Exchange Ltd.
Uni Building, Miller Tank, Vasanthanagar, Bangalore–560 052
Phone: (918–12) 220163/236567

The Bombay Stock Exchange
Phiroze Jeejeebhoy Towers, Dalal Street, Bombay–400 001
Phone: (91–22) 275860 Fax: (91–22) 202–8121

The Calcutta Stock Exchange Association, Ltd
7 Lyons Range, Calcutta–700 001
Phone: (91–33) 20–6957/20–6928 Fax: (91–33) 20–2514

Madras Stock Exchange Ltd
11 Second Line Beach, Exchange Building, Madras–600 001
Phone: (91–44) 521071 Fax: (91–44) 514897

The Delhi Stock Exchange Assoc. Ltd.
3 and 4/4B Asaf Ali Road, New Delhi–110 002
Phone: (91–11) 327–9000 Fax: (91–11) 326–7112

Jamaica
Jamaica Stock Exchange
Bank of Jamaica Tower, Nethersole Place, Kingston
Phone: (809) 922–0806 Fax: (809) 922–6966

Korea
Korea Stock Exchange
33 Yoido-Dong, Yongdeungpo-ku, Seoul 150–010
Phone: (82–2) 780–2271 Fax: (82–2) 786–0263

Malaysia
The Kuala Lumpur Stock Exchange
3rd-5th Fl., Exchange Square, Off Jalan Semantan, Damansara Heights, Kuala Lumpur 50490
Phone: (60–3) 2546433 Fax: (60–3) 2557463/2561291

Mexico
Bolsa Mexicana de Valores, SA de CV
Paseo de la Reforma, 255, Col. Cuauhtemoc, Mexico 06500
Phone: (52–2) 726–6600 Fax: (52–2) 591–0642

Pakistan
Karachi Stock Exchange (Guarantee) Ltd.
Stock Exchange Road, Karachi 2
Phone: (92–21) 24109146/242–8752 Fax: (92–21) 241–0825/242–8692

Lahore Stock Exchange
19 Khayaban-e-Aiwan-e-Igbal, Lahore, Punjab 54000
Phone: (92–42) 636–8111/636–8000 Fax: (92–24) 636–8484/636–8485

Paraguay
Bolsa de Valores y Productos de Asuncion SA
Calle Estrella 540, Asuncion
Phone: (595–21) 442–445 Fax: (595–21) 442–446

Peru
Lima Stock Exchange
Pasaje Acuna 191, Lima 100
Phone: (51–14) 327–939 Fax: (51–14) 337–650

Philippines
Makati Stock Exchange, Inc.
Makati Stock Exchange Building, Ayala Avenue, Makati, Metro Manila
Phone: (63–2) 810–1145/810–1146 Fax: (63–2) 810 5710

Manila Stock Exchange
12th Fl., Tekite Tower I, Tekite Road, Ortigas Center, Pasig, Manila
Phone: (63–2) 634–5112, 634–5113 Fax: (63–2) 634–6901

Poland
Gielda Papierow Wartosciowych
Bul. Nowy Swiat 6/12, Banking Center, 5th Floor, Warszawa 00–920
Phone: (48–2) 628-32–32/33 Fax: (48–2) 628–17–54, 628–81–91

Portugal
Bolsa de Valores de Lisboa
Rua dos Fanqueiros, 10, Lisbon 1100
Phone:: (351–1) 888–27–38/29–17 Fax: (351–1) 864231/877402

Bolsa de Valores Do Porto
Palcio da Bolsa, Rua de Ferreira Borges, Porto 4000
Phone: (351–2) 318–546, 202–6237 Fax: (351–2) 200–2475, 316–859

Taiwan, China
Taiwan Stock Exchange
85 Yen-Ping South Road, Taipei
Phone: (886–2) 311–4020 Fax: (886–2) 311–4004

Thailand
Stock Exchange of Thailand
Sinthon Building, 2nd Floor, 132 Wireless Road, Bangkok 10330
Phone: (66–2) 256–7100/254–0440 Fax: (66–2) 254–3040/256–7110

Turkey
Istanbul Stock Exchange
Rihtim Caddesi No. 245, Karakoy-Istanbul 80030
Phone: (90–1) 252–4800/251–7390 Fax: (90–1) 243–7425/252–4915

Uruguay
Bolsa de Valores de Montevideo
Misiones 1400, Montevideo
Phone: (598–12) 96–50–51 Fax: (598–12) 96–19–00

Venezuela
Bolsa de Valores de Caracas
Edificio Atrium, Calle Sorocoma, Urbanizacion, El Rosal, Piso 1, Caracas
Phone: (58–2) 905–5511 Fax: (58–2) 905–5829/905–5707

About depositary receipts

Companies listed as depositary receipts are normally the largest and most actively traded in their respective markets. These include privatized telephone and electric utilities, oil and chemical companies and banks. Global Depositary Receipts are registered, issued and traded in the US public markets and listed on major US and non-US exchanges, chiefly London and Luxembourg. International Depositary Receipts (sometimes called Continental or European Receipts) generally trade on London's SEAQ system. American Depositary Receipts trade in the US markets, with NASDAQ accounting for the majority. As NASDAQ is a global trading system with some 30,000 quotation terminals in 52 countries, it is a convenient way of giving a firm's stock global exposure. Non-US stocks, notably from the Netherlands, Israel and the Philippines, also trade on US markets as so-called New York shares. This appendix, updated through February 1996, includes American Depositary Receipts (ADRs), Global Depositary Receipts (GDRs) and New York shares:

some 1,800 such equities from 64 countries. As Canadian shares trade freely in the United States under a reciprocity agreement, they are omitted. So are bonds, for reasons explained in the first chapter. Each stock traded via a depositary receipt is normally identified by a ticker symbol or a so-called cusip number. Ticker symbols are given here in preference to cusip numbers.

Preference shares traded as ADRs can have fixed, adjustable or auction interest rates, set either in US dollars or another currency. Those with auction rates are targeted at institutional investors.

Here are four US money center banks that act as custodians for ADRs:

Bank of New York, 101 Barclay Street, New York, NY 10286; Citibank, 111 Wall Street, New York, NY 10043; Morgan Guaranty Trust Company, 60 Wall Street, New York, NY 10260–0060; Chemical Bank, 55 Water Street, New York, NY 10041.

Each bank publishes a list of ADRs for which it serves as custodian. By writing to the individual banks, you can obtain copies of their latest listings. US broker Merrill Lynch publishes *Global Research Review*, which provides a wealth of statistical information on ADRs. Director of the firm's Global Securities Research & Economics Group is Jeffrey Peek; Tel: + 1–212–449–8334.

More extensive information on ADRs is available from two sources in particular. Detail on each firm's activities plus a list of Canadian ADRs can be found in David Muller's annual *Directory of Foreign Stocks Traded in the US*, covering approximately 1,300 non-Canadian equities plus 400 from Canada. Mineral and oil exploration stocks make up about a third of that total. PO Box 75, Fairfax Station, VA 22039; Tel: + 1–703–425–5961.

For cusip numbers, sponsoring banks and market makers, you can consult Agorot's yearly *Comprehensive Guide to ADRs*, whose list of roughly 1,700 depositary receipts includes both corporate and government bonds. Agorot also publishes *Global Investing*, which each month provides information on new ADRs. 1040 First Avenue, Suite 305, New York, NY 10022; Tel: + 1–212–758–9480.

US discount broker Marquette de Bary, with many clients outside the US, has long specialized in ADRs. Trading European securities in the US saves the transfer and value-added taxes that apply in many countries. 488 Madison Avenue, New York, NY 10022; Tel: + 1–212–644–5300. In Europe, you can call toll- free: United Kingdom 0800–89–1972; France: 05.90.11.41; Germany 0130–81–1497; Switzerland 046–05–89–65; Luxembourg 0800–4213.

US discount broker JB Oxford & Company is also used to handling ADR trades for non-US residents, and has a multi-lingual staff. The head office is at 9665 Wilshire Boulevard, Beverly Hills, CA 90212, but the firm has a Swiss representative office at Peter Merian-Strasse 50, CH-4002 Basel; Tel: + 41–61–279–8840.

A word on the US Security Exchange Commission's Rule 144A, under which qualified institutions that manage more than a million dollars can trade unlisted securities via private placement networks. ADRs are available in the US this way via the Portal or 144A systems and internationally as International or Global Depositary Receipts. The drawback to 144A placements is their exclusion of individuals and smaller institutions. Moreover, liquidity on Portal is frequently inadequate. For these reasons, even qualified institutions increasingly tend to prefer public offerings. On the list which follows, some Dutch firms bear the cachet "Koninklijke," meaning "Royal." In Malaysia, "Berhad" is much the same as "Inc." WT stands for warrant. UT stands for unit: a share receipt from which a warrant has not yet been detached.

List of Depositary Receipts

Exchange	Company	Ticker	Industry
Argentina			
OTC	Alpargatas SAIC	ALPAY	Textiles
NASDAQ	Banco de Galicia y Buenos Aires B	BGALY	Banking
NYSE	Banco Frances del Rio de la Plata	BFR	Banking
OTC	Banco Quilmes de Argentina		Banking
NYSE	Bridas Energy Corp A	BDS	Utility
NYSE	Buenos Aires Emboteliadora SA Baesa	BAE	Food Proc
PORTAL	Capex SA 144A A SH		Utility
OTC	Celulosa Argentina		Pulp, Paper
PORTAL	Central Costanera SA 144A		
PORTAL	Central Puerto SA 144A		
OTC	Compania Naviera Perez Companc	CNPZY	Conglomerate
PORTAL	Electricidad de Argentina 144A		
OTC	Irsa Inversiones y Representaciones	IRSAY	Real Estate
OTC	Italo Argentine Electric Co		
NYSE	Metrogas SABSH	MGS	
PORTAL	Mircor SAIFIA 144A		
PORTAL	Molinos Rio de la Plata 144A		
PORTAL	Molinos Rio de la Plata WTS 144A		
OTC	Naviera Perez Companc, Compania	CNPZY	Oilfield Svc
LUX	Nortel Inversora SA		Telecom
PORTAL	Nortel Inversora SA A 144A		Telecom
PORTAL	Nortel Inversora SA PR B 144A		Telecom
PORTAL	Sociedad Comercial del Plata 144A	SCD	Energy
OTC	Sol Petroleo SA		Oil
OTC	Telecom Argentia Stet FR Telecom B	TAGBY	Telecom
NYSE	Telefonica de Argentina B GDR	TAR	Telecom
SEAQ	Telefonica de Argentina B GDR	TAR	Telecom
NYSE	Transportadora de Gas del Sur SA		Gas
NYSE	YPF Yacimientos Petroliferos Fiscales	YPF	Oil

Exchange	Company	Ticker	Industry

Australia

Exchange	Company	Ticker	Industry
OTC	APM (Australian Paper Mills)		Pulp, Paper
OTC	Agen Ltd	AGLTY	Pharmaceuticals
OTC	Airboss Ltd (Fomerly Altrack)	AIRBY	Tires
OTC	Amadeus Oil NL	AMDOY	Oil
OTC	Amcor Ltd	ARMLY	Pulp, Paper
OTC	Ashton Mining Ltd	ASHMY	Mining
OTC	Astro Mining NL	ASTOY	Mining
OTC	Atlas Pacific Ltd	APCFY	
OTC	Auridiam Consolidated NL	AURAY	Mining
OTC	Auspharm International Ltd		Pharmaceuticals
NYSE	Australia & New Zealand Banking Cap Securities	ANZ P	Banking
OTC	Australia & New Zealand Banking Group	ANEWY	Banking
OTC	Australia Wide Industries Ltd	AUWDY	Mineral Exp
OTC	Australian Cons Investments Ltd (Former Bell Resources Ltd)	ACIEY	Oil, Gas
OTC	Australian Consol Press Ltd	ACPL	Publishing
OTC	Australian Hydrocarbons Ltd	AUSHY	Oil, Gas
OTC	Australian Natl Industries Ltd	AUNTY	Machinery
OTC	Australian Oil & Gas Corp Ltd	AOGSY	Oil
OTC	BHP Gold Mines Ltd	BHGMY	Gold Mining
OTC	BH South Ltd (Formely Broken Hill South)	BHSOY	Oil
OTC	Barrack Energy Ltd	BAENY	Mining
OTC	Barrack Mines Ltd	BACKY	Gold Mining
OTC	Barrack Technology Ltd	BATEY	Automotive
OTC	Biota Holdings Ltd		Pharmaceuticals
OTC	Black Hill Minerals Ltd	BLKMY	Gold Mining
OTC	Bond Corp Holdings Ltd	BCHFY	Conglomerate
NASDAQ	Boral Ltd	BORAY	Bldg Matls
OTC	Bougainville Copper Ltd	BOCOY	Mining
OTC	Boulder Gold LP	BDRBY	Gold Mining
NYSE	Broken Hill Proprietary Ltd	BHP	Oil, Metals
OTC	Browns Creek Gold	BWCEY	Gold Mining
OTC	Burns (Philp) & Co Ltd	BPHCY	Food Proc
OTC	CRA Ltd	CRADY	Metal
OTC	CSR Ltd	CSRAY	Bldg Matls
OTC	Cameronics Tech Corp Ltd	CMRNY	
OTC	Cape Range Ltd	CPRNY	Energy
OTC	Capenter, WR Holdings Ltd	CAWRY	Conglomerate
OTC	Carr Boyd Minerals Ltd	CRBMY	Mineral Exp
OTC	Centaur Mining & Expl Ltd	CNXPY	Mining
OTC	Central Norseman Gold Corp	CNOGY	Gold Mining
NASDAQ	Central Pacific Minerals	CPMNY	Oil
OTC	Clarement Petroleum NL	CLPTY	Oil

Exchange	Company	Ticker	Industry
OTC	Clyde Industries Ltd	CYDNY	Elect Mach
OTC	Coaltech Ltd		
OTC	Coca-Cola Amatil Ltd	CCLAY	Beverages
NYSE	Coles Myer Ltd	CM	Retailing
OTC	Comalco Ltd A	CLMOY	Aluminum
PORTAL	Commonwealth Bank of Australia 144A	CBAUY	Banking
OTC	Condor Minerals & Energy Ltd	CNMAY	Oil, Gas
OTC	Consolidated Gold Mining Areas	CGMAF	Investment
OTC	Copperfield Gold NL		Gold Mining
OTC	Cord Holdings Ltd	CRHLY	Mineral Exp
NASDAQ	Cortecs International Ltd	DLVRY	Pharamaceuticals
OTC	Cox Bros	COXBY	
OTC	Crackow Gold Ltd	CRAKY	Gold Mining
OTC	Delta Gold NL	DEGOY	Gold Mining
OTC	Denehurst Ltd	DENHY	Metals, Coal
OTC	Dioro Explorations NL	DOROY	Gold Mining
OTC	Dominion Mining Ltd	DMNOY	Gold Mining
OTC	East West Minerals	EAWEY	Mining
OTC	Eastern Group Ltd	EAGRY	Mining
OTC	Email Ltd	EMALY	Appliances
OTC	Emperor Mines Ltd	EMPMY	Gold Mining
OTC	Energy Oil & Gas NL	EOGSY	Mineral Exp
OTC	Enserch Corp		
OTC	Erg Australia Ltd	ERGAY	Electronics
OTC	Euralba Mining Ltd	EURLY	Mining
OTC	FH Faulding & Co Ltd	FAFHY	Health Care
NYSE	FAI Iinsurances Ltd	FAI	Insurance
OTC	Federation Resources NL	FEREY	Gold Mining
OTC	First Australian Resources NL	FAR	Mining
OTC	Fosters Brewing Group Ltd	FBWGY	Brewing
OTC	Giant Bay Resources Ltd	GBYLF	Mining
OTC	Gold & Minerals Exploration NL	GMEXY	Mineral Exp
OTC	Gold Mines Kalgoorlie Ltd	GMKGY	Gold Mining
OTC	Golden Valley Mines NL	GVYMY	Gold Mining
OTC	Goodman Fielder Wattie Ltd	GMFIY	Baked Goods
OTC	Grants Patch Mining Ltd	GMPLY	Gold Mining
NASDAQ	Great Central Mines NL	GTCMY	Gold Mining
OTC	Great Fingall Mining Co	GRFMY	Mineral Exp
OTC	Greenbushes Tin Ltd		
OTC	Greenvale Mining NL	GVLMY	Mining
OTC	Griffths Bros Ltd	GFBOY	
OTC	Gwalia International Ltd	GWLRY	Mining
OTC	Gwalia Consolidated Ltd (Formely Gwalia Resources Ltd)		Mining
OTC	Hadfields Ltd		
OTC	Hallmark Gold NL (Formely Sirius Corp)	HLMGY	Gold Mining
OTC	Hardman Resources NL	HAR	Oil

Exchange	Company	Ticker	Industry
OTC	Hawk Investments Ltd		
OTC	Helm Corp	HELMY	Insurance
OTC	Hill Minerals NL		Mineral Exp
OTC	HMC Australasia NL	HMCAY	Mining
OTC	Hoyts Entertainment Ltd	HOYT	Film Distr
OTC	Hydromet Corp Ltd	HMCLY	
OTC	Inderpendent Resources Ltd	ITRSY	Investment
OTC	Indonesian Diamond Co Ltd	IDIMY	Diamond Exp
OTC	Intermin Resource Ltd		
OTC	International Mining Corp NL	IMNCY	Mining
OTC	James Hardie Industries Ltd	JHDEY	Bldg Matls
OTC	Jason Mining Ltd	JMIGY	Mineral Exp
OTC	Jones, David Ltd	JONDY	Retail
OTC	Julia Mines NL	JULIY	Gold Mining
OTC	Kalbara Mining	KALBY	Mining
OTC	Kern Corp Ltd	KECLY	Construction
OTC	Kidston Gold Mines Ltd	KSGMY	Gold Mining
OTC	Laverton Gold NL		Gold Mining
OTC	Lennard Oil NL (Formely Magnet Group Ltd)	LENOY	Oil
OTC	Lightning Jack Film Trust	LJFTY	
OTC	MIM Holdings Ltd	MIMAY	
OTC	Magellan Petroleum Australia	MAPAY	Oil
OTC	Materials Tech Ltd	MTLKY	
OTC	Matrix Telecommunications Ltd	MTXTY	Telecom
OTC	Mawson Pacific Ltd	MAWFY	
OTC	Msyne Nickless Ltd	MAYNY	Transport
OTC	McPhersons Ltd	MCFSY	Printing
OTC	Melcorp Securities Ltd	AGLOY	Precious Met
NASDAQ	Memtec Ltd	MMTCY	Water Treat
OTC	Merlin Mining NL	MNMGY	Mining
OTC	Metana Minerals NL	MEMNY	Mineral Exp
OTC	Mid-East Minerals NL	MESTY	Mining
OTC	Mincorp Petroleum NL	MCPEY	Oil
OTC	Mintaro Slate & Flagstone Ltd	MTSLY	Stone
OTC	Monarch NL	MONNY	Indust Sands
OTC	Mount Angelo Exploration NL		
OTC	Mount Burgess Gold Mining NL	MTBGY	Gold Mining
OTC	Mount Kersey Mining NL	MTKRY	
OTC	Mount Leyshon Gold Mines Ltd (formerly Pan Australian Mining)	MLYGY	Gold Mining
NYSE	National Australia Bank Ltd	NAB	Banking
OTC	Network Media Ltd	NFILY	Broadcasting
OTC	New Australian Resources NL	NAVSY	Mineral Exp
OTC	Newcrest Mining Ltd		Gold Mining
NYSE	News Corp Ltd	NWS PR	Broadcasting
NYSE	News Corp Ltd	NWS	Broadcasting
OTC	News Corp Plc Cayman 3.5% CV P (Reuters)	NWSF	Broadcasting

Exchange	Company	Ticker	Industry
OTC	Niugini Mining Ltd (Papua NG)	NGIMY	Mining
OTC	Normandy Oil & Gas	NRMDY	Oil, Gas
OTC	Normandy Poseiden Ltd	NDYPY	Gold Mining
OTC	North Broken Hill Peko Ltd	NBHKY	Forest Prod
OTC	North Flinders Mines Ltd		
OTC	North Queenlands Resources NL	NOQRY	Mining
OTC	Oil Search Ltd (Papua NG)	OISHY	Oil, Gas
NYSE	Orbital Engine Corp Ltd	OE	Technology
OTC	Otter Exploration NL	OTEYF	
NASDAQ	Pacific Dunlop Ltd	PDLPY	Footwear
OTC	Pact Resources NL	PACTY	Mineral Exp
NASDAQ	Palmer Tube Mills Ltd	PTMLY	Piping
OTC	Pancontinental Mining Ltd	PCTMY	Gold Mining
OTC	Pangea Resources Ltd	PGEAY	
OTC	Paragon Resources NL	PGORY	Gold Mining
NASDAQ	Pelsart Resources NL	PELRY	Gold Mining
OTC	Petrogulf Resources Ltd	PGULY	Oil
OTC	Petroz NL	PROZY	Oil, Gas
OTC	Philip Morris Australia Ltd		
OTC	Pioneer International PR A1		Petroleum
OTC	Pioneer International PR A2		Petroleum
OTC	Pioneer International PR B1		Petroleum
OTC	Pioneer International PR B2		Petroleum
OTC	Pioneer International Ltd	PONNY	Petroleum
OTC	Placer Pacific Ltd	PLCAY	Gold Mining
OTC	QNI Ltd	QNILY	Nonferrous
OTC	Queen Margaret Gold Mines NL		Gold Mining
OTC	Queensland Merchant Holdings	QSLDY	
OTC	Range Resources Ltd	RGRLY	Mineral Exp
OTC	SA Brewing Holdings Ltd	SABGY	Brewing
OTC	Samantha Gold NL	SMGOY	Gold
OTC	Samson Exploration NL	SAENY	Mineral Exp
NASDAQ	Santos Ltd	STOSY	Oil, Gas
OTC	Sapphire Mines NL (formerly Conex Australia NL)	SPHMY	Mining
OTC	Shomega Ltd	SEGAY	
OTC	Simsmetal Ltd	SIMEY	
OTC	Smith, Howard Ltd	SMHWY	Engineering
OTC	Sons of Gwalia NL	SOGAY	Gold Mining
OTC	Southcorp Holdings Ltd		
OTC	Southern Goldfields	STGFY	Gold Mining
NASDAQ	Southern Pacific Petroleum NL	SPPTY	Oil, Gas
OTC	Southern Ventures NL	SOVEY	Mining
OTC	Southwest Gold Mines NL	SOGMY	Gold Mining
OTC	Sovereign Oil Australia Ltd	SOALF	Gold, Oil
OTC	Spargos Mining NL	SPXFY	Gold
OTC	St Barbara Mines	STBRY	Mining
OTC	St George Bank Ltd	STGKY	Banking

Exchange	Company	Ticker	Industry
OTC	Striker Resources NL	SKRRY	
OTC	Sydney Oil Ltd		
OTC	TNT Ltd	TNTMY	Transport
OTC	Tabcorp Holdings Ltd	TABLY	
OTC	Tennyson Holdings Ltd	TENYY	Mineral Exp
OTC	Terrex Resources NL	TRXSY	Mineral Exp
OTC	Tolltreck Systems Ltd	TOLRY	Investment
OTC	Total Assets Protection Ltd	TOTAY	Computer Svc
OTC	Triad Minerals NL	TIDMY	Mineral Exp
OTC	Trust Co of Australia Ltd	TCAVY	Banking
OTC	Union Carbide Australia & New Zealand	UNAUY	
OTC	Vam Ltd	VAMLY	
OTC	Vanguard Petroleum Ltd	TOLRY	Oil
NASDAQ	Victoria Petroleum NL	VPTOY	Oil
OTC	Walhalla Mining NL	WALMY	Investment
OTC	Wattle Gully Gold Mines NL	WGGMY	Gold Mining
NYSE	Western Mining Corp Holdings	WMC	Oil, Metals
NYSE	Westpac Banking Corp Ltd	WBK	Banking
NYSE	Westpac Banking Corp P	WBK P	Banking
OTC	Woodside Petroleum Ltd	WDBOY	Oil, Gas
OTC	Zamex Ltd	ZANXY	Mineral Exp

Austria

Exchange	Company	Ticker	Industry
OTC	Bank Austria (Z-Laenderbank)	ZLAEY	Banking
OTC	Boehler-Uddenholm	BHDDY	
OTC	EVN Energieversorgung Niederoesterreich	EVNVY	Utility
OTC	Lauda Air Luftfahrt AG		Airline
OTC	Lenzing AG	LNZNY	Paper
PORTAL	Mayr-Melnhof Karton AG 144A		Paper
OTC	OMV (Oestereichischer Mineralverband) AG	OMVAY	Oil
OTC	VA Technologie AG	VATXY	
OTC	Veitsch-Radex (formerly Veitscher Magnesitwerke)	VEITY	Metals
OTC	Vienna International Airport	VIAAY	Airport

Bahamas

Exchange	Company	Ticker	Industry
OTC	Polydex Pharmaceuticals Ltd	POLXF	Pharmaceuticals

Belgium

Exchange	Company	Ticker	Industry
OTC	Gevaert Photo Produkten NV	GEVAY	Photography
NASDAQ	Lernout en Hauspie	LNSPF	Speech Tech.
OTC	Petrofina SA	PTRFY	Oil
OTC	Solvay	SLVVY	Chemicals
OTC	Union Miniere SA		Mining

Exchange	Company	Ticker	Industry

Belize

Exchange	Company	Ticker	Industry
NASDAQ	Belize Holdings Inc ORD	BZHKF	Holding Co

Bermuda

Exchange	Company	Ticker	Industry
NASDAQ	American Eagle Tankers Inc Ltd	AETIF	Transport
NYSE	Amway Asia Pacific (Hong Kong)	AAP	Retailing
NASDAQ	Arethusa (Offshore) Ltd	ARTHF	Oil Drilling
NASDAQ	BT Shipping	BTBTY	Transport
NYSE	Brilliance China Automotive (China)	CBA	Automotive
OTC	CP Pokphand (Hong Kong)	CPPKY	Food Proc
OTC	Central European Media Enterprises B		
NASDAQ	Challenger International Ltd	CSTIF	Firearms
NYSE	China Yuchai International Ltd (China)	CYD	Automotive
NASDAQ	Concordia Paper Ltd (Hong Kong)	CPLNY	Pulp, Paper
OTC	Dairy Farm International Ltd (Hong Kong)	DFIHY	
NASDAQ	Fairhaven International Ltd	NIMSY	
OTC	Fine Homes International PLC		
NASDAQ	First South Africa Corp	FSACF	Machinery
NASDAQ	GCR Holdings	GCREF	Reinsurance
OTC	General Resources Development International Ltd (Hong Kong)	GDRPY	
NASDAQ	Globalstar Telecommunications	GSTRF	Telecom
OTC	Golden Resources Dev Intl Ltd (Hong Kong)	GDRPY	
OTC	Hongkong Land (Hong Kong)	HKHGY	Real Estate
OTC	Jardine Matheson Holdings Ltd (Hong Kong)	JARLY	
OTC	Jardine Strategic Holdings Ltd (Hong Kong)	JDSHY	
OTC	Johnson Electric Holdings Ltd (Hong Kong)		
NASDAQ	Lesalle RE Holdings Ltd	LSREF	Reinsurance
NASDAQ	London & Overseas Freighters	LOFSY	Transport
OTC	Mandarin Oriental International (Hong Kong)	MAORY	
NASDAQ	Mid-Ocean Ltd	MOCNF	Reinsurance
NASDAQ	Nobel Insurance Ltd	NOBLF	Insurance
NASDAQ	Nord Pacific Ltd	NORPF	Minerals Exp
AMEX	Nordic American Tanker WTS	NAT.WS	Transport
OTC	Onfem Holdings Ltd (Hong Kong)	ONHLY	Real Estate
NASDAQ	Partner RE Holdings Ltd	PTREF	Reinsurance
OTC	Peregrine Inv Holdings Ltd (Hong Kong)	PGIGY	

Exchange	Company	Ticker	Industry
NASDAQ	Renaissance RE Holdings	RNREF	Reinsurance
OTC	Semi-Tech (Global) Ltd (Hong Kong)	SMIGY	
OTC	Smedvig Tankships Ltd	SVTKY	Transport
OTC	South China Morning Post (Hong Kong)	SCHPY	Publishing
NYSE	Sphere Drake Holdings Ltd	SD	Insurance
OTC	Starlight International Ltd (Hong Kong)		Electronics
NASDAQ	Van Diemen's Co Ltd	VANDF	Mineral Exp
OTC	Welback Holdings Ltd (Hong Kong)	WELKY	Electronics

Bolivia

NYSE	Compania Bolivana de energia Electrica SA	BLP	Utility

Brazil

OTC	Acesita (CIA ACOS Especiais Itabira)	ATASY	Spec Steel
OTC	Acesita (CIA ACOS Especiais Itabira)	ACSTY	Spec Steel
NYSE	Aracruz Celulose	ARA	Pulp, Paper
OTC	Bahia Sul Celulose	BHIAY	Pulp, Paper
OTC	Bombril SA PR	BMBBY	Hshld Prods
OTC	CTM Citrus	CTMMY	Citrus Grower
NYSE	Capco Automative	CAB	
OTC	Celesc Centrais Eletricas DA STA Catarina	CAIOY	Utility
OTC	Celesc Centrais Eletricas DA STA Catarina SAB	CAIBY	Utility
OTC	Celesc Centrais Eletricas DA STA Catarina SA PR	CAIAY	Utility
OTC	Centrais Eletricas Brasileiras (Electrobras)	CAIFY	Utility
OTC	Centrais Eletricas Brasileiras (Electrobras) PR	CIAGY	Utility
OTC	Ceval Alimentos SA	CVEAY	Food Proc
OTC	Ceval Alimentos SA PR	CVEPY	Food Proc
GDR	Companhia Brasileira de Distribuicao		Utility
SEAQ	Companhia Energetica de Minas Gerais Cemig	CEMIG	Utility
OTC	Companhia Energetica de Minas Gerais Cemig Nonvoting PR	CEMCY	Utility
OTC	Companhia Energetica de Minas Gerais Cemig Ord	CEMCY	Utility
OTC	Companhia Energetica de Sao Paulo (CESP)	CMPSY	Utility

Exchange	Company	Ticker	Industry
PORTAL	Companhia Siderugica de Tubarao (CST) PR B 144A		Steel
OTC	Companhia Siderurgica Nacional (CSN)	CSNNY	Steel
OTC	Companhia Suzano de Papel e Celulose PR	CSZPY	Pulp, Paper
OTC	Companhia Vale do Rio Doce	CVROY	Metals
OTC	Copene Petroquimica do Nordeste SA	CPEPY	Petrochem
OTC	Eucatex SA Industria e Comercio		Conglomerate
OTC	Industrias de Papel Simao	IDPSY	Pulp, Paper
OTC	Industrias Klabin de Papel & Celulose PR	IKBLY	Pulp, Paper
OTC	Iochpe-Maxion	IOCJY	Automotive
OTC	Lojas Americans	LOJAY	
PORTAL	Makro Atacadista SA		
OTC	Refrigeracao Parana		Refr Eq
GDR	Rhodia-Ster SA		
OTC	Sao Paulo Alpargatas SA	SAALY	Apparel
OTC	Sao Paulo Alpargatas SA PR	SAALZ	Apparel
OTC	Sementes Agroceres SA PR	SMTAY	Agrobiz
OTC	Tecelagem Kuehnrich (Teka) SA PR		Textiles
NYSE	Telebras	TBR	Telecom
OTC	Telecomunicacoes Brasileiras (Telebras) PR	TBRAY	Telecom
LUX	Usiminas Usinas Siderurgicas de Minas Gerais SA		Mining
PORTAL	Usiminas Usinas Siderurgicas de Minas Gerais PR 144A		Mining

British West Indies

NASDAQ	Chandler Insurance Co Ltd	CHANF	Insurance
NYSE	Club Med Inc	CMI	Resorts
OTC	IWI Holding Ltd	JEWL	Jewelry Mfr
AMEX	Norex America Inc	NXA	Oil Drilling

Cayman

NYSE	Espirito Santo Overseas PR A (Portugal)	ESB	
OTC	Truly International Holdings (Hong Kong)	TRUCY	

Chile

NYSE	Banco de A. Edwards	AED	Banking
NYSE	Banco O'Higgins	OHG	Banking
NYSE	Banco Osorno Y LA Union	BOU	Banking
PORTAL	Chilectra Quinta Region SA 144A	CQDS	Utility

Exchange	Company	Ticker	Industry
NYSE	Chilgener SA	CHR	Utility
NYSE	Chilquinta SA		Utility
NASDAQ	Compania Cervecerias Unidas	CCUUY	Brewing
NYSE	Compania de Telefonos de Chile	CTC	Telecom
NYSE	Cristalerias de Chile SA	CGW	Packaging
PORTAL	Distribuidora Chilectra Metropolitana 144A	DDCMY	Utility
NYSE	Embotelladora Andina SA	AKO	Bottler
NYSE	Empresa Nacional de Electridad Endesa	EOC	Utility
NYSE	Empresas Telex Chile SA	TL	Telecom
NYSE	Enersis SA	ENI	Utility
NYSE	Laboratorio Chile SA	LBC	Pharmaceuticals
NYSE	Madeco SA	MAD	Aluminium
NYSE	Maderas y Sinteticos SA Masisa	MYS	Wood products
NYSE	Provida (Administrador de Fondos de Pensiones)	PVD	
NYSE	Santa Isabel Inc	ISA	Supermarkets
NYSE	Sociedad Quimica y Minera de Chile B	SQM	Fertilizers
NYSE	Vina Concha y Toro	VCO	Vintner

China

Exchange	Company	Ticker	Industry
NYSE	Brillance China Automotive	CBA	Automotive
OTC	China Cellular Communication (Canada)	CNCMF	Telecom
NYSE	China Tire Holdings Ltd	TIR	Tire
NYSE	EK Chor China Motorcycle	EKC	
OTC	Guandong Investment Ltd	GGDVY	Real Estate
	Guangzhou Shipyard International Company Ltd		
PORTAL	Harbin Power Equipment Co Ltd 144A		
NYSE	Huaneng Power International Inc	HNP	Utility
NYSE	Jilin Chemical Industrial Co Ltd	JCC	
PORTAL	Maansham Iron & Steel Ltd H 144A		Steel
GDR	Qingling Motors Co Ltd GDR		
NYSE	Shandong Huaneng Power Development Co Ltd	SH	Utility
OTC	Shanghai Chlor-Alkali Chemical Co Ltd B	SLIBY	Chemicals
OTC	Shanghai Erfangji Co Ltd B	SHFGY	Machinery
PORTAL	Shanghai Hai Xing Shipping Co 144A		
NYSE	Shanghai Petrochemical Co Ltd H	SHI	Chemicals
OTC	Shanghai Tyre & Rubber B	STRCY	Automotive
OTC	Shenzhen Sspecial Economic Zone Real Estate & Proprieties	SZPRY	Real Estate
PORTAL	Yizheng Chemical Fibre Co 144A		Textile

Exchange	Company	Ticker	Industry

Colombia

Exchange	Company	Ticker	Industry
OTC	Banco de Los Andes		Banking
NYSE	Banco Ganadero PR	BGAPR	Banking
NYSE	Banco Ganadero SA	BGA	Banking
NYSE	Banco Industrial Colombiano	CIB	Banking
NYSE	Banco Industrial Colombiano SA PR	CIBPR	Banking
LUX	Cadenalco SA		
PORTAL	Cadenalco SA 144A		
PORTAL	Carulla & cia SA 144A	CARVY	
PORTAL	Cementos Diamante SA 144A		Cement
GDR	Cementos Paz de Rio 144A		Cement
OTC	Corporacion Financiera del Valle SA Nonvoting B	CFDVF	Financial
GDR	Corporacion Financier del Valle SA		Financial
PORTAL	Gran Cadena de Almacenes Colombianos (Cadenalco) B 144A		Dept Stores
GDR	Papeles Nacionales SA		

Denmark

Exchange	Company	Ticker	Industry
OTC	Den Danske Bank AF 1871 A/S	DEAFY	Banking
NYSE	ISS International Service System AS B	ISG	Cleaning Svcs
NYSE	Novo Nordisk AS	NVO	Pharmaceuticals
NASDAQ	Olicom AS	OLCMF	Computers
NYSE	Tele Danmark AS	TLD	Telecom
PORTAL	Unidanmark AS 144A	UNIDY	Banking
PORTAL	La Cemento Nacional CA 144A		Cement

El Salvador

Exchange	Company	Ticker	Industry
OTC	Compania de Alumbrado Electrico de San Salvador	ELSYF	Utility

Finland

Exchange	Company	Ticker	Industry
OTC	Amer Group Ltd	AMGPY	Conglomerate
OTC	Cultor Ltd	CULTY	Animal Feed
PORTAL	Espoon Sahko OY 144A		Utility
PORTAL	Huhtamaki OY 144A	HUHIY	Packaging
NASDAQ	Instrumentarium Corp	INMRY	Healthcare
PORTAL	Kemira OY		
OTC	Labsystems OY		
OTC	Nokia Corp	NKIAY	Telecom
NYSE	Nokia Corp PR	NOKPR	Telecom
NYSE	Rauma OY	RMA	
OTC	Repola Corp		Paper
PORTAL	Valmet Corp 144A	VMETY	Pulp, Paper

Exchange	Company	Ticker	Industry

France

Exchange	Company	Ticker	Industry
OTC	Accor Asia Pacific	AAPCY	Hotels
OTC	Air Liquide SA	LIQUY	Spec Chem
NYSE	Alcatel Alsthom	ALA	Elect Equip
PORTAL	Banque Nationale de Paris 144A	BNPRY	Banking
OTC	Beghin SA	BGHNF	Food Proc
OTC	Business Objects SA	BOBJY	Software
OTC	Canal Plus	CNPLY	Media
PORTAL	Ciments Francais B 144A	CIMFY	Cement
OTC	Ciments Francais PR B		Cement
OTC	Clarins SA	CLARY	Cosmetics
OTC	Clarins SA 144A	CLARF	Cosmetics
OTC	Club Mediterranee	CLMDY	Leisure
NASDAQ	Coflexip SA	CXIPY	Oil Serv
OTC	Compagnie Bancaire ORD	CMBNF	Banking
OTC	Compagnie de Saint-Gobain	GMGOF	
OTC	Compagnie de Suez	CSUZY	Banking
OTC	Compagnie des Machines Bull	CODMY	Computers
OTC	Compagnie Generale des Eaux	CDGEY	
PORTAL	Credit Lyonnais Capital Acc Inv GPS 144A	CLYOY	Banking
PORTAL	Credit Lyonnais Capital Group 144A	CLYOY	Banking
OTC	Danone Groupe (formerly BSN)	BSNOY	Food Proc
NYSE	Elf-Aquitaine, Societe Natle	ELF	Oil, Gas
NYSE	Elf Overseas Ltd PA (Cayman)	EOL PA	Oil, Gas
OTC	Eurodisney SA	EDISC	Tourism
OTC	Fiat France SA (FFSA)	FFSAY	Automotive
OTC	Havas, Agence	HAVSY	Adv/Publishg
NASDAQ	LVMH Moet Hennessy Louis Vuitton	LVMHY	Luxury Goods
NASDAQ	L'Oreal SA	LORLY	Cosmetics
NASDAQ	Lafarge Coppee SA	LFCPY	Bldg Mat
OTC	Lafarge Coppee WTS		Cement
OTC	Lagardere Group SCA	LGDDY	Media
OTC	Lyonnaise des Eaux-Dumez	LYNNF	
OTC	Michelin A	MCHAF	Automotive
OTC	Michelin B	MCHBF	Automotive
OTC	Pernod-Ricard SA	PDRDY	
OTC	Peugeot-Citroen SA	PEUGY	Automotive
OTC	Pixtech Inc	PIXT	
PORTAL	Renault 144A		Automotive
NYSE	Rhone-Poulenc PSSA Comb	RPPRC	Pharmaceuticals
NYSE	Rhone-Poulenc PSSA WTS	RP%	Pharmaceuticals
NYSE	Rhone-Poulenc SA	RP	Pharmaceuticals
NYSE	Rhone-Poulenc SA PF A		Pharmaceuticals
PORTAL	Roussel Uclaf SA 144A	ROU	Pharmaceuticals
OTC	Schneider SA	SCHNY	Engineering

Exchange	Company	Ticker	Industry
OTC	Schneider SA WTS		Engineering
OTC S	Societe Generale France		
PORTAL	Technip 144A		
NASDAQ	Thomson-CSF	TCSFY	Elect Equip
NYSE	Total SA B SH	TOT	Oil, Gas
PORTAL	Usinor Sacilor 144A		Steel
OTC	Valeo, Societe	VLEOY	Automotive

Germany

Exchange	Company	Ticker	Industry
OTC	AEG AG	AEGXY	Elec Equip
OTC	Allianz Versicherung	ALLZF	Insurance
OTC	BASF AG	BASFY	Chemicals
OTC	Bayer AG	BAYZY	Chemicals
OTC	Bayerische Hypotheken- und Wechsel Bank (Hypo-Bank)	BHYWY	Banking
OTC	Bayerische Vereinsbank AG	BYRCY	Banking
OTC	Berliner Handels Und Frankfurter Bank BHF	BHFFY	Fin Service
OTC	Commerzbank AG	CRZBY	Banking
OTC	Continental AG	CTTAY	Tires
NYSE	Daimler-Benz AG	DAI	Automotive
OTC	Deutsche Bank AG	DBKAY	Banking
OTC	Deutsche Lufthansa AG	DLAGY	Airline
OTC	Deutsche Texaco	DTEXY	
PORTAL	Dresdner Bank 144A	DMBKY	Banking
NASDAQ	Dresdner Bank AG	DRSDY	Banking
OTC	GMN Georg Muller Nurnberg AG		
OTC	Gelsenkirchner Bergwerks AG	GLSKY	
OTC	Hoechst AG	HOEHY	Chemicals
OTC	Hoesch AG	HAKTY	Industrial
OTC	Karstadt AG	KARDY	Retailing
OTC	Kaufhof AG PR	KAAZY	Retailing
OTC	Kaufhof Holding AG	KAAGY	Retailing
OTC	Kloeckner-Werke AG	KKWAY	Steel
OTC	Mannesmann AG	MNSMY	Engineering
OTC	RWE AG (Rhine Westphalia Electric)	RWAGY	Utility
OTC	Rheinische Stahlwerke AG	RHNSF	Steel
OTC	Rosenthal AG	RSTHY	Porcelain
OTC	SAP Ag PR	SAPHY	
OTC	Schering AG	SCHRF	
OTC	Siemens AG	SMAWY	
OTC	Stahlwerke Peine Salzgitter	SLHUY	Steel
OTC	Thyssen AG	THAGY	Conglomerate
OTC	VA Technologie AG		
OTC	Volkswagen AG	VLKAY	Automotive
OTC	Volkswagen PR		Automotive

Exchange	Company	Ticker	Industry

Ghana

PORTAL	Ashanti Goldfields 144A	ASHAY	Gold Mining

Greece

NASDAQ	Anangel-American Shipholdings	ASIPY	Shipping
NASDAQ	Astro Tankers Ltd	ASROF	Shipping
OTC	Boutari John, & Son Wines	BOUC	Food Proc
OTC	Boutari, John, & Son Wines PR	BJSPY	Food Proc
OTC	Credit Bank AE	CBAEY	Banking
AMEX	Global Ocean Carriers Ltd	GLO	Shipping
OTC	Globe Group SA	GLGPY	Conglomerate

Hong Kong

NASDAQ	AES China Generating	CHGNF	Utility
OTC	Amoy Properties Ltd	AMOPY	Real Estate
NYSE	Amway Asia Pacific Ltd	AAP	
OTC	Applied International Holdings	APIHY	Games, Toys
OTC	Asia Orient Co Ltd	AOCPY	Real Estate
OTC	Bank of East Asia Ltd	BKEAY	Banking
OTC	Bonso Electronics Int, UTS		Electronics
OTC	Bonso Electronics International	BNSOF	Electronics
OTC	Cathy Pacific Airways Ltd	CPCAY	Airline
OTC	Champion Technology Holding	CMPLY	Tel. Eq.
OTC	Cheung Kong Holdings Ltd	CHEUY	Real Estate
OTC	China Aerospace Intl Holdings	COIVY	Aerospace
NASDAQ	China Industrial Group	CIND	
OTC	China International Land & Inv. Ltd	CAOVY	Property
OTC	China Light & Power Ltd	CHLWY	Utility
OTC	China Strategic Inv. Ltd	CSILY	Conglomerate
NASDAQ	Chinatek	CTEK	
OTC	Chuangs Holdings Ltd	CHUNY	Holding Co
OTC	Companion Bldg Matl (Holdings)	CBMHY	
OTC	Consolidated Electronic Power Asia (CEPAL)	CWERY	Utility
NASDAQ	DSG International	DSGIF	Diapers
OTC	Deswell Industries	DSWLF	Plastic Products
NASDAQ	Electronic International Inc	EPLTF	Semiconductors
OTC	Emperor (China Concepts) Inv	EPCHY	
OTC	Emperor International Holdings	EPRRY	
OTC	Evergo Holdings Ltd	EVGOY	Investment
OTC	FP Special Assets	FPSAY	Investment
OTC	First Pacific Co Holdings	FPAFY	Investment
OTC	Frankie Dominion International	FKDMY	Novelties
OTC	Giordano Holdings Ltd	GRDHY	Apparel
OTC	Gold Peak Industries Holdings		Electronics
OTC	Grand Hotel Holdings Ltd	GHOAY	Hotel

Exchange	Company	Ticker	Industry
NASDAQ	Great Wall Elecronic International Ltd	GWALY	Electronics
OTC	HB International Holdings Ltd	HBIHY	
OTC	HSBC Hongkong & Shanghai Bank Holding	HSBHY	Banking
OTC	Hang Lung Development Co Ltd	HANLY	Banking
OTC	Hang Seng Bank Ltd	HNGSY	Banking
OTC	Hanny Magnetics Holdings Ltd		Magn Tapes
OTC	Henderson Land Development Ltd	HLDLY	Real Estate
OTC	HIH Cap Ltd		
OTC	Hong Kong & China Gas	HOKSY	Utility
OTC	Hong Kong Aircraft Engineering Co Ltd	HKAEY	Engineering
OTC	Hong Kong Daily News Holdings	HKDNY	Media
OTC	Hong Kong Electric Holdings Ltd	HONGY	Utility
NYSE	Hong Kong Telecom Ltd	HKT	Telecom
OTC	Hopewell Holdings	HOWWY	Construction
OTC	Hutchison Whampoa Ltd	HUWHY	Retailing
OTC	Hysan Development Ltd	HYSNY	Real Estate
OTC	International Pipe Ltd	IPPEY	
OTC	Jardine Matheson Holdings Ltd	JARLY	Marketing
OTC	Jardine Stragetic Holdings Ltd	JDSHY	Retailing
OTC	Jinhui Holdings Co Ltd	JHUHY	Ship Charter
OTC	Johnson Electric Holdings Ltd	JELCY	Micrometers
OTC	K. Wah International Holdings	KWAHY	
OTC	Keng Fong Sin Kee Constr & Inv		
OTC	Kumagai Gumi (Hong Kong) Ltd	KMGMY	
NASDAQ	L Rex International	LREXF	Printing
OTC	Lai Sun Development Co	LDVSY	
OTC	Legend Hdgs Ltd	LGHLY	
NASDAQ	M T C Electronic Tech (Canada)	MTCEF	
OTC	Mandarin Oriental International	MAORY	Hotels
OTC	Moulin International Hldgs Ltd	MLIJY	
NASDAQ	Nam Tai Electronics	NTAIF	Electronics
OTC	New World Development Co Ltd	NEWDY	Hotels
NASDAQ	OLS Asia Holdings	OLSAY	Construction
NASDAQ	Pacific Basin Bulk Shipping	PBBUF	Shipping
OTC	Pacific Concord Holdings Ltd	PFCHY	
OTC	Playmates Intl Holdings Ltd	PYMHY	Toys
OTC	Radica Games Ltd	RADAF	Games
OTC	Shun Tak Holdings Ltd	SHTGY	Restaurants
OTC	Sino Land Ltd	SNLAY	Real Estate
OTC	Siu-Fung Ceramics Holdings Ltd	SFCHY	Ceramics
OTC	South China Morning Post (Holdings)	SCHPY	Newspaper
OTC	Star Paging International Ltd	STPGY	
OTC	Sun Hung Kai & Co Ltd	SHGKY	Financial
OTC	Sun Hung Kai Properties	SUHKY	Real Estate
OTC	Swire Pacific Ltd A	SWRAY	Conglomerate

Exchange	Company	Ticker	Industry
OTC	Swire Pacific Ltd B	SPCBY	Conglomerate
OTC	Swire Properties Ltd	SWPPY	Real Estate
OTC	T V E Holdings Ltd	TVEHY	Media
OTC	Tai Cheung Holdings Ltd	TCHLY	Real Estate
OTC	Techtronic Industries Co Ltd	TTNDY	Hshold Elect
OTC	Television Broadcasts Ltd	TVBSY	Media
NYSE	Tommy Hilfiger Corp	TOM	Apparel
OTC	Trafalgar Housing Ltd		Real Estate
OTC	Varitronix International Ltd	VARXY	
OTC	Vtech Holdings Ltd	VTKHY	Electronics
OTC	Wah Kwong Shippg Holdings Ltd	WKSHY	Transport
NASDAQ	Wharf Holdings Ltd	WHARY	Holding Co
OTC	Wheelock & Co Ltd 144A	WHELY	
OTC	Wing Hang Bank Ltd	WGHGY	Banking
OTC	Winsor Industrial Corp Ltd	WIINY	Apparel
OTC	Wo Kee Hong (Holdings) Ltd	WKHHY	

Hungary

Exchange	Company	Ticker	Industry
OTC	Fotex RT First American-Hungarian Photo Servicing Ltd	FOTCY	Photography
GDR	Gedeon Richter Ltd		Chemicals
NASDAQ	Hungarian Telecom & Cable	HTCC	Utility
GDR	MOL Magyar Olaj-es Gazipari RT		Gas
GDR	OTP Bank Ltd		Banking
PORTAL	Pharmavit Pharmaceuticals & Food Industrl Stock Co 144A		Healthcare
GDR	Pick Szeged RT 144A		Food

India

Exchange	Company	Ticker	Industry
GDR	Arvind Mills Ltd		Textile
PORTAL	Arvind Mills Ltd 144A		Textile
PORTAL	Ballarpur Industries Ltd		Pulp, Paper
PORTAL	Ballarpur Industries Ltd CV of APR 1 1999 144A		Pulp, Paper
GDR	Bombay Dyeing & Mfg Co Ltd		Machinery
PORTAL	Bombay Dyeing & Mfg Co Ltd WTS 144A		Machinery
PORTAL	Century Textiles & Industries Ltd GDR		Textiles
GDR	Cesc Ltd		
PORTAL	Cesc Ltd 144A	CESCY	
PORTAL	Cesc Ltd 144A WTS	CESCW	
PORTAL	Chakwal Cement 144A		Cement
GDR	Core Healthcare Ltd		Health
PORTAL	Core Parentals 144A		Health
GDR	DCW Ltd		Chemicals
PORTAL	DCW Ltd 144A		Chemicals
GDR	Dr Reddy's Laboratories Ltd		Pharmaceuticals
PORTAL	Dr Reddy's Laboratories 144A	REDDY	Pharmaceuticals

Exchange	Company	Ticker	Industry
PORTAL	East India Hotels Ltd 144A		Hotels
GDR	EID Parry (India) Ltd		
PORTAL	EID Parry (India) Ltd 144A	EIDPY	
GDR	Finolex Cables Ltd		Wire, Cable
PORTAL	Finolex Cables Ltd 144A		Wire, Cable
GDR	Flex Industries Ltd		
GDR	Garden Silk Mills Ltd		Silk
GDR	Grasim Industries Ltd		Textiles
PORTAL	Grasim Industries Ltd 144A	GRSF	Textiles
GDR	Great Eastern Shipping Ltd		Shipping
GDR	Gujarat Ambuja Cement Ltd		Cement
PORTAL	Gujarat Ambuja Cement Ltd 144A		Cement
GDR	Gujarat Narmada Valley		Fertilizers
PORTAL	Gujarat Narmada Valley 144A		Fertilizers
GDR	Hindalco Industries Ltd		Aluminium
PORTAL	Hindalco Industries Ltd 144A		Aliminium
PORTAL	Hindalco Industries Ltd WT 144A		Aluminium
GDR	Hindusthan Development Corp Ltd		
PORTAL	Hindusthan Development Corp Ltd 144A		
GDR	ITC Ltd		
PORTAL	ITC Ltd 144A		
PORTAL	ITC Ltd 144A WTS		
GDR	India Cements Ltd		Cement
PORTAL	India Cements Ltd 144A		Cement
GDR	Indian Aluminium Co Ltd		Aluminium
PORTAL	Indian Aluminium Co Ltd 144A	IALCY	Aluminium
GDR	Indian Petrochemical Corp		Chemicals
GDR	Indian Rayon & Industries Ltd		Textiles
PORTAL	Indian Rayon & Industries Ltd 144A		Textiles
GDR	Indo Gulf Fertilisers & Chemicals Corp Ltd		Fertilizers
PORTAL	Indo Gulf Fertilisers & Chemicals Corp Ltd 144A		Fertilizers
GDR	JCT Ltd		
PORTAL	JCT Ltd 144A		
GDR	JK Corp Ltd		
IDR	Jain Irrigations Systems Ltd		
GDR	Larsen & Toubro Ltd		
PORTAL	Larsen & Toubro Ltd 144A		
GDR	Mahindra & Mahindra Ltd		
PORTAL	Mahindra & Mahindra Ltd 144A	MHMHY	
GDR	NEPC-Micon Ltd		
GDR	Nippon Denro Ispat Ltd		
GDR	Oriental Hotels Ltd		Hotels
GDR	Ranbaxy Laboratories Ltd		
PORTAL	Ranbaxy Laboratories Ltd 144A		
GDR	Raymond Woollen Mills Ltd		Textiles
PORTAL	Raymond Woollen Mills Ltd 144A		Textiles

Exchange	Company	Ticker	Industry
GDR	Reliance Industries Ltd		Textiles
PORTAL	Reliance Industries Ltd 144A	RELYP	Textiles
PORTAL	SIV Industries GDR		
GDR	Sanghi Polyesters Ltd		Textiles
PORTAL	Sanghi Polyesters Ltd 144A		Textiles
PORTAL	Shriram Industrial Enterprises Ltd 144A		
PORTAL	Shriram Industrial Enterprises Ltd UTS 144A		
PORTAL	Shriram Industrial Enterprises Ltd WTS 144A		
GDR	Southern Petrochemical Industries Corp Ltd		
PORTAL	Southern Petrochemical Industries Corp Ltd 144A	SPICY	
PORTAL	Sterlite Industries (India) Ltd 144A		
GDR	TATA Electric Companies		
PORTAL	TATA Electric Companies 144A	TATAF	
GDR	TATA Engineering & Locomotives		
PORTAL	TATA Engineering & Locomotives 144A	TATAY	
GDR	TATA Iron & Steel Co. Ltd		Steel
PORTAL	TATA Iron & Steel Co. Ltd 144A		Steel
GDR	Tube Investments of India Ltd		
PORTAL	Tube Investments of India Ltd 144A	TUBEY	
GDR	United Phosphorus Ltd		Chemicals
PORTAL	United Phosphorus Ltd 144A		Chemicals
GDR	USHA Beltron Ltd		
GDR	Videocon International Ltd		Hshold Elect
PORTAL	Videocon International Ltd 144A		Hshold Elect
GDR	Wockhardt Ltd		

Indonesia

NYSE	Indosat PT Indonesian Satellite	IIT	Telecom
OTC	PT Indah Kiat Pulp & Paper		Pulp, Paper
OTC	PT Indocement Tunggal Prakarasa		
OTC	PT Inti Indorayon Utama	PTIDY	Pulp, Paper
NASDAQ	PT Tri Polyta Indonesia	TPIFY	Petrochem

Ireland

NYSE	Allied Irish Banks Pref	ATELY	Banking
NYSE	Allied Irish Banks Plc	AIB	Banking
OTC	Anglo-Irish Bank corp	AGBKY	Banking
AMEX	Aran Energy Plc	ARANY	Energy
	Bank of Ireland Group		Banking
OTC	CBT Group Plc	CBTSY	Data Processing
OTC	CRH Plc	CRHCY	Bldg Matls
AMEX	Elan ATS UTS	ELNE	Pharmaceuticals
AMEX	Elan Corp Plc	ELN	Pharmaceuticals

Exchange	Company	Ticker	Industry
AMEX	Elan Corp Plc WTS	ELN X	Pharmaceuticals
OTC	GPA Group Plc		
OTC	GLENCAR Explorations Plc	GLNCY	Gold Mines
NASDAQ	Hibernia Foods Plc	HIBUF	Beef Proc
NASDAQ	Hibernia Foods Plc UT		Beef Proc
NASDAQ	Hibernia Foods Plc WTS A	HIBNY	Beef Proc
OTC	Independent Resources Ltd	ITRSY	
OTC	Institute of Clinical Pharmacology	ICPYY	Pharmaceuticals
PORTAL	Nale Laboratories Ltd 144A		
NASDAQ	Pharma Patch A WT	SKIWF	Biotech
NASDAQ	Pharma Patch B WT	SKIZF	Biotech
NASDAQ	Pharma Patch C WT	SKIMF	Biotech
NASDAQ	Pharma Patch Plc	SKINY	Biotech
NASDAQ	Pharma Patch Unit	SKIUF	Biotech
OTC	Phoenix Shannon Plc	PHNXY	
OTC	Power Corp Plc	PWRCY	Real Estate
OTC	Ryan Hotels Plc	RYHOY	Hotels
NASDAQ	Saville Systems Ireland	SAVEY	Data Processing
NASDAQ	Trinity Biotech Plc	HIVSY	Biotech
OTC	Trinity Biotech Plc UT	HIVUF	Biotech
NASDAQ	Waterford Wedgwood Plc	WATFZ	Hshold Eq
NASDAQ	Waterford Wedgwood Plc UT		Hshold Eq

Israel

Exchange	Company	Ticker	Industry
NASDAQ	Accent Software International	ACNTF	Data Processing
NASDAQ	Aladdin Knowledge Systems	ALDNF	Software
AMEX	American Israeli Paper Mills	AIP	Pulp, Paper
OTC	American Israeli Paper Mills PR4	AMPLO	Pulp, Paper
NASDAQ	American Israeli Paper Mills PR 6 1/2	AMPLP	Pulp, Paper
AMEX	Ampal America Israel A (US Company)	AIS A	Holding Co
AMEX	Ampal America Israel WTS	AIS.W	Holding Co
NASDAQ	Arel Communications & Software Ltd WTS	ARLWF	Software
NASDAQ	Arel Communications & Software Ltd	ARLCF	Software
NASDAQ	Ariely Advertising	RELEF	Advertising
NASDAQ	ARYT Optronics Industries	ARYTF	Electronics
OTC	BVR Technologies Ltd	BVRTF	
NASDAQ	Bank Leumi Le Israel B SH	BKLMY	Fin Serv
NASDAQ	Bio Technology General (US Company)	BTGC	Biotech
AMEX	Carmel Container Systems	KML	Transport
NASDAQ	Comet Software International	CMTTF	Software
NASDAQ	Comverse Technology	CMVT	Software
NASDAQ	Data Systems & Software Ltd (DSSI)	DSSIY	Software
NASDAQ	ECI Telecom Ltd	ECILF	Telecom
NASDAQ	Edunetics Educational Systems Ltd	EDNTF	Software
NASDAQ	Edusoft Ltd Ord	EDUSF	Software
NASDAQ	Elbit Computers Ltd	ELBTF	Electronics
NASDAQ	Electric Fuel	EFCX	
AMEX	Electrochemical Industries (Frutarom)	EIF	Chemicals

Exchange	Company	Ticker	Industry
OTC	Electrocon International Ltd	EPLTF	
NASDAQ	Electronics & Imaging	EFII	Software
OTC	Elite Industries Ltd ADR 1 NIS	ELEDY	Food, Snacks
AOTC	Elite Industries Ltd ADR 5 NIS	ELEIY	Food, Snacks
NASDAQ	Elron Electronic Industries Ltd	ELRNF	Biotech
NYSE	Elscint Ltd	ELT	Biotech
NASDAQ	ESC Medical Systems	ESCMF	Electromedical
NASDAQ	Eshed Robotec 1982 Ltd	ROBOF	Robotics
AMEX	ETZ Lavud Ltd	ETZ	Pharmaceuticals
AMEX	ETZ Lavud Ltd A	ETZ A	Pharmaceuticals
NASDAQ	Fibronics International	FBRX	Fibreoptics
NASDAQ	Fourth Dimension Software Ltd	DDDDF	Software
NASDAQ	Geotek Communications Inc (US Company)	GOTK	Electronics
NASDAQ	Gilat Satellite Networks Ltd	GILTF	Telecom
OTC	Healthcare Technologies Ltd	HCTLF	Biotech
NASDAQ	Healthcare Technologies WT	HCTWF	Biotech
NASDAQ	Home Centers	HOMEF	Hardware Stores
OTC	IDB Bankholding Ltd	IDBUY	Banking
OTC	IDB Bankholding Ltd B		Banking
NASDAQ	IIS Intelligent Info Sys Ltd	IISLF	Telecom
NASDAQ	ISG International Software Group Ltd	SISGF	Software
NASDAQ	Idan Software Ind	IDANF	Software
OTC	Industrial Bank of Israel D PR	IDDNF	Banking
OTC	Industrial Dev Bank 6% PR	IDDPF	Banking
NASDAQ	Interpharm Labs Ltd	IPLLF	Biotech
NASDAQ	Israel Land Development Co Ltd	ILDCY	Real Estate
NASDAQ	Isramco Inc Ord	ISRL	
OTC	ISRAS Investment Co Ltd NIS1	ISIMY	
OTC	ISRAS Investment Co Ltd NIS5		
NASDAQ	ISTEC Industries & Tech Ltd	ISTEF	Finance
NASDAQ	ISTEC Industries & Tech Ltd UTS	ISTUF	Finance
NASDAQ	ISTEC Industries & Tech WTS	ISTWF	Finance
OTC	Kopel (Drive Yourself) Ltd	KOPLY	Automotive
NASDAQ	Lannet Data Communications Ltd	LANTF	Telecom
NASDAQ	Lanoptics Ltd	LNOPF	Telecom
OTC	Laser Industries Ltd	LASGF	Biotech
NASDAQ	M-Systems Flash Disk	FLSHF	Computers
NASDAQ	Magal Security Systems Ltd	MAGSF	Security
NASDAQ	Magic Software Enterprises Ltd	MGICF	Software
NASDAQ	MEDIS EL Ltd	MDSLF	Biotech
NASDAQ	Netmanage	NETM	
NASDAQ	Nexus Telecommunication Systems Ltd	NXUSF	Telecom
NASDAQ	Nexus Telecommunication Systms Ltd UTS	NXUUF	Telecom
NASDAQ	Nexus Telecommunication Systems Ltd WT B	NXUZF	Telecom
NASDAQ	Nexus Telecommunication Systems Ltd WT A	NXUWF	Telecom

Exchange	Company	Ticker	Industry
NASDAQ	Nice Systems	NICEY	Computer Eq
NASDAQ	Nur Advanced Technologies	NURTF	Printing Eq
NASDAQ	Orbotech Ltd	ORBKF	
NASDAQ	OSHAP Technologies Ltd	OSHSF	Software
NASDAQ	OSHAP UTS	OSHUF	Software
NASDAQ	OSHAP WTS	OSHWF	Software
NYSE	PEC Israel Economic Corp (US Company)	IEC	Investment
OTC	Pharmos Corp (US Company)	PARS	
NASDAQ	RADA Electronic Industries Ltd	RADIF	Electronics
NASDAQ	Robomatix Ltd	RBMXF	
OTC	Scaiwec Co		Graphics
NASDAQ	Scan Vec Co	SVECF	Computers
NASDAQ	Scitex Corp Ltd	SCIXF	Printing
NASDAQ	Silicom WTS '98	SILZF	Computers
NASDAQ	Silicon Ltd	SILCF	Computers
NASDAQ	TVG Technologies	TVGTF	Graphics
OTC	TVG Technologies A WT	TVGWF	Graphics
OTC	TVG Technologies B WT	TVGZF	Graphics
OTC	TVG Technologies C WT	TVGLF	Graphics
OTC	TVG Technologies UTS	TVGUF	Graphics
NYSE	Tadiran Ltd	TAD	Telecom
OTC	Taro Pharmaceutical Industries	TAROF	Pharmaceuticals
NASDAQ	Tat Technologies Ltd (formerly Galagraph Ltd)	TATTF	Graphics
NASDAQ	Tat Technologies Ltd Unit	TATUF	Graphics
NASDAQ	Tat Technologies WT	TATWF	Graphics
NASDAQ	Technomatix Technologies	TCNOF	Software
NASDAQ	Teledata Communication Ltd	TLDCF	Telecom
NASDAQ	Telegraph Newspaper	TELGF	Publishing
NASDAQ	Telegraph Newspaper A WT	TELWF	Publishing
NASDAQ	Telegraph Newspaper B WT	TELZF	Publishing
TEVI	TEVA Pharmaceutical Industries	TEVIY	Pharmaceuticals
OTC	Tower Semiconductor Ltd	TSEMF	Electronics
NASDAQ	Vocal Tec	VOCLF	Data Processing

Italy

Exchange	Company	Ticker	Industry
OTC	Assicurazione Generali	ASSGF	Insurance
PORTAL	Banca Cimmerciale Italiana 144A	BCIAY	Banking
OTC	Bastogi B SH	BATGY	Hotels
NYSE	Benetton Group SPA	BNG	Apparel
PORTAL	Credito Italiano 144A	CIAOY	
OTC	Eridania Spa	ERIDY	Sugar
NYSE	Fiat Spa	FIA	
NYSE	Fiat Spa Pref	FIA P	
NYSE	Fiat Spa-Svgs	FIA P A	
NYSE	Fila Holdings Spa	FLH	
OTC	Finanziaria Agroindustriale Spa	FIN	Oils, Sugar
OTC	Finanziaria Agroindustriale Spa Svgs	FIS	Oils, Sugar

Exchange	Company	Ticker	Industry
NYSE	Gucci	GUC	Leatherware
NYSE	Industrie Natuzzi Spa	NTZ	Upholstery
NYSE	Istituto Mobiliare Italiano	ISI	Banking
NYSE	Istituto Nazionale Delle Assicurazione	INZ	Insurance
OTC	Italcementi Fabriche Reunite	ILMNY	Cement
OTC	La Rinascente	LARCY	
OTC	Ledoga Spa Pr		
NYSE	Luxottica Group	LUX	
OTC	Luxottica Spa	LUXOF	
NYSE	Montedison Spa Ord	MNT	Chemicals
NYSE	Montedison Spa Svgs	MNT S	Chemicals
OTC	Olivetti & Co Spa	OLIVY	Computers
OTC	Olivetti & Co Spa Non-conv Sh	OICCY	Computers
OTC	Olivetti & Co Spa Pr	OLIPY	Computers
OTC	Pirelli Spa	PIREY	Tires Cables
OTC	Simint Industria Spa	SMIIY	Apparel
OTC	Simint Industria Spa Pr		Apparel
OTC	SNIA Viscosa	SNIAY	
OTC	Societa Finanziera Siderugica (Finsider) A	SFIZY	Steel
OTC	Stet Soc Finanz Telef Spa WTS	STEWY	Telecom
NYSE	Stet Soc Finanziaria Telefonica Spa	STE	Telecom
NYSE	Stet Soc Finanziaria Telefonica Spa Svgs	STEA	Telecom
OTC	Stet Soc Finanziaria Telefonica Spa UTS	STEUY	Telecom

Jamaica

OTC	Caribbean Cement Co Ltd		Cement
OTC	Jamaica Broilers		Food
OTC	Jamaica Flour Mills Ltd		Flour Mill
OTC	Jamaica Telephone Co	JTELY	Telecom
OTC	Ciboney Group Ltd	CIB	Hotels

Japan

OTC	Aida Engineering Ltd	ADERY	Machinery
OTC	Ajinomoto Co Inc	AJINY	Food Proc
OTC	Akai Electric Co Ltd	AKELY	Hshold Elect
OTC	All Nippon Airways Co Ltd	ALNPY	Airline
OTC	Alps Electric Co Ltd	ALPSY	Hshold Elect
OTC	Amada Co Ltd	AMDLY	Hshold Elect
NYSE	Amway Japan Ltd	AJL	Retailing
OTC	Asahi Bank Ltd (formerly Kyowa Saitama Bank)	KATMY	Banking
OTC	Asahi Chemical Industry Co Ltd	ASHIY	Chemicals
OTC	Asahi Glass Co Ltd	ASGLY	Glass
OTC	Ashikaga Bank Ltd	AKGBY	Banking
OTC	Bandai Co Ltd	BNDCY	Toys
OTC	Bank of Fukuoka Ltd	BOFLY	Banking
OTC	Bank of Tokyo Ltd	BLKMY	Banking

Exchange	Company	Ticker	Industry
OTC	Bank of Yokohama Ltd	BKJAY	Banking
OTC	Banyu Pharmaceutical Co Ltd	BNYUY	Pharmaceuticals
OTC	Bridgestone Corp	BRDCY	Tire
OTC	Brother Industries Ltd	BRTRY	Hshold appl
NASDAQ	CSK Corp	CSKKY	Software
OTC	Calpis Food Industries Ltd	CPISY	Food Proc
NASDAQ	Canon Inc	CANNY	Off Eq
OTC	Casio Computer Co Ltd	CSIOY	Elect Eq
OTC	Dai Nippon Printing Ltd	DNPCY	Printing
NASDAQ	Dai'ei Inc	DAIEY	Retailing
OTC	Dai-Ichi Kangyo Bank Ltd	DAIKY	Banking
OTC	Daibiru Corp (formerly Osaka Bldg Co Ltd)	DIBUY	Property
OTC	Daiwa Danchi Co Ltd	DWADY	Construction
OTC	Daiwa House Industry Ltd	DWAHY	Construction
OTC	Daiwa Securities Ltd	DSECY	Finance
OTC	Daiwa Seiko Inc	DWASY	Sporting Gds
OTC	Ebara Corp	EBCOY	Machinery
OTC	Eisai Co Ltd	EISAY	Pharmaceuticals
OTC	Fuji Bank Ltd	FUJPY	Banking
OTC	Fuji Heavy Industries Ltd	FUJHY	Automotive
NASDAQ	Fuji Photo Film Ltd	FUJIY	Photography
OTC	Fujita Corp	FTACY	Construction
NTC	Fujitsu Ltd	FJTSY	Computers
OTC	Furukawa Electric Ltd	FUWAY	Wire, Cable
OTC	Hachijuni Bank Ltd	HACBY	Banking
OTC	Hino Motors Ltd	HINOY	Automotive
OTC	Hitachi Cable Ltd	HCBLY	Wire, Cable
OTC	Hitachi Koki Co Ltd	HKKIY	Power Tools
NYSE	Hitachi Ltd	HIT	Electronics
OTC	Hitachi Metals Ltd	HMTLY	Steel, Metals
OTC	Hochiki Corp	HHKIY	Telecom Eq
OTC	Hokuriku Bank Ltd	HKRBY	Banking
NYSE	Honda Motor Co Ltd	HMC	Automotive
OTC	Industrial Bank of Japan	ILBKY	Banking
OTC	Isuzu Motors Ltd	ISUZY	Automotive
NASDAQ	Ito-Yokado Co Ltd	IYCOY	Groceries
OTC	Itochu (formerly Itoh, C. & Co)	ITOHY	Trading
NASDAQ	Japan Air Lines Ltd	JAPNY	Airline
OTC	Japan Steel Works Ltd	JPSWY	Steel
OTC	Jusco Co Ltd	JUSCY	Groceries
OTC	Kajima Corp	KAJMY	Construction
OTC	Kanebo Ltd	KABOY	Textiles
OTC	Kankaku Securities (formerly Nippon Kangyo Kakumaru Sec Ltd)		
OTC	Kao Corp	KAOCY	Hshold Prod
NASDAQ	Kashiyama & Co Ltd		
OTC	Kawasaki Steel Corp	KWSTY	Steel

Exchange	Company	Ticker	Industry
OTC	Kikkomen Shoyu Ltd	KIKKF	
NASDAQ	Kirin Brewery Ltd	KNBWY	Brewing
OTC	Kobe Steel Ltd	KBSTY	Steel
OTC	Komatsu Ltd	KMATY	Machinery
OTC	Konica Corp	KNCAY	Leisure Gds
NYSE	Kubota Corp	KUB	Bldg Matls
OTC	Kumagai Gumi Ltd	KUMGY	Construction
NYSE	Kyocera Corp	KYO	Electronics
NASDAQ	Makita Corp	MKTAY	Power Tools
OTC	Marubeni Corp	MARUY	Trading
OTC	Marui Co Ltd	MAURY	Retailing
NYSE	Matsushita Electric Ind Ltd	MC	Appliances
OTC	Matsushita Electric Works Ltd	MSEWY	Appliances
OTC	Meiji Seika Kaisha Ltd	MSIKY	Candy
OTC	Mikuni Coca-Cola Bottling Ltd	MIKOF	Bottling
OTC	Minebea Ltd (formerly Nippon Minature Bearing)	MBEAY	Electronics
NYSE	Mitsubishi Bank Ltd	MBK	Banking
OTC	Mitsubishi Chem Machinery Ltd	MITCY	Chemicals
OTC	Mitsubishi Corp	MTSBY	Trading
OTC	Mitsubishi Electric Corp	MIELY	Electronics
OTC	Mitsubishi Estate Co Ltd	MITEY	Property
OTC	Mitsubishi Kasei Corp	MKASY	Petrochem
OTC	Mitsubishi Rayon Ltd	MTKOF	
OTC	Mitsubishi Trust & Banking Corp	MITTY	Banking
NASDAQ	Mitsui & Co Ltd	MITSY	Trading
OTC	Mitsui Marine & Fire Insurance	MMFIY	Insurance
OTC	Mitsui Mining & Smelting	MTMSF	Mining
OTC	Mitsui Toatsu Chemicals Inc	MTTTF	Chemicals
OTC	Mitsukoshi Ltd	MKOLY	Apparel
NASDAQ	NEC Corp	NIPNY	Electronics
OTC	NKK Corp	NKKCY	Steel
OTC	NSK Nippon Seiko KK	NISKY	
OTC	Nagoya Railroad Co Ltd	NARRY	Railroad
OTC	New Japan Securities Co Ltd	NEJSY	Brokers
OTC	Nifco Inc	NIFCF	Automotive
OTC	Nikko Securities Ltd	NIKOY	Brokers
AMEX	Nikon Corp	NINOY	Photography
OTC	Nintendo Co Ltd	NINTY	Games
OTC	Nippon Seiko KK Ltd	NISKY	Bearings
OTC	Nippon Shinpan Ltd	NSHPY	Credit Cd Svcs
OTC	Nippon Shokubai KK Ltd	NSHKY	Chemicals
OTC	Nippon Steel	NISTF	Steel
OTC	Nippon Suisan Kaisah Ltd	NISUY	Food
NYSE	Nippon Telegraph & Telephone	NTT	Telecom
OTC	Nippon Yusen Kabushiki Kaisha	NYUKY	Shipping
OTC	Nippon Denso Co Ltd	NIPDY	Automotive
NASDAQ	Nissan Motor Co Ltd	NSANY	Automotive

Exchange	Company	Ticker	Industry
OTC	Nisshin Steel Ltd	NHISY	Steel
OTC	Nitto Denko Corp	NDEKY	Sealants
OTC	Nomura Securities Co Ltd	NRSCY	Banking
OTC	Oji Paper Co Ltd	OJIPY	Pulp, Paper
OTC	Olympus Optical Co Ltd	OLYOY	Photography
OTC	Omron Corp (formerly Omron Tateisi Electronics)	OMTEY	Electronics
OTC	Onoda Cement Ltd	ONDAY	Cement
OTC	Onward Kashiyama Co Ltd	OKASY	Apparel
OTC	Osaka Building Co Ltd	OSAKY	Real Estate
NYSE	Pioneer Electronic Corp	PIO	Electronics
OTC	Ricoh Co Ltd	RICOY	Photography
OTC	Sakura Bank	STSUY	Banking
OTC	Sanko Steamship Co Ltd	SKSSY	Shipping
OTC	Sanwa Bank Ltd	SANWY	Banking
NASDAQ	Sanyo Electic Co Ltd	SANYY	Electronics
OTC	Sanyo Securities Ltd	SSECY	Brokers
OTC	Secom Co Ltd	SOMLY	Security Svcs
OTC	Sega Enterprises Ltd	SEGNY	Games
OTC	Sekisui House Ltd	SKIHY	Construction
OTC	Seven-Eleven Japan Co	SVELY	Groceries
OTC	Sharp Corp	SHCAY	Electronics
OTC	Shisedido Ltd	SHSDY	Cosmetics
OTC	Shizuoka Bank Ltd	SHZUY	Banking
OTC	Showa Sangyo Ltd	SHSGY	Edible Oils
NYSE	Sony Corp	SNE	Electronics
OTC	Sumitomo Bank Ltd	SUBJY	Banking
OTC	Sumitomo Electric Industries	SUMTY	Wire, Cable
OTC	Sumitomo Metal Industries Ltd	SMMLY	Steel, Const
OTC	Surugu Bank Ltd	SUGBY	Banking
NYSE	TDK Corp	TDK	Recording
OTC	Taisel Corp	TAISY	Construction
OTC	TaiyoYuden Ltd	TYOYY	Semiconductors
OTC	Teijin Ltd	TINLY	Chemicals
OTC	Teijin Seiki Co Ltd	TSEKY	Aircraft Parts
OTC	Toa Harbor Works Co Ltd	TOAHY	Engineering
OTC	Tokai Bank Ltd	TOKBY	Banking
NASDAQ	Tokio Marine & Fire Ins Ltd	TKIOY	Insurance
OTC	Tokyo Dome (formerly Korakuen Stadium)	TOKOY	Leisure
OTC	Tokyu Land Corp	TOLAY	Real Estate
OTC	Toppan Printing Co Ltd	TONPY	Printing
OTC	Toray Industries Inc	TRAYY	Chemicals
OTC	Toto Ltd	TOTOY	Plumbing Fixtures
OTC	Toyo Suisan Kaisha Ltd	TSUKY	Fish
OTC	Toyobo Co Ltd	TYOBY	Textiles
NASDAQ	Toyota Motor Corp	TOYOY	Automotive
OTC	Tsubakimoto Precision Products	TSPRY	Bearings
OTC	Tsugami Corp	TSGMY	Automotive

Exchange	Company	Ticker	Industry
OTC	Victor Co of Japan Ltd	VJAPY	Hshold Elect
NASDAQ	Wacoal Corp	WACLY	Apparel
OTC	Yamaichi Securities Ltd	YAMAY	Fin Serv
OTC	Yamazaki Baking Co Ltd	YMZBY	Food Proc
OTC	Yasuda Trust & Banking Co Ltd	YSUTY	Banking

Lebanon

GDR	Banque Audi SAL		Banking

Liberia

AMEX	B&H Maritime Carriers Ltd	BHM	Shipping
AMEX	B&H Ocean Carriers Ltd	BHO	Shipping
AMEX	Global Ocean Carriers Ltd	GLO	Shipping
AMEX	MC Shipping Inc	MCX	Shipping
NYSE	Royal Caribbean Cruises Ltd	RCL	Tourism

Luxembourg

NASDAQ	Anangel-American Shipholdings A	ASIPY	Transport
PORTAL	Arbed SA Steel		Steel Mfr
PORTAL	Credit Lyonnais Capital Acc Inc GPS	CLYACC	Banking
PORTAL	Credit Lyonnais Capital Quib GPS	CLYNYP	Banking
NASDAQ	Cronos	CRNSF	Eq Leasing
NYSE	Espirito Santo Finanical SA	ESF	Finance
PORTAL	Indosuez Holdings SCA PR A 144A (France)		Holding Co
OTC	Millicom International Cellular SA	MICCF	Telecom
NASDAQ	Minorco (South Africa)	MNRCY	Holding Co
OTC	Scandinavian Broadcasting System SA	SBTVF	Media
NASDAQ	Stolt Comex-Seaway SA	CSSWF	Oil Drilling
NASDAQ	Stolt-Nielsen SA	STLTF	Shipping

Malaysia

OTC	Amsteel Berhad (formerly Amalgamated Steel Mills)	AAGSY	Steel, Tires
OTC	Angkasa Marketing Berhad	AMB	Automotive
OTC	Bandar Raya Devs Berhad	BROBY	Conglomerate
OTC	Berjaya Corp Berhad	BRJAY	Conglomerate
OTC	Faber Group Berhad		
OTC	Genting Berhad	GEBEY	Plantations
OTC	Inter-Pacific Industrial Group Berhad	IPIGY	Food
OTC	Kesang Corp	KSGCY	Real Estate
OTC	Kuala Lumpar Kepong Berhad	KLKBY	Palm Oil
OTC	Lion Land Berhad	LONLY	Real Estate
OTC	MBF Holdings Berhad	MBFHY	Conglomerate
OTC	Malayan United Industries	MYLUY	Finance
OTC	Perlis Plantations Berhad	PPBHY	Sugar
OTC	Rersorts World Berhad	RSWSY	Hotels

Exchange	Company	Ticker	Industry
OTC	Selangor Properties Berhad	SGPBY	Investment
OTC	Sime Darby Berhad	SIDBY	Conglomerate
OTC	Supreme Corp Berhad	SCOBY	Investment
OTC	Tenaga Nasional Berhad	TNABY	Utility

Mexico

Exchange	Company	Ticker	Industry
PORTAL	Abaco Grupo Financiero SA de CV C 144A		Fin Serv
PORTAL	Aerovias de Mexico SA de CV 144A	AERMY	Airline
OTC	Altos Hornos de Mexico	ADEMY	Steel
OTC	Apasco SA de CV A	AASAY	Cement
OTC	Apasco SA de CV B	AASBY	Cement
NASDAQ	Banca Quadrum	QDRMY	Banking
NYSE	Bufete Industrial SA	GBI	Construction
OTC	Celanese Mexicana SA	CLMXF	Textile
OTC	Cemex SA A Partic A	CMXAF	Cement
OTC	Cemex SA B SH	CMXBY	Cement
PORTAL	Cifra SA de C V A SH 144A	CFRAY	Retailing
OTC	Cifra SA de C V B	CFRAB	Retailing
NYSE	Coca-Cola Femsa SA de CV L	KOF	Food Proc
NYSE	Consorcio G. Dina SA de CV	DIN	Automotive
NYSE	Consorcio G. Dina SA de CV L	DINL	Automotive
OTC	Contoladora Comercial Mexicana SA de CV	CRRXY	Retailing
PORTAL	Corporacion Geo SA 144A		
OTC	Corporacion Indl Sanluis Ser A-1	CORSY	Conglomerate
OTC	Corporacion Indl Sanluis Ser A-2	CILSY	Conglomerate
OTC	Corporacion Indl Sanluis A	CISAY	Conglomerate
OTC	Corporacion Mexicana de Aviacion	CMXVY	Airline
OTC	Desc (Sociedad de Fomento Industrial) C		Conglomerate
NYSE	Desc SA de CV	DES	Conglomerate
OTC	EPN SA de CV	EPNSY	Oil, Gas
OTC	El Puerto de Liverpool SA		Retailing
OTC	Empaques Pondero SA	EMQSY	Pulp, Paper
NYSE	Empresas ICA Soc Controladora	ICA	Construction
NYSE	Empresas La Moderna SA Cert	ELM	Tobacco
NYSE	Empresas La Moderna SA de CV UTS (4 CPOS+1 I SH)	ELM	Tobacco
OTC	Far Ben SA de CV		Pharmaceuticals
PORTAL	Fomento Economico Mexicano Femsa SA 144A	FEMXY	
PORTAL	Grupo Carso SA de CV 144A	GRPCY	Conglomerate
NYSE	Grupo Casa Autrey SA de CV	ATY	Retailing
NYSE	Grupo Elektra Participation Certs	EKT	Retailing
NYSE	Grupo Embotellador (GEMEX) SA de CV	GEM	Bottling

Exchange	Company	Ticker	Industry
PORTAL	Grupo Financiero Banamex Accival (Banacci) L 144A		Banking
PORTAL	Grupo Financiero Bancomer 144A	GPFBY	Banking
PORTAL	Grupo Financiero GBM Atlantico SA de CVL 144A		Fin Serv
OTC	Grupo Financiero Inverlat SA de CV C		Fin Serv
OTC	Grupo Financiero Invermexico SA de CV B CPO	GFIMB	Fin Serv
OTC	Grupo Financiero Invermexico SA de CV C	GFIMC	Fin Serv
OTC	Grupo Financiero Mexival Banpais C	MKXAY	Fin Serv
OTC	Grupo Financiero Prime Internacional SA L SH		Fin Serv
OTC	Grupo Financiero Probursa C	GRFNY	Fin Serv
OTC	Grupo Financiero Probursa Certs B	GRFPY	Fin Serv
NYSE	Grupo Financiero Serfin SA de CV	SFN	Banking
PORTAL	Grupo Gigante 144A	GPGTY	Retailing
NYSE	Grupo Industrial Durnago SA de CV CPO	GID	Packaging
NYSE	Grupo Industrial Maseca A	MSK	Food Proc
OTC	Grupo Industrial Maseca B	GRBMY	Food Proc
NYSE	Grupo Iuascell SA de CV D	CELD	Telecom
NYSE	Grupo Iuascell SA de CV L	CEL	Telecom
NYSE	Grupo Mexicano de Desarrollo SA B	GMD B	Construction
NYSE	Grupo Mexicano de Desarollo SA de CV L	GMD	Construction
PORTAL	Grupo Mexicano de Video SA de CV 144A		Video Retail
PORTAL	Grupo Posadas SA de CV L 144A	GPDGF	Hotels
NYSE	Grupo Radio Centro SA de CV	RC	Media
NYSE	Grupo Sidex SA de CV B	SDK B	Conglomerate
NYSE	Grupo Sidex SA de CV L	SDK	Conglomerate
AMEX	Grupo Simec SA de CV B	SIM	Steel
OTC	Grupo Situr SA de CV B	GPSMY	Tourism
OTC	Grupo Synkro C	GPSYF	Textiles
OTC	Grupo Synkro SA de CV B	GPSYY	Textiles
OTC	Grupo Syr SA de CV L	GSYRY	Real Estate
NYSE	Grupo Televisa SA de CV L	TV	Media
NYSE	Grupo Tribasa SA de CV	GTR	Construction
PORTAL	Hylsamex SA de CV 144A		
OTC	IEM (Industria Electrica de Mexico) SA	IEMEY	Utility
NYSE	Internacional de Ceramica B	ICM	Plumbing Fixtures
PORTAL	Internacional de Ceramica C 144A	CERMY	Plumbing Fixtures
OTC	Kimberly-Clark de Mexico Cert	KCDMY	Pulp, Paper
GDR	Mexico City Toluca Toll RD 144A		
NYSE	Panamerican Beverages Inc A (Panama)	PB	Bottling

Exchange	Company	Ticker	Industry
OTC	Ponderosa Industrial SA	PNDIY	Pulp, Paper
OTC	Sanluis, Corporacion Industrial (A1)	CORSY	Conglomerate
OTC	Sanluis, Corporacion Industrial (A2)	CORWY	Conglomerate
PORTAL	Sears Roebuck de Mexico B-1 144A	SMXBY	Retailing
NASDAQ	Servicios Financieros Quadrum SA de CV CPO	QDRMY	Fin Serv
OTC	Sociedad de Fomento Industrial SA de CV C		
NASDAQ	Telefonos de Mexico A	TFONY	Telecom
NYSE	Telefonos de Mexico L	TMX	Telecom
OTC	Tolmex SA de CV	TLMXY	Cement
PORTAL	Tolmex SA de CV Conv 144A		Cement
NYSE	Transportacion Maritima Mex CPO A	TMM A	Transport
NYSE	Transportacion Maritima Mex L	TMM	Transport
AMEX	Tubos de Acero de Mexico	TAM	Spec Steel
NYSE	Vitro SA de CV	VTO	Glass

Netherlands Antilles

NASDAQ	Orthofix International NV	OFIXF	
NYSE	Schlumberger Ltd	SLB	Oilfield Svc
NYSE	Singer Co NV	SEW	Sewing Mach
NASDAQ	Sunresorts Ltd NV	RSTAF	Tourism
NASDAQ	Velcro Industries NV	VELCF	Fasteners

Netherlands

NASDAQ	ASM Advance Semiconductor Materials NV	ASMIF	Semiconductors
NASDAQ	ASM Lithograpghy Holding	ASMLF	Wafer Steppers
OTC	ABN-Amro Bank	ARBLY	Banking
NYSE	Aegon NV	AEG	Insurance
NASDAQ	Affymax NV	AFMXF	Biotech
NYSE	Ahold NV, Koninklijke	AHO	Retailing
NASDAQ	Akzo Nobel NV	AKZOY	Chemicals
NASDAQ	Baan Co NV	BAANF	Software
NASDAQ	BE Semiconductor Industries	BESIF	Semiconductors
OTC	Bolswessanen, Koninklije	KNWSY	Food, Bev
PORTAL	Ceteco Holdings NV 144A		Appliances
NASDAQ	Core Laboratories	CRLBF	Research
OTC	DSM NV	DSMKY	Chemicals
OTC	DSM NV ORD	DSMVF	Chemicals
NYSE	ELSAG Bailey Process Automation	EBY	Automation
NYSE	Elsevier NV	ENZ	Publishing
OTC	Elsevier NV	ELSVF	Publishing
OTC	Fortis Amev	FAMVY	Fin Service
OTC	Gist Brocades NV	GISTF	Yeast
NASDAQ	Heidemij	HEIDF	
OTC	Heineken NV	HINKY	Brewing

Exchange	Company	Ticker	Industry
OTC	Heineken NV Ord	HEIKF	Brewing
OTC	Hoogovens EN Staalfabriek, Koninklijke Nederlands	HOOGY	Steel
OTC	Hunter Douglas NV	HDOUY	Blinds
OTC	Indigo NV (Israel)	INDGF	Printing
OTC	Internationale Nederlanden Group (Ing)	INGLY	Banking
OTC	KBB (Koninkljke Bijenkorf Beheer) NV	KBBNY	Retailing
NYSE	KLM Royal Dutch Airlines	KLM	Airline
OTC	KLM Royal Dutch Airlines Ord	KLMRF	Airline
OTC	KNP-BT, NV Koninklijke	NVKJY	Pulp, Paper
NASDAQ	KPN (Koninklijke PTT Nederland) NV		Telecom
PORTAL	KPN (Koninklijke PTT Netherland) NV 144A		Telecom
OTC	Madge NV	MADGF	Networking
NASDAQ	Oce-Van Der Grinten NV	OCENY	Photocopiers
NYSE	Philips Electronics NV	PHG	Appliances
NYSE	Polygram NV	PLG	Entertainment
OTC	Royal Nedlloyd Group NV	RNDGY	Transport
OTC	Sapiens International (Israel)	SPNSF	
NYSE	SGS – Thomson (France) Microelectronics NV Ord	STM	Electronics
OTC	Societe Generale Ltd NV WTS	SGGX	
NASDAQ	Triple P	TPPPF	Data Processing
NYSE	Unilever NV	UN	Food/Soap
OTC	Van Ommeren Ceteco NV	VAOSY	Transport
OTC	VNU, NV Verenigt Bezit	VNUNY	Publishing
OTC	VNU ORD, NV Verenigt Bezit	NVER	Publishing
OTC	Wolters Kluwer	WTKWY	Publishing

New Zealand

OTC	Brierly Investments Ltd	BYILY	Conglomerate
NYSE	Fletcher Challenge Forest Division	FFS	Lumber
NYSE	Fletcher Challenge Ltd	FLC	Pulp, Paper
OTC	Leisureland Corp	LLDLY	Hotels
NASDAQ	New Zealand Petroleum	NZPCY	Oil, Gas
NYSE	Telecom Corp of New Zealand	NZT	Telecom

Norway

OTC	Bergesen DY A/S-A SH	BEDAY	Transport
OTC	Bergesen DY AS Nonvoting B	BEDBF	Transport
PORTAL	Bona Shipbldg Ltd		Transport
OTC	Christiania Bank OG Kreditkasse	CBKRY	Banking
NYSE	Hafslund Nycomed AS B SH	HN	Cosmetics
OTC	Hafslund Nycomed AS A SH	HAFAY	Cosmetics
PORTAL	Helikopter Service AS 144A		Transport

Exchange	Company	Ticker	Industry
OTC	Kloster Cruise AS		Tourism
OTC	Kvaerner AS A	KVRAY	Transport
OTC	Kvaerner AS B	KVRBY	Transport
NASDAQ	Nera AS	NERAY	Laundry Eq
PORTAL	Norske Skog Iindustrier 144A		Pulp, Paper
NASDAQ	Petroleum Geo-Services AS	PGSAY	Oil Serv
NYSE	Saga Petroleum AS A SH	SPMA	Oil
OTC	Saga Petroleum AS B SH	SPMB	Oil
OTC	Skibsaksjeselskapet Storli	SRLIY	Transport
OTC	Smedvig Tankships Ltd AS	SMEMY	Shipping
OTC	Tomra Systems	TOSYY	Recycling
OTC	Unitor Ship Services	UTRSY	Ind Service
OTC	Vard AS A	VARDY	Transport
OTC	Vard AS B		Transport
OTC	Viking Media AS	VIKMY	Media

Pakistan

GDR	Hub Power Co Ltd		
PORTAL	Hub Power Co Ltd 144A		
PORTAL	Pakistan Telecom 144A		Telecom

Panama

NYSE	Banco Latinoamericano de Exportaciones Bladex E	BLX	Fin Service
NASDAQ	Ezcony Interamerica Inc	EZCOF	Electronics

Papua New Guinea

NASDAQ	Lihir Gold	LIHRY	Gold, Silver
OTC	Niugini Mining Ltd (Australia)	NGIMY	Mining
OTC	Oil Search Ltd (Australia)	OISHY	Oil, Gas

Peru

NYSE	Banco Wiese	BWP	Banking
OTC	Cementos Lima	CEMTY	Cement
OTC	Compania Peruana de Telefonos	PDTBF	Telecom
NYSE	Credicorp	BAP	Banking
NYSE	Southern Peru Copper	PCU	Mining
PORTAL	Tele 2000 144A	TELEY	Telecom

Philippines

GDR	Aboitiz Equity Ventures		
PORTAL	Aboitiz Equity Ventures 144A		
AMEX	Atlas Consolidated Mining & Development Corp	ACMB	Mining
GDR	Ayala Corp B		Conglomerate
PORTAL	Ayala Corp B 144 A	AYC	Conglomerate
NYSE	Benguet Corp B	BE	Metal
PORTAL	Benpress Holdings 144A		
GDR	JG Summit Holdings		Conglomerate
PORTAL	JG Summit Holdings 144A		Conglomerate

Exchange	Company	Ticker	Industry
OTC	Lepanto Consolidated Mining (B)	LECBF	Mining
GDR	Manila Electric Co (Meralco)		Utility
OTC	Manila Electric Co (Meralco)		Utility
GDR	Petron Corp		
PORTAL	Petron Corp 144A		
NYSE	Philippine Long Distance CV PR	PHL	Telecom
NYSE	Philippine Long Distance Tel	PHI	Telecom
GDR	Philippine Long Distance Tel		Telecom
OTC	Philodrill Corp (Philippine Overseas Drilling)	PHLOY	Oil
AMEX	San Carlos Milling Co	SAN	Sugar
OTC	San Miguel Brewieries	SMEGY	Brewing
GDR	SM Prime Holdings		
PORTAL	SM Prime Holdings 144A		

Poland

Exchange	Company	Ticker	Industry
NASDAQ	Polish Telephones & Microwave Corp	PTMC	Telecom
NASDAQ	Polish Telephones & Microwave Corp WTS	PTMCW	Telecom

Portugal

Exchange	Company	Ticker	Industry
NYSE	Banco Comercial Portugues	BPC	Banking
OTC	Portucel Industrial		
NYSE	Portugal Telecom SA	PT	Telecom

Russia

Exchange	Company	Ticker	Industry
NASDAQ	Petersburg Long Distance Inc (Canada)	PLDIF	Telecom

Slovakia

Exchange	Company	Ticker	Industry
GDR	Slovnaft AS		

South Africa

Exchange	Company	Ticker	Industry
OTC	AE & CI Ltd	AECLY	Chemicals
OTC	Afmin Holdings Ltd	AFHOY	Gold Mining
OTC	Afrikander Lease Ltd	AFKDY	Metal
OTC	Anglo-Alpha Ltd	ANGAY	Cement
OTC	Anglo-American Coal	ANAMY	Coal Mining
NASDAQ	Anglo-American Corp S Africa	ANGLY	Conglomerate
NASDAQ	Anglo-American Gold Inv Co Ltd	AAGIY	Gold Mining
OTC	Anglo-American Inv Trust	ANGVY	Holding Co
OTC	Anglo-American Platinum	AGAPY	Mining
OTC	Anglovaal Hdgs Ltd	ANAVY	Holding Co
PORTAL	Anglovaal Ltd 144A		Conglomerate
NASDAQ	Anglovaal Ltd CL A	ANVAY	Conglomerate
OTC	Anglovaal Ltd Ord	ANAVF	Conglomerate
OTC	Barlow Rand Ltd	BRRAY	Conglomerate
OTC	Beatrix Mines Ltd	BRTXY	Gold Mining

Exchange	Company	Ticker	Industry
OTC	Blue Circle Cement Ltd	BLUCY	Cement
NASDAQ	Blyvooruitzicht Gold Mining Ltd	BLYVY	Gold Mining
OTC	Bracken Mines Ltd	BRACY	Gold Mining
NASDAQ	Buffelsfontein Gold Mining Ltd	BFLEY	Gold Mining
OTC	CG Smith Ltd	CGSMY	
OTC	Consolidated Modderfontein Mines	CMMIY	Gold Mining
OTC	Consolidated Murchison Ltd	CNMUY	Gold Mining
OTC	Daggafontein Mines Ltd	DAGGY	
NASDAQ	De Beers Consolidated Mines Ltd	DBRSY	Diamonds
OTC	Deelkraal Gold Mining Ltd	DEELY	Gold Mining
OTC	Doorfontein Gold Mining Ltd	DORDY	Gold Mining
NASDAQ	Driefontein Cons	DRFNY	Gold
OTC	Duiker Exploration Ltd	DUKRY	Gold, Coal
OTC	Durban Roodepoort Deep Ltd	DURBY	Mining
OTC	East Daggafontein Mines Ltd	EDGNY	Gold, Uranium
OTC	East Rand Gold & Uranium Ltd	EASRY	Gold, Uranium
OTC	East Rand Proprietary Mines	ERNDY	Gold Mining
OTC	Eastern Transvaal Consol Mines	ETVLY	Gold Mining
OTC	Egoli Consolidated Mines Ltd	ELCMY	Gold Mining
OTC	Elandsrand Gold Mining Ltd	EGMLY	Gold Mining
OTC	Elsburg Gold Mining Ltd	ELSBY	Gold Mining
OTC	Engen Ltd	ENGNY	Energy
GDR	Energy Africa Ltd		Energy
	Ettington Investments Ltd		
OTC	Federale Mynbou Beperk	FDMBY	
OTC	Fedsure Holdings Ltd	FSURY	Insurance
OTC	Fedsure Holdings Ltd PR	FSUPY	Insurance
NASDAQ	Free State Consol Gold Mining	FSCNY	Gold Mining
OTC	Free State Development & Inv	FSDIY	
OTC	Geduld Investments Ltd		
OTC	Genbel Investments Ltd	GIVLY	Mining
OTC	Gencor Investments B SH	GNCLY	Investments
NASDAQ	Gencor Ltd	GIVLY	Holding Co
NASDAQ	Gold Fields of South Africa	GLDFY	Investments
OTC	Gold Fields Property Ltd	GFPYY	Property
OTC	Great Eastern Mines Ltd	GOLMY	
OTC	Grootvlei Prop Mines Ltd	GTPMY	Gold Mining
NASDAQ	Harmony Gold Mining Ltd	HMNYY	Gold Mining
OTC	Hartebeestfontein Gold Mines	HBGDY	Gold Mining
NASDAQ	Highveld Steel & Vanadium Ltd	HSVLY	Steel, Vanadium
OTC	Impala Platinum Holdings Ltd	IMPAY	Platinum
OTC	Iscor Ltd	ISCRY	
OTC	JCI Ltd	JICPY	
OTC	Jphannesburg Consol Inv Ltd	JOHNY	Investments
OTC	Kinross Mines Ltd	KNRSY	Mining
NASDAQ	Kloof Gold Mining Ltd	KLOFY	Gold Mining
OTC	Leslie Gold Mines Ltd	LESGY	Gold Mining
OTC	Liberty Life Assn of Africa Ltd	LTYLY	Insurance

Exchange	Company	Ticker	Industry
OTC	Loraine Gold Mines Ltd	LORAY	Gold Mining
NASDAQ	Lydenburg Platinum Ltd	LYDPY	Platinum
OTC	MTD Mangula Ltd	MTDGY	
OTC	Malbak Ltd	MLBAY	Food Proc
OTC	Messina Ltd	MSNAY	Platinum
GDR	Metro Cash & Carry Ltd		Retailing
OTC	Middle Witwatersrand (WN Areas)	MWWSY	Mining
TOR	Minorco Canada Ltd (Canada)		
OTCN	Modder B Gold Holdings Ltd	MBGOY	Gold Mining
IDR	Nampak Ltd		
OTC	Nedcor Ltd	NDCRY	Fin Serv
OTC	New Wits Ltd	NWITY	
AMEX	O Okief Copper Ltd	OKP	Copper
OTC	Ocean Diamond Mining Holdings	OCDIY	Diamonds
NASDAQ	Orange Free State Investments	OFSLY	Holding Co
OTC	Palabora Mining Co	PBMOY	Copper
OTC	Pepkor Ltd	PEPKY	
OTC	Premier Group	PRRGY	
OTC	Rand Estensions & Expl Ltd	RAXPY	
OTC	Rand Mines Properties Ltd	RDPPY	
OTC	Randex Ltd	RNDXY	Mining
OTC	Randfontein Estates Gold Mining Witwatersrand Ltd	RNDEY	Gold Mining
OTC	Recor Holdings Ltd	RCRHY	
OTC	Rembrandt Group Ltd	RBDGY	Investments
OTC	Rooderport Gold		
OTC	Rustenburg Platinum Holdings	RPATY	Platinum
NASDAQ	Saint Helena Gold Mines Ltd	SGOLY	Gold Mining
OTC	Samancor Ltd	SMNCY	Manganese
OTC	Sappi Ltd	SAPIY	
NASDAQ	Sasol Ltd	SASOY	Coal Mining
OTC	Sentrachem Ltd	SNTRY	
OTC	Servgro International Ltd	SVGRY	
OTC	Simmer & Jack Mines	SJACY	Mining
OTC	South African Breweries Ltd	SWBRY	Brewing
OTC	South Roodepoort Main Reef Areas Ltd	SROOY	Gold Mining
OTC	Southvaal Holdings Ltd	STHVY	Mining
OTC	Stilfontein Gold Mining Co Ltd	STILY	Gold Mining
OTC	Stocks & Stocks Ltd	STKKY	
OTC	Sub Nigel Gold Mining Co Ltd	SUBGY	Gold Mining
OTC	Tiger Oats Ltd	TIOAY	
OTC	Trans Hex Group Ltd	TRHXY	
OTC	Trans Natal Coal Corp Ltd	TNCCY	Coal Mining
OTC	Unisel Gold Mines Ltd	UNSLY	Gold Mining
NASDAQ	Vaal Reefs	VAALY	Gold Mining
OTC	Venterspost Gold Mining Ltd	VGMDY	Gold Mining

Exchange	Company	Ticker	Industry
OTC	Vereeniging Estates Ltd	VRNGY	
OTC	Vlakfontein Gold Mining Ltd	VLAKY	Gold Mining
NASDAQ	Welkom Gold Holdings Ltd	WLKMY	Gold Mining
OTC	West Rand Consolidated MNS Ltd	WRCMY	Gold Mining
OTC	Western Areas GLD Mining Ltd	WARSY	Gold Mining
NASDAQ	Western Deep Levels Ltd	WDEPY	Gold Mining
OTC	Winkelhaak MNS Ltd	WINNY	Gold Mining
OTC	Witwatersrand Nigel Ltd	WWRNY	Gold Mining
OTC	Zandpan GLD Mining Ltd	ZNDPY	Gold Mining

South Korea

Exchange	Company	Ticker	Industry
IDR	Dong AH Construction Corp Ltd		Construction
PORTAL	Goldstar Co Ltd 144A	SLSTY	
OTC	Goldstar Video	GVID	
GDR	Hankuk Glass Industries		Glass
PORTAL	Hankuk Glass Industries 144A		Glass
PORTAL	Hansol Paper GDR	HANPZ	Pulp, Paper
PORTAL	Hansol Paper 144A	HAP	Pulp, Paper
PORTAL	Hyundai Motor Co	HYMLZ	Automotive
PORTAL	Hyundai Motor Co GDR	HYMCY	Automotive
GDR	Kia Motors Corp		Automotive
PORTAL	Kia Motors Corp 144A		Automotive
NYSE	Korea Electric Power (Kepco)	KEP	Utility
IDR	Korea Express Corp Ltd		
GDR	LG Electronics Inc		Electronics
NYSE	Pohang Iron & Steel (Posco)	PKX	Metal
GDR	Samsung Co Ltd	SAMG	Trading
PORTAL	Samsung Co Ltd 144A	SSNG	Electronics
PORTAL	Samsung Electronics Co Ltd	SAME	Electronics
PORTAL	Samsung Electronics Co Ltd PR	SELC	Electronics
GDR	Samsung Electronics Co Ltd		Electronics
PORTAL	Samsung Electronics & Construction Co 144A		Construction
GDR	Yukong Ltd		
PORTAL	Yukong Ltd 144A		

Singapore

Exchange	Company	Ticker	Industry
NYSE	Asia Pacific Resources Intl Holdings Ltd	ARH	
NYSE	Asia Pulp & Paper	PAP	
NYSE	Asia Pulp & Paper Ltd	PAP	
OTC	City Developments Ltd	CDEVY	Real Estate
NASDAQ	Creative Technology Ltd	CREAF	Audio/Video
OTC	Cycle & Carriage Ltd	CYCAY	Vehicle Parts
OTC	Development Bank of Singapore	DEBSY	Banking
OTC	GB Holdings Ltd	GBHLY	
OTC	Hai Sun Hup Group Ltd	HISHF	
OTC	Inchcape Berhad	INCHY	Automotive

Exchange	Company	Ticker	Industry
OTC	Keppel Corp Ltd	KPELY	Shipyard
OTC	Malayan Credit Ltd	MYANY	Fin Serv
OTC	Malayan United Industries Berhad	MYLUY	
OTC	Neptune Orient Lines Ltd	NTOLY	Shipping
OTC	Overseas Union Bank Ltd	OUBYF	Banking
OTC	Pan-Electric Industries Ltd	PELCY	
OTC	Sembawang Shipyards Ltd	SBAWY	
OTC	Singapore Land Ltd	SINPY	Property
OTC	Singapore Telecom	SGTCY	Telecom
OTC	United Overseas Bank Ltd	UOVBY	Banking
OTC	United Overseas Land Ltd	UTOVY	Real Estate

Spain

Exchange	Company	Ticker	Industry
OTC	Acerinox SA	ACNXF	Steel
NYSE	Banco Bilbao Vizcaya Gibraltar PR	BBV P	Banking
NYSE	Banco Bilbao Vizcaya Gibraltar PR B	BVG PB	Banking
NYSE	Banco Bilbao Vizcaya Gibraltar PR C	BVG PC	Banking
NYSE	Banco Bilbao Vizcaya SA	BBV	Banking
NYSE	Banco Central Hispano-Americano SA	BCM	Banking
NYSE	Banco de Santander	BSTD	Banking
OTC	Banco Espanol de Credito (Banesto)	BSCRY	Banking
OTC	Bankinter SA	BKISY	Banking
OTC	Compania Sevillana de Electricidad	COVDY	Utility
NYSE	Corparacion Bancaria de Espana "Argentaria"	AGR	Banking
OTC	Corparacion Mapfre-Compania Internacional de Reaseguros	CRFEY	Insurance
NYSE	Endesa Empresa NACL de Electridad	ELE	Utility
NYSE	Repsol SA	REP	Oil
NYSE	Santander Overseas Bank P A (US Company)	SOPR P	Banking
NYSE	Santander Overseas Bank P B (US Company)	OPRpB	Banking
NYSE	Santander Overseas Bank P C S (US Company)	OPRpC	Banking
NYSE	Santander Overseas Bank PR D (US Company)		Banking
TEF	Telefonica de Espana SA	TEF	Telecom

Sri Lanka

Exchange	Company	Ticker	Industry
GDR	John Keells Holdings Ltd		Conglomerate
PORTAL	John Keells Holdings Ltd		Conglomerate

Sweden

Exchange	Company	Ticker	Industry
OTC	AGA AB A SH	AGAXY	Chemicals
OTC	AGA AB B SH	AGABY	Chemicals
OTC	Arjo AB	ARJOY	Pharmaceuticals

Exchange	Company	Ticker	Industry
OTC	Astra Holdings Plc	ASTHY	Pharmaceuticals
OTC	Atlas Copco AB A	ATLSY	Machinery
OTC	Atlas Copco AB B	ATLPY	Machinery
PORTAL	Autoliv 144A	ALIVY	
NASDAQ	Electrolux AB	ELUXY	Appliances
NASDAQ	Ericsson, LM Telecom AB B SH	ERICY	Telecom
OTC	Esselte AB B	ESLTY	Office Articles
OTC	Frontline AB	FROLY	
OTC	Gambro AB WTS		Medical Eq
NASDAQ	Gambro AB	GAMBY	Medical Eq
PORTAL	Kalmar Industrier AB 144A		Mech Eng
NASDAQ	SKF AB	SKFRY	Bearings
OTC	SAAB AB	SAABF	Automotive
OTC	Sandvik AB	SAVKY	Steel, Tools
OTC	Skandia International Hldg AB		
PORTAL	Svedala Industri AB 144A		
NASDAQ	Svenska Cellulosa AB B	SCAPY	Packaging
NASDAQ	Volvo AB B SH	VOLVY	Automotive

Switzerland

Exchange	Company	Ticker	Industry
NASDAQ	Adia SA	ADIAY	Temp Empl
OTC	Aluminium Suisse	ALSSF	Alum Smelter
NASDAQ	Asea Brown Boveri B SH	ASEAY	Elect Eq
OTC	BBC Brown Boveri	BBOVY	Machinery
OTC	CS Holding	CSHKY	Banking
OTC	Ciba-Geigy AG	CBGXY	Pharmaceuticals
PORTAL	Nestle SA 144A		Food Proc
OTC	Nestle SA Bearer Part Certs	NESAY	Food Proc
OTC	Nestle SA Reg SH	NSRGY	Food Proc
OTC	Roche Holding Ltd Prof SH Cert	ROHHY	Pharmaceuticals
OTC	Sandoz Ltd	SDOZY	Pharmaceuticals
OTC	Swiss Bank Corp	SWBKY	Banking
OTC	Swissair Schweizerische Luft	SWSAF	Airline
OTC	Union Bank of Switzerland	UBSUY	Banking

Taiwan

Exchange	Company	Ticker	Industry
GDR	ADI Corp		
GDR	Advanced Semiconductors Engineering Inc		Electronics
PORTAL	Asia Cement Corp 144A		Cement
GDR	Aurora Corporation		
SEAQ	Chia Hsin Cement Co		Cement
GDR	China Steel Corp 144A	CISEY	Steel
GDR	Hocheng Corp		Plumbing Fixtures
PORTAL	Hocheng Corp 144A		Plumbing Fixtures
GDR	Microelectronics Technology		Electronics
PORTAL	Microelectronics Technology Inc 144A		Electronics
GDR	Presidential Enterprises Corp	PRELY	Food, Bev

Exchange	Company	Ticker	Industry
GDR	Tung Ho Steel Enterprises		Steel
PORTAL	Tung Ho Steel Enterprises 144A		Steel
PORTAL	Tuntex Distinct Corp 144A	TNTXY	Chemicals
GDR	Walsin Lihwa Corp		
GDR	Yageo Corp		
PORTAL	Yageo Corp 144A		

Thailand

Exchange	Company	Ticker	Industry
OTC	Advanced Information Service Ltd	AVIFY	Telecom
OTC	Asia Fiber Co Ltd	ASFBY	Textile
OTC	Chareon Pokphand Feedmill	CPOKY	Food Proc
OTC	Hana Microelectronics Public Co Ltd	HANAY	Electronics
OTC	Shinawatra Computer & Communications	SHWCY	Computers
GDR	Telecomasia Corp Ltd		Telecom
PORTAL	Telecomasia Corp Ltd 144A		Telecom
GDR	Thai Telephone & Telcommunications Ltd		Telecom
PORTAL	Thai Telephone & Telcommunications Ltd 144A	TTTPY	Telecom

Trinidad

Exchange	Company	Ticker	Industry
OTC	Trinidad Cement Ltd	TDDCY	Cement

Turkey

Exchange	Company	Ticker	Industry
OTC	Garanti Bankasi		Banking
OTC	Net Hdgs Inc	NETHY	Banking
GDR	Tofas Turk Otomobil Fabrikasi		Automotive
PORTAL	Tofas Turk Otomobil Fabrikasi 144A	TOFAY	Automotive
PORTAL	Turkiye Garanti Bankasi 144A	TURKY	Banking

United Kingdom

Exchange	Company	Ticker	Industry
NYSE	ADT Ltd (Bermuda)	ADTA	Security Svcs
NYSE	ADT Ltd WTS (Bermuda)	ADT W	Security Svcs
OTC	Abbey National	ABYNY	
OTC	Aegis Group Plc	AEGSY	Advertising
NASDAQ	Airship Inds Ltd (Isle of Man)	AIRSY	Blimps
OTC	Airship International Ltd Com	BLMP	Blimps
OTC	Albert Fisher Group Plc	AFHGY	Food Dist
OTC	Allied Colliods Plc	AIEGY	
OTC	Allied-Domecq Plc	ALDCY	Conglomerate
OTC	Allied-Lyons Plc	ALLYY	Tobacco, Bev
OTC	Associated British Foods Plc	ASBFY	Food Dist
OTC	Associated British Foods PR 6%	ASBPF	Food Dist
OTC	Astec (BSR) Plc	ASTCY	Hshold Elect
NYSE	Attwoods Plc (Bermuda)	A	Waste Disposal
NYSE	Automated Security Holdings Plc	ASI	Security Svcs
OTC	BAA Plc	BAAPY	Airports
AMEX	BAT Industries Plc	BTI	Conglomerate
NYSE	BET Plc	BEP	Bus service

Exchange	Company	Ticker	Industry
OTC	BOC Group Plc	BOCNY	Spec Chem
OTC	BOM Holdings Plc (formerly Bristol Oil & Minerals)	BOMHY	Oil
OTC	BTR Plc	BTRUY	Conglomerate
OTC	Babcock International Plc	BCOKY	Medical Eq
NYSE	Barclays Bank CV Notes E	BCB P	Banking
NYSE	Barclays Bank Plc	BCS	Banking
NYSE	Barclays Bank PR A	BCBP A	Banking
NYSE	Barclays Bank PR B	BCBP B	Banking
NYSE	Barclays Bank PR C	BCBP C	Banking
NYSE	Barclays Bank PR D	BCBP D	Banking
NYSE	Bass Plc	BAS	Brewing
AMEX	Bat Industries Plc	BTI	Tobacco
NYSE	Beazer Plc	BZR	Construction
NASDAQ	Bell Cablemedia Plc	BCMPY	Telecom
OTC	Bespak Plc	BPAKY	Packaging
NYSE	BET Plc	BEP	Industrial Svcs
NYSE	BET Plc (A)	BCBPA	Industrial Svcs
NYSE	BET Plc (B)	BCBPB	Industrial Svcs
NYSE	BET Plc (C)	BCBPC	Industrial Svcs
NYSE	BET Plc (D)	BCBPD	Industrial Svcs
OTC	Bio-Isolates Holdings Plc	BISOY	Food Proc
OTC	Blenheim Exhibitions Group Plc	BHEHY	Conferences
OTC	Blue Circle Industries Plc	BCLEY	Bldg Matls
OTC	BOC Group Plc	BOCNY	Healthcare Prod
OTC	Body Shop International Plc	BDSPY	Cosmetics
OTC	Booker Plc	BKERY	Food Proc
OTC	Boots Co Plc	BOOTY	Retailing
OTC	Bowater Industries Plc	BWTRY	Packaging
OTC	Bowater Industries Plc PR A	BOWRP	Packaging
OTC	Brent Walker Group Plc	BWKGY	Leisure
OTC	Bristol Oil & Minerals Plc		Oil, Gas
OTC	Britannica Group Plc	BRITY	Real Estate
NYSE	British Airways Plc	BAB	Airline
NASDAQ	British Bio-Technology Group Plc	BBIOY	Biotech
NYSE	British Gas Plc	BRG	Gas Utility
NYSE	British Petroleum Plc	BP	Oil
NYSE	British Petroleum WTS	BPW	Oil
NYSE	British Sky Broadcasting Group	BSY	Broadcasting
NYSE	British Steel Plc	BST	Steel
NYSE	British Telecommunications New	BTY P	Telecom
NYSE	British Telecommunications Plc	BT	Telecom
NASDAQ	Burmah Castrol Plc	BURMY	Chemicals
OTC	Burton Group Plc	BRGPY	Retailing
OTC	CML Microsystems Plc	CMLMY	Telecom
NYSE	Cable & Wireless Plc	CWP	Telecom
OTC	Cadbury Schweppes Auction PR SER 3		Food Proc
OTC	Cadbury Schweppes Auction PR SER 4		Food Proc
OTC	Cadbury Schweppes Auction PR SER 5		Food Proc

Exchange	Company	Ticker	Industry
OTC	Cadbury Schweppes Auction PR SER 6		Food Proc
NASDAQ	Cadbury Schweppes Plc	CADBY	Food Proc
NASDAQ	Cantab Pharmaceuticals Plc	CNBTY	Pharmaceuticals
NASDAQ	Caradon, MB Plc	MBGRY	Printing
NASDAQ	Carlton Communications Plc	CCTVY	Audio/Video
NYSE	Central Transport Rental Group Plc	TPH	Transport
OTC	Charter Consolidated Plc	CHRTY	Conglomerate
OTC	Charterhall Plc	CHALY	
OTC	Chloride Group Ltd	CDGPY	Elec Eq
OTC	Christian Salvesen Plc	CSALY	Food Proc
OTC	Christies International Plc	CRSEY	Art Auctions
OTC	Chubb & Son Plc	CHUBY	
OTC	Cluff Resources Plc	CLFRY	Mining
OTC	Coats Viyella Plc	COATY	Textiles
OTC	Computerised Medical System	CMDSY	
OTC	Consloidated Gold Fields Plc	COGOY	Gold
NYSE	Cordiant Plc	CDA	
OTC	Corporate Service Group Plc		
AMEX	Courtaulds Plc	COU	Coatings
OTC	Crossroads Oil Group Plc	CRSOY	Oil, Gas
NASDAQ	Danka Business Systems Plc	DANKY	Office Eq
OTC	De La Rue Plc	DERUY	Printing
NYSE	Dixons Group Plc	DXN	Retailing
OTC	Dowty Group Plc	DOWTY	Electronics
NYSE	ECC Group (English China Clays)	ENC	Bldg Matls
OTC	ECC Group Auct Mkt PR Ser A		Bldg Matls
OTC	East Midlands Electric Plc	EMELY	Utility
OTC	Eastern Group	ESTNY	Utility
OTC	Egerton Trust Plc	EGTRY	
OTC	Elf Aquitaine UK Holdings PR A		Oil, Gas
OTC	Elf Aquitaine UK Holdings PR B		Oil, Gas
OTC	Elf Aquitaine UK Holdings PR C		Oil, Gas
OTC	Elf Aquitaine UK Holdings PR D		Oil, Gas
OTC	Elf Aquitaine UK Holdings PR E		Oil, Gas
OTC	Elf Aquitaine UK Holdings PR F		Oil, Gas
OTC	Elf Aquitaine UK Holdings PR G		Oil, Gas
OTC	Elf Aquitaine UK Holdings PR H		Oil, Gas
OTC	Elf Aquitaine UK Holdings PR I		Oil, Gas
OTC	Elf Aquitaine UK Holdings PR J		Oil, Gas
NYSE	English China Clays Plc	ENC	Bldg Matls
NYSE	English China Clays PR A	ENCYF	Bldg Matls
NYSE	Enterprise Oil Plc	ETP	Oil
NYSE	Enterprise Oil Plc PR A	ENTPP	Oil
OTC	Enterprise Oil Plc PR B	ETP PB	Oil
NASDAQ	Ethical Holdings Ltd	ETHCY	Phamaceuticals
OTC	Eurotunnel Plc/S A (France)	ETNLY	Channel Tunnel
OTC	FKB Group Plc	FKBGY	
OTC	Fairey Co Plc	FARYY	Electronics
OTC	Financial Systems Tech	FITPY	

Exchange	Company	Ticker	Industry
NASDAQ	Fisons Plc	FISNY	Pharmaceuticals
NASDAQ	Fuel-Tech Nv	FTEKF	Environmental
NASDAQ	Futuremedia Plc	FMDAY	Media Courses
NASDAQ	Futuremedia Plc Unit	FMDYZ	Media Courses
NASDAQ	Futuremedia Plc WT	FMDYW	Media Courses
OTC	GKN Plc	GKNPY	Automotive
OTC	Gateway Plc		
NASDAQ	Gemstar International Group	GNSTF	Audio/Video
NASDAQ	General Cable Plc	GCABY	Telecom
OTC	General Electric Co Plc	GNELY	Electronics
OTC	Gestetner Holdings Plc	GTETY	Office Eq
OTC	Gestetner Holdings Plc A	GTEYF	Office Eq
NYSE	Glaxo Holdings Plc	GLX	Pharmaceuticals
OTC	Gold Greenlees Trott Plc	GGTRY	Advertising
NASDAQ	Govett & Co Ltd	GOVTY	Fin. Serv
OTC	Govett Stategic Inv Trust Plc	GTSIY	Closed-End Fund
NYSE	Grand Metropolitan Plc	GRM	Restaurants
NYSE	Grand Metropolitan Plc PR A 9.42%	GRM PA	Restaurants
OTC	Great Universal Stores Plc	GRUSY	Retailing
OTC	Great Universal Stores Plc A	GUNVY	Retailing
OTC	Guinness Plc	GURSY	Brewing
OCT	HSBC Holdings Plc	HSBHY	Holding Co.
NYSE	Hanson A WTS	HAN WA	Conglomerate
AMEX	Hanson B WTS	HAN WB	Conglomerate
NYSE	Hanson Plc	HAN	Conglomerate
OTC	Hard Rock International Plc		Leisure
OTC	Hard Rock International Plc A		Leisure
OTC	Hartstone Group Plc	HSTEY	Apparel
OTC	Harvard Group Plc	HARVY	
OTC	Hawker Siddeley Group	HHWGY	Machinery
OTC	Hestair Plc		
OTC	Hillsdown Holdings	HDNHY	Food
OTC	Horace Small Apparel (formerly United Uniform Services)	HSMAY	Apparel
OTC	House of Fraser Ltd	HOFSY	Retailing
NYSE	Huntingdon Intl Holdings Plc	HTD	Research
OTC	ICL Plc	ILLIPY	Electronics
NYSE	Imperial Chem Industries Plc	ICI	Chemicals
NASDAQ	Insignia Solutions	INSGY	Data Processing
NASDAQ	Insituform Group Ltd	IGLSF	Sewer Rehab
NASDAQ	Integrated Micro Products Plc	IMPTY	Computers
OTC	International Capital Equipment	ICEYF	
OTC	Invesco Plc	ISCOY	Investment
OTC	Keller Industries Ltd	KILSF	Construction
OTC	Kingfisher Plc	KIFSY	Retailing
OTC	Ladbroke Group Plc	LADGY	Betting, Hotels
NYSE	Lasmo Plc	LSO	Oil, Gas
NYSE	Lasmo Plc PR	LSO P	Oil, Gas

Exchange	Company	Ticker	Industry
NYSE	Lasmo Plc RTS	LSO$	Oil, Gas
OTC	Laura Ashley Holdings Plc	LARAY	Apparel
NASDAQ	Learmonth & Burchett Management	LBMSY	Data Processing
OTC	Legal & General Group Plc		Insurance
NASDAQ	Leica Plc (formerly Cambridge Instruments)	CAMBY	Optics
NASDAQ	Lep Group Plc	LEPGY	Distribution
OTC	London & Overseas Freighters Plc (Bermuda)	LOVFY	Shipping
OTC	London Electricity Plc	LNDNY	Utility
OTC	London Finance & Inv Group Plc	LFVGY	Investment
NASDAQ	London International Group Ltd	LONDY	Photography
OTC	Lonrho Plc	LNROY	Auto Sales
OTC	MAI Plc		
OTC	MAI Plc PR	MAIPF	
NASDAQ	MB Caradon Plc	MBGRY	Printing
OTC	Management Agency & Music	MAMUY	
OTC	Manweb Plc	MANWY	Utility
OTC	Marks & Spencer Plc	MASPY	Retailing
OTC	Marling Industries Plc		
AMEX	Medeva Plc	MDV	Pharmaceuticals
NASDAQ	Micro Focus Group Plc	MIFGY	Computer Eq
NYSE	Midland Bank PR	MIBA	Banking
NYSE	Midland Bank Plc PR A		Banking
OTC	Midlands Electricty Plc	MIDEY	Utility
NASDAQ	Midstates Plc	MSADY	
OTC	Morgan Crucible Plc		Ceramics
AMEX	NFC Plc	NFC	Transport
AMEX	NFC Plc RTS		Transport
OTC	NMC Group Plc	NMGRY	
NASDAQ	Naid	NAIDY	Data Processing
NYSE	National Power Plc	NP	Utility
NYSE	National Westminister Bank	NW	Banking
NYSE	National Westminister Bank PR A	NWP A	Banking
NYSE	National Westminister Bank PR B	NWP B	Banking
OTC	Northern Electric Plc	NORLY	Utility
OTC	Norton Group Plc		
OTC	Norweb Plc	NORWY	Utility
NASDAQ	Nynex Cablecomms Group Plc	NYNCY	Cable TV
OTC	Omnimedia Plc	OMMDY	Media
OTC	Pearson Plc	PRSNY	Publishing
OTC	Peninsular & Oriental Steam Navigation	POSNY	Shipping
OTC	Pentland Group Plc	PNDL	Apparel
OTC	Pentos Plc	PENOY	Retailing
OTC	Pittencrieff Plc	PNCIY	Telecom
NYSE	Powergen Plc	PWG	Utility
OTC	Premier Consol Oilflds Plc	PMCDY	Oil, Gas
OTC	Prudential Corp Plc	PPLCY	Insurance
OTC	RR Realisations Ltd (formerly Rolls Royce)	RYCEY	Aerospace

Exchange	Company	Ticker	Industry
NYSE	RTZ Plc	RTZ	Mining
OTC	Racal Electronics Plc	RACLY	Electronics
NASDAQ	Rank Organisation Plc	RANKY	Movies, Hotels
OTC	Redland Plc	REDPY	Roofing, Brick
OTC	Redland Plc Ser A		Roofing, Brick
OTC	Redland Plc Ser B		Roofing, Brick
OTC	Redland Plc Ser C		Roofing, Brick
OTC	Redland Plc Ser D		Roofing, Brick
OTC	Redland Plc Ser E		Roofing, Brick
NYSE	Reed International Plc	RUK	Publishing
OTC	Regional Electric Co Unit	ELCUY	Utility
OTC	Rentokil Group Plc	RTOKY	Bus Serv
NASDAQ	Reuters Holdings Plc	RTRSY	News Service
NASDAQ	Rodime Plc	RODMY	Computer Eq
OTC	Rothmans International Plc	ROTHY	Tobacco
NASDAQ	Rowlands Corp (Ex-Eagle Corp)	Row	
NYSE	Royal Bank of Scotland PR A	RBS A	Banking
NYSE	Royal Bank of Scotland PR B	RBS B	Banking
NYSE	Royal Bank of Scotland PR C	RBS C	Banking
NYSE	Royal Dutch Petroleum (Netherl)	RD	Oil, Gas
OTC	Ryan Traders Distr Ltd	RYTDY	
NYSE	Saatchi & Saatchi Co Plc	SAA	Advertising
OTC	Sainsbury, J Plc	SABUY	Groceries
OTC	Saint John Del Rey Minning Plc		Mining
OTC	Scantronic Holdings Plc	SCTHY	Electronics
OTC	Scottish & Univ Investments Plc	SUVLY	
OTC	Scottish Hydro-Electric Plc	SHYAY	Utility
OTC	Scotttish Investment Trust	SIVTY	Investment
OTC	Scottish Power Plc	SPYAY	Utility
OTC	Sears Plc	SPLCY	Retailing
OTC	Securiguard Plc		
OTC	Sedgwick Group Plc	SGWKY	Insurance
OTC	Seeboard Plc	SEEBY	Utility
OTC	Select Appointments Holding		
NASDAQ	Senetek Plc	SNTKY	Med Research
OTC	Senetek Plc CL A WTS	SNTWF	Med Research
OTC	Senetek Plc CL B WTS	SNTZF	Med Research
OTC	Shandwick Plc		
NYSE	Shell Transportation & Trading	SC	Oil
OTC	Siebe Plc	SIBEY	Controls
NASDAQ	Signet CV P	SIGGZ	Retailing
NASDAQ	Signet Group Plc (formerly Ratners Plc)	SIGGY	Retailing
OTC	Signet Group VTP SER A		Retailing
OTC	Signet Group VTP SER B		Retailing
OTC	Signet Group VTP SER C		Retailing
OTC	Signet Group VTP SER D		Retailing
OTC	Signet Group VTP SER E		Retailing
OTC	Sir Speedy Printing Centres Plc		

Exchange	Company	Ticker	Industry
NYSE	Smithkline Beecham	SBE	Pharmaceuticals
NYSE	Smithkline Beecham A SH	SBA	Pharmaceuticals
NYSE	Smithkline Beecham UTS	SBE	Pharmaceuticals
OTC	Sotheby Parke Bernet Plc		Art Auctions
OTC	South Wales Electricity Plc	SOWLY	Utility
OTC	South Western Electricity Plc	SWSTY	Utility
OTC	Southern Electric Plc	SOELY	Utility
OTC	Southwest Resources Plc	SOUWY	
OTC	Summer International Plc	SUMPY	
GDR	Sun Brewing Ltd (Jersey)		Brewing
OTC	Swan Ryan International Ltd	SWRRY	
OTC	System Designer Plc	SYP	Electronics
OTC	Systems Connections Group Plc	SSCNY	
OTC	T & N Plc	TNNNY	Automotive
OTC	TI Group Plc	TIGRY	Engineering
OTC	Tarmac Plc Auctn Mkt P A		Bldg Matls
OTC	Tarmac Plc Auctn Mkt P B		Bldg Matls
OTC	Tarmac Plc Auctn Mkt P C		Bldg Matls
OTC	Tarmac Plc Auctn Mkt P D		Bldg Matls
OTC	Tate & Lyle Plc	TATYY	Food Proc
NASDAQ	Telewest Communications Plc	TWSTY	Cable TV
OTC	Tesco Plc	TESOY	Supermarkets
OTC	Thorn EMI Plc	THOMY	Conglomerate
OTC	Thorn EMI Plc 7% P		Conglomerate
NYSE	Tiphook Plc	TPH	Transport
NASDAQ	Tomkins Plc	TOMKY	Conglomerate
OTC	Trafalgar House Plc	TFLHY	Construction
OTC	Transco Exploration Partners	EXPC	Mining
OTC	Transport Development Group Ltd	TDVGY	Distribution
OTC	Trinity International Holdings	TNYLY	Publishing
OTC	Unigate Plc	UUGAY	Food Proc
NYSE	Unilever Plc	UL	Food/Soap
OTC	Unitech Plc	UNTKY	Electronics
OTC	United Biscuits Holdings Plc	UTBTY	Food Proc
NASDAQ	United News and Media Plc	UNEWY	Publishing
OTC	United Uniform Services Plc (now Horace Small Apparel)	HSACY	Uniforms
OTC	Utility Cable Plc	OMMDY	Wire, Cable
OTC	Vickers Plc	VKRSY	Automotive
NASDAQ	Videotron Holdings Plc	VRONY	Cable TV
OTC	Virgin Interactive Entertainment		
OTC	Virtuality Group Plc	VRTGY	Leisure
NYSE	Vodafone Plc	VOD	Telecom
NASDAQ	WPP Group Plc	WPPGY	Advertising
OTC	Wace Group Plc	WCCRY	Printing
NYSE	Waste Management International	WME	Waste Disposal
NYSE	Wellcome Plc	WEL	Pharmaceuticals
PORTAL	Wellington Underwritting Plc 144A		Insurance

Exchange	Company	Ticker	Industry
OTC	Wembley Plc	WMBYY	Sporting Events
OTC	Whitbread & Co Plc A	WTBRY	Brewing
OTC	Williams Holdings Plc	WIHLY	Bldg Matls
NYSE	Willis Corroon Plc	WCG	Insurance
NASDAQ	Xenova Plc	XNVAY	Biotech
OTC	Yorkshire Electricity Group Plc	YOREY	Utility
NYSE	Zeneca Group Plc	ZEN	Pharmaceuticals

Uruguay

GDR	Banco Comercial de Uruguay		Banking

Venezuela

PORTAL	Banque Indosuez Luxembourg-Sivensa 144A WTS	SVNSWYP	Steel
OTC	CA Venezolana de Pulpa y Papel SA (Venepal)	CVNZY	Pulp, Paper
GDR	CA Venezolana de Pulpa y Papel SA (Venepal)	VNPLY	Pulp, Paper
OTC	Ceramica Carabobo A	C RCAY	Bldg Matls
OTC	Ceramica Carabobo B	CRCBY	Bldg Matls
NYSE	Corimon SA	CRM	Chemicals
OTC	Dominguez y CIA Caracas	DOMZY	Containers
OTC	Dominguez y CIA PR A	DOMZP	Containers
OTC	Mantex SAICA	MTXSY	Textiles
OTC	Mavesa SA	MVSAY	Food
OTC	Siderurgia Venezolanal Sivensa SAICA	SVNZY	Steel
OTC	Sudamtex de Venezuela SA	SUDTY	
NASDAQ	Venezuelan Goldfields Ltd	VENGF	Gold Mining
PORTAL	Venprecar	VPRCF	Steel

Virgin Islands

NASDAQ	Fonic Inc (Hong Kong)	FONCF	
NASDAQ	Fonic Inc Units (Hong Kong)	FONUF	
OTC	New World Dev Ltd (Hong Kong)	NEWDY	

Zambia

0TC	General Mining & Finance		
OTC	Zambia Consol Copper Mines Ltd	ZAMBY	Copper, Lead
OTC	Zambia Copper Investments Ltd (Bermuda)	ZMBAY	Holding Co

Zimbabwe

OTC	Mhangura Copper Mines Ltd		Mining

BIBLIOGRAPHY

Articles

Arbel, A. and Strebel, P. "Pay attention to neglected firms!" *The Journal of Portfolio Management* (Winter 1983): 37–42.

Arbel, A., Carvell S. and Strebel, P. "Giraffes, Institutions and Neglected Firms," *Financial Analysts Journal* (May/June 1983): 57–63.

Arnott, R.D. "What hath MPT wrought: Which risks reap rewards?" *The Journal of Portfolio Management* (Fall 1983): 5–11.

Bailey, W. and Lim, J. "Evaluating the Diversification Benefits of the New Country Funds," *The Journal of Portfolio Management* (Spring 1992): 74–80.

Banz, R. "The Relationship Between Return and Market Values of Common Stock," *Journal of Financial Economics* 9 (1981).

Bercel, A. "Consensus Expectations and International Equity Returns," *Financial Analysts Journal* (July/August 1994): 76–80.

Bernoulli, D. "Exposition of a New Theory on the Measurement of Risk," *Econometrica* 22, January 1954 (translation by Dr. Louise Sommer of an address at Petersburg's Imperial Academy of Sciences, "Specimen Theoriae Novae de Mensura Sortis," published 1738 in Petersburg): 23–36. Evanston, Illinois: The Econometric Society.

Bernstein, P.L. "How True are the Tried Principles?" *Investment Management Review* 3 (March/April 1989): 17–24.

Bernstein, P.L. "Risk as a History of Ideas," *Financial Analysts Journal* (January/February 1995): 7–11.

Bernstein, P.L. "The Surprises of Risk," *The Journal of Portfolio Management* (Summer 1984): 4.

Black, F. "Universal Hedging: Optimizing Currency Risk and Reward in International Equity Portfolios," *Financial Analysts Journal* (July/August 1989): 16–22.

Black, F. and Litterman, R. "Global Portfolio Optimization," *Financial Analysts Journal* (September/October 1992): 28–43.

Black, F. and Scholes, M. "The Pricing of Options and Corporate Liabilities," *The Journal of Political Economy,* (May–June 1973): 637–654.

Brinson, G.P. "Asset Allocation," *Investing Worldwide IV*, summary of the February 1993 annual conference on global investing: 7–14.

Brinson, G.P. "Setting the Global Asset Allocation Mix," *Initiating and Managing a Global Investment Program* (Institute of Chartered Financial Analysts: speeches from a November 1990 seminar): 35–39.

Brinson, G.P. "You Can't Access Local–Currency Returns," *Financial Analysts Journal* (May/June 1993): 10.

Brown, S. and Goetzmann, W. "Mutual Fund Styles," *Western Finance Association* (June 1995)

Brown, S., Goetzmann, W. and Ross S. "Survival," *Journal of Finance* (July 1995).

Buffett, W.E. "Mr. Market, Investment Success and You," *Chairman's Letter, Berkshire Hathaway,* Inc. 1987 Annual Report

Burchill, A. "Reluctant converts," *Institutional Investor* (April 1994): 45–51.

Capaul, C., Rowley, I. and Sharpe, W.F. "International Value and Growth Stock Returns," *Financial Analysts Journal* (January/February 1993): 27–36.

Carman, P. "The Psychology of Investment Decision–Making," Exerpted from a speech at the Sanford C. Bernstein Company's Third Annual Pension Conference, September 9, 1985, in *Classics II* (Homewood, Illinois: Business One Irwin, 1991).

Celebuski, M.J., Hill, J.M. and Kilgannon, J.J. "Managing Currency Exposures in International Portfolios," *Financial Analysts Journal* (January/February 1990): 16–23.

Christie, W. and Schultz, P. "Why Do Nasdaq Market Makers Avoid Odd–Eighth Quotes?" *Journal of Finance* (December 1994): 1813–1840.

Clarke, R.G., FitzGerald, M.T. and Statman, M. "Market Timing with Imperfect Information," *Financial Analysts Journal* (November/December 1989): 27–36.

Clayman, M.R. and Schwartz, R.A. "Falling in Love Again – Analysts' Estimates and Reality," *Financial Analysts Journal* (September/October 1994): 66–68.

Craig, D., Johnson, G. and Joy, M. "Accounting Methods and P/E Ratios," *Financial Analysts Journal* (March/April 1987): 41–45.

Davis, N. "Reflections of Reality," *A Ned Davis Research Historical Perspective* (January 1995).

Davis. E. and Kay, J. "Assessing Corporate Performance," *Business Strategy Review* (Summer 1990).

De Bondt, W.F.M. and Thaler, R.H. "Financial Decision–Making in Markets and Firms: A Behavioral Perspective," in *Handbook of Finance* (Amsterdam, the Netherlands: Elsevier Science BV).

Dreman, D.N. and Berry, M.A. "Analyst Forecasting Errors and Their Implications for Security Analysis," *Financial Analysts Journal* (May/June 1995): 30–41.

Dreman, D.N. and Berry, M.A. "Overreaction, Underreaction, and the Low–P/E Effect," *Financial Analysts Journal* (July/August 1995): 21–30.

Dropsy, V. and Nazarian–Ibrahimi, F. Macroeconomic Policies, "Exchange Rate Regimes, and National Stock Markets," *International Review of Economics and Finance*, vol. 3, no. 2 (1994): 195–220.

Drummen, M. and Zimmermann, H. "The Structure of European Stock Returns," *Financial Analysts Journal* (July/August 1992): 15–26.

Ellis, C.D. "The Loser's Game," *Financial Analysts Journal* (July/August 1975): 19–26.

Elton, E.J., Gruber, M.J. and Gultekin, M. "Expectations and Share Prices," *Management Science* (September 1981): 975–987.

Emanuelli, J.F. and Pearson, R.G. "Using Earnings Estimates for Global Asset Allocation," *Financial Analysts Journal* (March/April 1994): 60–72.

Erb, C.E., Campbell, H.R. and Viskanta, T.E. "Forecasting International Equity Correlations," *Financial Analysts Journal* (November/December 1994): 32–45.

Erickson, H.L. and Cunniff, J.M. "A Comparative Look at Consensus Earnings in World Markets," *Journal of Investing* (Spring 1995).

Errunza V. and Losq, E. "How Risky Are Emerging Markets? Myths and Perceptions Versus Theory and Evidence," *Journal of Portfolio Management* (Fall 1987).

Errunza, V. "Emerging Markets: A New Opportunity for Improving Global Portfolio Performance," *Financial Analysts Journal* (September–October 1983).

Errunza, V. and Padmanabhan, P. "Further Evidence on the Benefits of Portfolio Investments in Emerging Markets," *Financial Analysts Journal* (July–August 1988).

Evans, J.H. and Archer, S.H. "Diversification and the Reduction of Dispersion: An Empirical Analysis," *Journal of Finance* (December 1968).

Fama, E.F. "Random Walks in Stock Market Prices," *Financial Analysts Journal* (September/October 1965).

Farrelly, G.E. and Reichenstein, W.R. "Risk Perceptions of Institutional Investors," *The Journal of Portfolio Management* (Summer 1984): 5–12.

Ferguson, R. "An efficient stock market? Ridiculous!" *The Journal of Portfolio Management* (Summer 1983): 31–38.

Ferguson, R. and Hitzig, N.B. "How to Get Rich Quick Using GAAP," *Financial Analysts Journal* (May/June 1993): 30–34.

Frankel, R. and Lee, C.M.C. "Accounting Valuation, Market Expectation, and the Book-to-Market Effect," *I/B/E/S Academic Research Program* (September, 1995).

Froot, K. "Currency Hedging Over Long Horizons," *National Bureau of Economic Research* (Working Paper No. 4355, 1993).

Gastineau, G.L. "Beating the Equity Benchmarks," *Financial Analysts Journal* (July/August 1994): 6–11.

Gastineau, G.L. "The Currency Hedging Decision: A Search for Synthesis in Asset Allocation," *Financial Analysts Journal* (May/June 1995): 8–17.

Gastineau, G.L., Holterman, G. and Beighley, S. "Equity Investment Across Borders: Cutting the Costs" (Swiss Bank Corporation, February 1993).

Grubel, H.G. "Internationally Diversified Portfolios," *American Economic Review* (December 1968).

Hackel, K.S., Livnat, J. and Rai, A. "The Free Cash Flow/Small–Cap Anomaly," *Financial Analysts Journal* (September/October 1994): 33–42.

Hawkins, E., Chamberlin, S. and Daniel, W. "Earnings Expectations and Stock Prices," *Financial Analysts Journal* (September/October 1984).

Hendricks, D., Patel, J. and Zeckhauser. R. "Hot Hands in Mutual Funds: The Persistence of Performance," *National Bureau of Economic Research* (Working Paper No. 3389, June 1990)

Heston, S. and Rouwenhorst, G. "Does Industrial Structure Explain the Benefits of International Diversification?" *Journal of Financial Economics* (August 1994).

Ippolito, R.A. "Efficiency with Costly Information: A Study of Mutual Fund Performance, 1965–1984," *Quarterly Journal of Economics 104* (1989): 1–23.

Ippolito, R.A. "On Studies of Mutual Fund Performance, 1962–1991," *Financial Analysts Journal* (January/February 1993): 42–50.

Jaffee, J.F. "Special Information and Insider Trading," *Journal of Business*, July 1974.

Jeffrey, R.H. "The Folly of Stock Market Timing," *Harvard Business Review* (July/August 1984).

Jensen, M.C. "The Performance of Mutual Funds in the Period 1945–1964," *Journal of Finance 23* (May 1968): 389–416.

Keim, D.B. "A New Look at the Effects of Firm Size and E/P Ratio on Stock Returns," *Financial Analysts Journal* (March/April 1990): 56–67.

Kerrigan, T.J. "When forecasting earnings, it pays to watch forecasts," *The Journal of Portfolio Management* (Summer 1984): 19–26.

Kester, G.W. "Market Timing with Small versus Large–Firm Stocks," *Financial Analysts Journal* (September/October 1990): 63–69.

Kirby, R.G. "The Coffee Can Portfolio," *The Journal of Portfolio Management* (Fall, 1984): 76–79.

Klemkosky, R.C. and Miller, W.P. "When forecasting earnings, it pays to be right!" *The Journal of Portfolio Management* (Summer 1984): 13–18.

Kothare, M. and Laux, P.A. "Trading Costs and the Trading Systems for Nasdaq Stocks," *Financial Analysts Journal* (March/April 1995): 42–53.

Kritzman, M. "About Uncertainty," *Financial Analysts Journal* (March/April 1991): 17–21.

Kritzman, M. "About Utility," *Financial Analysts Journal* (May/June 1992): 17–20.

Kritzman, M. "Asset Allocation for Individual Investors," *Financial Analysts Journal* (January/February 1992): 12–13.

Kritzman, M. "The Minimum–Risk Currency Hedge ratio and Foreign Asset Exposure," *Financial Analysts Journal* (September/October 1993): 77–78.

Kurz, M. "Asset Prices with Rational Beliefs," CEPR publication No. 375, Stanford University, Stanford, CA. February 1994.

Kurz, M. "Asset Prices with Rational Beliefs," draft, Stanford University 1996 (to appear in a forthcoming monograph entitled "*Rational Beliefs and Endogenous Uncertainty*," Studies in Economic Theory, Springer–Verlag).

Lerner, E.M. and Theerathorn, P. "The Returns of Different Investment Strategies," *The Journal of Portfolio Management* (Summer 1983): 26–28.

Lessard, D. "World, Country and Industry Relationships in Equity Returns," *Financial Analysts Journal* (January/February 1976).

Levy, H. and Sarnat, M. "International Diversification of Investment Portfolios," *American Economic Review* (September 1970).

Litterman, R.B. "Currency Impacts on Global Portfolios," *Initiating and Managing a Global Investment Program* (Institute of Chartered Financial Analysts: speeches from a November 1990 seminar): 46–53.

Livingston, M. and O'Neal, E. "Soft dollars and fund performance," *Journal of Financial Research* (Blacksburg, Virginia, Winter 1995).

Loeb, T.F. "Is There a Gift from Small–Stock Investing?" *Financial Analysts Journal* (January/February 1991): 39–44.

Malkiel, B. "Risk and Return: A New Look," in *The Handbook of Corporate Earnings Analysis* (Homewood, Illinois: Irwin, 1994).

Markowitz, H. "Portfolio Selection," *Journal of Finance* (March 1952).

McWilliams, J.D. "Watchman, tell us of the night!" *The Journal of Portfolio Management* (Spring 1984): 75–80.

Muller, F.L. "Equity Securities Analysis in the U.S." *Financial Analysts Journal* (January/February 1994): 6–9.

Nagy, R.A. and Obenberger, R.W. "Factors Influencing Individual Investor Behavior," *Financial Analysts Journal* (July/August 1994): 63–68.

Nesbitt, S.L. "Currency Hedging Rules for Plan Sponsors," *Financial Analysts Journal* (March/April 1991): 73–81.

Niederhoffer, V. and Regan, P.J. "Earnings Changes, Analysts' Forecasts and Stock Prices," *Financial Analysts Journal* (May/June 1972): 65–71.

Odier, P. and Solnik, B. "Lessons for International Asset Allocation," *Financial Analysts Journal* (March/April 1993): 63–77.

Ogishima, S. "Empirical Test for the 'Mochiai' Effect in Japan," *Securities Analysts Journal* (June 1993): 19–32.

Oyvind, B. and Michalsen, D. "Corporate Cross–Ownership and Market Aggregates," *Journal of Banking and Finance* (September 1994): 687–704.

Peavy III, J.W. "Closed–End Fund IPOs: Caveat Emptor," *Financial Analysts Journal* (May/June 1989): 71–75.

Peavy III, J.W. and Goodman, D.A. "The Significance of P/Es for Portfolio Returns," *The Journal of Portfolio Management* (Winter 1983): 43–47.

Perold, A.F. and Schulman, E.C. "The Free Lunch in Currency Hedging: Implications for Investment Policy and Performance Standards," *Financial Analysts Journal* (May/June 1988): 45–50.

Phillips, M.J. "Expanding the Universe of Opportunities," *Initiating and Managing a Global Investment Program* (Institute of Chartered Financial Analysts: speeches from a November 1990 seminar): 7–13.

Pratt, S. and DeVere, C. "Relationship Between Insider Trading and Rates of Return for NYSE Common Stocks, 1960–66," in *Modern Developments in Investment Management* (New York: Praeger Publishers, 1972).

Rahman, H. and Yung, K. "Atlantic and Pacific Stock Markets–Correlation and Volatility Transmission," *Global Finance Journal* (Summer 1994): 103–119.

Rea, J.B. "Remembering Benjamin Graham – Teacher and Friend," in *Security Selection and Active Portfolio Management* (New York: Institutional Investor Books, 1978): 108–125.

Regan, P.J. "Insider Transactions: Watch What They Do," *Financial Analysts Journal* (January/February 1991): 13–15.

Reichenstein, W. "Touters Trophies: Ranking Economists' Forecasts," *Financial Analysts Journal* (July/August 1991): 20–21.

Reinganum, M.R. "Portfolio Strategies Based on Market Capitalization," *The Journal of Portfolio Management* (Winter 1983): 29–36.

Schultz, P. "Transaction Costs and the Small Firm Effect," *Journal of Financial Economics* 12 (1983).

Senchack, Jr., A.J. and Martin, J.D. "The Relative Performance of the PSR and PER Investment Strategies" *Financial Analysts Journal* (March/April 1987): 46–56.

Shaked, I. "International Equity Markets and the Investment Horizon," *The Journal of Portfolio Management* (Winter 1985): 80–84.

Sharpe, W.F. "Likely Gains from Market Timing," *Financial Analysts Journal* (March/April 1975): 60–69.

Sharpe, W.F. "Mutual Fund Performance," *Journal of Business* 39 (1966): 119–38.

Sharpe, W.F. "Risk, Market Sensitivity and Diversification," *Financial Analysts Journal* (January/February 1972): 74–79.

Shilling, A.G. "Market Timing: Better than a Buy–and–Hold Strategy," *Financial Analysts Journal* (March/April 1992): 46–50.

Siebels–Kilnes, J. "Emerging Markets: Why, When, and How," *Investing Worldwide IV*, summary of the February 1993 annual conference on global investing: 23–29.

Siegel, J.J. "The Equity Premium: Stock and Bond Returns Since 1802," *Financial Analysts Journal* (January/February 1992): 28–38.

Siegel, J.J. "The Nifty–Fifty Revisited: Do Growth Stocks Ultimately Justify Their High Prices?" *The Journal of Portfolio Management* (Summer 1995): 8–20

Simon, H.A. "A Behavioral Model of Rational Choice," *Journal of Economics* (1955): 91–118

Sinquefield, Rex A. "Are Small–Stock Returns Achievable?" *Financial Analysts Journal* (January/February 1991): 45–50.

Slovic, P. "Analyzing the Expert Judge: A Descriptive Study of a Stockbroker's Decision Processes," *Journal of Applied Psychology* 53 (No. 4, August 1969): 225–263.

Solnik, B. "Why Not Diversify Internationally Rather than Domestically?" *Financial Analysts Journal* (July/August 1974): 48–54.

Sorensen, R.A. "An 'Essential Reservation' about the EMH," *The Journal of Portfolio Management* (Summer 1983): 29–30.

Thorley, S.R. "The Time–Diversification Controversy," *Financial Analysts Journal* (May/June 1995): 68–76.

Traynor, J. "The Only Game in Town," *Financial Analysts Journal* (January/February 1995): 81–83.

Umstead, D.A. "Selecting a Benchmark for International Investments," *Financial Analysts Journal* (March/April 1990): 8–9.

Umstead, D.A. "The Portfolio Management Process," *Initiating and Managing a Global Investment Program* (Institute of Chartered Financial Analysts: speeches from a November 1990 seminar): 40–45.

Uppal, R. "The Economic Determinants of Home Country Bias in Investors' Portfolios," *Journal of International Financial Management and Accounting* (Autumn 1992): 171–189.

Vaga, T. "The Coherent Market Hypothesis," *Financial Analysts Journal* (November/December 1990): 36–49.

Ware, J.W. "Quantum Investing," *Financial Analysts Journal* (March/April 1992): 10–14.

White, R.F. "The Dangers of Falling in Love with a Company," *Institutional Investor,* November 1975.

Wilcox, J.W. "Global Investing in Emerging Markets," *Financial Analysts Journal* (January/February 1992): 15–19.

Wilcox, J.W. "Practice and Theory in International Equity Investment," *Financial Analysts Journal* (January/February 1986).

Wood, A.S. "Behavioral Risk: Anecdotes and Disturbing Evidence," *Investing Worldwide VI,* summary of the February 1995 annual conference on global investing: 74–78.

Wood, A.S. "Fatal Attractions for Money Managers," *Financial Analysts Journal* (May/June 1989): 3–5.

Zacks, L. "EPS Forecasts – Accuracy is Not Enough," *Financial Analysts Journal* (March/April 1979): 53–55.

Zeikel, A. "Forecasting and the Market," *Financial Analysts Journal* (November/December 1991): 15–18.

Books

Band, R.E. *Contrary Investing for the 1990s* (Alexandria, Virginia: Alexandria House Books, 1989).

Bavishi, V. *International Accounting and Auditing Trends,* 4th edition (Princeton: Center for International Financial Analysis and Research, 1995).

Bernstein, P.L. *Capital Ideas* (New York: The Free Press, 1992).

Bernstein, P.L., ed. *International Investing* (New York: Institutional Investor Books, 1983).

Bernstein, P.L., ed. *Security Selection and Active Portfolio Management* (New York: Institutional Investor Books, 1978).

Berryessa, N. and Kirzner, E. *Global Investing the Templeton Way* (Homewood, Illinois: Irwin, 1988).

Block, W., Gwartney, J. and Lawson, R. *Economic Freedom of the World: 1975–1995* (Copublished by 11 institutes including the Fraser Institute in Vancouver, the Cato Institute in Washington, DC, and the Institute of Economic Affairs in London, 1996).

Bruce, B.R. and Epstein, C.B., ed. *The Handbook of Corporate Earnings Analysis* (Homewood, Illinois: Irwin, 1994).

Carroll, L. *Alice's Adventures in Wonderland and Through the Looking Glass* (London: Macmillan & Co., 1898).

Chorafas, D.M. *Chaos Theory in the Financial Markets* (Chicago, Illinois: Probus Books, 1994).

Day, A. *International Investment Opportunities* (New York: William Morrow and Company, 1983).

Dessauer, J.P. *International Strategies for American Investors* (New York: Prentice Hall Press, 1986).

Dessauer, J.P. *Passport to Profits* (Chicago, Illinois: Dearborn Financial Publishing, 1991).

Dreman, D. *Contrarian Investment Strategy* (New York: Random House, 1979).

Drew, G.A. *New Methods of Profit in the Stock Market* (Boston: Metcalf Press, 1941).

Ellis, C.D. *Institutional Investing* (Homewood, Illinois: Irwin, 1971).

Fosback, N.G. *Stock Market Logic* (Fort Lauderdale, Florida: The Institute for Econometric Research, 1987).

Francis, J.C. *Investments Analysis and Management* (New York: McGraw–Hill, 1976).

Gastineau, G.L. *The Stock Options Manual* (New York: McGraw Hill, 1979).

Getty, J.P. *How to Be Rich* (Chicago, Illinois: Playboy Press, 1973).

Graham, B. *The Intelligent Investor*, 4th revised edition (New York: Harper & Row, 1973).

Graham, B., Dodd, D.L., Cottle, S. and Tatham, C. *Security Analysis* (New York: McGraw–Hill, 1934).

Kahneman, D., Slovic, P. and Tversky, A. *Judgment under Uncertainty: Heuristics and Biases* (New York: Cambridge University Press, 1982).

Keynes, J.M. *A Treatise on Probability* (London: Macmillan and Co., 1921).

Levine, S.N., ed. *Financial Analyst's Handbook* (Homewood, Illinois: Irwin, 1975).

Livermore, J.L. *How to Trade in Stocks* (Palisades Park, New Jersey: Indicator Research Group, 1966; originally published 1940).

Loeb, G.M. *The Battle for Investment Survival* (New York: Simon and Schuster, 1965).

Lowe, J. *Benjamin Graham on Value Investing: Lessons from the Dean of Wall Street* (London: Pitman Publishing, 1995).

Lucas, R. and Sargent, T.J., ed. *Rational Expectations and Econometric Practice* (Minneapolis, Minnesota: University of Minneapolis Press, 1981).

Malkiel, B. *A Random Walk Down Wall Street* (New York: W.W. Norton & Company, 1973).

Mintz, S.L. *Five Eminent Contrarians: Careers, Perspectives and Investment Tactics* (Burlington, Vermont: Fraser Publishing Company, 1994).

Morton, J., ed. *The Financial Times Global Guide to Investing* (London: Pitman Publishing, 1995).

Nix, W.E. and Nix, S.W. *International Securities, Futures, and Options Markets* (Homewood, Illinois: Irwin, 1988).

O'Neill, E. *A Moon for the Misbegotten* (New York: Random House, 1952).

Prechter, Jr. R.R. *At the Crest of the Tidal Wave* (Gainesville, Georgia: New Classic Library, 1995).

Proctor, W. *The Templeton Touch* (New York: Doubleday, 1983).

Saroyan, W. *The Time of Your Life* (New York: Samuel French, 1939).

Schwartz, D. *Schwartz Stock Market Handbook* (Stroud, Gloucestershire: Burleigh Publishing Company, 1996).

Sharpe, W.F., Alexander, G. and Bailey, J. *Investments*, 5th edition (Englewood Cliffs, New Jersey: Prentice–Hall, 1995).

Siegel, J.J. *Stocks for the Long Run* (Homewood, Illinois: Irwin, 1994).

Skousen, M. *Economics on Trial* (Homewood, Illinois: Irwin, 1991).

Skousen, M. *Scrooge Investing* (Chicago, Illinois: Dearborn Financial Publishing, 1992).

Smith, A. *Supermoney* (New York: Random House, 1972).

Solnik, B.H. *European Capital Markets* (New York: Lexington Books, 1973).

Solnik, B.H. *International Investments* (New York: Addison Wesley, 1991).

Strebel, P. and Carvell, S. *In the Shadows of Wall Street* (Englewood Cliffs, New Jersey: Prentice–Hall, Inc, 1988).

Taylor, J.H. *Global Investing for the 21st Century* (Chicago, Illinois: International Publishing Corporation, 1995).

Thaler, R.H., ed. *Advances in Behavioral Finance* (New York: Russell Sage Foundation, 1994).

Train, J. *The Money Masters* (New York: Harper & Row, 1980).

Von Neumann, J. and Morgenstern, O. *Theory of Games and Economic Behavior* (Princeton: Princeton University Press, 1947).

Zweig, M.E. *Winning on Wall Street* (New York: Warner Books, 1986).

INDEX